OVID IN THE AGE OF CERVANTES

EDITED BY FREDERICK A. DE ARMAS

Ovid in the Age of Cervantes

— Prof. Lillo

Many thanks for your assistance with this essay and for guiding me to Vico in the first place. Hope to see you out in Berkeley sometime in the next few years.

Best,
Keith

UNIVERSITY OF TORONTO PRESS
Toronto Buffalo London

©University of Toronto Press Incorporated 2010
Toronto Buffalo London
www.utppublishing.com
Printed in Canada

ISNB 978-1-4426-4117-4

Printed on acid-free, 100% post-consumer recycled paper with vegetable-based inks.

Library and Archives Canada Cataloguing in Publication

Ovid in the age of Cervantes / edited by Frederick A. de Armas.

Includes bibliographical references and index.
ISBN 978-1-4426-4117-4

1. Ovid, 43 B.C.–17 or 18 A.D. – Influence.   2. Ovid, 43 B.C.–17 or 18 A.D.
– Appreciation – Spain.   3. Spanish literature – Classical period, 1500–1700
– History and criticism.   4. Renaissance – Spain.   I. De Armas, Frederick A.

PQ6066.O785 2010   860.9'003   C2009-907358-7

University of Toronto Press acknowledges the financial assistance to its
publishing program of the Canada Council for the Arts and the Ontario
Arts Council.

University of Toronto Press acknowledges the financial support for its
publishing activities of the Government of Canada through the Book
Publishing Industry Development Program (BPIDP).

Contents

Preface

In exile, far from Rome, Ovid writes the *Tristia*, where he addresses his own book: 'Go, my book, and in my name greet the beloved places' (1996, 1.15). In spite of his displacement, disgrace, and inability to partake of the culture of Rome, the *Tristia* and indeed all of Ovid's works have enjoyed remarkable fame.[1] Ovid is said to be 'the most imitated and influential classical author in the Renaissance' (Burrow 2002, 301). While in the Middle Ages his texts were consistently allegorized, the Renaissance searched for mysteries hidden in his many myths and conceits. His impact was deeply felt through the seventeenth century and beyond.[2] Spain is no exception. In addition to many Latin editions and commentaries, a number of translations of the *Metamorphoses* were available during the sixteenth and seventeenth centuries, pointing to its unrivalled popularity. These include translations by Jorge de Bustamante (c. 1543), Antonio Pérez Sigler (1580), and Pedro Sánchez de Viana (1589). The *Ars amatoria*, the *Ibis*, the *Heroides*, the *Epistulae ex Ponto*, the *Remedia amoris*, and the *Tristia* were also available (at least in part) in the vernacular (Beardsley 1970, 154).[3] Even Ovid's puzzling and lesser-known *Fasti* was utilized in Spain during this period, in spite of the fact that there was no Spanish translation. Ovid's tales, his powerful images, and startling transformations were imitated and refashioned by the leading Spanish writers of the period: Cervantes, Calderón de la Barca, Góngora, Lope de Vega, and Quevedo. His *Heroides* became key to the elaboration of the sentimental romances.[4] His *Tristia* led many to speculate on the reasons why he was banished from Rome.[5] His *Metamporhoses* was the model for many poetic fables composed by writers from Diego Hurtado de Mendoza to the Count of Villamediana.[6] His advice on love was often cited or imitated; and his myths were turned into sonnets. They were also the subject of countless mythological plays.[7]

And yet, not since Rudolph Schevill penned his *Ovid and the Renascence in Spain* in 1913 has there been another comprehensive look at Ovid's vast impact on Spain. We catch glimmers of his imposing presence in José María de Cossío's work on Spanish poetry of the Golden Age, or in Juan Antonio Martínez Berbel's study of Lope's mythological plays. Marsha Welles shows how the mythological vision, often derived from Ovid, was burlesqued in the literature and art of seventeenth-century Spain; Mary Barnard turns to the grotesque as one of the keys to Ovid's reception; Carolyn Nadeau looks at the women in the Prologue with an eye on Ovid; John McCaw points to Ovid when studying the Clavileño episode in *Don Quijote*. This collection of essays, then, attempts a more comprehensive vision of Ovid and is thus a first step in filling a major gap in the relations between Spain and the classics.

I have titled this volume *Ovid in the Age of Cervantes* for two reasons. First, I use the 'Age of Cervantes' as an alternative for the traditional term used to designate this period: 'Golden Age.' Secondly the title seeks to foreground Cervantes' wide-ranging utilization of Ovid, from the *Metamorphoses* to the *Tristia*, and from the *Heroides* to the *Fasti*. As I have discussed in previous studies, I am quite comfortable using the term 'Golden Age' to refer to sixteenth- and seventeenth-century Spain since I view it, first of all, as an aesthetic term that points to the immense flowering of literature and the arts during this period. Second, I find it to be a correct term given the mythology it foregrounds. It derives from the Augustan Golden Age in Rome (and thus Ovid would fit very well under such a rubric). Imperial Rome believed that a new mythical age was dawning with the reign of Augustus Caesar. It would be the highest of the four ages of humankind (gold, silver, bronze, and iron). Roman poets thus asserted that Augustus presided over an age that was akin to the first flowering of humankind where it was said that gods commingled with men on earth and there was universal peace and happiness. This mythical concept was then transferred to Spain where the Catholic kings, Charles V and even Philip IV, were said to have brought back an age of perfection, peace (and empire). The repeated usage of the term during Spain's sixteenth and seventeenth centuries can thus authorize its use today. But, in doing so, critics and historians must be aware that rulers used it as propaganda for their regimes, and that this period was a time of conflict, not of peace. As James Parr has shown, the usage has created discomfort among some critics because 'it is considered unseemly and undemocratic, not to say politically incorrect to privilege one period over others, particularly when the period was associated with territorial expansion by force of arms and the exploitation of indigenous peoples' (2001, 406). However, the most common alternative that has been proposed, 'early modern,' poses some problems. It can be interpreted as a reference to an age that is related to modern times but is not quite there. Thus, it becomes an appendage to a 'better' and more recent age.[8] However, there are times when this term becomes particularly useful, as when an author wishes to separate epistemic changes or modes of thinking. For example, Marina Brownlee's essay chooses to consider the transformation from myth to science using this term. And Keith Budner questions why the first 'modern' novel has need to garb itself with the classics, as Cervantes becomes a 'Spanish Ovid' / 'español Ovidio' (Cervantes 1978, 1.64). Given the complexities of choosing the correct name for the period, some, like John Beusterien and Barbara Fuchs, have thus turned to terms such as 'imperial' or 'imperium studies.'[9]

But, without abandoning 'Golden Age,' I prefer as an alternative 'the Age of Cervantes' because this writer, located temporally in the middle of what is called the Spanish Golden Age, has become a symbol of change, experimentation, and a breaking with the past. Thus, he looms above others, questing, questioning, and satirizing a quixotic episteme and an empty mythologizing. These qualities led him to invent or at least reinvent a key genre, the novel, where, as Foucault states, he questions and breaks with the episteme of analogy. Analogy is no longer a source of knowledge but becomes the weapon of poets and madmen. And, Cervantes' Don Quijote is a work that, for many, brings into question relations of power and the link between the mythical Golden Age and Spanish imperial aspirations. Labelling the Golden Age as the Age of Cervantes would then provide an appropriate balance in the terminology of periodization. It both points to the recurrence of the term 'Golden Age' as propaganda for empire and questions the link through Cervantes' polyvalent text. The 'Age of Cervantes' also foregrounds a new episteme without colonizing the past in terms of the present. Furthermore, the term incorporates the innovations of Cervantes' precursors, contemporaries, and immediate followers.[10]

While these general reasons allow for the usage of this term, there are very specific reasons why I consider it essential for this book. One of the reasons why I would move from 'Golden Age' to the 'Age of Cervantes' in this study has to do with Ovid. Even though in his Metamorphoses he does indeed narrate the myth of the four ages of humankind, and even though he lived in what Virgil labelled as a Golden Age, he was never able to pluck the fruits of his labours peaceably. Losing the emperor's favour, Ovid is exiled to what he believed was the very edge of civilization. In spite of years of poetic pleadings, he is never allowed to return to Rome, languishing and dying in the 'barbaric' outpost of Tomis on the Black Sea. Ovid, then, did not experience a Golden Age, but a time of injustice and exile. He is thus very much like Cervantes; hence the title of the book. Indeed, in *Don Quijote* the knight, warning of the dangers of poetry, points to Ovid's exile at Pontus, cautioning satirists to avoid personal allusions and admonitions directed against the powerful (1978, 2.157). At the same time Cervantes, in a metafictional move within the novel, is labelled by a fictitious character as 'nuestro español Ovidio' [our Spanish Ovid] (1978, 1.64). Perhaps the warning and the label are a kind of self-fashioning. Through these allusions, Cervantes exhibits himself as a new Ovid, as an author that always seems exiled from the benevolence of the powerful; an author who in his lifetime never gained a canonical status. This Ovidian reference clashes with Cervantes' many attempts to fashion himself as a Virgilian poet. He first points to his Virgilian career in *La Galatea*, comparing himself to the young author of *Eclogues*. Having announced his career moves, Cervantes becomes a prose Virgil by moving through an apprenticeship to epic (*Don Quijote*), to epic (*Persiles y Sigismunda*). But this clash of authorities should not come as a surprise. After all, he claims that his posthumous prose epic is an imitation of Helidorus rather than Virgil. Indeed, Cervantes is consistently ambiguous as to his self-fashioning and his imitative models. In his early play, *La Numancia*, for example, he underscores the clash of different authorities in the creation of this text: Virgil's *Aeneid* (which is the focus of the first act), clashes with Lucan's *Pharsalia*, the central motif of the second act.[11] This contrast between Virgil and Lucan also appears in Grisóstomo's pastoral tale within *Don Quijote* (de Armas 2002, 276–7). Thus, it should come as no surprise that Cervantes problematizes his literary career by exhibiting himself as a new Virgil while at the same time becoming a new Ovid.

Indeed, Cervantes' *Don Quijote* is a deeply Ovidian text. Like the antique text, the Spanish novel evokes fears of exile. It also feigns to condemn satirical passages on would-be modern Ovids. Indeed *Don Quijote* recalls Ovid through its uses of myth and the prevalence of transformation. Even Sancho is suffused with Ovidian wit. The squire will choose Ovid for two of his major fabrications – Dulcinea's enchantment, and his voyage to the Pleiades on a wooden horse. Both are taken from Ovid's *Fasti* and reveal Sancho as a new Mercury.[12] The wondrous transformations that take place in the novel, starting with the rustic Sancho who becomes a knight's squire, are thus linked to the *Metamorphoses*. In the frontispiece of the 1632 edition by George Sandy we can see how Apollo and Mercury transform Ovid into a great writer, with fame trumpeting his name above. In Cervantes, the gentleman from La Mancha is transformed into a knight, seeking such fame as a solar hero accompanied by the eloquence of Mercury. It is this transformation that will grant fame to Cervantes, a new Ovid.

In Cervantes' novel, both Don Quijote and Sancho transform themselves, taking on new roles. Don Quijote, followed by his squire, proceeds to travel through a rural landscape that he moulds through his metaphorical, metamorphic, and mythic thinking process. It is as if an Ovidian universe is being renewed in these adventures, one that is, of course, mediated in part by the romances of chivalry. But the novel, while elevating the quotidian, does so only in the mind of the knight. Cervantes and his knight thus enter into a conversation with the ancients. Ovid himself had recast ancient tales into new forms, giving shape to his *Metamorphoses*. Cervantes delegates authority for most transformations to his crazed knight, thus creating a kind of dialectic imitation where Don Quijote seeks to make a better world just as the modern text seeks to surpass the ancient through a new vision of the world. In doing so, the ancient text also comes to the fore struggling for its own presence in the narrative.[13] Thus, metamorphosis does not fully point to the mythical, unless the knight's madness is taken as a Platonic furor, a type of divine inspiration that suffuses the world with a new kind of Ovidian magic.

But there is a key difference between Ovid's and Cervantes' uses of transformations. While in Ovid transformations usually move downwards, that is, from a divine, semi-divine, or human figure to the animal and plant world, in Cervantes the transformations move upwards, from inns to castles, from prostitutes to ladies.[14] Thus Cervantes' imitation of Ovid is a way to surpass the ancient classic with new and surprising metamorphoses that arouse not only wonder but also laughter, as they move, in the mind of a crazed knight, from the quotidian to the ideal. These transformations stay in the mind of the reader since they were probably intended as mnemonic images. Let us recall that the 'art of memory' was very important at the time. Cervantes, I would argue, used at least one Italian Renaissance text on the subject, Giambattista della Porta's *L'Arte del ricordare* (de Armas 2006, 17–21). This volume was published only four years before Cervantes' 1570 arrival in Naples, a city that viewed Della Porta as one of its greatest writers. For Della Porta and others, the artificial memory can be enhanced by having the subject paint images in his mind and place them in appropriate places so as to remember them. And these ought to be strong images, easy to remember. The metamorphoses in Ovid's book, then, can be easily recalled since they often describe amazing and visually appealing transformations. So we can think of Cervantes' novel as a new way to write of transformations. Cervantes' images are as visually striking as those in Ovid, and thus equally easy to remember. But their heroism is tainted with foolishness. The knight most often fails as he attacks images that are transformed in his mind. And indeed, Della Porta reminds us that both heroic and humorous images, when particularly vivid and pictorial, stay in the mind. Thus Cervantes' imitation of Ovid is a way to surpass the ancient classic with new and surprising metamorphoses that arouse not only wonder but also laughter, as they move in the mind of a crazed knight from the quotidian to the ideal.

Of course, this book is not just about Ovid and Cervantes, but Ovid in the Age of Cervantes. The collection is divided into four parts. The first section of the book seeks to look at how Ovid was transformed from the Middle Ages to the Age of Cervantes. It also discusses how Ovid's texts were translated, and how they were utilized in compendia that spread his fame even more. This section is composed of four essays. In the first one, Ryan D. Giles, taking as a point of departure Lope de Vega's epithet for Ovid as a 'Galen for lovers,' reviews the reception of the *Remedia amoris*. In this rich and learned overview, he discusses the links between Ovid, pseudo-Ovid, and the medical profession. This essay begins with Andrea Capellanus's *De Amore*, continues with the fourteenth-century *Libro de buen amor*, and concludes with *La Celestina*. The second essay begins where the first one leaves off. John Parrack associates the many cultural changes taking place in the sixteenth century with the popularity of the *Metamorphoses*. He then analyses in detail the last translation of the century by Sánchez de Viana. For Parrack, the profuse annotations serve as literary artifice. These notes contain fragmented commentaries reflecting what many others have said about specific passages. In so doing, the annotator does not provide meaning but invites the reader to do so. While on the one hand, meaning is constructed, on the other hand, Sánchez de Viana uses poetry rather than prose for the purposes of self-legitimacy and self-fashioning. Translation, then, is a powerful tool, and the uses of Ovid are many, even within such a work.

The last two essays in the first part of this volume turn to miscellanies and compendious works. Marina Brownlee focuses on Torquemada's

Jardín de flores curiosas (1568), studying it as an encyclopedia of exotica. The natural and the supernatural, the mind and nature are here explored. Indeed, Brownlee shows that Torquemada's Ovidian exploration is one that goes well beyond myth and extends to modern concerns with science and the use of empirical rather than bookish concerns in the search for truth. Brownlee argues that Torquemada uses Ovid since he was a sceptical observer of human experience. Much less 'modern' is the discussion of witches and demons, which, although present in Ovid, reaches a new state of paranoid fears in the sixteenth century. But exotic metamorphoses are viewed through a more modern perspective, providing scientific rather than magical explanations for apparently unexplainable phenomena. While Brownlee stresses the carefully cultivated garden of Torquemada's narrative, in my own study I begin with a much more chaotic forest grown by Pedro Mexía in his *Silva de varia lección* (1540/50). The essay continues with Juan Pérez de Moya's *Philosophía secreta* (1585), then turns to Bartolomé Jiménez Patón's *Elocuencia española en arte* (1604/21), and concludes with Baltasar Gracián's *Agudeza y arte de ingenio* (1642/8). These compendious texts are utilized in order to assess the importance of the *Fasti*, Ovid's one major text that was not translated into Spanish during the Age of Cervantes. One key element found in all four texts is a discussion of the figure of Janus, the god that brings in the New Year as he presides over January. Janus, as a god of portals, provides a double vision, one that foregrounds the antique in Ovid, and a second that projects the anxieties of the Age of Cervantes upon the ancient writer.

Part Two of this collection deals specifically with Ovid and Cervantes. The first essay here focuses on Narcissus and the mirror. Timothy Ambrose analyses *El curioso impertinente*, an interpolated tale in Part One of Cervantes' *Don Quijote* as it relates to the third book of Ovid's *Metamorphoses*. Reflecting Ovid, Ambrose weaves in a series of myths and motifs in order to provide us with a new vision of this curious tale. Bacchus and Narcissus, Tiresias and Pentheus, blindness and prophecy, madness and tragedy, the impossible and the liberating, mirrors and tapestries are all carefully interwoven in order to show how the Narcissus story, located at the centre of Ovid's third book serves to mirror Anselmo and his 'double,' Lotario, much like Bacchus mirrors Apollo in the Ovidian mirror. While Timothy Ambrose probes Anselmo's Dionysian imagination and uncovers the working of the gods, Keith Budner, ponders why Cervantes utilizes the ancients to create something new, showing how 'beneath the shell of mythic figures lies Cervantes' early-modern

Spain.' Focusing on the episode of the fulling hammers in *Don Quijote*, Budner asks why two myths seem to coalesce here, that of the ages of humankind and that of Mars. He centres his discussion on the Age of Iron, a place for fulling mills (with iron chains) and technical inventions and modernity. He then shows how the image of Mars in the episode is used to connote the triumph of valour. However, the clanging chains of the fulling mills also become the chains, forged by Vulcan, that trap Mars. Thus, for Budner, Don Quijote's Iron Age is closer to Vulcan's ugly industry than to the valour of the war-like Mars. The third essay, by William Worden, gives us a panoramic view of what he labels as the 'dubious' metamorphoses of the main characters in the novel, including Alonso Quijano, Sancho Panza, Aldonza Lorenzo, Dorotea, Sansón Carrasco, and Ginés de Pasamonte. Worden demonstrates that, while Ovid conditions the reader of his *Metamorphoses* to accept the transformations, Cervantes leads his readers to scrutinize the transformation of his characters. But doubt does not only come from outside the text – even the Cervantine characters may not fully believe their transformations. While Ovid's transformations are the prerogative of the gods, Cervantes' changes are the result of a ruse, disguises, and mental metamorphoses. It is no wonder then that the *Metamorphoses* and *Don Quijote* have themselves become metamorphosed into a number of new visions and adaptations.

Part Three of the collection turns to specific myths in Ovid. As in Part Two, this section begins with Narcissus. Mary Barnard looks at the Ovidian myth of Echo and Narcissus in Garcilaso's *Second Eclogue* through the Renaissance invention of the flat mirror. This object is also a metaphor for self-imaging. Barnard enjoins the reader to observe her views through the art of Parmigianino where the mirror is key to some of his paintings. In Garcilaso Albanio/Narcissus shares the reflecting waters with Camila, thus obscuring and problematizing Ovid's watery mirror. While for Albanio the mirror/fountain is one that reflects inner discord, Camila appropriates it to create a self-portrait, but one based on an unreflecting surface. While Mary Barnard reflects upon Narcissus and the mirror of self-imaging, Kerry Wilks turns to an Ovidian Circe in order to propose a political reading of Lope de Vega's *La Circe*. For her, this Ovidian witch serves to praise and criticize the Count-Duke of Olivares. But Circe is also an emblem of creation that can transform the poet into a swan. Thus, the poem uses Ovid not only to examine the most powerful political figure during the reign of Philip IV, but also to develop a laudatory image of the poet.

The third essay in this section turns away from Garcilaso and Lope de Vega in order to focus on Cristóbal de Castillejo, a poet who is generally considered to be a traditionalist, being singled out for his rejections of Garcilaso's innovations. Wagschal, however, reads Castillejo's use of Ovid's *Metamorphoses* through Appiah's notions of cosmopolitanism. While Wagschal metamorphoses a traditionalist into a cosmopolitan poet, Pablo Restrepo-Gautier discusses how the sexualities of Ovid's *Metamorphoses* created anxieties and new perspectives. Taking as a point of departure the monster of Ravenna carefully described in Mateo Alemán's picaresque novel, *Guzmán de Alfarache*, Restrepo-Gautier shows the fascination and abhorrence created in early modern Europe toward intersexuality. Ovid's Hermaphroditus is located in numerous Spanish texts, such as the mythographies of Perez de Moya and Baltasar de Vitoria, as well as in Sebastián de Horozco's poems and Sebastián de Covarrubias's emblems. Restrepo-Gautier exhibits the many ways in which this myth could be interpreted, from the moral to the pseudo-scientific. Indeed, many writers excluded Hermaphroditus, a figure that caused unease, from gender categories.

The fourth and last section of the book centres on Ovid and questions of poetic fame and self-fashioning. We have already seen glimpses of this in Kerry Wilks's essay. But now, Benjamin J. Nelson takes us to Garcilaso's poetry and to Montemayor's pastoral in order to carefully examine the myth of Orpheus and the fashioning of poetic fame. Nelson reveals how the Orpheus story found in these works comes closer to the Ovidian than the Virgilian tale, although with elements of *contamino*. In the *Third Eclogue,* Garcilaso provides the kind of poetry needed for a rising empire as he fashions himself as a sixteenth-century Ovidian Orpheus. Jorge de Montemayor follows suit. Felicia's temple praises not only valour in arms but the role of women in crafting empire through dynastic succession. As Orpheus praises Maria and Juana (daughters of Charles V), he is praising both their link to the Spanish monarchy and their contribution to the growth of empire through marriage. While Benjamin J. Nelson analyses the fashioning of an Ovidian poet through the myth of Orpheus, Julio Vélez-Sainz inquires as to the political implications of the Apollo and Daphne tale. Pointing out that the Ovidian tale begins with lust and ends with an elegy to Augustus Caesar, he discovers an answer to this curious trajectory through the trinomial eros, *imperium*, and *vates*. While the myth's ambiguities diminish Augustus, the poet (Ovid) is lauded through his connection to Apollo. Vélez-Sainz then shows how Lope takes up the image of the Ovidian poet in *El amor enamorado*, creating a carnivalesque Apollo, and a comical poet (Bato). Only when he learns to be subservient to Daphne and accept the laurel does Apollo/Philip IV learn to prize the poet. On the other hand, Calderón, in *El laurel de Apolo*, prefers to dramatize the myth as a mirror of princes, a mirror of the Spanish sun king.

In the third essay in Part Four, Christopher Weimer moves from the problematization of Ovidian myth to a rejection of Ovid as the subject for self-fashioning. Weimer reminds us that while numerous poets use Virgil to structure their literary career, playwrights tend to follow Ovid. And this may be what Tirso de Molina had set out to do, culminating in the overt Ovidianism and eroticism of his miscellany *Los cigarrales de Toledo*, which includes one of his best known plays, *El vergonzoso en palacio*. But Tirso, like Ovid, was exiled. Late in life, Tirso writes another miscellany, the neglected *Deleitar aprovechando* (1635). In this work, Tirso no longer delights his audience with secular novellas and plays. Instead, he turns to religious images and stories, emphasizing Christian devotion. Indeed, his frame characters are pious members of the nobility who flee from the licence of carnival. While the daughters of Minyas in Ovid are found wanting in their rejection of Bacchic feasts, here Tirso lauds those pious souls who turn away from carnival. Weimer thus clearly shows how Tirso takes a counter-Ovidian turn and thus fashions himself as a poet of pious exile. The last of the essays in this volume seeks to expand Ovid's domain. We move from Spain to America, and from Ovid's realms to Africa. Here, Jason A. McCloskey studies Juan de Miramontes Zuázola's *Armas antárticas*, a poem where an African slave explains to an English pirate how he and his community are descendants of Andromeda and Apollo. For McCloskey, these Ovidian myths serve a double purpose. First, the slave's community becomes a more worthy opponent of the Spaniards since they are now part of the classical tradition – they are whitened. Second, Miramontes himself acquires authority (and, he hopes, future fame) by placing his text and himself as descending from Ovid. This is a most intriguing work that creates a new myth for Apollo, who after Daphne is transformed into a laurel, wanders through Africa, and falls for Andromeda. Apollo's light and the feigned whiteness of Andromeda provide a suitable background for this fascinating epic that turns to Ovid to reimagine the slave.

I would like to express my appreciation to all who made this volume possible. The sessions on Ovid in the Age of Cervantes at the Renaissance Society of America during the last several years have contributed much to the discussion of this topic. Many of those present encouraged me to undertake this collection. My thanks in particular go to Mary Barnard, Anne J. Cruz, Lía Schwartz, Steven Wagschal, and William Worden. To Martha Roth, Dean of Humanities at the University of Chicago, I owe a debt of gratitude for her support of this project. Finally, I would like to thank Felipe Rojas for his help in assembling and editing this volume. When citing Spanish works, this volume includes the original plus the translation. When citing Ovid only the translation is included unless there is need for the Latin in the essay's argument. If the Loeb Classical Library edition is used, then book and verse are given. If other translations of Ovid are utilized, then the page number is included.

NOTES

1 Baltasar Gracián, in his thirty-fourth chapter or *discurso* of his *Agudeza y arte de ingenio*, discusses conceits that derive from adapting lines from an ancient text to a new context. Erudition and subtlety are key to these *conceptos* (1969, 2.62). Thus, the burning of one of Francisco Suarez's books in England, the *Defensio fidei catholicae*, evokes the famous first line of Ovid's *Tristia*: 'Parve (nec invideo) sine me, liber, ibis in Urbem' [Little book, you will go without me – and I grudge it not – to the city] (1996, 1.1).
2 Although Burrow sees a kind of banishment of Ovid in England around 1601, he argues: 'Changed anew, he again becomes a major presence in Shakespeare's work around 1609, at about the same time as Thomas Heywood's dramatizations of tales from the *Metamorphoses* were being performed at the popular playhouse the Red Bull' (2002, 310). This new Shakesperean Ovid has to do with the powers of the imagination. Ovid achieved new heights in seventeenth-century Spain as evinced by Isabel Torres's collection of essays on myth.
3 Although Beardsley begins his volume with 1482, decades earlier Ovid had already become fashionable. As Schevill points out, the *Epístolas de Ovidio* (or *Bursuario*) 'represents one of the first steps of the process by which the works of Ovid, notably the *Metamorphoses* and the *Heroides*, assumed a modern garb and so became a part of Spanish fiction of the Renascence' (1913, 115–16).
4 Brownlee shows how the *Bursuario* author points to the Spanish sentimental romances by using the *Heroides* in unexpected ways, even creating a 'literary counterfeit' by attributing three of his own letters to Ovid (1990, 39).
5 Colin Burrow notes that many of the lives of the poet 'frequently speculated on what the "error" was. Politian's elegy on the death and exile of Ovid

(composed in the 1490s) found a place among the prefatory matter of editions of Ovid's works … The *Tristia* themselves were often among the first Latin poems studied at school' (2002, 308).

6 José María de Cossío asserts that Hurtado de Mendoza's *Adonis* was the first great Ovidian fable in Spanish verse (1952, 90).

7 For Ovid in Calderón's spectacle plays, see Greer and O'Connor.

8 These last sentences come from my essay 'Simple Magic' (2005, 20–1).

9 John Beusterien asserts: 'In this study I use "imperial," rather than "Golden Age."' He then points to Barbara Fuchs, who 'sees an advantage to connecting Spanish literature to the Augustan and Roman period, but rejects the aesthetic suggestiveness of the term and proposes "imperium studies"' (2006, 176, note 7).

10 Once again, I am echoing my previous study, 'Simple Magic' (2005, 21). Studying jealousy as a way of 'working through a series of political and cultural problems involving power' (2006, 2), Steven Wagschal also has recourse to the term 'Age of Cervantes' in his book on jealousy.

11 While the third act commingles Homer, Virgil, and Seneca in epic fires and textual ashes, the fourth act turns to Cicero and Macrobius for questions of epic and poetic fame (see de Armas 1998, 154–90).

12 For a discussion of these two fabrications and their Ovidian models, see de Armas 2008. For a discussion of the *Clavileño* episode in terms of Ovid's Phaeton, see McCaw.

13 According to Greene, we move to dialectic imitation when there is a current of mutual aggression as the modern text exposes the 'vulnerability' of its model, 'while exposing itself to the subtext's potential aggression' (1982, 45). There are times when the modern text seeks to trivialize the ancient, as when a 'humanist' in part 2 decides to write a rather ridiculous book entitled *Metamorfoseos o Ovidio español* (1978, 2.206).

14 Elaine Fantham asserts: 'Most traditional tales of metamorphosis dealt with humans changed downward, into lower forms of life – animals or plants – or even into inanimate rocks and water. Yet for centuries before Ovid there had been tales about men or women transformed into stars as a kind of deification, as Bacchus had deified Ariadne, or changed into immortal demigods and nymphs. A very few were even raised to heaven, to join the Olympians, as Heracles and Castor and Pollux, heroes with divine fathers, were reputed to have become gods' (2004, 15). There are, of course, some exceptions: Io regains her human shape, Pygmalion's statue becomes a woman, and Hercules, Caesar, Augustus, Aeneas, and Romulus become gods, etc.

WORKS CITED

Barnard, Mary. 1987. *The Myth of Apollo and Daphne from Ovid to Quevedo: Love, Agon and the Grotesque*. Durham: Duke University Press.

Beardsley, Theodore. 1970. *Hispano-Classical Translations*. Pittsburgh: Duquesne University Press.

Beusterien, John. 2006. *An Eye on Race: Perspectives from Theater in Imperial Spain*. Lewisburg: Bucknell University Press.

Brownlee, Marina Scordilis. 1990. *The Severed Word: Ovid's Heroides and the Novela Sentimental*. Princeton: Princeton University Press.

Burrow, Colin. 2002. 'Re-embodying Ovid: Renaissance Afterlives.' In *The Cambridge Companion to Ovid*, ed. Philip Hardie, 301–19. Cambridge: Cambridge University Press.

Cervantes, Miguel de. 1978. *El ingenioso hidalgo don Quijote de la Mancha*. Ed. Luis A. Murillo. 2 vols. Madrid: Castalia.

– 1998. *Don Quixote*. Trans. Charles Jarvis. Oxford: Oxford University Press.

Cossío, José María de. 1952. *Fábulas mitológicas en España*. Madrid: Espasa-Calpe.

De Armas, Frederick A. 1998. *Cervantes, Raphael and the Classics*. Cambridge: Cambridge University Press.

– 2002. 'Cervantes and the Virgilian Wheel: The Portrayal of a Literary Career,' In *European Literary Careers: The Author from Antiquity to the Renaissance*, ed. Patrick Cheney and Frederick A. de Armas, 268–85. Toronto: University of Toronto Press.

– 2005. 'Simple Magic: Ekphrasis from Antiquity to the Age of Cervantes.' In *Ekphrasis in the Age of Cervantes*, ed. Frederick A. de Armas, 13–31. Lewisburg: Bucknell University Press.

– 2006. *Quixotic Frescoes: Cervantes and Italian Renaissance Art*. Toronto: University of Toronto Press.

– 2008. 'Sancho as a Thief of Time and Art: Ovid's *Fasti* and Cervantes' *Don Quixote* 2.' *Renaissance Quarterly* 61:1–25.

Fantham, Elaine. 2004. *Ovid's Metamorphoses*. Oxford: Oxford University Press.

Gracián, Baltasar. 1969. *Agudeza y arte de ingenio*. Ed. Evaristo Correa Calderón. 2 vols. Madrid: Castalia.

Greene, Thomas M. 1982. *The Light in Troy: Imitation and Discovery in Renaissance Poetry*. New Haven: Yale University Press.

Greer, Margaret. 1991. *The Play of Power: Mythological Court Dramas of Calderón de la Barca*. Princeton: Princeton University Press.

Martínez Berbel, Juan Antonio. 2003. *El mundo mitológico de Lope de Vega: Siete comedias mitológicas de inspiración ovidiana*. Madrid: Fundación Universitaria Española.

McCaw, John R. 2007. 'Transforming Phaethon: Cervantes, Ovid, and Sancho Panza's Wild Ride.' In *The Changing Face of Ovid's Metamorphoses in Medieval and Early Modern Europe*, ed. Alison Keith, 236–52. Toronto: Centre for Reformation and Renaissance Studies.

Nadeau, Carolyn A. 2002. *Women of the Prologue: Imitation, Myth, and Magic in 'Don Quixote I.'* Lewisburg: Bucknell University Press.

O'Connor, Thomas Austin. 1988. *Myth and Mythology in the Theater of Calderón de la Barca*. San Antonio, TX: Trinity University Press.

Ovid. 1996. *Tristia. Ex Ponto*. Ed. and trans. A.L. Wheeler. Rev. G.P. Goold. Cambridge, MA: Harvard University Press.

Parr, James A. 2001. 'A Modest Proposal: That We Use Alternatives to Borrowing (Renaissance, Baroque, Golden Age) and Leveling (Early Modern) in Periodization.' *Hispania* 84.3:406–16.

Schevill, Rudolph. 1913. *Ovid and the Renascence in Spain*. Berkeley: University of California Press.

Torres, Isabel. 2007. 'Introduction: *Con pretension de Fénix*.' In *Rewriting Classical Mythology in the Hispanic Baroque*, ed. Isabel Torres, 1–16. London: Tamesis.

Wagschal, Steven. 2006. *The Literature of Jealousy in the Age of Cervantes*. Columbia: University of Missouri Press.

Welles, Marcia. 1986. *Arachne's Tapestry: The Transformation of Myth in Seventeenth-Century Spain*. San Antonio, TX: Trinity University Press.

PART ONE

Alternatives, Diagnoses, and Translations

1 A Galen for Lovers: Medical Readings of Ovid in Medieval and Early Renaissance Spain

RYAN D. GILES

A memorable reference to Ovid's amatory fiction can be found in part two of *Don Quijote de la Mancha*, when Altisidora pretends to grow faint at the sight of the famous gentleman, prompting him to sing a love song about Dulcinea in order to assuage the passions of the swooning maid: 'yo consolaré lo mejor que pudiere a esta lastimada doncella; que en los principios amorosos los desengaños prestos suelen ser remedios calificados' [I shall consol this afflicted maid as best I can; for when love is dawning, to be soon undeceived is the best cure] (1990, 894; 2000, 792).[1] Editors have noted that this passage refers to the *Remedia amoris*, the same poem that Don Quijote evokes in the lyrics of his ballad:

> Suelen las fuerzas de amor
> sacar de quicio a las almas,
> tomando por instrumento˙
> la ociosidad descuidada.
> Suele el coser y el labrar
> y el estar siempre ocupada
> ser antídoto al veneno
> de las amorosas ansias.
>
> [The soul, by Love's most mighty power,
> can often be upset
> if Love can count on careless sloth
> to aid and to abet.
> Much sewing and embroidery
> and ceaseless occupation
> are antidotes to the virulence
> of amorous inclination.]   (1990, 894; 2000, 793)

Ovid similarly advises lovers who are ready to give themselves over to his 'medicabilis arte' to keep busy and not to leave themselves vulnerable to 'otia,' Cupid's secret weapon (1957, vv. 135–9). Of course, the *Remedia amoris* is not the only text being implicated in this scene. Knights like Amadis and Tristan were known to play musical instruments, and medical treatises commonly advised patients suffering from lovesickness to listen to music as a way of distracting themselves.[2]

Don Quijote could even be alluding to medical readings of Ovid, in addition to the actual text of the *Remedia amoris*. The works of physicians like Bernardo de Gordonio, whose *Lilium medicinae* was still being reprinted and studied during the time of Cervantes, frequently cite the Roman poet as a *doctor amoris* or what Lope de Vega calls a 'Galeno de los amantes' [Galen of lovers] (1980, 250). It is the historical background of this textual intersection that will concern me in the pages that follow, and in particular, Ovid's dual influence on medical writing and satirical literature during the later Middle Ages. While adaptations of Ovidian material by physicians and storytellers have tended to be set apart and treated as discrete cultural productions, we will see how these modes of discourse overlapped and productively cross-contaminated each other in medieval and early Renaissance Spain.

Lovesickness was first systematically introduced into Western medical discourse by Galen, the second-century physician of Emperor Marcus Aurelius. As Mary Wack has observed, Galenic commentary on Hippocrates strikes a somatic balance between views of mad love as divinely inspired by beauty, and lovesickness as a physiological response (1990, 7–9).[3] Whereas earlier treatments for this disorder had involved bed rest and dietary restrictions, Galen, like Ovid, advises sufferers to distract themselves with pleasurable activities until the symptoms of feverishness, loss of appetite, insomnia, and melancholy subside. Subsequent Roman physicians further recommend that melancholic patients rehabilitate themselves by engaging in sexual intercourse, a remedy that is also found in Ovid's work.[4] Classical descriptions of lovesickness as a form of mania and melancholy were later synthesized and expanded on by Arabic writers, before being translated in Toledo and Montecassino during the eleventh and twelfth centuries.

One of the most significant medical treatises to be produced during this period is the *Viaticum peregrinantis* of Constantine the African, an adaptation of the tenth-century Arabic medical handbook by Ibn al-Jazza, *Kitāb Zād al-musāfir wa-qūt al-hādir* [Provisions for the Traveller and Nourishment for the Sedentary]. In his chapter on lovesickness,

Constantine uses the phrase, 'amor qui est eros dicitur' [love that is also called eros], to translate the word *ishk* – a term that, in fact, signified a more Platonic concept of the soul's irresistible attraction to that person or thing which most conforms to its nature (Wack 1990, 35–8, 186–7). He then defines the illness as a sexual desire as well as a melancholic disease or *morbus* caused by an obsession with what is perceived as a beautiful form and associated with an imbalance of bodily humours. After listing common symptoms of *amor eros*, Constantine gives an elaborate description of therapeutic activities, including poetry reading and listening to music. During the twelfth and early thirteenth centuries, the *Viaticum* spread from the Schola Medica at Salerno to other centres of medical learning such as Paris and Montpellier.[5] By this time, students of Constantine had renamed the disease *amor heroes* as a way of conveying what was perceived as the greater susceptibility of 'heroic' nobles to the ravages of love (Wack 1990, 46–7).

Later commentators cite Ovid's *Remedia amoris* in their interpretation of diagnoses and remedies for lovesickness found in the writings of Galen and Constantine, as well as Avicenna (Ibn Sīnā) and Rhazes (Al-Rāzī), whose works had been translated in Toledo by Gerard of Cremona.[6] In doing so, they draw serious medical conclusions from a burlesque poem in which the speaker, himself a notorious advocate for Cupid, warns youthful readers, 'do not trust me too far,' as he teaches them how to avoid falling in love and how to overcome amorous despair (1957, v. 426).[7] This can be seen as part of what Ioan Couliano has called the 'hermeneutic filter' through which Arabic knowledge was received, altered, and retransmitted by scholastic commentators (1987, 11). For example, Wack has edited the commentaries of two early Iberian physicians: Giles of Portugal (Gil de Santarém), a Dominican friar who studied medicine at Coimbra and Toledo and worked in Paris in the 1220s; and Peter of Spain (Pedro Julião), another Portuguese scholar who taught at Siena before being elected Pope John XXI in 1276. In the *Glose super Viaticum*, Giles draws on the authority of Ovid's *Remedia amoris* in his discussion of whether wine will exacerbate or mollify the effects of these kinds of passions. In spite of the poet's warning, 'wine prepares the heart for love,' he agrees with Constantine that drinking in moderation 'will carry away bad thoughts' and is thus 'beneficial for sufferers of *heros*' (1957, v. 805; Wack 1990, 209–11).[8] In his *Questiones super Viaticum*, Peter engages in a more sophisticated reading of the same Ovidian verses, arguing that the Roman poet advises lovers to either abstain or drink wine to the point of drunkenness: 'one is returning the estimative faculty to rightly ordered love ... the other is the taking away and removal of care and worry' (Wack 1990, 248–9).[9] These kinds of commentaries show how medieval physicians engaged in literal readings of passages selected from the *Remedia amoris*, consulting the poem as a reliable source for instructions on how to cure lovesickness.

One of the most striking examples of how imaginative writers from the same period interpreted Ovid can be found in the late twelfth-century *De amore* of Andreas Capellanus. This influential work became widely popular in medieval Spain and elsewhere in Europe, as testified by numerous extant copies and translations, including one in Catalan. The narrator, who identifies himself as a French royal chaplain, advises a neophyte named Walter about the uplifting nature of courtly love, and tells him how it can be maintained. Not surprisingly, among the most important sources for *De amore* are Ovid's amatory works, and in particular the *Ars amatoria* – the ancient author's tongue-in-cheek manual on seduction that often preceded the *Remedia amoris* in medieval manuscripts.[10] Scholars have also found that Capellanus's portrayal of love as a *passio* is indebted to the writings of Constantine (and possibly Avicenna).[11] In fact, this interrelation of the literary and the scientific influences is so strong that it becomes difficult at times to distinguish between them. For instance, Wack notes that the same verse from the *Amores* – concerning Ovid's famous depiction of his affair with Corinna – appears both in medical *Questiones* and in the *De amore* when Capellanus describes how unrequited love 'increases beyond all measure and drives the lovers to lamenting their terrible torments, because "we strive for what is forbidden, and always want what is denied us"' (1986, 109; 1990, 34).[12]

Having praised all the good that comes from satisfying love's *passio*, the narrator reverses himself at the end of the *De amore* by writing what Peter Allen has aptly called an 'analogue to the extensive disillusioning of the *Remedia amoris*' (1992, 74). This final *De reprobatione amoris* engages in theological and medical arguments against worldly love, warning of the grave physiological dangers that lovers face: 'physiologists tell us ... love causes one to eat less and drink less ... takes away a man's sleep and deprives him of all rest. Lack of sleep is followed in a man by bad digestion and great weakening of the body' (1992, 199).[13] In recent years, critics like Allen and Catherine Brown have embraced the contradictions of *De amore* as a strategy for teaching readers how to interpret *duplex sententia* and create their own fictions. The text's unreliable narrator, in other words, prescribes counteracting medicines, leaving it to the victim of love to bring about his own cure, in keeping with the biblical proverb, 'physician, heal thyself' (Luke 4:23). In this way, the *De amore* draws on a confluence of Ovid's *auctoritas* in medieval poetics and medicine – the problematic authority of a narrator who admits in the *Remedia amoris* that not long ago the doctor 'was sick, and applying his own medication,' and then later cautions his audience not to place too much trust in 'Ovid, giver of love, Ovid, reliever of lovers,' for 'if you don't want to love, don't expose yourself to contagion ... looking at those who are sick, you also may suffer infection' (1957, vv. 313, 557, 613–15).[14] In contrast to the medical writers discussed earlier, who seem to have ignored the irony of such passages, poets like Capellanus drew inspiration from Ovid's contradictory image as a *medicus aeger* or 'sick doctor' who at once spreads the poison and the antidote of love (1957, v. 314).[15]

The impact of this authorial persona can also be seen in anonymous texts that were falsely attributed to Ovid and widely circulated during the twelfth and thirteenth centuries, a time that has been called the *aetas Ovidiana*. Chief among these are the *Pamphilus de amore* (c. 1150) and *De vetula* (1220–70), interrelated works that were often compiled together in the same manuscript, that creatively imitate elements of Ovid's amatory fiction, and may have been initially written as rhetorical exercises.[16] They can also be related to *accessa* and imaginative commentaries explaining how the long-nosed poet was exiled for the 'carmen et error' of writing about his illicit sex life, spying on the naked empress Livia, falling in love with her, and committing adultery (1988, 2.207).[17] The *Pamphilus* recycles material from the *Ars amatoria*, telling the story of a lover who complains to Venus that his health and vitality have suffered as a result of his passionate love for Galatea (Burkard 1999, 145). After enlisting the aid of a go-between, he manages to force himself on Galatea and the elegiac comedy ends with their impending marriage. The *Pamphilus* character seems to have been devised as an outgrowth of Ovid's medieval biography or 'afterlife' as a famed libertine, and was in some cases even viewed as synonymous with the Roman author himself (Hexter 1999, 329).[18] This kind of association can be seen, for example, in the Spanish *Libro de confesiones* (c. 1316), which warns scholars to be on their guard against the potentially corrupting influence of exercises in Latin grammar: 'ca meten en el coraçon de los escolares amores malos e carnales con ellos asi commo Ovidio mayor *De arte amandi* e *Panfilio*' [because they plant in the hearts of students examples of sinful, carnal love such as Ovid the Greater (in) *The Art of Love* and *Pamphilus*] (Pérez 2002, 440).

In the *De vetula*, which builds on the *Pamphilus* and was also widely read in fourteenth-century Spain, a lovesick narrator named Ovid hires an old woman to help seduce his neighbour's virginal daughter, but the messenger instead secretly arranges to take the girl's place and have him for herself, not unlike the trick Anna Perenna plays on Mars in the *Fasti* (1989, 3.15).[19] The resulting encounter, with its grotesque description of the *vetula*, dramatizes the cure in *Remedia amoris* of turning 'attractions into defects or possibly worse,' and also could have evoked Avicenna's popular therapy of finding an 'old woman to disparage the beloved, speaking of her stinking dispositions' (1957, vv. 320–50; Wack 1990, 70). This seems even more likely considering that the Ovidian narrator cites passages from the Persian doctor's *Canon medicinae* just before his ill-fated tryst, and later when he curses the health of the deceitful old woman, before undergoing his supposed conversion to Christianity (Robathan 1969, 12, 96, 443). It has also been pointed out that the *accessus* to *De vetula*, which claims that the text was found in a 'capsella eburnean' or ivory capsule at the Roman poet's tomb, was based on the spurious legend of a medical treatise entitled *Capsula eburnea* being enclosed in ivory at the grave site of the physician Hippocrates (Colker 1970, 323). Such a borrowing may have seemed natural, as similar scientific texts were sometimes attributed to Ovid, as in the case of *De quator humoribus* and *De medicamine aurium* (Rico 1967, 307). What the *De vetula* and related Ovidian apocrypha demonstrate is how the ancient author had been by this time mythologized and transformed into a lovesick poet-physician.

Such a development can be seen not only in secular Latin literature, but also in vernacular works like *Libro de buen amor* that were written during the fourteenth century – what Francisco Rico has called the 'siglo de oro de los Ovidios apócrifos' [golden age of apocryphan Ovids] (1967, 307). In a well-known section of this pseudo-autobiographical poem, the Archpriest of Hita famously assumes the identity of a mad lover called Don Melón and hires a go-between to help him woo the widow Doña Endrina – and, after consummating the affair, attributes 'lo feo de la estoria' to 'Pánfilo e Nasón' [Pamphilus and Ovid supplied the wordly parts of the story] (1988, stanza 891d; 1972, 181).[20] An association between the ancient poet and his medieval alter ego is also made by Don Amor, who names Ovid as the favourite student and servant of Love, 'si leyeres Ovidio el que fue mi criado, en él fallarás fablas que le ove yo mostrado, muchas buenas maneras para enamorado. Pánfilo et Nasón yo los ove castigado' [If you read Ovid, who was an apprentice of mine, you will find many good examples for a lover: Pamphilus and Ovid both learned from me] (1988, stanza 429ad; 1972, 112).[21] Whether or not the author of these verses was familiar with the authentic *carmina amatoria*, scholars like Rico and Richard Burkard have shown that elements of the poem were probably modelled after the *pseudo-Ars Amatoria*, the *Pamphilus*, and *De vetula* – as suggested in a passage in which the Archpriest describes his book, 'por amor *de la vieja* por decir razón, / Buen amor dixe al libro e a ella toda saçón' [For the old woman's sake and to speak the truth, I have called my book *Good Love*, and so do I call her always]; and later when the narrator recounts a humiliating sexual encounter described in the rubric, '*De la vieja* que vino a ver al Arçipreste' [The Old Woman Who Came to the Archpriest] (1988, 933ab, 945; 1972, 188, 190).[22] It has also been shown that the *Libro* is comparable to the *De amore* of Capellanus in its approach to Ovid's questionable authority, as both combine counsel on the pursuit of worldly love with calls to renounce the vanities of the flesh and prepare for the divine betrothal of the soul (Clarke and Wise). Michelle Hamilton has also pointed to intriguing parallels between the *De vetula*, the widow in the *Libro*, and encounters with aged female lovers in the *maqāmāt* tradition. Her findings suggest that – in keeping with the Western reception of medical writers like Ibn al-Jazza, Avicenna, and Rhazes – the amorous tropes of Judaeo-Arabic literature had been received by Europeans through an Ovidian 'hermeneutical filter.'

What has yet to be considered in discussions of influence is whether the author of the *Libro* might have also been familiar with medical readings of Ovid – readings that, as we have seen, had a significant influence on Capellanus and pseudo-Ovidian works. The Archpriest's prose prologue invites readers to approach the text as a poetic model, a practical *ars amatoria*, and a cautionary tale that promotes spiritual growth – competing approaches that John Dagenais has linked with the *intentio auctoris* in the *accessa* to Ovidian manuscripts. Recently, Marcelino Amasuno has posited that the debilitating concept of 'amor loco' [mad love] introduced in the prologue as 'apocando la vida e dando ... muchos daños a los cuerpos' [shortening the lifespan and causing much harm to the body] could have been informed by knowledge of the symptoms and pathology of the condition known as *amor heroes*, in addition to the Augustinian principle of *cupiditas* or fallen desires versus the *caritas* or redemptive love of God (2004, 109).[23] Sections of the *Libro* discussed earlier that adapt from the *pseudo-Ars amatoria* and the *Pamphilus* would seem to support Amasuno's thesis.

The Archpriest first accuses Amor of maddening and ruining the health of lovers by afflicting them with insomnia, a loss of appetite, and severe pains that cannot be treated with common remedies like balms and plasters: 'traes enloqueçidos a muchos con tu saber: / fazes les perder el sueño, el comer y el bever ... non lo sana mengía, enplasto nin xarope' [By your arts you drive people crazy, making them sleepless, ruining their appetites, drying up their throats ... there is no medicine, no balm, no plaster that can stop the hurt] (1988, stanzas 184–7b; 1972, 71–2). Later, he claims that his suffering over Doña Endrina is taking a devastating toll on his body, and – in keeping with Galen, Constantine, and Avicenna – lists such symptoms as madness, sallow skin, sunken eyes, and weakness of the limbs: 'con dolor et tristura, / el grand amor me fase perder salud e cura. / El color he perdido, mis sesos desfallesçen, / la fuerza non la tengo, mis ojos non paresçen ... mis membrios desfallesçen' [in pain and anguish: this great love is ruining my health and my spirit. See how sallow and confused I have become; I have no strength, my eyes are sunken ... all my limbs give out] (1988, stanza 607; 1972, 138). Having taken the pseudonym Don Melón, the Archpriest follows the Ovidian example of 'Pánfilo,' mentioned earlier, and hires a go-between to help him heal his sickened heart and overcome his mental and physical weakness (1988, stanzas 785–6). Trotaconventos informs Doña Endrina of his enfeebled, anorexic condition and unhealthy complexion, somatically attributing these symptoms to his mental obsession with the widow: 'mesquino e magrillo ... su color amarillo, e la su fas mudada / en todos los sus fechos vos trae antojada' [(He is) miserable and scrawny ... You should see how pale he is; his face is sallow. You obsess him in everything he does] (1988, stanzas 829–31; 1972, 171–2). Endrina soon after grows pale and reveals that she is herself overcome with the *eros* and *morbis* of lovesickness (1988, stanzas 855, 859). Trotaconventos warns that this disease can be fatal if not treated right away, and advocates the remedy of sexual intercourse. Before relating his next amorous adventure, the narrator urges readers to spiritually rehabilitate themselves 'en amor de Dios linpio' [with the pure love of God], a healing power that is later invoked in the prayer 'Dominus tecum ... melesina de coydados' [*Dominus tecum* ... consolation of the afflicted] (1988, stanzas 904, 1663; 1972, 321).[24] As indicated in the prologue, therapy in the *Libro* can be understood in Augustinian and Ovidian terms, allowing the Archpriest to pursue the spiritual restoration of *Christus medicus* while at the same time taking on the narrative voice of pseudo-Ovid, the *doctor amoris* turned lovesick patient of medieval lore.

It has been hypothesized that Fernando de Rojas read the *Libro de buen amor* at the University of Salamanca, where he claims to have found the anonymous, unfinished play that would form the basis for his 1499 *Tragicomedia de Calisto y Melibea* or *Celestina* (Gerli 1995, 30). Whether or not Rojas came across the *Libro* as a student, it is certain that he was influenced by Ovid's amatory fiction, as well as elegiac and humanistic comedies, and medical literature. His tragicomedy tells how the lovesick Calisto relies on the machinations of servants and hires a go-between named Celestina to help him seduce Melibea, the daughter of a nobleman. The couple soon after meets a tragic end, when Calisto falls to his death as he descends from a ladder, and Melibea ends her life by jumping from a tower. In 1502, Rojas added a prologue, which is addressed to an anonymous friend who has suffered love's blight, and appended it with an acrostic identifying the author and describing the medicinal function of his text in Horatian terms: 'como al doliente, que píldora amarga / o huye o rescela o no puede tragar / métenla dentro de dulce manjar; / engáñase el gusto, la salud se alarga' [Just like the sick man, who from a bitter pill flees, has misgivings or cannot swallow it (and so) puts it in a sweet treat; (he) fools his taste buds, prolonging his life] (Rojas 1994, 190). In this way, as Bienvenido Morros Mestre has suggested, the author presents the tragicomic function of his work as comparable to the honeyed-pill relationship between the *Ars amatoria* and *Remedia amoris* in medieval manuscripts, and the poet-physician role of Ovid in the *accessus* tradition (2004, 81–3).

Interlinked 'cures' for Calisto and Melibea's love are then offered over the course of the *Celestina*, one of them based on the remedies of physicians, and another drawn from Ovid's *Remedia amoris*.[25] In act 1 of the 1502 edition, Calisto cries out to 'Erasístrato medico' and calls for his lute, before settling for the dubious therapeutic expertise of his servant Sempronio (Rojas 1994, 54). According to an ancient story retold in Petrarch's *Trionfo d'Amore*, Erasistratos diagnosed the sickness of Antiochus, who had fallen in love with his stepmother. In later versions of the *Celestina*, Calisto invokes two physicians: Eras, as an ancient healer of the eyes – through which the image of the beloved enters the imagination – and Galen, still considered the first and foremost medical authority on lovesickness.[26] After retrieving an out-of-tune lute, Sempronio first wonders whether his heartbroken master will be driven to commit suicide and then vows to provide an antidote, reminiscent of Ovid's promise to cure sick lovers before they kill themselves (1957, vv. 15–22). The servant chooses to denigrate the object of Calisto's affections, following the earlier-cited directive in the *Remedia amoris* to 'call those attractions of hers defects or possibly worse' along with the misogynistic logotherapy of contemporary medical treatises like the Castilian translation of the *Lilium medicinae,* which repeatedly cites Ovid, in addition to Galen and Avicenna 1957, vv. 325–6, 108–9).[27] When Calisto rejects this treatment, Sempronio offers to bring Melibea to his bed through the aid of a go-between, thereby facilitating a humoural, coital remedy that will indirectly lead to Calisto's death, as Michael Solomon has shown. This outcome can also be associated with Ovid's recommendation to indulge in sexual intercourse, and his unreliability as a 'sick doctor' whose 'remedies' are not only ironically implicated in act 1, but will also inform Celestina's later prescription of sexual healing, when the old bawd – in words similar to Don Quijote's later warning to Altisidora – warns Melibea: 'más presto se curan las tiernas enfermedades en sus principios, que cuando an hecho curso en su perseveración' [for tender illnesses at their beginnings are more easily cured than those which are well established in their office] (Rojas 1994, 54).

Scholars have found that the *Celestina* sets the stage for later Renaissance satire insofar as the pathology of Rojas's characters can also be understood as a subversion of the medieval code of courtly love developed in *De amore,* and popularized through the suffering of enamoured heroes in sentimental and chivalric romance.[28] Building on the work of Alan Deyermond and others, Ivy Corfis has attributed this parodic effect to a 'tension between courtly and Ovidian love' in which the amorous writings of the ancient poet serve to unmask and expose the unreal pretence of lovers like Calisto. For many sixteenth-century readers of the *Celestina,* this age-old convention of the noble, lovesick suitor would have already seemed outmoded and 'laughable' (Corfis 1996, 396). My findings suggest that Rojas's parody extends beyond the tension between expressions of *fin amour* and Ovid's ironic approach to love and its antidote, to reflect the Roman poet's 'afterlife' as a medical authority and *praeceptor amoris.* The construction of this persona by medieval readers exemplifies a key characteristic of what Michel Foucault has called the 'author-function':

> not formed spontaneously through the simple attribution of a discourse to an individual. It results from a complex operation whose purpose is to construct the rational entity we call an author ... projections ... of our way of handling texts: in the comparisons we make, the traits we extract as pertinent, the continuities we assign. (1977, 127)

Through the course of Calisto's harmful and ultimately fatal therapy, Rojas and his characters not only exploit the texts of the *Ars amatoria* and *Remedia amoris*, but also the medical, satirical reception and reconstruction of Ovid and his works that has concerned me over the course of this discussion. For Rojas, and later Renaissance writers, the lovesick 'Galeno de los amantes' had come to represent an ironic intersection of poetic and medicinal discourse, and a convergence in the arts of infection and healing.

NOTES

1 Specifically, this passage coincides with Ovid's advice that lovers immediately undertake treatment at the onset of their passion (1957, vv. 79–81). All translations are by the author unless otherwise referenced in the appropriate passage.

2 This in contrast to Ovid, who warns against the provocative sounds of musical instruments and singing (1957, vv. 754–5).

3 Unless otherwise indicated, citations of Wack refer to her study, *Lovesickness in the Middle Ages*.

4 Oribasius, personal physician of Julian the Apostate, prescribes diversions and follows Rufus Ephesus in recommending intercourse – as does the famous al-Rāzī, known in the West as Rhazes (Wack 1990, 10–11). Other early medical writers, such as Caelius Aurelianus, take issue with this application of *similia similibus curantur*, or prescriptions of love-making as a kind of *pharmakon* (1990, 11–12).

5 As Luis García Ballester has shown, although Hispano-Arabic translators played a pivotal role in disseminating medical knowledge, the systematic study of Latin translations was carried out primarily in Italy and France during this period ('Medical Science' 1987).

6 Avicenna's eleventh-century Persian *Al-Qanun fi al-Tibb* [Canon of Medicine] was first translated in Toledo under the auspices of Archbishop Raimundus (c. 1150).

7 'Non sunt iudiciis omnia danda meis.' All English translations of the *Remedia amoris* are from the edition of Rolfe Humphries (1957). On the problem of Ovid's *auctoritas*, see the study of Jeremy Dimmick.

8 'Vina parant animum Veneri.' 'Affert cogitationes malas ... propter hoc competit heriosis.' Translations of the *Viaticum* commentaries are from Wack's edition (1990). Both Giles and Peter of Spain specifically cite 'Ovidius' in

'Remedio amoris' (1990, 208, 248). See also the Ovidian cure offered by an anonymous thirteenth-century glossator of *Viaticum* (1990 15, 270).

9 'Unum est reductio virtutis estimative ad rectitudinem et ordinatam dilectionem ... Aliud est ablatio et ereptio cure et sollicitudinis.' Peter of Spain's reading is also more accurate as the Roman poet explicitly recommends drinking in excess as it deadens the spirit of love (1990, vv. 132, 805–9).

10 On Capellanus's use of Ovidian material, see Francis Cairns and Peter Allen.

11 See Paolo Cherchi and in particular Wack ('Imagination'), who discusses the role of 'the *platea ymaginacionis*' in erotic desire in *De Amore* – along with the salutary and harmful effects of sexual activity.

12 See also the discussion in Wack's book (1990, 61–2). Translations of Capellanus, *De Amore*, are by John Joy Parry. 'Amor, quum non possit sua solatia capere, immoderata suscipit incrementa et in immanium lamenta poenarum deducit amantes, quia "nitimur in vetitum cupimus semperque negatum"' (Capellanus 1964, 1.6.7). The oft-cited verse from Ovid's *Amores* reads: 'nitimur in vetitum semper cupimusque negata' (2003, 4.17).

13 'Physicalis monstrat auctoritas ... amorem corpus minoris cibi et potus assumptione nutritur ... Praeterea tollit amor etiam somnum et omni solet hominem privare quiete. Sed ex privatione somni sequitur in homine digestio mala et corporis debilitatio multa' (2003, 3.57–8).

14 'Curabar propriis aeger Podalirius herbis, / Et, fateor, medicus turpiter aeger eram ... O qui sollicitos modo das, modo demis amores, / Adice praeceptis hoc quoque, Naso, tuis ... Siquis amas, nec vis, facito contagia vites; / Haec etiam pecori saepe nocere solent. / Dum spectant laesos oculi, laeduntur et ipsi.'

15 Walter of Châtillon, a well-known contemporary of Capellanus, uses the same trope in his anticipation of critics, 'Turpiter nos mordes, cum sis eger medicus' [Disgracefully you attack us, for you are a sick doctor] (1925, 7A vv. 49–50).

16 The construction of female voices in the text appears to draw on other Ovidian materials, such as the *Heroides* (1990, 20.145), and – as Anne Howland Schotter has shown – the story of Philomela in *Metamorphoses* (2004, 6.424–74).

17 For details on the construction of the Roman poet's legendary vita in the Middle Ages, see, for example, Fausto Ghisalberti and Ralph Hexter ('Ovid's Body').

18 Medieval scribes attributed the work to both Ovid and his alter ego Pamphilus (Burkard 1999, 30–1). More than sixty manuscript witnesses of *Pamphilus* and forty of *De vetula* are extant. On the reception of these texts in Spain, see Francisco Rico.

19 Mars sends Anna Perenna to convince Minerva to be his lover. Anna assures him that the young goddess will accept his advances and a wedding is arranged. When Mars lifts the veil of his new bride, he finds that she is not Minerva but his aged go-between.

20 The comparison with Pamphilus has already been made earlier in the poem, 'Doña Venus por Pánfilo non pudo más faser' [Lady Venus could not have done more for Pamphilus] (1988, 698c; 1988, 151–2). All translations of the *Libro* are based on that of Rigo Mignani and Mario A. Di Cesare. Don Melón breaks down the widow's door, but the subsequent rape scene is missing from manuscripts. In his early study, Rudolph Schevill was the first to examine the Ovidian character of the *Libro* in depth. The subject was again taken up by Félix Lecoy.

21 The Archpriest goes on to name Ovid as Don Amor's teacher and advisor: 'castigo con Ovidio concuerda … el amor leó a Ovidio' [I agree with Ovid on this point … Sir Love taught Ovid] (1988, 446c, 612a; 1972,114, 139).

22 The old woman's humiliating visit with the Archpriest takes place in the month of March, in keeping with Anna Parenna's festival in the *Fasti*, 'El mes era de março, salido el verano' [It was March; spring has arrived] (1988, 945ab; 1972, 190). It is possible that the author was aware of a connection between the *De vetula* topic and the portrayal of March/Mars in Ovid's textual calendar – a connection that would have contributed to the sinful connotations of this particular month elsewhere in the poem (1988, stanzas 951a, 1281d–2a, and 1618ab). On the influence of Ovidian elegiac comedy on the *Libro*, see also the recent study of Bienvenido Morros Mestres ('La comedia').

23 Combining these meanings would not have seemed unnatural, as St Augustine often employs the metaphor of *Christus medicus* in his writings (Arbesmann). On the relationship between medical views of lovesickness and religious passion in the Middle Ages, see Wack (1990, 18–30).

24 The *topos* of divine medicine was also frequently applied to the Virgin Mary during this period, as can be seen in the Archpriest's invocation: 'Tú, Virgen, del çielo Reyna, / e del mundo melesina' [Virgin, Queen of Heaven, Medicine for the world] (1988, stanza 33ab; 1972, 45).

25 On Ovidian sources in the *Celestina*, see, in addition to Schevill, Edwin Webber and Florentino Castro Guisasola (1924, 66–79).

26 In the 1499 version, the victim of love invokes Eras 'y Crato,' an ancient healer of the ears. See the study of Castells (2000, 47–62). The use of medical discourse in Rojas's tragicomedy has also been studied by Amasuno ('Calisto') and Morros Mestres ('La *Celestina*'). The fifteenth century has been described by medical historians as a time of Galenist renewal in Spanish universities. See García Ballester ('Galenismo').

27 'Qua potes, in peius dotes deflecte puellae, / Iudiciumque brevi limite
   falle tuum.' Michael Solomon has studied the exploitation of this kind
   of medical discourse by medieval misogynists. Bernardo de Gordonio repeatedly cites Ovid in his chapter on *amor heroes*: 'Dize Ovidio, "de la viga
   alta se decuelga la carga triste ... da al vazío de la memoria algund afán
   que lo detenga ... vé por lugares fermosos resplandescientes e fallarás mill
   colores de las cosas ... Fermosa cosa es tener dos amigas, pero más fuerte
   es si pudiere tener muchas"' [from the high beam hangs the woeful bur-
   den ... fill the mind with some delight that will distract it ... go to beautiful places and you will find all kinds of new things ... it's a nice thing to
   have two lovers, but having many is stronger medicine] (1957, vv. 17–18,
   169–94; 441–2; Gordonio 1993, 107–9).
28 On the role of lovesickness in romance and its influence on Cervantes, see
   Robert Folger.

WORKS CITED

Allen, Peter L. 1992. *The Art of Love: Amatory Fiction from Ovid to the 'Romance
   of the Rose.'* Middle Ages Series. Philadelphia: University of Pennsylvania
   Press.
Amasuno Sárraga, Marcelino V. 2000. 'Calisto, entre *amor heroes* y una terapia
   falaz.' *DICENDA: Cuadernos de filología hispánica* 18:11–49.
– 2004. 'El saber médico tras el prólogo del *Libro de buen amor*: "loco amor" y
   "amor hereos."' In *Juan Ruiz, Arcipreste de Hita, y el 'Libro de buen amor'*:
   *Actas del Congreso Internacional del Centro para la Edición de los Clásicos Es-
   pañoles*, ed. Francisco Toro Ceballos and Bienvenido Morros Mestres, 247–
   70. Alcalá la Real: Ayuntamiento de Alcalá la Real.
Arbesmann, R. 1954. 'The Concept of *Christus medicus* in St. Augustine.' *Trad-
   itio* 10:1–28.
Brown, Catherine. 1998. 'Sophisticated Teaching: The Double-Talk of Andreas
   Capellanus.' In *Contrary Things: Exegesis, Dialectic, and the Poetics of Didacti-
   cism*, 91–115. Stanford: Stanford University Press.
Burkard, Richard. 1999. *The Archpriest of Hita and the Imitators of Ovid: A Study
   in the Ovidian Background of the 'Libro de buen amor.'* Newark, DE: Juan de la
   Cuesta.
Cairns, Francis. 1993. 'Andreas Capellanus, Ovid, and the Consistency of *De
   amore.'* *Res Publica Litterarum* 16.2:101–17.
Capellanus, Andreas. 1964. *De amore libri tres.* Ed. E. Trojel. 2nd ed. Munich:
   Eidos.

– 1990. *The Art of Courtly Love [De amore]*. Trans. John Joy Parry. New York: Columbia University Press.

Castells, Ricardo. 2000. 'Calisto's Lovesickness and the Diagnosis of Heras and Crato, *Médicos*.' *Fernando de Rojas and the Renaissance Vision: Phantasm, Melancholy, and Didacticism in 'Celestina*,' 47–62. Pennsylvania State Studies in Romance Literatures. University Park, PA: Pennsylvania State University.

Castro Guisasola, Florentino. 1924. *Observaciones sobre las fuentes literarias de 'La Celestina*.' Revista de filología española. Anejo 5. Madrid: Jiménez y Molina.

Cervantes Saavedra, Miguel de. 1990. *El ingenioso hidalgo don Quijote de la Mancha*. Barcelona: Planeta.

– 2000. *The Ingenious Hidalgo Don Quixote de la Mancha*. Trans. John Rutherford. New York: Penguin.

Châtillon, Walter. 1925. *Die gedichte Walters von Chatillon*. Ed. Karl Strecker. Berlin, Weidmann.

Cherchi, Paolo. 1979. 'Andreas' *De amore*: Its Unity and Polemical Origin.' In *Andrea Cappellano, i trovatori e altri temi romanzi*, 83–111. Roma: Bulzoni.

Clarke, Dorothy C. 1972. 'Juan Ruiz and Andreas Capellanus.' *Hispanic Review* 40:390–411.

Colker, M.L. Rev. of 1970. *The Peudo-Ovidian 'De vetula*,'. Ed. D.M. Robathan. *Speculum* 45.2:322–6.

Corfis, Ivy A. 1996. 'Celestina and the Conflict of Ovidian and Courtly Love.' *Bulletin of Hispanic Studies* (Glasgow) 73.4:395–417.

Couliano, Ioan. 1987. *Eros and Magic in the Renaissance*. Trans. Margaret Cook. Chicago: University of Chicago Press.

Dagenais, John. 1986. 'A Further Source for the Literary Ideas in Juan Ruiz's Prologue.' *Journal of Hispanic Philology* 11.1:23–52.

Dimmick, Jeremy. 2002. 'Ovid in the Middle Ages: Authority and Poetry.' In *The Cambridge Companion to Ovid*, ed. Philip Hardie, 264–87. Cambridge Companions to Literature. Cambridge: Cambridge University Press.

Folger, Robert. 2002. *Images in Mind: Lovesickness, Spanish Sentimental Fiction and Don Quijote*. North Carolina Studies in the Romance Languages and Literatures 274. Chapel Hill: University of North Carolina Press; Dept. of Romance Languages.

Foucault, Michel. 1977. *Language, Counter-Memory, Practice*. Ed Donald F. Bouchard. Ithaca: Cornell University Press.

García Ballester, Luis. 1987. 'Medical Science in Thirteenth-Century Castile: Problems and Prospects.' *Bulletin of the History of Medicine*. 61.2:183–202.

– 2000. 'Galenismo y enseñanza médica en la universidad de Salamanca del siglo XV.' *Dynamis: Acta hispanica ad medicinae scientiarumque historiam illustrandam*. 20:209–47.

Gerli, E. Michael. 1995. 'Complicitous Laughter: Hilarity and Seduction in *Celestina.*' *Hispanic Review*. 63.1:19–38.

Ghisalberti, Fausto. 1946, 'Mediaeval Biographies of Ovid.' *Journal of the Warburg and Courtauld Institutes* 9:10–59.

Gordonio, Bernardo de. 1993. *Lilio de la medicina* [*Lilium medicinae*]. Ed. Brian Dutton, Jineen Krogstad, and María Nieves Sánchez. Madrid: Arcos.

Hamilton, Michelle M. 2007. 'Rereading the Widow: The Pseudo-Ovidian *De Vetula*, the Endrina Episode of the *Libro de buen amor* and Their Possible Judeo-Iberian models.' *Speculum* 82.1:97–119.

Hexter, Ralph J. 1986. *Ovid and Medieval Schooling: Studies in Medieval School Commentaries on Ovid's 'Ars amatoria,' 'Epistulae ex Ponto,' and 'Epistulae heroidum.'* Münchener Beiträge zur Mediävistik und Renaissance-Forschung 38. München: Bei der Arbeo-Gesellschaft.

– 1999. 'Ovid's Body.' In *Constructions of the Classical Body*, ed. James J. Porter, 327–54. Ann Arbor: University of Michigan Press.

Hyatte, Reginald. 1982. '*Ovidius, doctor amoris*: The Changing Attitudes Towards Ovid's Eroticism in the Middle Ages as Seen in the Three Old French Adaptations of the *Remedia amoris*.' *Florilegium* 4:123–36.

Kenaan, Vered Lev. 2005. 'The Contribution of *Ars* and *Remedia* to the Development of Autobiographical Fiction.' *Classica et Mediaevalia* 56:167–84.

Lecoy, Félix. 1938. *Recherches sur le 'Libro de buen amor' de Juan Ruiz, Archiprêtre de Hita*. Paris: E. Droz.

Morros Mestres, Bienvenido. 2003. 'La comedia elegíaca y el *Libro de Buen Amor*.' *Troianalexandrina: Anuario sobre literatura medieval de materia clásica* 3:77–121.

– 2004. '*La Celestina* como *remedium amoris*.' *Hispanic Review* 72.1:77–9.

Ovid. 1957. *The Art of Love* [*Ars amatoria, Remedia amoris, Medicamina faciei feminae*]. Trans. Rolfe Humphries. Bloomington: Indiana University Press.

– 1988. *Tristia*. Trans. Arthur Leslie Wheeler. Ed. G.P. Goold. 2nd ed. rev. Cambridge, MA: Harvard University Press.

– 1989. *Fasti*. Trans. James George Frazer. Eed. G.P. Goold. 2nd ed. Cambridge, MA: Harvard University Press.

– 1990. *Heroides*. Trans. Harold Isbell. New York: Penguin.

– 2003. *Carmina amatoria: Amores, Medicamina faciei femineae, Ars amatoria, Remedia amoris*. Ed. Antonio Ramirez de Verger. Bibliotheca scriptorum Graecorum et Romanorum Teubneriana. Munich: Saur.

– 2004. *Metamorphoses*. Trans. Charles Martin. New York: W.W. Norton.

Pérez, Martín. 2002. *Libro de las confesiones: una radiografía de la sociedad medieval española*. Ed. Antonio García y García, Bernardo Alonso Rodríguez, and Francisco Cantelar Rodríguez. Madrid: Biblioteca de Autores Cristianos.

Petrarch, Francesco. 1996. *Trionfi, Rime estravaganti.* Ed. Vinicio Pacca e Laura Paolino. Milan: A. Mondadori.

Rico, Francisco. 1967. 'Sobre el origen de la autobiografía en el *Libro de buen amor.' Anuario de estudios medievales* 4:301–25.

Robathan, Dorothy M. 1969. *The Pseudo-Ovidian 'De vetula.'* Amsterdam, A.M. Hakkert.

Rojas, Fernando. 1994. *La Celestina.* Ed. Dorothy S. 8th ed. Severin. Letras hispánicas 4. Madrid: Cátedra.

– 2004. *Celestina.* Trans. John Clifford. London: Nick Hern Books.

Ruiz, Juan. 1988. *Libro de buen amor.* Ed. G.B. Gybbon-Monypenny. Clásicos Castalia 161. Madrid: Castalia.

– 1972. *The Book of Good Love.* Trans. Rigo Mignani and Mario A. Di Cesare. Albany: State University of New York Press.

Schevill, Rudolph. 1913. *Ovid and the Renascence in Spain.* Berkeley: University of California Press.

Schotter, Anne Howland. 1998. 'The Transformation of Ovid in the Twelfth-Century *Pamphilus.'* In *Desiring Discourse: The Literature of Love, Ovid through Chaucer.* Ed. James J. Paxson and Cynthia A. Gravlee, 72–86. Selinsgrove, PA: Susquehanna University Press.

Solomon, Michael. 1997. *The Literature of Misogyny in Medieval Spain: The 'Arcipreste de Talavera' and the 'Spill.'* Cambridge Studies in Latin American and Iberian Literature 10. Cambridge: Cambridge University Press.

Ulrich, Jakob, ed. 1893. *Pamphilus de amore: comoedia elegiaca medioaevalis.* Turici: Typis Zuercheri et Furreri.

Vega, Lope de. 1980. *La Dorotea.* Ed. Edwin S. Morby. Madrid: Castalia.

Wack, Mary Frances. 1986. 'Imagination, Medicine, and Rhetoric in Andreas Capellanus' *De Amore.'* In *Magister Regis: Studies in Honor of Robert Earl Kaske,* ed. Arthur Groos, 101–15. New York: Fordham University Press.

– 1990. *Lovesickness in the Middle Ages: The 'Viaticum' and Its Commentaries.* Philadelphia: University of Pennsylvania Press.

Webber, Edwin J. 1958. 'The *Celestina* as an *arte de amores.' Modern Philology* 55.3:145–53.

Wise, David O. 1980. 'Reflections of Andreas Capellanus's *De reprobatio amoris* in Juan Ruiz, Alfonso Martínez, and Fernando Rojas.' *Hispania* 63.3:506–13.

2 Mythography and the Artifice of Annotation: Sánchez de Viana's *Metamorphoses* (and Ovid)

JOHN C. PARRACK

From pastoral to picaresque and *novela sentimental* to lyric poetry, Ovid is everywhere in early modern Spain. His cultural stature signals a noteworthy transformation from his condemnation by Isidore of Seville in the seventh century (Keith and Rupp 2007, 28) and underscores both the intrinsic nature of change during this period and the degree to which the *Metamorphoses* came to be emblematic of a period in which neither the church nor the crown could control the representation of culturally divergent viewpoints. Even as they confronted the threat of Protestantism abroad, the Hapsburg kings sought to control everything from the exhibition of *morisco* identity (in 1526 and 1568) to noble male dress (in 1594, 1600, and 1623). The printing press contributed further to this loss of control as the diffusion of standardized editions promoted private and often divergent interpretations (Eisenstein 1979, 84). For its part, the Catholic Church sought to reassert its control over universal truths even as it was forced to issue numerous *índices* of censorship (Kamen 1985, 80–6), debate the use of the vernacular during the Council of Trent (1547–61) (Eisenstein 1979, 343), or discard the Julian calendar in the fall of 1582 (Gimpel 1976, 191–2).[1] As Jane Tylus observes, '[C]hurch and state alike were aware of their own vulnerability amid historical change and disruption. They therefore turned to those intellectuals who worked for them to articulate the myth – and increasingly the reality – of monolithic status' (1993, 5).

Given a historical context preoccupied with so much change, it is not surprising that the *Metamorphoses* held a unique fascination for sixteenth-century Spaniards. The many fragmented *fábulas* recount transformation and implicitly reassure the reader paradoxically that change is one of the few constants that exist. Sánchez de Viana makes this point

explicitly in the *Anotaciones* when he declares: 'la naturaleza continua-
mente se sirve de la ordenada mudança de los siete Planetas para las
continuas mudanças del mundo inferior' [nature continually helps itself to the ordered change of the seven planets for the continued changes in the world below] (Ovid 1589, 47r). As a result, the *Metamorphoses*
were translated into Castilian by Jorge de Bustamante (c. 1543), Francisco
de Guzmán (1578), Antonio Pérez Sigler (1580), and Pedro Sánchez de
Viana (1589) (Ovid, ed. Alcina 1990, xxvi; Schevill 1913, 245–9; McCaw
2007, 242).[2] It is the last of these translations that has proven the least
understood and elicited the most divergent reactions. Notwithstanding
recognition of the translation's artistic accomplishment then and now,
the only sixteenth- or seventeenth-century edition was the *princeps*.[3]
This chapter describes how Sánchez de Viana sought to contribute to
this illusive order by using his annotations as literary artifice – a device,
in this case, that contrives to obscure the mysteries and truths in Ovid
through a game of intertextuality. In place of textual exegesis, Sánchez
de Viana employs the edition in order to displace Ovid and portray
himself as a classical figure that can triumph over his classical subject.
He competes with Ovid by projecting himself into the collection as an
active participant in the Ovidian mythography.

Over the past two centuries, critical response to Sánchez de Viana's
enterprise has varied. Such critics as George Ticknor, Marcelino Menéndez y Pelayo, and most recently, John Turner have noted the translation's poetic achievement and commitment to Ovidian tone and detail
while describing the *Anotaciones* rather ambiguously as 'a mass of learned and allegorical commentary' (Turner 1976, 38). The most strident view
of the annotations is offered by Schevill, who tersely observes:

> Unfortunately almost two thirds of this bulky work of Viana consists of
> comments, learned explanations and references to authorities … The in-
> terpretations of the myths are practically worthless from a scholarly stand-
> point, and merely show that even during the later Renascence students of
> the classics could not slough off the traditional attitude toward the
> *Metamorphoses*. (1913, 152)

As it pertains to the understanding of Ovid in early modern Spain, this
observation is fundamentally true. Filling 288 folios, the annotations establish intertextual and subtextual references within the realm of Ovidian
exegesis but do not offer original insights or readings. Schevill, nevertheless, dedicates some pages to the edition not because it is good, but

because it is overlooked: 'Since this translation was printed in only one edition, as far as I am aware, and, though not rare, is not generally accessible to readers, a few examples of its style will perhaps show why it does not deserve to be wholly forgotten' (1913, 149).[4] Juan Francisco Alcina, however, views the annotations in a much more positive light. As he states in the introduction to his 1990 edition of the Sánchez de Viana translation of Ovid: 'El segundo tomo con las *Anotaciones* sobre los quince libros es interesantísimo y siento realmente no poderlo publicar' [The second volume with the *Annotations* of the fifteen books (i.e., *Metamorphoses*) is very interesting and I really am sorry to not be able to publish it] (1990, xxvii). In this study, then, we seek to read the annotations far more broadly than Schevill did in order to examine their preoccupations and decipher their implications in sixteenth-century Spain. Although the *Anotaciones* may not advance early modern readings of Ovid, they can further our understanding of the cultural currency Ovid enjoyed in the sixteenth century. Since Ovid was already a classic literary figure whose *Metamorphoses* had already been translated into Castilian by at least three editors,[5] Sánchez de Viana employs the *Anotaciones* in order to monumentalize himself rather than to contribute to the 'consecration' of Ovid.[6] Ovid himself welcomes this game of intertextual competition through the fragmentation and openness of the *Metamorphoses* that invites the readers' 'contribution' (Lanham 1976, 59). This process serves as a corollary to the work of literary figures such as Juan Boscán or José González de Salas who published the works of contemporary poets such as Garcilaso de la Vega or Francisco de Quevedo posthumously, thereby monumentalizing them as modern classics. In this case, Sánchez de Viana seeks to privilege his own social and literary status.

As I will seek to demonstrate, the divergent readings of the *Anotaciones* are predicated on their length and many internal contradictions – factors that provide some degree of evidence for whatever reading a critic may wish to attribute to them. Contradiction is emblematic of Sánchez de Viana's *Anotaciones*, a text that is both dependent on the *Metamorphoses* as its underlying literary point of reference, but also independent from it. Organized as an entirely separate part of the edition, it offers a digressive, derivational, and tangential reading of Ovid that makes little direct reference to the translation it accompanies. In semiotic terms, the edition essentially dissociates the signifier – his translation – from the signified – his annotations.[7] Neither part makes direct reference to the other.

Internal contradictions abound. One point of conflict relates to the startling dimension of the *Anotaciones* and the repeated motif of *brevitas*.

Although such promises are often made to be broken, the contradiction here achieves almost ludic proportion. Even as the annotations dramatically overshadow the actual translation of Ovid, Sánchez de Viana underscores their brevity through the repetition of formulae such as 'por no ser largo no refiero' [in order to not be long-winded I will not relate] (1589, 162v, 202v, 213r, 302 [272]r,[8] 305 [275]v), or 'por no ser prolixo' [in order to not be excessively long] (1589, 21v, 98r, 194v). Throughout the *Anotaciones*, he reasserts this point: 'Sucintamente está la interpretación desta fábula declarada en este libro, quando tratamos de la dignidad de la poesía, y en esta parte tampoco seré largo' [the interpretation of this fable is succinctly stated in this book, when we address poetic dignity, and in this part, I will not be long-winded either] (1589, 130r); 'el qual no quiero yo recontar por evitar prolijidad' [which I do not wish to tell to avoid verbosity] (1589, 260r); 'Otras muchas opiniones hay en este negocio, las quales dexo por la brevedad' [there are many other opinions about this matter which I will leave for the sake of brevity] (1589, 305 [275]r); and 'por no multiplicar escriptura passo en silencio' [I will pass (them) by in silence in order to not multiply the amount of writing] (1589, 176v–r).

A second point of internal contradiction relates to the poetic form of the translation itself. Like Pérez Sigler a decade earlier, Sánchez de Viana chooses poetic verse over prose, translating the *Metamorphoses* into *tercetos* and *octavas rimas*. His goals, however, are not at all clear. In the Prologue to the translation itself, he attributes this choice to the preservation of literary artistry: 'Embebecido pues con la dulzura de su proceso me parece cosa digna de un buen espíritu traducirla en romance castellano, y verso más proporcional a la elegancia del latino, que la lengua española admite' [entertained with the sweetness of its process, it seems worthwhile for a good spirit to translate it into Castilian, and into a poetic verse more proportional to the elegance of the Latin one that the Spanish language allows] (1589, ¶¶2v). The *Prólogo a los lectores* [Prologue to the readers] of the *Anotaciones*, however, suggests a different purpose. The use of poetic verse is not to honour the Ovidian form but rather to monumentalize his own translation: 'Y porque cosas de tanto peso se conservasen en su entereza sin variación del tiempo o diversos entendimientos de los hombres ... fueron escritas en versos ... por no dar lugar a que inadvertidos y poco curiosos escritores las corrompiessen o alterassen' [and so that things of such weight may be preserved in their entirety without variation over time or the different interpretations of men, they were written in poetic verse so as not to give unobservant and unquestioning writers the opportunity to corrupt or alter them] (1589, A4v). So, how do we make sense of these contradictions or the length of the annotations?

The answer, I believe, centres on the various motivations of the edition: first, Sánchez de Viana's own project of self-legitimacy and self-fashioning and, second, the invitation to construct meaning.[9] Given the instability and contingency of Spanish life in the latter half of the sixteenth century, it is not surprising that Sánchez de Viana eschews the imposition of monolithic and allegorical readings of Ovid.[10] He readily acknowledges the polysemy of Ovid. In the annotations to book 14, he affirms the validity of these divergent interpretations: 'los dichos de los sabios de una manera se dizen, y de muchas, y todas verdaderas se pueden interpretar' [wise men's sayings are only said in one way and can be interpreted in many truthful ways] (1589, 249r). As a result, Sánchez de Viana inserts himself into the mythography much like a conductor who writes his own arrangement and then leads the orchestra in playing the piece. His goal is to link his fortunes to the popularity of Ovid, to elevate himself to Ovid's cultural status, and to compete with him both intertextually and subtextually through the annotations and the translation.[11] This artifice of self-promotion should not be surprising because Ovid was also a 'show-off' (Lanham 1976, 52, 56). In the case of a fragmented narrative such as the *Metamorphoses*, it is precisely Ovid's style that is the most salient feature of his writing (Lanham 1976, 56). Sánchez de Viana acknowledges this through an edition that seeks to both emulate Ovid's style and compete with his authorial subject. As Sánchez de Viana declares in the *dedicatoria* to Hernando de Vega, his fortunes are linked to the success of this edition of Ovid: 'He yo hecho aprovechando los momentos ... que otros llaman ratos perdidos en componer y publicar esa obra debajo del amparo de v.S. De la cual espero lustre y renombre perpetuo ... por su ventura y la mía, que a tan seguro puerto supimos acogernos' [I have made the most of the moments ... that other people call lost time, in writing and publishing this work with the support of your lordship, from which I expect glory and perpetual fame ... for its fortune and mine, since we learned how to welcome ourselves to such a certain port (i.e., Ovid)] (1589, A2r). His self-representation as annotator is predicated on his role as active participant, not passive observer. Ovid's *fábulas* constitute the 'corteza' (1589, 153v), the superficial narrative 'crust' that is *dulce*, while the annotations seek to penetrate the external stories and ascribe meaning, that which is *utile*. In the process of fashioning this subject position,

Sánchez de Viana misrepresents and privileges his own role in the literary enterprise of translating and annotating Ovid. In the opening lines of the *Anotaciones*, he (mis)characterizes the state of Ovidian study in Spain as follows:

> Cosa es digna de admiración, siendo como son las fábulas tan dulces en su proceso y tan útiles si se entiende lo que debajo de aquel sayal se esconde, y estando los libros, no solamente griegos y latinos, pero aun los de nuestro romance, y otras lenguas vulgares llenos de ellas [las fábulas], lo poco que hasta ahora en nuestra lengua se haya cultivado este inculto campo.

> [It is a thing worthy of admiration, being that the fables are so sweet in their reading and so useful if one understands what is hidden beneath that wool robe, and that not only Greek and Latin books but even those of our language (i.e., Castilian) and other vernacular languages are full of fables, how little this unknown field has been cultivated]. (1589, A3r)

He does not acknowledge any of the most important complete Spanish translations that precede his own, and casts himself as an innovator.

The creation of this pioneering authorial subject emerges also from the dedicatory sonnets that precede his translation. Although such a device is certainly common, there are no less than ten sonnets written by four different authors.[12] Collectively, they transform Sánchez de Viana into a classical figure that explains Ovid, gives new life to Ovid, makes Ovid relevant, and triumphs over Ovid. As this description of their function suggests, these sonnets confirm how Sánchez de Viana seeks to represent himself. He is the actor, Ovid is the passive object. While Ovid simply recounts entertaining stories of transformation, it is Sánchez de Viana who exposes the construction of meaning by both ancient and contemporary writers. In the first of these sonnets by López Maldonado, Sánchez de Viana not only competes with but triumphs over his classical source: 'Dos verdades se muestran principales, / Ovidio en vuestras fábulas ahora, / la una, que con voz blanda y sonora / os las haze un mortal ser inmortales. / Viana, con acentos celestiales, / con ser tan buenas, tanto las mejora, / que en el lugar adonde el bien no mora, / augmentará la Invidia vuestros males' [Two primary truths show themselves, the first, Ovid, is that a mortal being now makes your stories immortal. (Sánchez de) Viana, making the stories so good with celestial accents, improves them so much that in the place where good does not live, envy will increase your ills] (1589, ¶4v). At the end of the sonnet, López

Maldonado recognizes the symbiotic relationship between Ovid and Sánchez de Viana when he asserts that this translation and its annotations will do more for how people esteem Ovid's stories than what the stories will do for Sánchez de Viana himself. In the fourth and sixth sonnets, Martínez Polo portrays Sánchez de Viana as a literary figure who gives new life to Ovid and thereby makes him relevant in sixteenth-century Spain. Martínez Polo's first sonnet is an apostrophe directed to Ovid in which he addresses him as an 'Autor de mil marañas, y mentiras, / eras, liviano, torpe, deshonesto, / mas Viana te ha dado vida nueva ...' [Author of a thousand tangles and lies, you were frivolous, clumsy, dishonest, but (Sánchez de) Viana has given you new life] (1589, ¶4r). Two sonnets later, Martínez Polo portrays Ovid as a discredited figure due to his exile from Rome, suggesting: 'Bien así Ovidio (que por sospechoso / en su materna lengua fue juzgado) / por mano de Viana trasladado, / en la España es útil y gustoso' [So Ovid who was judged to be suspicious in his mother language, is useful and appealing in Spain because of being translated by Viana's hand] (1589, ¶5v). It is Sánchez de Viana who legitimates Ovid through his translation and annotations – a literary artifice that both translates the *Metamorphoses* from Latin to Spanish and also transubstantiates a text by a discredited author into one that is emblematic in sixteenth-century Spain. The ninth sonnet, by Marcos Dorantes, underscores the nebulous and fragmented nature of the *Metamorphoses* and represents Sánchez de Viana as a source of clarity. As the sonnet explains: 'Viana con sus versos sonorosos / deshaze la tiniebla que tenía / encubierta de Ovidio la Poesía, / debajo de conceptos milagrosos' [Viana with his sonorous verses undoes the fog that had covered Ovid's poetry] (1589, ¶6v).

These assertions of achievement in the dedicatory sonnets bolster Terry Eagleton's suggestion that Harold Bloom's theory of the anxiety of influence may well afflict translators just as much as poets (1977, 73). Although we now generally conceive that translations only emulate, they can and did lead to 'competitive imitation' in early modern Europe (Bizer 1995, 175). In the case of Sánchez de Viana, the publication of numerous Castilian translations of the *Metamorphoses* earlier in the sixteenth century only exacerbates this sense of belatedness. One result of this cultural anxiety is that Sánchez de Viana forges connections between himself and Ovid, and attributes his own pursuit of personal fame to Ovid as well: 'No se olvida de su tema el Ovidio, que es acumular fábulas, y dar muestra con la continuación de ellas, de su extraordinario ingenio' [Ovid does not forget his purpose which is accumulating fables and proving his extraordinary talent with the continuation of them] (1589, 134v). Certainly, this use of art as personal artifice is not at all uncommon in early modern Spain, a period in which the establishment of patronage networks is essential to the economic and political survival of the artist.[13] Sánchez de Viana inserts himself into the Ovidian mythography in much the same way that Vermeyen portrays himself in the tapestries representing the conquest of Tunis in 1535, or, that Velázquez will paint himself into *Las Meninas* a century later.[14] Indeed, while Vermeyen asserts his own role in making sense of the invasion, Sánchez de Viana employs a similar artifice, asserting that his *Anotaciones* are the figurative 'key' to unlocking the process of meaning in Ovid.

This artifice of annotation, however, is ironic and perhaps even ludic because Sánchez de Viana refuses to fully turn the key – to reveal the truths contained in the *Metamorphoses*. Rather, he invites the reader to participate in a game of intertextual reference in which he alludes in an almost tangential way to the works of León Hebreo, Marsilio Ficino, and particularly Natale Conti. Given the growth in private reading, the spread of print editions, and the rise in vernacular literacy, Sánchez de Viana seems to be keenly aware of both his inability to control the reading process and the danger presented by granting access to such knowledge to the uneducated. His position, however, is ironic, if not paradoxical, because translations and commentaries such as his were predicated on a larger reading public (Weinberg 1995, 229). As we will see, this threat is mitigated by two major aspects of the *Anotaciones*: their lack of revolutionary insights regarding Ovid and their fragmented, tangential, and derivative nature. Indeed, the *Anotaciones* exemplify a new and fragmented vision of the commentary in which the allegorical gloss is replaced by annotations that, as Michel Jeanneret has noted:

> favored a more technical understanding and provided documentary materials without prejudging the deeper meaning of the book. No longer was a moral or instructive outlook imposed on readers; readers were instead to be given the means to undertake an interpretation for themselves. Historical and critical analysis replaced ideology; assimilation was followed by respect for difference. (1993, 94)

Sánchez de Viana does not seek to impose a single allegorical reading of the *fábulas* as would be characteristic of medieval commentaries

(Brancaforte 1990, xix); he concedes the need for interpretation, and allows for the possibility of divergent readings, and to guide the humanist reader in this process. He accepts this fragmentation and does not seek to impose a unity precluded by what Liz Oakley-Brown calls 'Ovid's narrative method' (2006, 192).

The *Anotaciones* reveal this purpose through both what they discuss and what they censor. When Sánchez de Viana declines to explore the story of Pyramus and Thisbe because it is well-known and not necessary, he justifies the silence or omission. As he explains: 'Yo no la quiero recontar, pues en el testo se entiende claramente' [I do not want to retell it (i.e., the fable) since it is clearly understood in the text] (1589, 80r). On two later occasions, the clarity of the Ovidian text again precludes the need for any exegesis (1589, 131r, 298 [268]r). Sánchez de Viana also omits commentary in order to censure a poor reading, as occurs with Orologio: 'la alegoría de esta fábula la pone Orologio, y por no parecer muy buena no lo refiero' [Orologio writes the allegory of this fable, and, because it does not seem very good, I do not relate it] (1589, 199r).

On the many occasions when he does provide commentary, he corrects classical errors, seeks to expose 'modern' achievements, and guides the reader in discovering the meaning hidden within the Ovidian *fábulas*. By subjugating classical errors to sixteenth-century modernity, Sánchez de Viana not only competes with but triumphs over Ovid. As he declares early in the *Anotaciones*: 'Pero en nuestros tiempos se ha manifestado (como en algunas otras cosas) el error y engaño de los antiguos, porque se sabe que no ay más fértil tierra, ni más idónea para ser habitada, que la que cae debaxo de la equinocial' [But in our times it has become clear (as in some other things) the error and deception of classical authors, because it is known that there is no more fertile and suitable land to be inhabited than that which is beneath the celestial equator] (1589, 10v). When he addresses the columns of Hercules in the annotations to book 3, Sánchez de Viana again contrasts the mistakes of classical antiquity with the accomplishments of 'nuestros Españoles' [our Spaniards] (1589, 10r) – in this case, the Catholic kings. He writes: 'Nil ultra. El qual después nuestros Reyes católicos de gloriosísima memoria, mostraron ser falso, pues descubrieron el nuevo mundo, y mudando, el rétulo dixeron, Plus ultra' ['Nothing beyond,' which our Catholic kings of most glorious memory later showed to be false, as they discovered the new world and, changing the inscription, said 'More beyond'] (1589, 77v). Throughout the *Anotaciones*, Sánchez de Viana privileges modernity and cultivates this corrective discourse by ascribing the verb 'fingir' [to pretend] to classical authors.[15] Covarrubias's definition of the verb underscores both the lack of truth and the will to mislead: 'lo más recibido y usado es to-marse esta palabra fingir por disimular y fabricar alguna mentira' [the most accepted and used is to take this word 'fingir' as to pretend and to fabricate some lie] (1995, 547).

Since the annotations guide the reader in the construction of meaning rather than offering Sánchez de Viana's own interpretation, there is very little Christian rhetoric. While Sánchez de Viana does occasionally allude to Christian truths, Alcina privileges this function excessively in his edi-tion when he declares that Sánchez de Viana 'se esfuerza constantemente en hacer concordar el mito con las enseñanzas de la Biblia. Es un esfuerzo de sincretismo religioso' [makes an effort to reconcile the myth with bib-lical teachings. It is an act of religious syncretism] (1990, xxix). As already suggested, I would argue that the *Anotaciones* underscore a far broader and fragmented pursuit of truth that encompasses the secular more than the religious. Sánchez de Viana confirms this point in book 1 when he abruptly ends the thirty-eighth annotation by saying: 'ay mucha men-ción en la sagrada escriptura ... que por ser fuera de mi propósito no re-fiero' [there is much mention in Holy Scripture ... that I do not tell because it lies outside of my purpose] (1589, 34v).

For Sánchez de Viana, the *Metamorphoses* transcend Christian truth, combining both the history that seeks to benefit the reader – 'apro-vechar' – and the poetry that strives to entertain – 'deleytar' (1589, ¶¶7r). '[N]uestro Poeta,' as he refers to Ovid, 'lo tiene todo, pues es-cribe historia universal desde el principio del mundo a su estado y tiempo' [Our poet has it all, since he writes universal history from the beginning of the world up to his position and time] (1589, ¶¶7r). Christianity constitutes the only constant in this world of emblematic change. As he writes in the annotations to book 1: 'por eso amo a la Virgen pura, e incorrupta, que es el orden estable y duradero de las cosas del mundo ... por ser el mundo inferior, tan inestable, y que se muda siempre sin orden' [for this reason I love the pure and incorrupt Virgin, who is the stable and lasting order of the things in the world ... since the world beneath is so unstable and always moves without or-der] (1589, 47r). The *Metamorphoses*, then, may be read as a guide to living in this unstable world. As its lessons centre on transformation, they can only rarely be read as Christian allegory. Several annotations, for example, promote the *aurea mediocritas* (1589, 129v, 222v). In book 12, for example, Sánchez de Viana ascribes this secular lesson to the story about centaurs: 'Quisieron los antiguos darnos a conocer en esta fábula, que no devemos usar inmoderadamente del vino ni dexarnos vencer de los deseos ni por fuerça hazernos señores de las cosas agenas, y que conviene en todos nuestros actos usar de moderación y justicia' [The ancients wanted us to know in this fable that we should not abuse wine immoderately or let ourselves be overcome by desire or to enslave ourselves to things that belong to others, and that it is fitting in all our actions to use moderation and justice] (1589, 222v). One book later, when he analyses the story of Ulysses, the reading has no explicit Christian significance. The story, nevertheless, exposes the mysteries and promotes our understanding of human existence, what Sánchez de Viana describes as 'un retrato de la vida humana universal, y que a la sombra de estas patrañas están documentos divinísimos para instruirla' [a portrait of universal human life and that in the shadow of these tales are the most divine documents for instructing it] (1589, 229v). What these documents contain are secret truths that must be extracted and explained. As he writes in book 1: 'oficio proprio de poetas, es a las cosas verdaderas añadirles colores y adornos, y haciendo a las veces mezclas de muchas ficciones, para debajo de ellas significar grandes secretos de naturaleza, o misterios morales, como en el discurso de este comento se verá' [it is a proper duty of poets to add colour and decoration to true things, and, at times, making mixtures of many fictions in order to signify great natural secrets, or moral mysteries, as one will see in the course of this commentary] (1589, 45r). While annotators do seek to unlock these hidden truths, Sánchez de Viana recognizes that the process will never be complete. Some mystery will always remain. He explicitly addresses the truths that remain hidden in the *Metamorphoses* in book 13: 'Y esto se fingió porque no solo las cosas buenas y prósperas de los hombres muchas veces se acaban y destruyen pero aun los considerados y muy mirados consejos no tienen cierto paradero. Pues hay muchas cosas que de ninguna manera podemos entenderlas' [And this was fabricated not only because the good and favourable things of men often end and are destroyed but also because considered and careful advice does not have a certain end since there are many things that we cannot understand in any way] (1589, 236v).

Given the polysemy and mystery surrounding the moral – 'la moralidad' (1589, 51r) – and meaning – 'la significación' (1589, 77r), it is the duty of 'graves varones antiguos y modernos' [serious ancient and modern men] (¶¶8v), such as Sánchez de Viana, to decipher, debate, and even protect the content. There is freedom to interpret and to disagree, but Sánchez de Viana urges his humanist reader to understand that such knowledge is not for everyone because these hidden truths can be dangerous. In the *Prólogo a los lectores* (Prologue to the readers), he warns:

> Pues decir claramente verdades apuradas a los que no lo están para oírlas, es dar ocasión que en el entendimiento de los tales se corrompa la ciencia como suele el precioso vino en mal lavada vasija: de donde se sigue la destrucción universal de las doctrinas.

> [Since clearly telling difficult truths to those who are not for hearing them gives occasion for the corruption of their understanding, just as precious wine often does in a poorly washed vessel, whence follows the universal destruction of doctrine]. (1589, A3r)

One must be vigilant that only the educated have access to 'cosas divinas … conforme a su capacidad, porque no menosprecien lo que no entienden' [divine things … in accordance with their capacity so that they do not scorn what they do not understand] (1589, A3r). We must take care, however, not to equate these divine truths simply with Christian truth, since all truth emanates from God. Sánchez de Viana writes in book 1:

> Ansí que las Ideas descienden de Dios en el Angel, y porque cualquiera cosa alejándose de su principio y fuente, y mezclándose a naturaleza contraria, queda menos perfecta, las ideas apartándose de Dios su original, y juntándose con la naturaleza sin forma en todo diversa y ajena de su forma, necesariamente quedaron imperfectas.

> [So ideas descend from God in the angel, and because everything becomes less perfect when it is removed from its origins and source and when it is mixed with its opposite, ideas necessarily became imperfect through separation from God, their source, and affiliating themselves with a Nature without form, different and alien to its form]. (1589, 41r)

What is equally significant, however, is that truth – whether secular or religious – becomes more and more imperfect as it is removed from its divine source. This ever-present imperfection illustrates the need for interpretation and the diverse opinions that often surface as humanists seek to expose or recover the secret *moralidad*. Ironically, however, Sánchez de Viana does not endeavour to unlock the truths hidden within the Ovidian *fábulas* by offering his own interpretations. Rather, the *Anotaciones* simply organize, cross-reference, and privilege existing readings. When he addresses the origins of the universe, Sánchez de Viana seeks to include all points of view but does not draw any explicit conclusion.

> Dicho avemos tres opiniones de la produción del universo, una de Aristóteles, otra de Platón, y la de los fieles, nuestro poeta siguió la de Platón, y Hesiodo, que de las de los gentiles, fue la más conforme a nuestra verdad Cristiana.

> [We have presented three opinions about the production of the universe, one from Aristotle, another from Plato, and the opinion of the faithful; our poet follows Plato's, and Hesiod's, which was the opinion of the Gentiles most consistent with our Christian truth]. (1589, 6v)

On many occasions, he alludes to the divergence of opinion and only references their presentation in other written sources, declaring 'mucha duda ay entre los escriptores' [there is a lot of doubt among the writers] (1589, 46v), or 'no ay mucha conformidad entre los escriptores' [there is not a lot of agreement among the writers] (1589, 32r). Given the doctrinal acceptance of free will after the Council of Trent, Sánchez de Viana recognizes that these disagreements are natural, even defining 'la discordia' [discord] as 'la variedad' [variety] (1589, 40r).[16]

A central aspect of this literary artifice is its fragmentation. Sánchez de Viana does not explicitly include many interpretations or offer his opinion very frequently. Rather, he offers a fragmented commentary that references existing opinion among his European contemporaries in order to ensure that this knowledge does not fall into the wrong hands. To that end, the *Anotaciones* are a portal through which only the humanist reader can gain access to these interpretations. The fragmented nature of the annotations ensures that the reader must construct the interpretation for himself. The most important source by far to which Sánchez de Viana makes reference is the Italian mythographer Natale Conti (1520–82) who published his *Mythologiae* in 1551. Both the nature and frequency of Sánchez de Viana's allusions to Conti point to how much he respected the Italian's work. The annotations make dozens of direct references to Conti, effectively consecrating him as an authority through their unquestioned acceptance of his views. His authority stands by itself without the need of classical or contemporary verification. As Sánchez de Viana writes: 'La moralidad desta fábula pone Natal Comite' [Natale Conti writes the moral of this fable] (1589, 190v, 201v); 'Otra interpretación da Natal Comite' [Natale Conti gives another interpretation] (1589, 94r); and 'Comite alegoriza esta fábula muy bien' [Conti allegorizes this fable very well] (1589, 186r). At one point, Sánchez de Viana presents Conti rhetorically as an equal of Ovid: 'considerando la espina de un pescado, según Ovidio y según Comite a imitación de los dientes de una culebra, o serpiente que auía roýdo una tabla' [considering the spine of a fish, according to Ovid and to Conti, [it is] in imitation of a snake's teeth, or a serpent that had gnawed a plank of wood] (1589, 164v). The primary implication of this reverence for Conti is Sánchez de Viana's propensity to refer only tangentially to any detailed interpretations of Ovid and to outsource his own interpretation to Conti. As he writes in the annotations to book 13, 'Otras cosas demás de las dichas fingieron los fabuladores desta gente. Quien las quisiere ver lea a Natal Comite. La verdad que se puede sacar desta fábula pone él mismo' [The chroniclers of these people fabricated other things besides what they said. Whoever wants to see them should read Natale Conti. He writes the truth that one can get from this fable] (1589, 246v).

I hope to have demonstrated the degree to which Ovid permeated sixteenth-century Spanish culture, influencing not only writers from Garcilaso de la Vega to Cervantes, but also translators and annotators. This 'influence,' however, must be interpreted critically as the purpose of these writers, translators, and annotators often included far more than emulating Ovid. As I have suggested, Sánchez de Viana's translation of and annotations to the *Metamorphoses* seek to leverage the cultural currency that Ovid enjoyed in the second half of the sixteenth century. Read as a cultural document in its own right, the *Anotaciones* are as fragmented as the *Metamorphoses*. They allude ad infinitum to divergent and contradictory interpretations of Ovid from which the only clear lesson revealed to the reader is the literary genius and cultural *gravitas* of Pedro Sánchez de Viana.

NOTES

* I would like to acknowledge the University Research Council at the University of Central Arkansas for support in the acquisition of a copy of Sánchez de Viana's 1589 edition from the Houghton Library at Harvard University, and for a research stipend to complete this project.
1 Sánchez de Viana explicitly refers to the adoption of the Gregorian calendar

at the end of book 1 of the *Anotaciones*: 'Acaba su carrera en trescientos y sesenta y cinco días y seis horas menos ciertos minutos: y de las seis horas se hace el día bisextil, que se añade al año de cuatro en cuatro años, y los minutos corridos se descontaron en el Octubre del año de 1582, igualando el tiempo, nuestro muy santo padre Gregorio décimo tercio' [It ends its race in three hundred sixty-five days and six hours minus a few minutes: and from the six hours comes the leap day which is added to the year once every four years, and the minutes were deducted in October of 1582 when our Holy Father Gregory XIII recalibrated time] (1589, 49r). All translations from Spanish in this essay are my own.

2 Apart from these most important translations, Schevill alludes to several other editions that are either derived from the Italian (e.g., the 1586 edition edited by Felipe Mey), lack a clear provenance (e.g., the 1595 edition published by Pedro Bellero), or were published abroad (e.g., the 1561 edition published in the Netherlands) (1913, 245–9).

3 In the *Aprobación*, the maestro Lazcano not surprisingly provides a favourable review of the volumes. He declares: 'el primero está muy bien traduzido, y por estilo puro y muy elegante castellano: y en el otro (donde se declaran las alegorías de las fábulas) muestra varia y diversa erudición, de que se podrán aprovechar, assí los Preceptores como los curiosos discípulos para entender muchos lugares de Poetas que sin esto se pueden mal entender' [the first part is translated very well with pure style and in very elegant Castilian: and in the other (where the fables' allegories are declared) it shows varied and diverse erudition of which both the Preceptors and the curious students will be able to take advantage so as to understand many poetic common places that can be poorly understood without this volume] (1589, ¶3r).

4 McCaw also describes Sánchez de Viana's translation as 'considerably less popular' (2007, 242, note 8).

5 Lanham characterizes Ovid as the 'poet's poet,' revered in both the Middle Ages and the Renaissance (1976, 49).

6 Bizer uses the term 'consecration' to describe how Belleau ratifies Ronsard's status as a poet (1995, 176, 191).

7 In the context of the *novela sentimental*, Marina Brownlee ascribes this semiotic separation to the glosses in Pedro de Portugal's *Sátira de felice e infelice vida* (1990, 13). Instead of functioning exegetically, the glosses fulfil a narrative function (1990, 112), similar to Sánchez de Viana's *Anotaciones*.

8 A mistake in the pagination of the *Anotaciones* begins with folio 265, which is incorrectly numbered 295. This error continues to the end of the annotations. In this case, 302 is the printed folio error while [272] is the actual folio number.

9 Our limited knowledge of Sánchez de Viana's personal background provides little insight to guide our reading of the annotations. He was from the area around Valladolid, became a *bachiller* in medicine in 1564, a *licenciado* in 1583, and a doctor in 1591 (Alcina 1990, xxiii).

10 Such readings are problematized by what Lanham refers to as 'holes in the middle' (1976, 50).

11 Bizer asserts a similar mode of competition in Belleau's translation of and commentary about Ronsard (1995, 192–6).

12 The sonnets are written by López de Maldonado (2), Antonio de Baeza (1), Martínez Polo (3), and Marcos Dorantes (4).

13 While the use of art as a device for self-fashioning may be limited to literary or artistic figures, political figures have sought to privilege themselves at least as early as Castiglione's *Il Cortegiano* (1528), translated by Boscán in 1534. One historical example of this self-fashioning is Fernando de Valor, who advanced his own political standing during the rebellion in the Alpujarras (1568–71) by (re)adopting his Muslim subject position – as Aben Humeya (see Harvey 2005, 219).

14 I am indebted to Luis Avilés for his insightful investigation of Vermeyan's self-representation in this series of tapestries.

15 Sánchez de Viana employs the verb 'fingir' more than sixteen times to underscore the mistakes of classical antiquity.

16 Sánchez de Viana makes numerous references to free will, declaring at one point that not only ancient philosophers and mathematicians but the Bible 'affirman ser el alma humana libre, y en su albedrío esenta y señora' [affirm the human soul to be free and in its will to be independent and noble] (1589, 237v).

WORKS CITED

Bizer, Marc. 1995. 'Ronsard the Poet, Belleau the Translator: The Difficulties of Writing in the Laureate's Shadow.' In *Translation and the Transmission of Culture Between 1300 and 1600*, ed. Jeanette Beer and Kenneth Lloyd-Jones, 175–226. Kalamazoo, MI: Medieval Institute Publications.

Brancaforte, Benito, ed. 1990. *Las Metamorfosis y Las Heroidas de Ovidio en La General Estoria de Alfonso el Sabio*. Madison, WI: Hispanic Seminary of Medieval Studies.

Brownlee, Marina. 1990. *The Severed Word: Ovid's* Heroides *and the novela sentimental*. Princeton: Princeton University Press.

Covarrubias Orozco, Sebastián de. 1995. *Tesoro de la lengua castellana o española*. Ed. Felipe C.R. Maldonado. Madrid: Castalia.

Eagleton, Terry. 1977. 'Translation and Transformation.' *Stand* 19:72–7.

Eisenstein, Elizabeth. 1979. *The Printing Press as an Agent of Change. I: Communications and Cultural Transformations in Early-Modern Europe.* Cambridge: Cambridge University Press.

Gimpel, Jean. 1976. *The Medieval Machine: The Industrial Revolution of the Middle Ages.* New York: Holt, Rinehart, and Winston.

Harvey, L.P. 2005. *Muslims in Spain, 1500 to 1614.* Chicago: Chicago University Press.

Jeanneret, Michel. 1993. 'Modular Narrative and the Crisis of Interpretation.' In *Critical Tales: New Studies of the Heptameron and Early Modern Culture*, ed. John D. Lyons and Mary B. McKingley, 85–103. Philadelphia: University of Pennsylvania Press.

Kamen, Henry. 1985. *Inquisition and Society in Spain in the Sixteenth and Seventeenth Centuries.* Bloomington: Indiana University Press.

Keith, Alison, and Stephen Rupp. 2007. 'After Ovid: Classical, Medieval, and Early Modern Receptions of the *Metamorphoses*.' In *Metamorphosis: The Changing Face of Ovid in Medieval and Early Modern Europe*, ed. Alison Keith, 15–32. Toronto: Centre for Reformation and Renaissance Studies.

Lanham, Richard. 1976. *The Motives of Eloquence: Literary Rhetoric in the Renaissance.* New Haven: Yale University Press.

McCaw, R. John. 2007. 'Transforming Phaethon: Cervantes, Ovid, and Sancho Panza's Wild Ride.' In *Metamorphosis: The Changing Face of Ovid in Medieval and Early Modern Europe*, ed. Alison Keith, 236–52. Toronto: Centre for Reformation and Renaissance Studies.

Oakley-Brown, Liz. 2006. *Ovid and the Cultural Politics of Translation in Early Modern England.* London: Ashgate.

Ovid. 1589. *Anotaciones sobre los quince libros de las transformaciones de Ovidio.* Trans. and ed. Pedro Sánchez de Viana. Valladolid: Diego Fernández de Córdoba.

– 1990. *Las metamorfosis.* Ed. Juan Francisco Alcina. Trans. Pedro Sánchez de Viana. Barcelona: Planeta.

Schevill, Rudolph. 1913. *Ovid and the Renascence in Spain.* Berkeley: University of California Press.

Turner, John H. 1976. *The Myth of Icarus in Spanish Renaissance Poetry.* London: Tamesis.

Tylus, Jane. 1993. *Writing and Vulnerability in the Late Renaissance.* Stanford: Stanford University Press.

Weinberg, Florence M. 1995. 'Fischart's Rabelais.' In *Translation and the Transmission of Culture between 1300 and 1600*, ed. Jeanette Beer and Kenneth Lloyd-Jones, 227–57. Kalamazoo, MI: Medieval Institute Publications.

3 Torquemada's Ovidian Alternatives

MARINA S. BROWNLEE

Myths are designed to be tautologous.[1] They offer transparent explanations of material phenomena, both natural and unnatural (e.g., monstrous, metamorphosed humans), of abstract ideas and values that define political, social, and religious communities, and of human nature, perception, and emotion. And, though we tend to associate myths with the discourses of primitive societies, they extend far beyond. If we consider Freud and Jung, for example, we recall that when they sought to communicate their insights on the human psyche in the modern world, they too turned to ancient myths – to Oedipus, Electra, and others, endowing old myths with new contexts. Both Ovid in the first century and Antonio de Torquemada in the sixteenth are keenly aware of the transformative power of myth.

Unquestionably acknowledged as the paradigmatic mythographer of the Western tradition, Ovid (43 BC to 17 AD) produced an anomalous epic that lacks virtually all the features we would expect – a continuous narrator, plot, character, and chronology. Despite the absence of these narratological attributes, what captivates the reader of the fifteen books of his *Metamorphoses* is their timeless appeal, their unique meditation on a number of conceptual and experiential possibilities: the natural world and its myriad wonders, its origin and its workings, human behavior and agency. The unifying thread of Ovid's lengthy text is the transformation of bodies into new forms – the *nova corpora* (1977, 1.1–2).[2] Zeus transformed into a golden shower or Daphne into a tree are but two of the many graphic transformations revealed by the *Metamorphoses* which opens with an Ovidian invocation that promises to sing of events and changes from the beginning of time until the present:

My mind is bent to tell of bodies changed into new forms. Ye gods, for you yourselves have wrought the changes, breathe on these my undertakings, and bring down my song in unbroken strains from the world's very beginning even unto the present time. (1977, 1.1–4)[3]

Clearly, Ovid understood the cognitive complexities that myth can reveal, as well as its endless fascination, and so did Torquemada, as his *Jardín de flores curiosas* (1568) makes clear – from an updated, early modern perspective. Cognizant of its potential for commenting on contemporary society and its beliefs, Torquemada exploits mythic discourse to offer rational explanations of natural events and phenomena, and to explore the supernatural realm and the intricacies of the human mind and its nature. From the two zones of the skies that Ovid considered to be uninhabitable (an issue with which he will take issue), to the truth about human hybrids like tritons and centaurs, to attestations of contemporary *nova corpora* reported in the tabloid press,[4] the *Jardín* can be read as an anatomy of Ovidian myth placed into a new socio-political reality.

While Ovid was writing in the context of drastic paradigm shifts in the transition from the late Republic to the early Roman empire, the end of the civil wars and unprecedented views codified in new legislation – a time when the symbolic no longer matched the real – Torquemada was likewise living in an age of radical change regarding the boundaries of knowledge and belief – political, religious, and scientific upheavals – and their representation.[5] This essay explores his experience and articulation of instability, and his sixteenth-century rethinking of Ovidian myth, and the ethnographic and epistemological reasons for the *Jardín*'s pan-European appeal.[6]

Traditionally characterized as a 'miscellany,' a continuation of an ancient and medieval form, the *Jardín* offers the reader a new kind of book instead. The 'flowers' Torquemada offers us are intellectual rather than natural *flora*; as he tells us explicitly, each flower represents 'an idea' (1982, 356). While the medieval *florilegium* reflects the association of narratives with flowers, Torquemada's are carefully collected and presented ideas (the product of human artifice and design), not chaotically strewn, as in the case of his predecessor Pedro Mexía in his influential *Silva de varia lección* (1540), who sees no problem in justifying the disorder of his *Silva* 'porque en los bosques están las plantas y árboles sin orden ni regla' [because in the forests there exist plants and trees lacking order or rule] (1989, 161–2).

By contrast with Mexía's forest, Torquemada's garden is carefully cultivated, divided into six days of logically conceived discussions between three humanist friends in a literal garden setting. In their humanist trialogue, Antonio, Luis, and Bernardo dwell on such daunting topics as the natural world, the supernatural realm of ghosts and witches, the meaning of Fate, and the regions of the far north – the Septentrionis. Torquemada's text is centrally concerned with the status of myth and reality, and he is an innovator in combining such authorities as Ovid, Pliny, and Olaus Magnus with an emphasis on autochthonous and timely issues; narratives pertaining not only to contemporary witch trials and the cultural paranoia they reflect, but also to the social and political implications of Moors and Jews, to Spain's imperial ventures in the New World, and to uniquely Spanish monstrosities and events.

Torquemada's is a cognitive, analytical garden devoted to the thorny problem of objects and objective truth – offering a highly original meditation on progress, 'modern' science, and the value of empirical (rather than bookish) experience in the detection and correction of human error and the pursuit of truth. Reflecting on the epistemological valence of humanistic dialogue in general, but I think, equally applicable to Torquemada's trialogue, François Rigolot observes: 'The use of the dialogue form cannot be dissociated from the expression of free will – it being the product of a liberal God, who created a world of contingency and singularity' (2002, 175).[7]

The interrogation of authority from a sceptical perspective was, of course, central to early modern thought. Moreover, as Claude Levi-Strauss affirms, it was a by-product of the discovery of the New World. This unique and extraordinary event precipitated a revolutionary rethinking: 'a human community which had believed itself to be complete and in its final form suddenly learned ... that it was not alone, that it was part of a greater whole, and that, in order to achieve self-knowledge, it must first of all contemplate its unrecognizable image in this mirror' (1979, 102).

It is this radical (modern) epistemological fissure that compelled everyone – from contemporary thinkers to consumers of tabloid fiction – to become invested in (consumed by) the desire to rethink old assumptions and beliefs in the wake of geographic and ethnographic discoveries, and of scientific and technological advances; they were no longer content to adopt the wisdom of ancient and medieval auctores at face value. In the literary domain, the exploration of truth and fiction

– truth *in* fiction, especially the possible legitimacy of the marvellous debated so hotly in the *romanzi* polemic waged by the so-called Ancients and Moderns, was also crucial to its enterprise.

The legitimacy of the marvellous posed an immediate, additional concern for Spain that was unparalleled by any other country, given that sacred books (like romances also) were being construed by New World Indians as wonder-books. Clearly, what differentiated sacred from profane works was the frequently unpredictable and unstable perspective of the reader. As a result, New World councils in 1556 and 1565 determined that not only should Indians be refused induction into Christian religious orders, but in addition, they should be denied the possibility of reading printed texts or manuscripts. For the same reason, the king in 1580 was advised to forbid Jesuits from even offering higher education to Indians (Fuchs 2001, 23). After all, as Luis laments to his interlocutors, look at the trouble Luther had caused by his misreading of the Bible – a global issue that Torquemada writes about rather pointedly.[8]

Torquemada was a careful reader of Ovid, whose *Metamorphoses* are valuable to the *Jardín*'s epistemological project for several reasons. Not only is he a mythographic *auctor* who suggests many inviting transformational narratives that delight his readers, but he is also an astutely sceptical observer of human nature. His observation regarding the primacy of virtuous agency over noble lineage, for example, illustrates his wisdom in a way that many literary authors, politicians, and social theorists in the age of Cervantes will echo. Of this perspective Torquemada writes:

> No dirá uno: 'soy virtuoso o soy bueno'; sino: 'soy de los godos, o soy de tal linaje, descendiendo de tal casta o de tal parentela'; y no miran lo que dice Ovidio en el libro XIII de sus *Metamorphoseos*: Et genus, et proavos, et quae non fecimus ipso, Vix ea nostra voco.

> [One tends not to say: 'I am virtuous or a good man'; but instead, 'I am descended from the Goths, from this lineage, descended from that house or family': they do not heed what Ovid says in book XIII of his *Metamorphoses*: 'For as to race and ancestry and the deeds that others than ourselves have done, I call those in no true sense our own.'] (1982, 172)[9]

It is not difficult to understand how this preference for inherent rather than genealogical nobility would resonate with those who were not *viejos cristianos*, that is, the Moors and Jews who had been forced to convert to Christianity as a consequence of the obsession with blood purity – the *limpieza de sangre* that had overtaken every aspect of early modern Spanish law and society. Torquemada's inclusion of this Ovidian passage in his discussion here shows his strategic use of Ovid's *auctoritas* to reflect one of the most hotly contested national and imperial issues in his day.

Indeed, Torquemada alludes to the criterion of *limpieza* not only in general terms of titular pedigree versus inherent nobility, but from the perspective of race and skin colour, as when he speaks of human reproduction. In the *Jardín*'s first book, Torquemada recalls the celebrated case cited in chapter 12 of Augustine's *City of God*, of a white couple that engendered a black child. He explains that Augustine accounts for this striking racial disparity by concluding that the woman in question, at the moment of conception, must have been thinking about/imagining the portrait of a Moor represented in a painting on the wall. He also explains that in addition to Augustine's attribution of this racial anomaly to the power of the imagination, other thinkers both ancient (e.g., Plutarch) as well as modern (Amboise Paré) concur with this diagnosis. Yet he takes issue with their thinking, affirming that it is instead a question of genetics:

> Eso no fue por esta vía, sino porque naturaleza hizo un salto del abuelo al nieto, que pareció haber sido la madre concebida de un etíope en adulterio, y lo que en ella encubrió naturaleza por salir blanca, descubrió en el hijo, saliendo de ella negro.

> [It did not happen that way, but instead, because nature skipped from the grandfather to the grandson. It seems that the mother must have been conceived in adultery, and what nature concealed in her since she was born white, was revealed in the black son whom she bore.] (1982, 123)

Torquemada adds that Aristotle, Pliny, and 'otros muchos autores' [many other authors] bring up another celebrated case of race change with the example of the famous poet, Bizantino, who was the black offspring of white parents (1982, 162). And, though he does not offer explicit commentary regarding the relativity of racial and skin-tone attributes in his contemporary Spain, he is obviously raising a volatile topic during the very time when the tragic Morisco Rebellion was being fought (1568–71).[10] Clearly, metamorphosis of this kind is not the result of deceitful or vindictive deities – as it was with Ovid – but a scientific fact, the product of recessive genes, but one that also has timely and seriously destabilizing implications for the validity of the statutes of *limpieza*.[11]

Within the category of abstract ideas for which the *Jardín* draws on the *Metamorphoses*, Torquemada also recalls Ovid in his animated treatment of the extensively debated matter of demonology: whether and to what extent demons exist, what can only be construed as superstition, and the relationship of demons to the Christian belief system. This fiercely debated inquisitorial matter is treated extensively by Torquemada who refers to Ovid's Circe, Medea, and other demonic beings who transform themselves: 'hechiceros, nigrománticos y encantadores, que … dejando de ser hombres, se vuelven demonios' [witches, necromancers and enchanters who … ceasing to be humans, turn into demons] (1982, 323). Medea's ability to fly through the air with her dragons (*Metamorphoses* 6.350–403) is echoed by the contemporary account of a husband who accompanies his wife to a convocation of demons, flying more than 1,000 miles from home (1982, 322). After the wife confesses to the officials of the Holy Office, she and many other offending women are punished for their diabolical activities.[12]

The witch paranoia, evident not only in Iberia but throughout Europe at the time,[13] is addressed in the *Jardín* in a variety of graphic contexts, including the debate over whether witches actually drink the blood of children (1982, 315), and the undeniable fact that demon worship has been a constant since antiquity (1982, 320–3). Once again we see Torquemada rethinking Ovidian myth in the context of his own society's preoccupations – in this case, the Inquisition, its purview, and its validity.

Material and physical phenomena addressed by Ovid are also compelling subjects for Torquemada, ones he scrutinizes from the perspective of 'modern' cultural and scientific understanding. Pygmies, mentioned in *Metamorphoses* 6.70–102, are alleged to be barely two feet high (1977, 137). Torquemada cites Pliny, Juvenal, Aristotle, even Ezekiel, in his discussion to document discrepancies reported as to their size, physiognomy, and location. To this impressive list of *auctores* he adds the first-century Iberian cosmographer Pomponius Mela and the Italian Gemma Frisius from the sixteenth century. Among these authors there circulate reports claiming that female pygmies bear children between the ages of three to five, and that they die by the time they reach their eighth year. As to their location, they are situated by cosmographers either in Norway, Africa, or on a small island, and that their ears are as long as their bodies.

Weighing the accuracy of these exotic and frequently conflicting reports on pygmies, Torquemada concludes that though no consensus can be reached by the discussion with his two colleagues, Luis and Bernardo, it does not pose a problem: 'cada uno podrá creer lo que le pareciere, sin cometer pecado en ello' [each one can believe what he chooses, without committing a sin] (1982, 139). In other words, perspectivism is inescapable – and it is 'not a sin' to disagree. Thus, the relativity of human perception is acknowledged by Torquemada here (and at several other junctures in his text),[14] and it is a remarkably modern attitude. The additional acknowledgment that it is not 'a sin' to believe different accounts is a striking choice of terminology given the ubiquitous reach of the Inquisition into the daily life of its citizens. While Torquemada does not wish to be heretical, he does want to actively rethink received ideas from antiquity to the present, and to make an important point about the inescapable complexities of human perception.

Even a cursory reading of the *Jardín* reveals Torquemada's programmatic fascination with metamorphosis, an engagement with this discourse that is as serious as that of Ovid himself – yet for epistemologically different reasons; not the deceit or retribution of the deities, but scientific explanation afforded by his progressive, modern perspective. If we consider the notable metamorphosis of men into wolves in the muscovite province of Neuros, we are given the ancient authority of Solinus in addition to Pomponius Mela regarding the lupine transformation during 'ciertos meses del verano' [some summer months], after which they assume their human form once more (1982, 420). Torquemada muses that perhaps enchanters effected the dramatic transformation – which clearly transgresses the laws of biology. Ultimately, though, he prefers to reserve judgment about these sometime werewolves.[15]

Here as elsewhere, proof by the laws of nature is sought by Antonio as the three discussants try to explain the staggering amount of ethnographic, geographic, historical, medical, and supernatural information they process. The phenomenon of metamorphosis – of rocks that grow and shrink – offers another dramatic example of the 'modern' endeavour by Antonio, Bernardo, and Luis to explain mysterious natural phenomena. His interlocutors express astonishment at this seemingly organic attribute of such inorganic materials, as Bernardo explains: 'engañado estaba yo, que pensaba que las piedras no se criaban, sino que eran como huesos de la tierra, que siempre estaban en una manera, sin crecer ni descrecer' [I was deceived to have thought that rocks were not raised, but instead were like the bones of the earth, that were always in one way, without growing or ungrowing] (1982, 203). Adopting the discourse of a naturalist, Antonio addresses Bernardo's perplexity by explaining that there is no magic at issue, only a difference in quality; some rocks are characterized by sedimentation, which makes their size increase, while others are affected by erosion, which diminishes them.

One final example of exotic metamorphosis that the *Jardín* and also Cervantes' *Trabajos de Persiles y Sigismunda* include is recorded by the illustrious Italian Pope Pius II, Enea Silvio Piccolomini. He reports that in Scotland there exists on the banks of one river a particular type of tree whose leaves when they wither from age, drop into the water, where they are metamorphosed into worms that ultimately morph into birds that mature and take wing (1982, 205). Realizing that such a hybrid of *flora* and *fauna* strains the imagination, Torquemada comments that no such birds have ever been observed in the sixteenth century, and that such extraordinary metamorphosis may, in fact, be a miracle rather than a natural occurrence.

While critics routinely invoke phenomena like the 'bird-producing tree' – as an object shared by the *Jardín* and *Persiles* – there are others that could be included as well.[16] Beyond this coincidence, however, the anomalous tree is instructive in signalling the distance that separates Cervantes' arborial excursus from that of his predecessor. Torquemada records this striking avian metamorphosis with an intensely analytical eye, indicating that according to one source – Alejandro in the *Días geniales* – on the western shores of England the debris from shipwrecks gives rise to mushrooms [hongos] that turn into birds. Citing a different source thereafter, Antonio recounts that Piccolimini offers an appreciably different explanation for the origin of these birds in Scotland, namely, trees growing by the water's edge whose leaves dry up, rot, and fall into the water, thereafter producing worms that become birds, which take to the skies. A third explanation is given by Casanius in the *Catalogus gloriae mundi*, alleging that these birds, native to England, are the result of an *árbol milagroso* that grows next to the water's edge. The fruit it bears rots and if it falls to the ground it decomposes, and yet if it falls into the water, it turns into a bird that takes wing, and flies away. Some sources claim that many such trees existed, resulting in numerous 'wood-birds' of this sort.

Torquemada does not stop his excursus here, however, with the catalogue of sources. Instead he adds one more detail, culled from a *mapa mundi* printed by the Venetian cartographer Andreas Valvasor, claiming that his neighbour Andreas Rofo had in his possession at the time during which the *mapa mundi* was produced not one but two of these birds: 'tenía al presente dos de estos pájaros de tamaño de dos ánades pequeñas, y que se los habían llevado de España' [he had, at present, two such birds, the size of two small ducks that he had taken to Spain] (1982, 205). Antonio takes issue with this account as a result of what he assumes to be a scribal error [debe estar errada la letra] (1982, 205), assuming that the journal entry should have referred to England or Scotland rather than Spain, 'pues no estaría tan encubierto este milagro, si en España estas aves se engendrasen o se criesen' [this miracle (*sic*) could not have been kept secret if such birds were either born or raised in Spain] (1982, 225).

The semantic fields of the words 'marvel' and 'miracle,' and their usage in the *Jardín* (and in its translations as well) is striking. Torquemada uses both in his text, as illustrated by Luis's questioning of Antonio's word choice early in the text:

Haciéndolo todo tan fácil en la mano y voluntad de Dios, a quién habéis llamado la misma naturaleza, cuando por ella viene a obrar cosas grandes y milagrosas, como las que habéis referido, las llamáis sobrenaturales, en lo cual parece que os contradecís, pues tan natural es a Dios lo uno como lo otro.

[Since the hand of God does everything so effortlessly, which you have also called nature, when He brings about great and miraculous things such as you have indicated, you call them supernatural, which seems contradictory since both miracles and the supernatural are equally natural to God.] (1982, 107)

Antonio justifies this polynomasia by saying that since we do not understand and have never before witnessed such astounding occurrences, 'por la grandeza de ellas las llamamos milagros, que quiere decir cosa de maravilla, y sobrenaturales' [because of their amazing nature, we call them miracles, which means marvels and the supernatural] (1982, 107).

Speaking in general terms, Jacques Le Goff explains that to speak of the 'marvellous' was 'a form of resistance to Christian ideology during the later Middle Ages (1988, 34). He adds:

there were at least three ways in which the marvelous was reclaimed for other ends: Christian, scientific, and historical. Christians ... recast marvels as miracles and ... used them as moral symbols. The evolution of the Latin texts of the *Physiologus* provides a good example. The earlier versions tell of animal marvels without ascribing any symbolic significance to them. Both later versions incorporate so much moral symbolism that the marvelous intent is all but lost. (1988, 34)

It is interesting that Torquemada chooses not to distinguish between 'marvels' and 'miracles,' leaving it to the reader to determine whether logic and scientific observation or the supernatural is to be credited.

Voicing scepticism concerning widely differing accounts of the inter-species *rara avis* that originates in leaves and worms, Bernardo suggests that though it might, in fact, be a miraculous phenomenon [milagro], it may also be nothing more than a verbal fabrication [cosa fingida] (1982, 205). This is another striking example of the scepticism Torquemada occasionally stages for his reader. Not only does he acknowledge perspectivism, which is striking in a text presenting itself as a chronicle of natural and supernatural wonders, but this indeterminacy is marked by an additional, decidedly religious valence as well. Here as elsewhere, Torquemada is bold in averring that disagreement about the ultimate phenomenal category of the object 'would not be a sin' [no sería pecado].[17]

This perspectival admission, the acknowledgment that insoluble disagreement among interpreters can occur, is a frequently articulated Cervantine observation as well. With respect to this episode, the *Persiles* simply mentions the tree's existence, without dwelling on the discrepancies among different accounts, viewing them as the product of submerged wood and a tasty fowl found most abundantly in England and Ireland (Avalle-Arce 1969, 110–11).

Unlike Torquemada's text, Cervantes' abundant focus on exotic objects and exotic ethnographic communities in the *Persiles* is not designed to question their objective existence, but instead to use them as ways of projecting the contradictions of his central focus on the human subject. The emphasis for Cervantes is not placed on sorting out the phenomenal existence of a novel object per se, but from the other side, on dramatizing the unpredictable human responses to a world of astounding phenomena in the 'age of the deceiving senses,' as Foucault characterizes the time in which Cervantes wrote (1972, 23). For Cervantes, complexities inherent in the human subject – and human as object – are what need to be articulated, not scientific accuracy or the congruence of the material and the symbolic.

While it is science – not sin or magic – that makes rocks appear to grow and shrink, and accounts for black offspring being born to white parents, it makes Antonio sceptical as to the existence of the leaf-worm-bird;

it also accounts for the existence of centaurs in a scientific manner that incorporates the Spanish conquest of the New World. These creatures, referred to five times in the *Metamorphoses*,[18] as well as in other sources, were defined as half man and half horse, native to the mountains of Thessaly, the sons of Ixion by a cloud in the form of Juno. Luis explains that they never existed, in reality, but rather were the product of ignorance both in antiquity and in the New World, of an easily explained optical illusion: 'era cosa tan nueva que no la entendían ... en las Islas e Indias occidentales pensaron los indios cuando vieron a los españoles en los caballos. Teniendo por cierto que el hombre y el caballo eran todos un mismo animal' [it was such a new thing that the Indians didn't understand it ... in the islands and West Indies. They were convinced that the man and the horse were one and the same animal] (1982, 173).

Tritons are a further example of hybridity treated by Ovid in three books of the *Metamorphoses* that come under scrutiny in the *Jardín* in a different way.[19] In Ovid, Triton is a singular sea and river god who is half man and half fish. He was begotten by Neptune and Amphitrite, the Nereid, and he had the noteworthy ability to calm the angry seas with the sound of his conch shell. Over time, the figure of this singular Triton was transformed into a race of 'fish men' [tritones o hombres marinos] (1982, 175), as documented among others, by Olaus Magnus (the Latinized form of Olaf Mansson), the influential Swedish ethnographer and cartographer (1490–1557), who was also archbishop of Upsala.[20] According to him, there existed an abundance of tritons in the *mar Septentrionis*, and they were characterized by a serious nautical curiosity that prompted them to jump into small boats and even large ships, much to the surprise of the mariners on board:

> Es verdad que se suelen meter en los navíos pequeños, de los cuales trastornan algunos con su gran peso; y que, asimismo, se suben en los navíos grandes, y A lo que parece, no para hacer daño, sino que están mirando lo que va dentro de ellos.

> [It is true that they enter small boats, capsizing some of them because of their considerable weight; likewise, they board large ships and, it seems, they mean no harm by this action, being prompted simply by curiosity.] (1982, 175–6)

We are informed, in addition, that they travel in large groups, 'pareciendo encima del agua algún gran ejército de muchas gentes' [seeming like a large human army on the surface of the water] and that they are concerned for the welfare of their fellow fish, defending them faithfully:

> cuando sienten que alguno de su compañía es tomado o preso, hacen aquella muestra, de manera que ponen temor a los marineros, de que se atreverán a subir y entrar muchos en la nao y los pondrán a todos en algún notable peligro, y, por esta causa, los tornan a soltar, y con esto, cesa el miedo, porque también cesan las voces y el ruido, y todos se tornan a esconderse debajo del agua.

> [when they sense that one of their group has been captured, they enter the boat in order to provoke fear among the sailors. As a result of this action, the sailors are stricken by fear, which prompts them to release the captive and, by this action, the fear is abated because the noise and shouts also cease; then the fish disappear beneath the water.] (1982, 177)

Being supremely curious, these fish-men sometimes board a vessel 'no con intención de hacer daño' [not to cause harm] but rather to get a close view of 'los hombres que son de su hechura' [the men, who are like them] (1982, 176). Hence, it is an unanticipated intellectual curiosity about humans that the fish-men demonstrate. They often capsize the boats they enter, not with a malicious intent, but rather because of their substantial weight which, at the moment they fling themselves on board, has an undesired destabilizing effect. Admittedly, these aquatic creatures, their surprising curiosity and pacifism, seem hard to accept. And it is a phenomenon about which Antonio ultimately suspends judgment after clearly taking pleasure in the narration of a form of marine life and behaviour that is hard to believe. Rather than affirming or denying their existence and habits, he defers to Divine understanding instead, commenting that 'estos secretos dejémoslos a Dios, que sabe la verdad, que nosotros juzgamos por conjeturas' [we will leave these secrets for God, who knows the truth that we can only guess] (1982, 176–7). Though he defers here to the wisdom of God rather than man's limited understanding (in a rather uncharacteristic move), Antonio soon takes up the matter of *hombres mariños* once again from the perspective of the human intellect, which he is relentlessly compelled to exercise.

Reflecting the *Jardín*'s keen regional interest in reviewing autochthonous Iberian lore, Bernardo brings up the topic of the Galician Mariños ('los cuales se dice y afirma por cosa muy cierta') [of whom it is affirmed as true] and whether they are not only real, but descendants of one of the tritons who ambushed a woman, after which 'tuvo sus ayuntamientos libidinosos con ella,' [he had intercourse with her], with the result that she became pregnant, giving birth to a rational fish-man (1982, 177). Luis doubts this genealogy, indicating that such a union would result not in a being capable of human reason, but a monster (1982, 178). The issue of whether the Mariño would be a son of Adam is debated, and whether two species so different as human beings and fish can procreate is left ultimately unanswered when Antonio concludes the discussion by observing that 'acaecen muchas veces muchas cosas notables en el mundo' [amazing things frequently occur in the world] (1982, 179).

Near the end of the *Jardín*, the topic of fish with human intellect is tellingly presented by Torquemada for a different motive – in dramatic geopolitical terms. It was widely believed that dolphins not only loved music, but were so tame that they would give rides to children on their backs (1982, 479). One such dolphin off the island of Santo Domingo (known as Española once it became conquered by the Spanish), was transported from the ocean to a lake, where it attained the size of a horse. It was given a name by its caregivers, and became so docile that it would literally eat from their hands 'como si fuera un animal doméstico' [as if it were a domesticated animal] (1982, 479). It enjoyed playing with the children as much as they did, being careful not to submerge itself while carrying its human playmates. All this changed, however, when a group of Spaniards approached, wanting to see this marvellous animal. Without any provocation, one of the Spaniards injured the dolphin with a lance, which forever changed its behaviour. It could discern the Spaniards from their clothes, and whenever one of them appeared, the fish would disappear. The dolphin managed to return to the ocean, and was never seen again (1982, 479).

Though Torquemada does not gloss the meaning of this extraordinary fish and its high level of socialization, it is clear that the Spanish colonizers bring unprovoked harm, and, ultimately, the extinction of the creature from the native culture. It would be difficult to miss this loaded political observation. Both because Torquemada revels in the ethnographic diversity of exotic lands, and in the extraordinary *flora* and *fauna* they contain (irrespective of their reality), the disappearance of this anthropocentric animal as a consequence of the unprovoked brutality of the conquistadores is poignant. And in Spain, where the effects of the New World conquest continued to be so hotly debated, we see how Torquemada exploits myth to address the sixteenth-century cultural crisis of empire during which he lived.

From this selection of largely Ovidian figures, we see that Torquemada is equally invested in metamorphosis and the pleasures of its narration. Unlike Ovid, he confronts exemplary discourse, reflecting sceptically on its exhausted nature. It is not the deception or wrath of angry deities that results in human or animal transformations, but genetic and biological issues. Alternatively, some of the putative transformations are dismissed as fictions because they do not conform to reason and scientific observation. There are, finally, matters, like the supernatural existence of witches, necromancers, and enchanters, that only God can comprehend because they defy human reason.

What is also strikingly modern about Torquemada's enterprise is that he acknowledges the inevitability of change, of progress. Speaking in the final pages of the *Jardín* of the Castilian language, he admits that it too will change inevitably:

> tened por cierto que aun en los lenguajes tendrá esta propiedad y fuerza [del cambio]: que aunque ahora nos parezca que se habla en Castilla el más polido y delicado romance que se pueda hablar, los que vendrán después de nosotros algunos años lo hablarán tan diferentemente que lo que se hallare escrito de nuestros tiempos les parecerá a ellos tan bárbaro como a nosotros nos parece el romance de algunas historias antiguas que se hallan de España; y entenderéis esto porque de treinta o cuarenta años a esta parte hallaréis muy grand multitude de vocablos mudados e inventados ahora nuevamente, perdiéndose los unos y usándose los otros.

> [know for certain that in languages [change] is a constant: even now, though it seems to us that in Castile the most polished and nuanced Romance speech imaginable is spoken, what will come soon after us will be so different that our writing will seem barbarous, just the way we consider the language of some ancient Spanish stories; and you will understand that because in thirty of forty years from now you will find a multitude of words that are changed or invented, some are abandoned and others become current.] (1982, 497–8)

In the introductory essay to his valuable edition, Giovanni Allegra describes the *Jardín* as 'un almacén o un museo en que a la acumulación, casual, a pesar de todo, de los objetos, supple el innato entusiasmo y la buena sensibilidad (ya que no siempre la conciencia) del guía' [a storehouse or museum in which the casual accumulation of objects is supplemented by the inherent enthusiasm and good sense (if not always the conscience) of the guide] (1982, 79). It can be argued that the accumulation, however, is not casual, given its thematic subdivision into six coherent books. What is even more noteworthy about the *Jardín* than its function as wonder-book is its surprisingly modern epistemological dimension – the desire to reconsider ancient, medieval, and modern sixteenth-century myths and ideas and phenomena from the more informed perspective of his age, and its calculatedly organized encyclopedic dimension. This conceptual framework makes the book truly innovative in the history of the encyclopedia as genre. As Richard Yeo explains, the Enlightment provided a revolution in the development of the encyclopedic venture. In the Middle Ages, and indeed since antiquity, the 'cyclopedia' or 'encyclopedia' involved the 'cycle' (κύκλος) of the Εγκύκλιος παιδεία, the 'circle of subjects considered the basis of a liberal education' (2007, 48).[21] This is what Quintillian called 'a round of learning,' thereby Latinizing the Greek term and concept. This circular (circumscribed) metaphor representing the body of knowledge that any educated man should possess came to be replaced by a different spatial referent – the field. Jeremy Bentham justifies this transformation, explaining: 'By the image of a circle is presented the idea of a limited extent, determined by the circumference. By the image of a field no limitation whatsoever is presented' (1843, 8:73).

In his stunning essay, Yeo points to two major developments pertaining to the encyclopedia's evolution, its premodern as opposed to modern nature. He writes: 'From the early 1700s, the "modern" encyclopedia was in the ascendant. During the next half century this term came to signify the total of all knowledge, encapsulated in summary form, rather than the prescribed learning of an educated individual' (2007, 50). The *Jardín* does not conform to either category. It clearly exceeds the limited boundaries of knowledge that an educated individual should know, but, as Torquemada points out several times, his text is by no means offering 'the total of all knowledge.' The other development Yeo documents in the modern as opposed to premodern encyclopedia is the choice of alphabetical organization rather than a cosmological scheme (2007, 50). Here too, we note that Torquemada offers a different structure: six books corresponding to six days of conversations stemming from a profusion of phenomena and uncommon events: ethnography, nature and its human wonders, rivers, lakes, and the location of the Earthly Paradise of Christian belief, the supernatural world; Fate, fortune, and happiness; astronomy and time; secrets of the *terra septentrionis*. This subject matter – though encyclopedic in its scope – is avowedly selective.

Torquemada admits that logically one could never address all the wonders of the universe. Nonetheless, he does offer a transitional phase both between the limited curriculum of the cyclopedia and the sum of all knowledge in encapsulated form and an intermediate stage also from the cosmological ordering of the premodern encyclopedia and the alphabetically ordered modern form. The *Jardín* offers an encyclopedia of *exotica* in the service of epistemological and phenomenological learning.

NOTES

1 According to the *Oxford English Dictionary*, myth is defined thus: 'A traditional story, typically involving supernatural beings or forces, which embodies and provides an explanation, aetiology, or justification for something such as the early history of a society, a religious belief or ritual, or a natural phenomenon.' Myth is strictly distinguished from allegory and legend by some scholars, but in general use it is often used interchangeably with these terms.

2 All quotations refer to the Frank Justus Miller edition. For a general study of the text, see Karl Galinsky.

3 Torquemada read Ovid in Latin: 'In nova fert animus mutatas dicere formas corpora; di, coeptis (nam vos mutastis et illas) / adspirate meis primaque ab origine mundi / ad mea perpetuum deducite tempora carme!' Translations from the *Metamorphoses* are taken from Miller's edition. All other translations are by the author unless otherwise referenced in the appropriate passage.

4 See, for example, the work of Henry Ettinghausen. See also the online *Biblioteca de relaciones de sucesos* based at the Universidad de la Coruña http://rosalia.dc.fi.udc.es/RelacionesSucesosBusqueda/.

5 For a concise treatment of the tumultuous changes undergone by Spain during this period, see J.H. Elliott.

6 Torquemada finished writing his *Jardín* in 1568, and it was published in 1570, 1571, 1573, 1575, 1577, 1587, 1589, 1599, 1621, 1943, 1955, and 1982. The text was, in addition, widely translated: into French in 1579, 1582, 1583, 1610, and 1625; into Italian in 1590, 1591, 1597, 1600, 1604, 1612, 1620, and 1628. There were two German translations, in 1626 and 1652, and two translations into English, in 1600 and 1618.

7 'l'emploi … du dialogue n'est pas dissociable de l'exercise qu'il prone pour le libre arbitre, lui-même redevable de la conception d'un Dieu liberal, qui a

créé le monde sous le signe de la contingence et de la singularité' [The use
… of dialogue cannot be dissociated from the exercise of free will, which is
itself dependent on a conception of a liberal God, who has created the
world under the sign of contingency and singularity] (2002, 175).

8 Luis remarks: 'la mala Christiandad de los Luteranos y su pertinacia, sin
averse querido someter al sancto Concilio que se celebró en Trento, basta
para tener estragado el mundo mucho tiempo' [the bad form of Christianity practised by the Lutherans and their obstinacy, without having wished
to submit themselves to the holy Council celebrated at Trent, has corrupt-
ed the world for a long time] (1982, 244).

9 Ovid's continued prestige in the sixteenth-century is attested to by Zapata,
who writes at the end of the century: 'Ovidio en su *Metamorphoseos* ninguna reprehension padece, antes en ingenio, en invención, en disposición
hace a todos los poetas ventaja. En elocución Virgilio se la hace; mas en las
otras obras Ovidio' [Ovid does not deserve any reproach; rather, in originality, invention, and disposition he surpasses all the other poets. In elocu-
tion Virgil reigns supreme, but in the other categories it is Ovid] (quoted
in Schevill 1913, 209).

10 For a consideration of this embattled population, see, for example, Antonio Domínguez Ortiz and Bernard Vincent.

11 For a lengthy discussion of this issue, see Albert Sicroff.

12 In the notes to his edition of the *Jardín*, Giovanni Allegra points to a similar episode told by Paolo Grillando in his *Tractatus de hereticis et sortilegiis*
(Lyon, 1545), fols XXXIX r–XL v. (1982, 313–14).

13 See Hugh Trevor Roper for documentation of the obsession with witchcraft at the time.

14 Cf. pp. 186, 205, 296, 443–4. It comes as no surprise that the *Jardín* was
placed on the Inquisition's *Indice de libros prohibidos* in Portugal in 1581 and
then in Spain in 1643. Ironically, though Torquemada's *Coloquios satíricos*
offers far more critical material that should have triggered the censorship
of the Inquisition, that text was not subject to condemnation by the
Holy Office.

15 He chooses this moment in his discussion to voice frustration at the name
changes undergone by kingdoms, cities, even mountains and rivers, which
makes his scholarly sleuthing difficult if not inconclusive: 'no se pueden
acabar de verificar bien las cosas que por los antiguos están escritas de lo
qur toca a esta tierra septentrional; y no tanto por la poca noticia que tenemos de ella, como pore star tan mudados los nombres de reinos, provin-
cias, ciudades, montes, ríos, que no se puede atinar cuál sea una, cuál sea
otra … Y entenderéis esto, por lo que toca a nuestra España, que si tomáis a

Tolomeo y a Plinio. Que más particularmente escriben de ella, nombrando los principales pueblos que tienen, no hallaréis cuatro que ahora se conozcan por aquellos nombres, que todos están trocados y mudados' [The observations written by the ancients regarding the Septentrionis cannot be easily substantiated. Such is the case not because the accounts are too brief, but because the place names of the kingdoms, provinces, cities, mountains and rivers have been changed so that they are difficult to find ... You will understand this because it applies to our Spain as well, if you consider Ptolemy and Pliny. If you consider the important places they name, you will find four at most that are still referred to in the same way. All the rest have been changed] (1982, 421).

16 For example, talking wolves, flying horses and flying carpets, and skis, not to mention a variety of witches.

17 On the other hand, he is quite pointed in terms of church doctrine. He remembers better times when 'todos los cristianos conformes en conocer y obedecer a la iglesia Católica, y estar debajo del amparo de ella, y no como muchos que tinen solamente el nombre de cristianos, y son miembros apartados por obedecer a otras iglesias y seguir nuevas opinions y herejías' [all the Christians who know and obey the Catholic church, and are protected by it, unlike many who are Christians in name only, who are distant because they obey other religions and follow heretical beliefs] (1982, 244). He is outspoken against 'la mala cristiandad de los luteranos' [the bad form of Christianity practiced by Lutherans] (1982, 244).

18 *Met.* II: 633–76, IX: 89–158, IX: 159–210, XII: 210–44, XII: 563–79.

19 *Met.* I: 313–47, II: 1–30, XIII: 898–968.

20 *Historia de gentibus septentionalibus* (Rome, 1555), and *Charta marina* (Venice, 1539), which also dealt with the Septentrionis.

21 This article offers a wealth of information and valuable commentary on the evolution of the encyclopedia, ending with a thoughtful meditation on the encyclopedic function of the internet.

WORKS CITED

Avalle-Arce, Juan Bautista, ed. 1969. *Los trabajos de Persiles y Sigismunda*. Madrid: Clásicos Castalia.

Bentham, Jeremy. 1843. *Chrestomathia: Being a Collection of Papers, Explanatory of the Design of an Institution*. In *The Works of Jeremy Bentham*. 11 vols. Edinburgh: William Tait.

Domínguez Ortiz, Antonio, and Bernard Vincent. 1978. *Historia de los moriscos: vida y tragedia de una minoría*. Madrid: Revista de Occidente.

Elliott, J.H. 1989. *Spain and Its World, 1500–1700*. New Haven: Yale University Press.

Ettinghausen, Henry. 1993. 'The Illustrated Spanish News: Text and Image in the Seventeenth-Century Press.' In *Art and Literature in Spain,1600–1800: Studies in Honor of Nigel Glendinning*, ed. Charles Davis and Paul Julian Smith, 117–33. London: Tamesis.

– 1995. *Noticias del siglo XVII: Relaciones españolas de sucesos naturales y sobrenaturales*. Barcelona: Puvill.

Foucault, Michel. 1972. *The Archeology of Knowledge*, trans. A.M. Sheridan. New York: Harper and Row.

Fuchs, Barbara. 2001. *Mimesis and Empire*. Cambridge: Cambridge University Press,

Galinsky, Karl. 1975. *Ovid's 'Metamorphoses': An Introduction to the Basic Aspects*. London: Blackwell.

Le Goff, Jacques. 1988. *The Medieval Imagination*, trans. Arthur Goldhammer. Chicago: University of Chicago Press.

Levi-Strauss, Claude. 1979. *Tristes Tropiques*, trans. John and Doreen Weightman. New York: Atheneum.

Mexía, Pedro. 1989. *Silva de varia lección*. Madrid: Cátedra.

Ovid. 1977. *Metamorphoses*. Ed. Frank Justus Miller. Cambridge, MA: Harvard University Press.

Poster, Mark, ed. 1988. *Jean Baudrillard: Selected Writings*. Stanford: Stanford University Press.

Rigolot, François. 2002. *L'Erreur de la Renaissance*. Paris: Champion.

Roper, Hugh Trevor. 1969. *The European Witch-craze of the 16th and 17th Centuries, and Other Essays*. New York: Harper and Row.

Schevill, Rudolph. 1913. *Ovid and the Renascence in Spain*. Berkeley: University of California Press.

Sicroff, Albert. 1985. *Los estatutos de sangre: controversias entre los siglos XV y XVII*. Madrid: Taurus.

Torquemada, Antonio de. 1982. *Jardín de flores curiosas*. Ed. Giovanni Allegra. Madrid: Castalia.

Yeo, Richard. 2007. 'Lost Encyclopedias Before and After the Enlightenment.' *Book History* 10:47–68.

4 Ovid's Mysterious Months: The *Fasti* from Pedro Mexía to Baltasar Gracián

FREDERICK A. DE ARMAS

Ovid, the most cited and imitated classical author during the Renaissance, was often translated and utilized in Spain during the Age of Cervantes. Most of his works were readily available, as writers attempted to emulate, burlesque, or simply borrow from the countless myths and conceits found in his writings. But the same cannot necessarily be said of Ovid's most puzzling work, the *Fasti*. Carole E. Newlands explains: 'Literary critics have generally regarded the *Fasti* as an artistic failure' (1995, 2). The *Fasti* follows the Roman calendar and its feasts for the first six months of the year, from January to June. Some have asked if the work purposefully stops here, before the two months dedicated to the Caesars: Julius (July) and Augustus (August). He would not write extended praise of the powers that exiled him. Amid calendared events, astrological ponderings, hints of exile, and even praise for Augustus and Germanicus, the text also includes numerous metamorphoses, as well as other forms of conjoining the divine and the quotidian. Its many tones and visions have puzzled readers. Its apparently unfinished state and the notion that an almanac could supply material for a major poem further undermined its prestige. It should not come as a surprise, then, that the *Fasti* was not translated into Spanish during the Age of Cervantes and beyond.

And yet, any reader of the *Fasti* must admit to the richness of its language, the lavishness and allure of its feasts, and the majestic progression of the months, each ruled by a deity. Readers have been moved by the poem's shifting moods; by its laudatory images and subversive moments; and by its rustic, bawdy, and sacred myths. They have puzzled over the *Fasti*'s polyphonic meanings as they learned of the myriad ways in which deities can be propitiated (and angered). Indeed, each month with its presiding deity takes on complex meanings as the reader is told why it is named after a particular god or goddess. As Newland states: 'The *Fasti* is both serious and humorous, both panegyrical and subversive' (1995, 6). This essay, then, will turn away from Ovid's most popular works in order to consider the impact of the *Fasti* in the Age of Cervantes, showing how its imitators were concerned with its mysteries and its mysterious months. In order to provide a preliminary assessment of the importance of Ovid's text, this essay will veer from the main literary works of the period and investigate instead the presence of the *Fasti* in two important Spanish compendia of the sixteenth century, and in two works from the seventeenth century that collect many examples of ancient and modern texts. Thus, we will begin with Pedro Mexía's *Silva de varia lección* (1540/1550); continue with Juan Pérez de Moya's *Philosophía secreta* of 1585; then move to Bartolomé Jiménez Patón's *Elocuencia española en arte* (1604/1621); and conclude with Baltasar Gracián's *Agudeza y arte de ingenio*. Having analysed the presence of the *Fasti* in these four texts that span a century (from 1540 to 1648), we will then conclude with an Ovidian subject that connects several of these works: the figure of Janus, the god that brings in the New Year as he presides over January.

Each of these four texts utilizes Ovid's *Fasti* in a variety of ways. By pointing out indebtedness to the *Fasti*, a text can partake of the authority of Ovid. The work can also evoke a certain curiosity on the part of the reader who is presented with a rather obscure text that tells of the religious practices of a culture that flourished long before. At times, a line or more of the Latin text or Spanish translation is given as a 'sacramental' gesture, a way to further authorize a statement or notion.[1] The Spanish writer may take the lines out of context, thus increasing the desire for the ancient, the need to discover the mysterious text. Some passages often comment on the ancient work, establishing a textual conversation which can lead the learned reader to ponder differing meanings (a heuristic imitation).[2] More elaborate imitations are also to be found here. The Spanish text can even deviate from the original and provide a new vision of the events or notions from the *Fasti*, thus exemplifying what Thomas Greene has called a dialectical imitation.[3] Most of these imitative passages will foreground an estrangement from the ancients, the desire to repossess a lost civilization, and to surmount the historical gap.[4] The gap allows these writers to respond to Ovid in many different ways. Centring on the notion of mystery, we will see that for some, it is the curiosity aroused by the ancient as enigmatic that is most important. Mysteries are not just mysteries that arise from a cultural gap or the mysteries of ancient religion; there are also literary or cultural mysteries, the veiling through myth of holy or philosophical insights.[5] Finally, some Spanish writers would transform ancient mysteries into Christian ones with concepts that would seal the gap and garb the ancients in modern fashions. No matter what strategy is used, what Leonard Barkan has called the heart of myth seems to preside over these allusions and imitations – the merging of the divine and the quotidian.[6] A new year, a marriage, prostitution, a woman's blemishes, the reversals of fortune, the desire to know what is to come – these are things that are part of life, but they are suffused with divinity in Ovid.

Pedro Mexía's *Silva de varia lección* (1540/50) was one of the most popular works of the sixteenth-century with dozens of editions published in Spanish and other languages such as Italian, French and German (Mexía 1989, 1:53). Mexía was the foremost Spanish writer of the genre called the miscellanies, one which according to its modern editor, Antonio Castro: 'pretendía indagar sobre el mundo y el hombre y alcanzar la verdad por medio del descubrimiento de sus enigmas, divulgando los conocimientos que, por estar escondidos hasta entonces, podían provocar, dado su carácter extraordinario o sorprendente, la curiosidad intelectual' [sought to search the world and mankind and reach truth by way of the unveiling of its enigmas, popularizing knowledge that, having been hidden until then, could provoke intellectual curiosity given its extraordinary or surprising character'] (Mexía 1989, 1:62).[7] In this work, Mexía searches for these curiosities in ancient and modern writers, Pliny becoming one of his most prized models from antiquity. Ovid is also among the frequently cited authors, with at least twenty-six direct mentions. Mexía cites from the *Fasti*, the *Metamorphoses*, the *Heroides*, *Ibis*, *Remedia amoris*, and *Tristia* (Mexía 1989, 1:208, note 42).

Since Mexía is less interested in myth per se than in curious or extraordinary occurrences of any kind, the number of citations from the *Metamorphoses* does not overwhelm other texts by Ovid. There are six moments taken from the *Fasti*, showing that, even though the text was not translated into Spanish, it was certainly used by humanists such as Mexía. He never cites the Latin text, but gives the gist of a story, anecdote, or curious custom as found in the *Fasti*. Of course, Mexía uses the *Fasti* to describe calendared moments and their implications – different mysteries or curiosities that arise in different months. He expounds, for example, on the notion that May is inauspicious for weddings – it is between April, dedicated to Venus (goddess of love), and June, dedicated to Juno (goddess of marriage) (1989, 1:34). Thus, Romans must advance or delay their marriages so as to celebrate them in an auspicious month. While revealing this little-known belief, Mexía undercuts its authority, labelling these deities, Venus and Juno, 'vanidad' [vain], and ending the passage with a rejection of 'la vana idolatría' [vain idolatry] (1989, 1:635). And yet, this recurring term does not dampen curiosity over an ancient calendar that survived until his times. Mexía's purpose, then, may be as conflictive as that of the *Fasti*. The Spanish humanist wants to arouse interest in the classical past; he wishes to unveil ancient notions and the significance of months that still carry their ancient names. At the same time, he must somehow condemn as 'vain' an antique world that fascinates him. Obviously aware that his times were still 'contaminated' with a pagan past (as in the names of the months and the days of the week), Mexía provides his audience a glimpse of how the ancients viewed the passing of the year, a mysterious and alluring vision that foregrounds antique practices.[8]

May was not the only month that interested Pedro Mexía. We will turn to his discussion of January at the end of this essay. But he also draws from the *Fasti*'s astronomical or astrological images as when he warns of the noxious days of the Dog Star (1989, 1:368); or when he tells of the orrey built by Archimedes and described by Cicero (1989, 1:830). Although seeming to move away from the gods, Mexía still images them through the celestial sphere. There are also two references to Fortuna, a major motif in the *Fasti* (1989, 1:795–6). Mexia calls on Ovid's authority as he tells how women disrobed in front of the statue of Fortuna 'y, descubriendo allí cualquier deffecto y tacha que tuviessen creýan que la Fortuna se la encubriría ... Assí lo dize Ovidio en sus *Fastos*' [and showing whatever defect or blemish that they had, they believed that Fortuna would cover it up ... Thus says Ovid in his *Fasti*] (1989, 1:796). The passage does indeed come from *Fasti* (1989, 4. v. 148). The direct reference to the Roman poet may grant authority to the past practice of this curious custom. At the same time, it distances Ovid from Mexía's audience; it also casts doubts on ancient beliefs by using the verb *creýan* (to believe). Ancient miracles are thus curiosities, the stuff of fiction.

In a second allusion to Fortune in Ovid, Mexía states: 'Ovidio en los *Fastos*, la llama fuerte y también dibdosa' [Ovid in his *Fasti* calls her strong and also doubtful] (1989, 1:795). The reference here is to the June festival of *Fors Fortuna* described in the *Fasti* (1989, 6. v. 773ff). The goddess's strength is perceived through Servius Tullius, who rose to kingship although born of a slave woman. But nothing is said in Ovid's passage of Fortuna's trait as doubtful or inconstant. Indeed, it is not clear from the passage if Mexía means that the reader should doubt her existence or see her as changeable. Earlier, his meaning is clear: 'con no ser nada la fortuna, sino una cosa ymaginaria y sin ser' [Fortune being nothing, but something imaginary and without being] (1989, 1:790). Mexía's addition again places the gods in a liminal position, between admiration and derision, between curiosity and disbelief. Mexía, then, has established a conversation with the antique work. His dialectical imitation impels his readers to turn to the mysteries of ancient worship, while creating a certain distance from his own culture.

Juan Pérez de Moya, one of the first, if not the first great Spanish mythographer, wrote his famous treatise, the *Philosophía secreta* (1585), more than three decades after Pedro Mexía's miscellany. Like Mexía, he relies heavily on Ovid, although he often borrows his classical citations from other important mythological treatises, such as Boccaccio's *Genealogia deorum* and Natale Conti's *Mythologia*.[9] Indeed, there are passages that even resemble Mexía's *Silva*. There are more than two hundred references to the *Metamorphoses* in Pérez de Moya, overwhelming all other works by the Roman poet. The *Fasti*, on the other hand, is cited more than sixteen times – a substantial number of instances, although minuscule when compared to the *Metamorphoses*.[10] Indeed, Pérez de Moya prefers the *Metamorphoses* even when little is said of a particular myth there – perhaps this comes from his heavy reliance on other mythological manuals.[11] But, he uses the *Fasti* to narrate or allude to quite a number of myths: Arion, Castor and Pollux, the two Cupids, Flora, Janus, the Lars, Mars, Oceanus, Sisyphus, Tethys, Venus, and Vesta. There is no question that Pérez de Moya wishes to infuse the divine into everyday life. Although his work is all about the ancient gods, the allure of paganism pales when compared to Pedro Mexía. As Jean Seznec asserts: 'His scholarship has a distinctly medieval cast' (1972, 317). The *Philosophía secreta* proposes to reveal secrets and mysteries. But he follows Boccaccio in maintaining that 'ancient poets were divinely inspired to prophesy the Christian mysteries' (Green 1970, 113). Thus, Pérez de Moya ends up showing the reader how to interpret the pagan gods in a way that is compatible with Christianity. His euhemerism and his allegories rationalize the ancient.[12]

Some of his uses of Ovid have to do once again with the intellectual value of the antique. He cites the *Fasti* to establish a genealogy,[13] or buttress authority for the name of a god or goddess.[14] Given the importance of sacred architecture in the Renaissance, and the popularity of Vitribius, it should come as no surprise that Pérez de Moya imitates an important element of the *Fasti*, a discussion of the temples of antiquity.

These include the temple of Vesta and the temple of Venus (1995, 385). Both Ovid and the Spanish mythographer tell how one of Venus's temples was transferred from Sicily to Rome. But while Pérez de Moya keeps his citation focused on this transfer as an explanation of a specific name attributed to the goddess, Ovid goes on to explain that this day is sacred to wenches and 'ladies of a liberal profession' (1989, 4. v. 866). It is difficult to say if the Spanish mythographer made this a deliberate omission or if he was simply borrowing from an intermediary and did not know the context for this feast. Imitation, then, is problematized by possible contamination.

Pérez de Moya's discussions of another temple lead us back to Pedro Mexía. Both writers describe at length the way Fortuna is depicted and worshipped. Without referring to Mexía or to Ovid, Pérez de Moya repeats and expands the story of the founding of one of her temples (which he states was Fortuna's first): 'El primero que entre los romanos la honró fue Servio Tulio ... y atribuyendo su estado a la fortuna le hizo un suntuoso templo en el Capitolio y mandó a todos que la honrasen por deesa' [The first among the Romans who honoured her was Servius Tullius ... and attributing his state to Fortune he made her a sumptuous temple in the Capitol and ordered everyone to honour her as goddess] (1995, 430). Pérez de Moya's lengthy description seems to echo the religious, social, and political contexts of the *Fasti*, thus making this a fuller and more satisfying imitation. It foregrounds, like the *Fasti*, the common people (*plebs*) and their relation to their rulers and their gods. Carole Newlands believes that here Ovid contrasts a virtuous man with a negative contemporary example: 'Ovid ... stresses the king's humble origins ... Unlike Tiberius, Tullius rises to power through merit, not through family connections' (1995, 222). Pérez de Moya may have knowingly or unwittingly brought into play the ambiguities of Ovid and thus the ambiguity of this passage in terms of the role of the people in the Spanish empire.

Like Mexía, Pérez de Moya utilizes the term 'vanidad' [vanity] to refer to Fortuna (1995, 430). But he is much more damning than Mexía when it comes to Fortuna. Instead of describing the ceremonies parents performed for their children in order to propitiate this deity, Pérez de Moya merely states that such rites are laughable ['mueven a risa'] (1995, 429). Indeed, he portrays this deity as one the great errors of antiquity (1995, 428). He rebels against the notion of Fortuna: 'como a tal le hacían templos y estatuas, en que el demonio, por engañar e introducir en el mundo su idolatría, entrando en ellos daba respuestas' [as such they built temples to her and sculpted statues in which the devil, to deceive and to introduce into the world his idolatry, entered into them and gave answers] (1995, 429). Thus, Fortuna is one of the least fortunate deities in Pérez de Moya. Many of the other antique myths derived from Ovid are given a more appropriate garb to survive a new age. What they acquire in 'rationality' they lose in allure and authenticity. The myth of Zephyrus's erotic passion for the nymph Chloris is found in Boccaccio and Ovid's *Metamorphoses*. But there could well be in the narrative of Pérez de Moya some contamination with the *Fasti*, where the story is treated at length (Ovid 1989, 5. v. 195ff). This is a clear use of natural or physical allegory, the transformation of myth into a natural phenomena, the arrival of spring: 'Esta fábula significa la virtud natural deste viento ser engendrar las flores' [This fable signifies the natural quality of this wind to engender flowers] (1995, 341). Ovid had been used to establishing genealogy when discussing Oceanus and Tethys, but these deities are also reshaped into a physical allegory: 'Por Oceano se entiende la virtud activa para la generacion que del agua hace, y por Tethys, la pasiva o la material de la generación' [The term Ocean can be understood as the active virtue of generation that derives from the water, while the term Tethys is the passive or material aspect of generation] (1995, 171).

As for the story of Arion told in the *Fasti* (1989, 2. vv. 85–118), Pérez de Moya gives us a moral allegory, that even the most hidden of sins will be discovered and punished by God (1995, 563). While Pedro Mexía sought to arouse curiosity with little-known tales and have readers ponder on what is truth and what is vanity, Pérez de Moya 'paints' (1995, 650) stories and myths from antiquity to create wonder and to make them more palatable to his Christian audience. But his constant allegorization foregrounds the historical gap between times and cultures, one that seems much more insurmountable than in Mexía's appeal to curiosity.

Two decades after Pérez de Moya, Bartolomé Jiménez Patón, a humanist from La Mancha, published the first version of *Elocuencia española en arte*. A revised version of the 1604 text became part of his *Mercurius Trimegistus* in 1621. Jiménez Patón's book was not addressed to a public in search of curiosities and mysteries. Instead, he wrote his work as a textbook on rhetoric for the schools. In order to teach tropes from metaphor to hyperbaton and in order to deal with memory, eloquence, and levels of meanings, he draws his examples from a number of Spanish writers as well as key classical authorities. Among the Spanish authors, he favours Lope de Vega, although even Pedro Mexía and Pérez de Moya are cited (1993, 144, 234). Since Jiménez Patón is dealing with rhetoric, it makes sense that the most cited classical author is Cicero. Horace and Virgil are frequently cited, followed by Ovid and Terence. Of the seven references to Ovid that I have found, three are too general to pinpoint, two derive from the *Metamorphoses*, one from the *Ars amatoria*, and one from the *Fasti*. Thus, even school children were exposed, to a very minor degree to be sure, to this least known of Ovid's works.

The reference to Ovid's *Fasti* is found in his chapter 'Antifrasis,' which he defines as 'cuando la palabra se recibe en contrario significado' [when the word is taken to mean its opposite] (1993, 144).[15] He includes euphemisms among this type of trope and it is here that he provides a Latin citation from the *Fasti*. Given the subject and the purpose of the book, it would seem that mystery is far from Jiménez Patón's range. And yet, this is precisely what we encounter. Euphemisms, he explains, come from the ancient notion that positive words are positive omens. In order to render authoritative this startling statement meant for youths at Spanish schools, Jiménez Patón alludes to five ancient writers. He begins with the Athenian orator Demetrius Phalereus, continues with Cicero, Horace, and Tibullus, and concludes with a paraphrase of verses 70 and 71 of the first book of Ovid's *Fasti*: 'Día de fiesta es, donde no solo hay necesidad de buenos deseos, mas aún de buenas palabras' [A feast day is one where there is need not only of good intentions but also of positive words] (1993, 147). Since these are words spoken by Janus, let us leave for later Jiménez Patón's startling interest in Ovidian mysteries.

Agudeza y arte de ingenio was published more than three decades after Jiménez Patón's rhetoric, half a century after Pérez de Moya's treatise, and a full century after Mexía's miscellany. The first version came to light in 1642, while a revised and expanded text was published in 1648.[16] For Lía Schwartz this book 'codified types of conceits that were available to the writers of the seventeenth century, who believed that creativity depended upon the artist's intelligence and erudition' (2004, 279). Thus, this treatise expounds the many ways through which the inventive mind, the mind that is suffused with *ingenio*, uses wit [*agudeza*] to develop conceits [*conceptos*].[17] These conceits 'did not designate objects with their names; in fact, objects remained hidden under the successive figurative descriptions that were pressed into service to build conceits' (Schwartz 2004, 280). While *agudeza* is a mental procedure that searches for connections between things or subjects, the conceit is the use of rhetorical figures to come up with the concrete verbal or textual result, one where the hidden must be perceived.[18] With countless examples from classical antiquity and from his own times, Gracián brings together the very different styles of the brothers Argensola, Camoens, Carrillo y Sotomayor, Garcilaso, and Lope de Vega in order to develop his theories and classify the many forms of wit or *agudeza*.[19] Among his contemporaries or near-contemporaries, the works of Góngora are the most cited, while among the ancients, Gracián foregrounds Martial's epigrams. Gracián also makes extensive use of Horace, Virgil, and Julius Caesar.[20] Ovid, surprisingly, only merits eight clear allusions in the second expanded version of the work.[21] Of these, two are from *Tristia* while one citation derives from the *Fasti*.[22]

Gracián's sixth chapter or *discurso* is entitled 'De la agudeza por ponderación misteriosa' [Of wit based on mysterious correspondences] (1969, 1:88). This type of wit is particularly enchanting since it promises to reveal a hidden truth, one that is often understood by connecting opposites or extremes. However, the connection proposed by the writer must be subtle in order to be fully appreciated. Gracián's introduction to this type of wit serves to arouse not only the readers' curiosity, but also their highest expectations. To satisfy them, Gracián gives the reader but one verse from Ovid's *Fasti*: 'Ne celeri fieret victima tarda Deo' [for no sluggard victim may be offered to the swift god] (1969, 1:386). This is followed by an account of what makes this verse subtle and mysterious: Gracián explains that there are two parts to the wit encountered in Ovid's line. First, the reader is led to ponder two very different types of sacrificial animals. The contrast in their qualities provides the extremes needed for a good conceit. Secondly, the reader is treated to the subtle mystery of why the horse is appropriate to the sun god – both animal and god share the quality of swiftness: 'Examinó, ingenioso, Ovidio el sacrificio que se le hacia al sol, que era de un veloz caballo, y satisface sentencioso, que al Dios de la ligereza no se le habían de ofrecer animales tardos y perezosos' [Ingenious Ovid examined the sacrifice that was made to the sun, which was of a fleet horse, and he satisfies us sententiously noting the one could not offer him lazy and sluggish animals] (1969, 1.89). Gracián's prose lacks the repeated, yet seemingly hollow condemnations of paganism found in Pedro Mexía's miscellany, although Gracián often compares classical examples to modern ones which centre on Christian mysteries. It is as if he were equally at ease revealing pagan and Christian mysteries. Thus, as opposed to Pérez de Moya's *Philosofía secreta*, Gracián initiates the reader into the secrets of

the ancients and not into how ancient fables and forms of worship reveal elements of Christianity, history, and science. By looking at ancient
poetry and pondering sacrificial mysteries, he images the ancient gods
for the seventeenth-century reader. And this image is tied to the temple
where the sacrifice is to take place, thus sharing with Mexía and Pérez
de Moya a certain curiosity about ancient temples.

As a way of concluding, let us look at the way each of the four writers
views the Ovidian mysteries of January/Janus. Pedro Mexía's interest in
the *Fasti* may derive from his desire to deal with calendared matters. He
has a lengthy discussion concerning the precise date of Christ's birth,
where he also shows the problems with the ancient calendar and even
the revision of the calendar made by Julius Caesar [the Julian Calendar]
(1989, 1:736–44). We have seen how Mexía has a long disquisition on the
month of May. He is also very interested in January. Mexía asserts that
the month of January begins the year because of the Romans' 'devoción
y vanidad que tenían con su dios Jano' [vain devotion that they had toward their god Janus] (1989, 2:183). In his usual manner he utilizes the
term 'vanidad' to refer to pagan practices. The repetitive use of the term,
as noted, minimizes its impact since it is given so often as a negative explanation for everything that is non-Christian that it becomes a commonplace. Mexía goes on to insist that for the Romans, the year began with
the month of March, alluding to the *Fasti* among his authorities.[23]
Although it is true that the Latin poem tells that in ancient times 'the
month of March was the first and that of Venus the second' (1989, 1. v. 39),
Ovid also contends that the two months were 'prefixed' to that of March
(1989, 1. vv. 43–4). The Spanish text dialogues with the antique and a
reader must know both in order to fully understand the tensions that
occur between and within the works.

  Mexía argues that it is more suitable to have the year commence with
March or the beginnings of spring since Adam and Eve would have
thus come out of paradise at a beneficial time, one that consoled them
for their loss. And yet, in this apparently Christian move away from
January to March, he is still echoing Ovid's poetic voice in the *Fasti*,
which asks Janus: 'Come say, why doth the New Year begin in the cold
season? Better had it begun in spring. Then all things flower, then time
renews his age, and new from out other teeming vine-shoot sells the
bud' (1989, 1. vv.149–51). Janus's response is twofold. First, January
brings the new sun, which will grow in power for the next six months.
Second, the year should begin with Janus since he is the god who

guards the threshold. Janus himself asserts: 'It is that through me ...
you may have access to whatever gods you please' (1989, 1. vv. 173–4).
But there is a third answer. As Denis Feeney reminds us, Ovid clearly
states that 'Mars' month used to come first, put there by his son
Romulus, but it has been displaced by Greek science, which taught the
Romans that there were actually twelve months in the year, not ten'
(2007, 205). Nature, rites, and science come together in a fragile coali-
tion. A similar conjoining can be found in Mexía's text. A Christianized
echo of Janus flickers in this *Silva* when the author reasons that January
comes shortly after the birth of Christ (1989, 2:183). Christ was imaged
as a new sun and as a figure that brings about a new age to humankind.
It is through him that Christians would have access, not to other gods
but to the vision of the 'true' God. Mexía, then, seems to lessen Ovid's
authority by quoting a statement that the Roman poet later rejects and
by using Christianity as a response to the vain gods of old. The two
texts thus battle for authority, as Ovid seeks to be heard over Mexía's
obvious Christianization. And yet, the Spanish humanist is actually
echoing a number of motifs from Ovid's calendared poem. The evocation of Christianity does not fully hide the ancient myths and the mysteries of this first month. Both new and old beliefs are conjoined – Mexia's
Silva cannot fully expel the ancient gods. Indeed, curiosity provides
them a forum through which they can reveal some of their mysteries.

Pérez de Moya is also very interested in Janus, devoting a full chapter
to this god (chapter 32 in part 2). His lengthy commentary on this deity
begins in a euhemeristic manner, making him into a historical figure,
the first king of Italy. As such, he had many temples built and invented
sacrifices to the gods. He was then made into a god (1995, 323). Pérez de
Moya argues that it is because of many of these traits that the Romans
never sacrificed to other gods without sacrificing to him first. He cites
Cicero and Macrobius as authorities here, neglecting Ovid's *Fasti*,
where Ovid explicitly states that Janus is first worshipped because he is
the god of thresholds. While Pedro Mexía, as noted, leaves out this trait
completely, Pérez de Moya includes it when dealing with how the god
is 'painted' or depicted: Janus holds keys or a sceptre (1995, 324).[24] But
Pérez de Moya is not content with a portrait of the god; he must find an
allegorical key. He thus explains that Janus is the sun that governs the
world and serves as guardian of the doors of the East and West where
the sun rises and sets (1995, 324). These roles, sovereign and doorkeep-
er, are reflected in the sceptre and keys. The Spanish mythographer
then cites the *Fasti* to describe the two faces of Janus. It is true that Ovid

claims that the two faces derive from the fact that Janus was one part of Chaos until the elements dispersed and 'a shapeless lump assumed the face and members of a god' (Ovid 1989, 1. vv. 111–12). But, Pérez de Moya embellishes Ovid by arguing that one of his faces is bearded, dark, and terrifying while the other is handsome and happy (1995, 325). It is now that we learn that he is the god of beginnings, since he emerged from Chaos.

It is through both the pictorial and the natural perspectives that the calendared and somewhat Ovidian Janus emerges. Indeed, Pérez de Moya provides an interesting pictorial and scientific detail, saying that a statue of Janus shows him with three hundred fingers in one hand and sixty-five in the other, thus adding to the number of days in the year (1995, 325). He immediately points to his own *Arithmética práctica y speculativa* (Salamanca, 1562), where he 'demonstrates' how and why the year has three hundred and sixty-five days (1995, 325), and thus recalls Ovid's use of Greek science. Pérez de Moya was particularly interested in popularizing science during the sixteenth century. He thought of it as a social necessity and he set out to educate his society. Although he revels in the many curious images found in Ovid and many other classical authors, he uses the *Fasti* as a springboard for scientific speculation and popularization. While acknowledging the book's importance as a calendared text, he discards its scientific elements so as to propound his own knowledge.

From a text that arouses curiosity over Janus and calendared mysteries (albeit with certain Christianized analogies), we have moved to a work that foregrounds physical or natural readings as well as the proliferation of images. Both Mexía and Moya have imitated lengthy passages from Ovid's *Fasti*. The third text by Jiménez Patón provides us with only one citation from the Roman poem, which is freely translated into Spanish. And yet, his passage is crucial to the rhetorical figure he is discussing. Euphemisms are important because words can be omens. Turning to Cicero, Jiménez Patón explains that the Pythagoreans 'querían en cualquier cosa que se hiciese no se dijese palabra antes mal sonante, por tenerla por azarosa, sino bien sonante, felice, fausta, bien afortunada' [wanted that in whatever thing was being done, there would not be uttered a harsh-sounding word because it was dangerous; instead they should be sweet-sounding, happy, prosperous, and bringers of good fortune] (1993, 147). The citation from Ovid closely follows: 'Now must good works be spoken on a good day' (Ovid 1989, 1. v. 71). Later, Janus will explain to 'Ovid': 'Omens are wont … to wait upon beginnings. At the first word you prick up anxious ears; from the first bird he sees the augur takes his cue. (On the first day) the temples and ears of the gods are open, the tongue utters no fruitless prayers, and words have weight' (1989, 1. vv. 178–83). Although Jiménez Patón does not make clear that the first day of the month is important since words uttered then have a greater impact, he never rejects the implication that words have an ominous component, that they can sway events. Indeed, this is the very origin of euphemisms if we accept the implications of Jiménez Patón's narrative. Euphemisms can be magical in that they bring forth positive and fortunate results. Let us recall that the second version of Jiménez Patón's work is called *Mercurio Trismegisto*, the title itself being an evocation of ancient Egyptian wisdom. Thus, it might be possible to further research this textbook on rhetoric as one that conceals ancient mysteries.

Turning to the last text, we are again faced with one citation from the *Fasti*. And, the very economy of Gracián's example makes it unique and thus more treasured amid the verbal outpourings of his text. Nothing is said of the context of the line. Turning to the *Fasti* a reader would discover that this line appears in the description of the month of January, and recalls Mexía's discussion of why this month comes first. But Gracián is not interested in what traits allow this deity to appear first in the calendar. Instead, he takes a line from a discussion of the feast of the Agonal, when Janus must be appeased with a sacrifice. After explaining that the day is called the 'Agonal' because of the sheep that are to be sacrificed, Ovid goes on to detail why different animals are sacrificed at different feasts: swine to Ceres; a goat to Bacchus; a heifer to Proteus; a horse to Hyperion; and a hind to Diana.[25] All the analogies between gods and animals in Ovid are developed through stories. Only that of the sun god is left without a narrative, being compressed into two verses. Of these, as noted, Gracián only gives us one: 'Ne celeri fieret victima tarda Deo' [for no sluggard victim may be offered to the swift god] (1969, 1:386). Gracián fails to mention that the sacrifice is to Hyperion, and not to Apollo.[26] Thus, mystery piles upon mystery in Gracián's terse allusion to the *Fasti*. And Hyperion himself is a shadowy figure. A Titan, son of Gaia (Earth) and Uranus, he is sometimes associated with the sun. And yet, it is his son Helios who is most often referred to as the solar orb.[27] Gracián, then, is keenly aware of the literary, religious, and philosophical aspects of pagan mysteries and how they can be utilized to develop wit, to create conceits and to lead us to mysterious analogies where words and gods veil and reveal the analogical foundations of thought. Even though the *Fasti* is cited only once in the *Arte y agudeza de ingenio*, its presence is a thoughtful tribute to Ovid's poem. Gracián's brief allusion leads to 'ponderación misteriosa' [mysterious ponderings] and 'verdad escondida y recóndita' [hidden and recondite truth] (1969, 1:88).

To conclude: Ovid begins his lengthy praise of Janus by calling him *Ianes biformis* and asking: 'But what god am I to say thou art, Janus of double shape? For Greece has no divinity like thee' (1989, 1. vv. 89–90). Janus is unique in that he both provides entrance into the classical pantheon and looks in two directions. Four authors from the Age of Cervantes have sought to enter the mysteries of antiquity using Janus. While Mexía and Pérez de Moya use him as one of their guides, Jiménez Patón and Gracián evoke the *Fasti* only once to reveal the uniqueness of Ovid's paean to this deity. Janus's 'double vision' (Newlands 1995, 7) is of key importance for all four writers since they bring to their texts a glimmer of the ancients as well as a perspective of those living some sixteen centuries after the Roman poet. Each imitates Ovid, each attempts to close the historical gap in different ways. While Pedro Mexía stresses the double vision of curiosity and vanity, Pérez de Moya paradoxically seeks to turn curiosity away from the ancients in a book dedicated to their mythology by including moral and physical allegories. Even though he calls his text *Philosphía secreta*, his vision of the secrets of the past is tempered by an emerging science and by Christianity. Jiménez Patón is perhaps the one writer closest to Ovid's mysteries, showing how a rhetorical device derives from Janus's feast, and how ancient magic imbues language. Baltasar Gracián is also interested in such devices, and also reveals ancient mysteries and hints at hidden truths. The god of the threshold, centuries later, has thus allowed an entrance into his mysteries.

NOTES

1 I am adapting Greene's notion of sacramental imitation to the simple use of a passage that calls for the veneration of the original text as authoritative.
2 These passages, according to Greene, 'Come to us advertising their derivation from the subtexts they carry with them, but having done that, they proceed to distance themselves from the subtexts and force us to recognize the poetic distance traversed' (1982, 40).
3 According to Greene, we move from heuristic to dialectic imitation when there is a current of mutual aggression as the modern text exposes the

'vulnerability' of its model, 'while exposing itself to the subtext's potential aggression' (1982, 45).

4 On the historical gap, see Thomas M. Greene's chapter, 'Historical Solitude' (1982, 4–27).

5 Edgar Wind cites Dionysius the Areopagite: 'All those who are wise in divine matters ... and are interpreters of the mystical revelations prefer incongruous symbols or holy things, so that divine things may not be easily accessible' (1968, 12–13). Thus, the antique myths and their ceremonies veil insights on the divine.

6 'But in the image of magical transformation there is always the mystery of the divine embedded in the real, the natural, the quotidian ... For a mythic view of the universe depends upon seeing the divine in the familiar' (Barkan 1986, 18).

7 All translations are by the author unless otherwise referenced in the appropriate passage.

8 As Otis Green notes, Tertullian attempted 'ineffectually' to do away with the pagan names of the days of the week (1970, 114). Others sought to change the names of the twelve signs of the zodiac to that of the twelve apostles.

9 According to his modern editor, Carlos Clavería, Pérez de Moya also follows *Las catorze cuestiones del Tostado* by Alonso de Madrigal. He could have consulted editions of 1506–7, 1545, and 1551 (Pérerz de Moya 1995, 22).

10 In contradistinction to the *Philosophía secreta*, there are numerous allusions to the *Fasti* in Italian mythological treatises such as Boccaccio's *Genealogia deorum*. Some thirty citations to the *Fasti* appear in Natale Conti's mythology. For Pérez de Moya's utilization of Conti, see M.C. Álvarez Morán and R.M. Iglesias Montiel.

11 When recounting the myth of Zephyr and Chloris, for example, the mythographer says nothing of the *Fasti*, where the myth gains great prominence as Ovid tells of the feast of the Floralia. He cites instead a brief passage from book I of the *Metamorphoses*. 'The wind Zephyrus created flowers which were born without seeds' [El viento Céphiro criava las flores nacidas sin simiente] (Pérez de Moya 1995, 601).

12 In the second chapter of the *Philosophía secreta*, the author provides a guide for the different interpretations of myth he will follow, but his fivefold classification is reduced in practice to three: historical (euhemeristic), physical, and moral (Seznec 1972, 316).

13 See, for example, the lineage of Mars (Pérez de Moya 1995, 288) and the status of Tethys as wife of Oceanus (171–3).

14 Venus as Ericina (1995, 385).

15 As an example, he refers to Pedro Mexía who 'dice que es no mal escriptor' [says he is not a bad writer] (1993, 144), while meaning that he is a very good writer.

16 Correa Calderón claims that the second version of Gracián's treatise 'va a adquirir una amplitud mucho mayor, acaso excesiva' [will acquire a much larger range, if not excessive] (Gracián 1969, 1:18).

17 Gracián clarifies that the conceit is the expression of wit: 'un acto del entendimiento que expresa la correspondencia que se halla entre los objetos' [an act of understanding that expresses the correspondence that is found between objects] (1969, 1:55).

18 Gracián notes that there are three types of *agudeza*. First, there is the *agudeza de perspicacia*, dealing with useful truths of arts and sciences. Second, there is the *agudeza de accion*, where witty actions are the result, and finally, there is the *agudeza artificiosa*, which is the subject of his current book (1969, 1:58). This last *agudeza* is further divided into simple or pure ['artificio menor'] and compound ['artificio mayor'] (1969, 1:62–3).

19 Even prose fiction is included: Don Juan Manuel's *exemplos* and Mateo Aleman's picaresque.

20 Already the first edition of 1642 included fifty-two epigrams by Martial, the most cited and favoured example.

21 However, one of these references actually cites five different passages from book II of the *Metamorphoses*, citations which Gracián views as *sententiae*. They are examples of how Apollo is able to counsel his son Phaeton: 'en que Apolo aconseja al temerario hijo a llevar el gobierno de su luz con mucha moderacion y prudencia' [in which Apollo counsels his reckless son to manage and steer his luminary with great moderation and prudence] (1969, 2:29).

22 Gracián also includes two references to the *Tristia*. The first tells how a new conceit can emerge by changing a word from a verse, as in the first elegy in Ovid's *Tristia* (1969, 2:65). The second reference has to do with the relation between author and mythological event. Ovid becomes a new Acteon who must pay for having contemplated what he should not have seen (1969, 2:223).

23 He also cites Varro and Macrobius (Mexía 1989, 2:183).

24 In this he echoes Ovid's *Fasti* (1989, 1:99).

25 Ovid concludes his sacrificial catalogue by returning to Bacchus and explaining why an ass is also an appropriate sacrificial victim. The latter led Bellini to paint his famous canvas, *Feast of the Gods*.

26 It is curious that Gracián cites Ovid three times in connection with the sun. Gracián tells us that he calls the luminary 'espejo del dia' [mirror of the

day] (1969, 1:128); he cites five *sententiae* pronounced by Apollo to counsel his son (1969, 2:29). This, of course, is in addition to the Hyperion passage.

27   Ovid claims that the horse sacrifice to Hyperion derives from Persia. This allusion (which Gracián also omits) is equally mysterious. It may derive from the unhappy love of Helious for Leucothoe, princess of Persia or Babylon, who was transformed into frankincense, according to Ovid's *Metamorphoses* (1976, 4:255).

WORKS CITED

Álvarez Morán, M.C., and R.M. Iglesias Montiel. 1990. 'Natale Conti, estudioso y trasmisor de textos clásicos.' In *Los humanistas españoles y el humanismo europeo*, 35–49. Murcia: Universidad de Murcia.

Barkan, Leonard. 1986. *The Gods Made Flesh: Metamorphosis and the Pursuit of Paganism*. New Haven: Yale University Press.

Beardsley, Theodore. 1970. *Hispano-Classical Translations*. Pittsburgh: Duquesne University Press.

Brownlee, Marina Scordilis. 1990. *The Severed Word: Ovid's* Heroides *and the Novela Sentimental*. Princeton: Princeton University Press.

Burrow, Colin. 2002. 'Re-embodying Ovid: Renaissance Afterlives.' In *The Cambridge Companion to Ovid*, ed. Philip Hardie, 301–19. Cambridge: Cambridge University Press.

Conti, Natale. 1988. *Mitología*. Ed. and trans. Rosa María Iglesias Montiel and María Consuelo Álvarez Morán. Murcia: Universidad de Murcia.

Feeney, Denis. 2007. *Caesar's Calendar: Ancient Time and the Beginnings of History*. Berkeley: University of California Press.

Gracián, Baltasar. 1969. *Agudeza y arte de ingenio*. Ed. Evaristo Correa Calderón. 2 vols. Madrid: Castalia.

Green, Otis H. 1970. *The Literary Mind of Medieval & Renaissance Spain*. Lexington: University Press of Kentucky.

Greene, Thomas A. 1982. *The Light in Troy: Imitation and Discovery in Renaissance Poetry*. New Haven: Yale University Press.

Greer, Margaret. 1991. *The Play of Power: Mythological Court Dramas of Calderón de la Barca*. Princeton: Princeton University Press.

Jiménez Patón, Bartolomé. 1993. *Elocuencia española en arte*. Ed. Francisco J. Martín. Barcelona: Puvill.

Martínez Berbel, Juan Antonio. 2003. *El mundo mitológico de Lope de Vega: Siete comedias mitológicas de inspiración ovidiana*. Madrid: Fundación Universitaria Española.

Mexía, Pero. 1989. *Silva de varia lección*. Ed. Antonio Castro. 2 vols. Madrid: Cátedra.

Newlands, Carole E. 1995. *Playing with Time: Ovid and the* Fasti. Ithaca: Cornell University Press.

O'Connor, Thomas Austin. 1988. *Myth and Mythology in the Theater of Calderón de la Barca*. San Antonio, TX: Trinity University Press.

Ovid. 1976. *Metamorphoses*. Ed. Frank Justus Miller. 2 vols. Revised G.P. Goold. Loeb Classical Library. Cambridge, MA: Harvard University Press.

– *Fasti*. 1989. Trans. James George Frazer. Revised G.P. Goold. Loeb Classical Library. Cambridge, MA: Harvard University Press.

– 1996. *Tristia. Ex Ponto*. Trans. A.L. Wheeler. Revised G.P. Goold. Loeb Classical Library. Cambridge, MA: Harvard University Press.

Pérez de Moya, Juan. 1995. *Philosophía secreta*. Ed. Carlos Clavería. Madrid: Castalia.

Schevill, Rudolph. 1913. *Ovid and the Renascence in Spain*. Berkeley: University of California Press.

Schwarts, Lía. 2004. 'Linguistic and Pictorial Conceits in the Baroque: Velazquez between Quevedo and Gracián.' In *Writing for the Eyes in the Spanish Golden Age*, ed. Frederick A. de Armas, 279–300. Lewisburg: Bucknell University Press.

Seznec, Jean. 1972. *The Survival of the Pagan Gods: The Mythological Tradition and Its Place in Renaissance Humanism and Art*. Trans. Barbara F. Sessions. Princeton: Princeton University Press.

Torres, Isabel, ed. 2007. 'Introduction: *Con pretension de Fénix*.' In *Rewriting Classical Mythology in the Hispanic Baroque*, 1–16. London: Tamesis.

Wind, Edgar. 1968. *Pagan Mysteries in the Renaissance*. 2nd ed. New York: W.W. Norton.

PART TWO

Ovid and Cervantes

5 Ovid, Cervantes, and the Mirror: Narcissus and the Gods Transformed

TIMOTHY AMBROSE

In the following essay, I will consider a series of stories in book 3 of Ovid's *Metamorphoses* and the possible connections between them and *El curioso impertinente*, the interpolated novella in chapters 33–5 of *Don Quijote*, Part 1. Frederick de Armas and Diana de Armas Wilson have previously noted models for the *Curioso* in the tale of Giges from Herodotus, in Ariosto's *Orlando furioso*, and in the story of Cupid and Psyche found in Apuleius's *Golden Ass*.[1] De Armas has added to these models Renaissance art works by Raphael and Giulio Romano (2006, 189–204). In what follows, I would like to suggest the possibility that Cervantes also had Ovid in mind when composing the *Curioso*.[2]

Book 3 of the *Metamorphoses* tells the stories of Bacchus, Tiresias, and Narcissus. The first story in the series is that of the birth of Bacchus (1993, 86–9).[3] In a manner similar to that in which the birth of Bacchus begins a series of interlocking stories in the *Metamorphoses*, the eruption of what may be called a Bacchic force is the point of departure for the events narrated in *El curioso impertinente*: Anselmo's initial irrational desire to test his wife sets the action of the story in motion, provoking the chain of events that will affect Anselmo, his friend Lotario, and Anselmo's wife, Camila.

Immediately following the birth of Bacchus in the *Metamorphoses*, and rhetorically connected to it,[4] the story of Tiresias is told, how the famous soothsayer came to be both blind and able to see the future, his powers of inner vision compensating for his lack of eyesight (1993, 89–90). Juno blinds Tiresias because he favours her husband, Jupiter, in a dispute. This situation arises because Tiresias possesses a special kind of knowledge: he has had the experience of being both a man and a woman; for this reason, Juno and Jupiter call upon him to judge whether a man or a woman enjoys more pleasure in love-making.

In her examination of the story of Narcissus, Patricia B. Salzman-Mitchell states that, 'the story actually begins with another story of seeing ... In Tiresias' case ... seeing is connected with knowledge ... Tiresias knows more than what is allowed to mortals ... Tiresias' doom has to do with knowing, knowing something forbidden or inappropriate' (2005, 56). In the *Curioso*, Anselmo, in addition to his Bacchic qualities, may be likened to Tiresias, because his tragic fate, as well as that of his friend and his wife, stems from a desire to know 'something forbidden or inappropriate': 'Anselmo's desire to render visible his wife's invisible qualities (her fidelity) brings about his destruction' (de Armas 2006, 191). This similarity between Anselmo and Tiresias connects them both to Bacchus (Dionysus), for one of the fundamental attributes of Dionysus is 'to reveal the invisible and the future' (Otto 1965, 97).

Tiresias's first use of his powers of prophecy introduces the story of Narcissus (Ovid 1993, 90–1). Tiresias prophesies to Narcissus's mother that her son will live to see old age 'if he never knows himself. / For many years his words seemed meaningless; / but then what happened in the end confirmed / their truth: the death Narcissus met when he / was stricken with a singular, strange frenzy' (91). The Latin words, 'novitasque furoris' used by Ovid,[5] which Allen Mandelbaum renders as 'strange frenzy,' could also be translated as 'strange madness' or 'strange insanity.' This allusion to madness links Narcissus to Bacchus, the god most associated with madness.[6] Within the sequence of stories from the *Metamorphoses* that we are here considering, the motif of madness thus evoked not only recalls the birth of Bacchus in a previous story, but also looks forward to Bacchus's triumph over Pentheus and the establishment of the god's cult in Thebes in a later story (1993, 98–106). The presence or atmosphere of a similar 'Bacchic' madness begins with Anselmo's desire to test Camila and ends with the destruction of Anselmo, Camila, and Lotario.

After the story of Tiresias's prophecy about Narcissus, the poet recounts the story of Echo and of Echo's tragic love for Narcissus (1993, 91–3),[7] which in turn leads into the story of Narcissus's infatuation with his own image mirrored in a pool of water and his consequent death as prophesied by Tiresias (1993, 93–7). We will return to the story of Narcissus presently.

At the end of Narcissus's story, Ovid again mentions Tiresias: 'And once his prophecy had come to pass / and all the towns of Greece had heard of that, / renown – well earned – now crowned Tiresias' (1993, 97). This reference to the seer comes at a point of transition between the tale of Narcissus and that of Pentheus. Pentheus is the ruler of Thebes, an important man, but his chief importance in the *Metamorphoses* is that he disdains Bacchus and the god's ritual celebrations. But, first he belittles Tiresias.

Pentheus even derides Tiresias's blindness. In response, Tiresias prophesies that Pentheus will perish because of his refusal to worship Bacchus. 'You will not honor the new god; and then / you will complain that, in my blindness, I / saw far too well' (1993, 98). An inversion of the play on the motif of seeing found in this passage occurs in the *Curioso*: Anselmo sees, from behind some tapestries, what he believes to be proof of his wife's fidelity, but what is in fact a demonstration of her infidelity (1978, 428–37; 2003, 297–305); in his blindness, Tiresias sees the truth, while in his seeing, Anselmo is blind to the truth. In both instances, attention is drawn to the phenomenon of seeing, which, as we will see, is of paramount importance in the *Curioso*.

Book 3 of the *Metamorphoses* concludes with the triumph of Bacchus when Pentheus, in hiding, secretly watches the maenads' frenzied revelries: 'Pentheus spies / the sacred rites with his profaning eyes' (1993, 105). Discovered by his own mother, Agave, herself one of the maenads, Pentheus is torn to pieces by the ecstatic bacchantes (1993, 106). Anselmo, in addition to his likeness to Bacchus and Tiresias, also resembles Pentheus. Like Pentheus, Anselmo secretly witnesses a Dionysian spectacle, one in which Camila artfully arranges a scene to authenticate her virtue and, like Pentheus, Anselmo is subsequently destroyed by Dionysian forces.[8] Cervantes' text suggests the Bacchic nature of the scene that Anselmo observes by foregrounding the motif of madness present in the scene as well as the scene's theatrical nature, Dionysus being the god not only of madness, but also of theatre.

Bacchus appears at the beginning and end of the series of stories in the *Metamorphoses*; in the beginning he is born and at the end he triumphs.[9] In parallel fashion, the eruption and triumph of Bacchic forces in the *Curioso* begins with Anselmo's request that Lotario attempt the seduction of Camila and ends with the destruction of all three.

As seen above, Ovid's story of Narcissus appears between two references to Tiresias: 1) how Tiresias lost his sight and came to have the power to foretell the future; and 2) Pentheus's disparagement of Tiresias and the latter's prophecy of Pentheus's doom. Before and after these references to Tiresias, two stories about Bacchus appear: 1) that of the god's birth; and 2) that of Bacchus's triumph over Pentheus and the acceptance of the god's cult by the Theban women (1993, 106). Thus, the story of Narcissus is framed on either side by stories about Tiresias and these stories are in turn framed on either side by stories about Bacchus. The tale of Narcissus appears at the centre of this layering of stories and is, as we have seen, connected to them. The stories that precede the story of Narcissus, with its central motif of the mirroring pool, may be thought of as reflecting the stories that immediately follow Narcissus. This narrative mirroring with its central pivotal point of the reflecting pool that captures Narcissus's gaze suggests that Ovid may have constructed these stories with the metaphor of the mirror in mind, implying both that Ovid intended to capture our gaze with his stories and that we should see our own reflection in them.

This symmetrical framework of stories surrounding the tale of Narcissus in Ovid is duplicated – perhaps we could even say, mirrored – by a symmetrical framework of six other interpolated stories that surround the *Curioso* in *Don Quijote*, part 1. Raymond Immerwahr discusses the placement of the *Curioso* at the centre of these stories, as well as the interconnectedness of the *Curioso*, the six other tales, and Cervantes' novel as a whole (1958, 126–7).

Immerwahr uses the metaphor of the mirror, one that he borrows from Friedrich Schlegel (1958, 129, note 35, and 133), to speak of the interrelationship between these interlocking elements: 'The seven intercalated narratives are thus like a series of mirrors, symmetrically placed at different angles around the main action, so as to reflect from different facets the general relation of literature to life' (1958, 129). Whether or not Cervantes had in mind book 3 of the *Metamorphoses* as he composed *Don Quijote*, Part 1, the centrality of the story of Narcissus as it is flanked on either side by the stories of Tiresias and Bacchus and the centrality of the *Curioso* as it is flanked by three stories on either side is an intriguing parallel.[10] The fact that these stories may be said to 'mirror' the action of Cervantes' entire novel, a metaphor that immediately calls to mind the central element of the central story of the series in the *Metamorphoses*, lends to this parallel an even greater interest.

The centrality of the stories of Narcissus and the *Curioso* in the *Metamorphoses* and *Don Quijote* suggests an identification of the *Curioso* with the tale of Narcissus, an identification that is justified, to some extent, by elements common to both. The motifs of the mirror, seeing, strangeness, and madness that are central to Narcissus's story also hold a place of importance in the *Curioso*. In addition, the opposition between a Dionysian (Bacchic) and an Apollonian force or presence, suggested by Ovid in a comparison of these two gods to Narcissus's image in the pool (1993, 94) – a suggestion that foreshadows the struggle between these forces in the story of Pentheus – is also found, as we will see, in the *Curioso*.

The title *El curioso impertinente* has been translated into English in different ways. The troublesome word for the translator is *impertinente*. Most literally, the title could be translated as *The Impertinent Curious Man*. However, the word *impertinente* and its English cognate impertinent have several possible meanings. Literally, this adjective characterizes that which does not pertain. To pertain, from the Latin *pertinere*, also the root of the Spanish verb *pertenecer*, means 1) to have relevance; 2) to belong; or 3) to be suitable.[11] That which is impertinent, therefore, is that which is not relevant, does not belong, or is not suitable.

I would like to focus attention on the meaning of *impertinente* denoting that which does not belong. I choose this particular meaning, because one aspect of all three of the protagonists of the *Curioso* is that, by virtue of their thoughts, speech, and actions, they are transformed from those who have a place in the world into those who no longer belong. This transformation, from belonging to not belonging, undergone by the characters of the *Curioso* parallels the transformation of Narcissus. Even before his transformation into a flower, Narcissus undergoes a transformation by means of which he ceases to feel at home in the world he inhabits; he becomes, by means of his reflected image in the pool, a stranger to himself, perhaps the most profound expression of not belonging.

By the end of the *Curioso*, not only have Anselmo, Camila, and Lotario lost their homes, they have also, like Narcissus, lost their identities. They no longer have a place in the world. This happens because, like Narcissus, each of the characters is 'stricken with a singular, strange frenzy.'

On the brink of initiating his 'novitasque furoris,' Anselmo himself refers to his wish to test Camila as 'un deseo tan estraño y tan fuera del uso común de otros, que yo me maravillo de mí mismo' [a desire so strange and out of the ordinary that I am amazed at myself] (1978, 1.33.402; 2003, 274). Anselmo's words emphasize his strange madness, linking him to Bacchus, together with his sense of being a stranger to himself, linking him to Narcissus. Anselmo's madness is explicitly mentioned on several occasions: Lotario speaks of his 'manifiesta locura' [patent madness] (1978, 1.33.406; 2003, 278), and Anselmo refers to 'mi locura' [my own madness] (1978, 1.33.402; 2003, 275). Lotario restates and expands the idea of being a stranger to oneself: 'yo pienso que no eres el Anselmo que solías, y tú debes de haber pensado que tampoco yo soy el Lotario que debía ser, porque las cosas que me has dicho, ni son de aquel Anselmo mi amigo, ni las que me pides se han de pedir a aquel Lotario que tú conoces' [I think you are not the Anselmo you used to be, and you must have thought I was not the same Lotario, either, because the things you have said to me would not have been said by my friend Anselmo, and what you have asked of me would not have been asked of the Lotario you knew] (1978, 1.33.404; 2003, 276).

Near the end of the *Curioso*, the theme of strangeness and alienation is repeated. Speaking to Anselmo without knowing who he is (an example of Anselmo's loss of identify), a Florentine citizen says of the recent events involving Camila, Anselmo, and Lotario that they are 'las más estrañas que muchos días ha se han oído' [the strangest heard there in many days] (1978, 1.35.444; 2003, 311), and later Anselmo, overwhelmed to the point of dying, wants to leave in writing 'noticia de la causa de su estraña muerte' [some explanation of his strange death] (1978, 1.35.445; 2003, 312).

In addition to the themes of strangeness, of not belonging, and of madness, Ovid's Narcissus and the *Curioso* also foreground the sense of sight and the special instance of that sense found in the mirror. An understanding of the relationship of these divergent themes one to another is fundamental to our discussion of the mirror and the sense of sight. We may discover the relatedness of these themes in a personal experience recounted by Sigmund Freud: 'I was sitting alone in my sleeping compartment when the train lurched violently. The door of the adjacent toilet swung open and an elderly gentleman in a dressing gown and traveling cap entered my compartment. I assumed that on leaving the toilet, which was located between the two compartments, he had turned the wrong way and entered mine by mistake. I jumped up to put him right, but soon realized to my astonishment that the intruder was my own image, reflected in the mirror on the connecting door. I can still recall that I found his appearance thoroughly unpleasant' (2003, 162).

Freud uses this story in his essay 'The Uncanny' as an example of the uncanny nature of the experience of encountering one's double.[12] In the *Curioso*, Anselmo and Lotario are characterized as so close, so attuned to one another, that they may be considered to be doubles: 'andaban tan a una sus voluntades, que no había concertado reloj que así lo anduviese' [their desires were so attuned that a well-adjusted clock did not run as well] (1978, 1.33.399; 2003, 272). The theme of the double also emerges in Ovid, when he compares Narcissus's image to both Bacchus and Apollo, who are doubles or mirror images of each other. Anselmo, as previously stated, may be identified with Bacchus, while Lotario resembles Apollo, especially in the beginning of the *Curioso*. A synonym for the word 'uncanny' is the word 'strange.' Freud's experience connects a sense of strangeness and of not belonging to the double and the mirror.[13] The German word used by Freud and translated by the word 'uncanny' is *unheimlich*. *Heimlich* means, 'belonging to the house, not strange, familiar.' *Unheimlich* is, therefore, that which does not belong to the house, that which is unfamiliar, that which is strange.[14] As the story told in the *Curioso* unfolds, Anselmo, Camila, and Lotario progressively enter into the realm of the *unheimlich*. This is, indeed, the domain of Bacchus/Dionysus. When speaking of the god, Otto refers to this domain as 'the world bewitched,' and states that, 'the world man knows, the world in which he has settled himself so securely and snugly – that world is no more. The turbulence which accompanied the arrival of Dionysus has swept it away. Everything has been transformed' (1965, 95). This passage could be taken as a fairly accurate description of the fictional world created in the *Curioso*.

The three protagonists go so far in the direction of the *unheimlich* that the priest, when he finishes reading the manuscript of their story, criticizes the events of the story because of they are impossible (1978, 1.35.446; 2003, 313). A reference to this extreme degree of strangeness – impossibility – also appears within the novella. At one point, the narrator of the *Curioso* admonishes Anselmo for his foolish plan: 'Mira que el que busca lo imposible, es justo que lo posible se le niegue' [Remember that if a man seeks the impossible, the possible may justly be denied him] (1978, 1.33.416; 2003, 286).

For Georges Bataille, the impossible is that phenomenon which breaks free from the established norms of society (1991, 10). He states that such a moment of defiance leads to the 'abyss,' to 'the inevitable fall' (1991, 20). Nonetheless, Bataille declares, it is only by embracing such a moment of defiance, by ignoring the established limits of society, that we achieve freedom. Anselmo's senseless desire and the events that it initiates may be seen, therefore, as a sort of liberation from the limits of the sensible world personified by the priest, even though they lead the protagonists into the abyss.

As the instigator of this 'liberating' chain of events, events which result in a tragic destruction, Anselmo further identifies himself with Dionysus; one of the Roman names for Dionysus, that used, in fact, by

Ovid when he has Tiresias prophesy Pentheus's doom, is 'Bacchus Liber' (1993, 98), and in book 3, line 512, of the *Fasti*, we learn that 'Libera' is another name for the deified Ariadne, the wife of Bacchus (2004, 69). Anselmo incites his friend and wife to precisely the sort of wild breaking of the established societal order we find in the *Metamorphoses* with the advent of Bacchus Liber (1993, 98–9).

The mirror, essential to Narcissus's story, provokes Freud's experience of the uncanniness of the double. The *Curioso* mentions not one but three important mirrors, all of them figurative, and the novella also foregrounds the sense of sight, so intimately connected to the mirror. In sixteenth-century Europe, sight was gradually replacing touch as a 'privileged erotic sense,'[15] as demonstrated in the diffusion of prurient images of women in engravings and etchings. Sabine Melchior-Bonnet relates this heightened erotic value of sight to an increase in the moralistic condemnation of Narcissus for 'reveling in the image of his own beauty' (2001, 158). The use of mirrors for erotic seeing was known even in antiquity. Seneca tells the story of Hostius Quadra who, 'surrounded himself with mirrors, by means of which he was able to distinguish and orchestrate all his degenerate acts';[16] Seneca quotes Hostius Quadra as saying, 'Let my eyes also take part in this lust, becoming its witnesses and executors.'[17] About Hostius Quadra, Maurizio Bettini comments, 'This notorious Roman voyeur thus realized the dream of autoscopy: the ability to have a vision of one's own body, replicated externally. A depraved variant of Narcissus, Hostius Quadra managed to make himself into his own object of pleasure' (1999, 229).

In the *Curioso*, Anselmo may be said to aspire to what Hostius Quadra achieved, because from a hiding place, he twice attempts to watch Lotario seduce his wife, once through a keyhole (1978, 1.33.415; 2003, 285) and again from behind some tapestries (1978, 1.34.428–9; 2003, 298). Both instances underscore the erotic dimension of sight. And, since Lotario is his double, Anselmo's attempted voyeurism suggests his desire to see himself making love to Camila, to watch himself with Camila as though in a mirror.[18]

Another example of the eroticism of seeing takes place when Lotario decides to lay siege in earnest to the fortress of Camila's virtue. Anselmo is not watching this time. However, Camila's virtue is so overwhelming that it prevents Lotario from speaking. Because of this imposed silence, Lotario's sense of sight is aroused all the more: 'Mirábale Lotario en el lugar y espacio que había de hablarla ... quiso ausentarse de la ciudad ... mas ya le hacía impedimento y detenía el gusto que hallaba en mirarla'

[Lotario looked at her when he should have been speaking to her ... he wanted to leave the city ... but the pleasure he found in looking at her had already become an impediment to his doing so] (1978, 1.33.417; 2003, 288). It is, the text implies, the sense of sight that is Lotario's, as well as Camila's undoing, just as it is the undoing of Narcissus.

As in the story of Narcissus, the sense of sight is intensified in the *Curioso* by the phenomenon of mirroring. The novella contains three metaphorical mirrors. The first appears when Lotario attempts to reason with Anselmo. Speaking of Camila's virtuous nature and its possible fragility, Lotario says, 'Es asimesmo la buena mujer como espejo de cristal luciente y claro ... Hase de usar con la honesta mujer el estilo que con las reliquias: adorarlas y no tocarlas' [the chaste woman is like a mirror of clear, shining glass ... One must treat the virtuous woman as one treats relics: adore them but not touch them] (1978, 1.33.409; 2003, 280). The word 'relics,' as we will see, will be reiterated in connection with another metaphorical mirror.

Sabine Melchior-Bonnet cites the above passage from the *Curioso* to exemplify the close relationship between mirrors and femininity. She goes so far as to state that, 'femininity is a creation of the mirror' (2001, 214). The idea that there is an intimate connection between the mirror and femininity recalls the ancient mythical association of certain goddesses with the moon, the celestial mirror. 'Venus is born in the water, her first mirror' (Melchior-Bonnet 2001, 213). About Lotario's speech comparing Camila to a mirror and a sacred relic, Melchior-Bonnet comments, 'goddess or concubine, she consents to this double role when she carries out the magic ceremony that is beauty's due, priestess of a mystery that surpasses her. This ambivalent status is precisely that of the mirror' (2001, 215). Some might label Camila, after she becomes Lotario's lover, a concubine, but few perhaps would find in her anything to suggest the goddess or priestess. Nonetheless, in Renaissance Europe the combination of woman and mirror created not only a profane and at times lascivious image, but also a sacred presence. Within the Petrarchan tradition, 'The mirror and the woman together, as a repository of beauty, guide the poet's aspirations toward the sacred, pointing toward a celestial reality. The woman and the mirror become an absolute end, more goddess than woman, an inaccessible idol' (Melchior-Bonnet 2001, 213).

Right after Lotario compares the virtuous woman to a mirror, he continues the metaphor by reciting a brief poem that begins with the words, 'Es de vidrio la mujer' [Woman is made of fragile glass] (1978, 1.33.409;

2003, 281). The poem's conclusion implicitly compares Camila to Danae. Danae was not a goddess. She was, however, ravished by the god Zeus who came to her as a shower of gold, and she subsequently gave birth to Zeus's offspring Perseus. Because of this, Danae is linked to the gods. Lotario's poem, by comparing Camila to Danae, therefore, connects Camila to the gods, the feminine to the divine.

The second example of a metaphorical mirror in the *Curioso* occurs, not surprisingly, in a Petrarchan sonnet recited by Lotario. In this sonnet the word 'relic' again appears in relation to Camila: 'Podré yo verme en la región de olvido, / de vida y gloria y de favor desierto, / y allí verse podrá en mi pecho abierto / cómo tu hermoso rostro está esculpido. / Que esta reliquia guardo' [When I am in the land of the forgotten, / deserted by glory, favor, and by life, / there, in my open bosom, you will see, / a sculpted image of your lovely face. / I keep this holy relic] (1978, 1.34.423; 2003, 293). If Camila were to look at the 'sculpted image' mentioned in the sonnet, she would see her own face, thus converting the image into a mirror. This mirror has a sacred dimension, because it is a 'holy relic.' The conceit fashioned in Lotario's sonnet represents a sacred feminine persona reflected in a mirror. On two occasions, here and in the passage we examined earlier, Lotario associates Camila with the phenomenon of mirroring and also with the sacredness of a divine memento or relic. These associations link Camila to the sacred, thereby designating Camila as goddess, and to the mirror with its generative, magical properties: 'the mirror retains its magical, mystifying, and creative power' (Melchior-Bonnet 2001, 6).

In the novella, there is yet another instance of Camila being compared to a mirror. This Camila-as-mirror conceit is voiced not by Lotario, as in the previous two examples, but by Camila herself, and it occurs during a theatrical performance that is a stratagem, one that Camila alone orchestrates and executes with consummate skill, to such an extent that Lotario, 'se admiró de la sagacidad, prudencia y mucha discreción de la hermosa Camila' [marveled at the great sagacity, prudence, and intelligence of the beautiful Camila] (1978, 1.34.434; 2003, 303). The need for Camila's theatrical stratagem stems from the fact that Lotario, having seen a man – the lover of Camila's maid, Leonela – leaving Anselmo and Camila's house, wrongly presumes that Camila has taken another lover. As a consequence, he becomes enraged and accuses Camila to Anselmo. The description of Lotario's rage places him within the context of the same sort of Dionysian madness that Anselmo exhibits: 'le faltó a Lotario en este punto todo su buen entendimiento, y se le fueron de la memoria todos sus advertidos discursos; pues, sin hacer alguno que bueno fuese, ni aun razonable ... ciego de la celosa rabia que las entrañas le roía, muriendo por vengarse de Camila ... se fue a Anselmo' [Lotario lost his good sense and forgot all his skillful reasoning; without a second or even a rational thought ... blinded by the jealous rage gnawing at his entrails and driving him to take his revenge on Camila ... he went to see Anselmo] (1978, 1.34.426; 2003, 296). Lotario, bereft of the rational thinking that earlier led him to oppose Anselmo, is now transformed into an irrational, crazed lover. He is, after all, Anselmo's double, and now he takes on the quality of Anselmo's Dionysian madness, his 'novitasque furoris.'

After telling Anselmo of Camila's unfaithfulness, Lotario immediately regrets his rash action. Not knowing what to do, he goes to Camila to tell her everything: 'Pidióle perdón desta locura, y consejo para poder remedialla y salir bien de tan revuelto laberinto como su mal discurso le había puesto' [He begged her forgiveness for this act of madness and asked her advice on how to repair the damage he had done and emerge safely from the intricate labyrinth into which his foolish talk had led them] (1978, 1.34.428; 2003, 297). The metaphor of the labyrinth provides another link between Camila and the divine feminine.

One of the names given to the ancient Cretan goddess Ariadne, long before she appeared in mythical stories as a mortal girl abandoned by Theseus on the island of Naxos, was 'Mistress of the Labyrinth' (Kerényi 1976, 98). Ariadne was also, 'no doubt the Great Moon Goddess of the Aegean world' (Kerényi 1976, 124).[19] Ariadne thus unites the elements of labyrinth, goddess, and the celestial mirror of the moon. Camila ingeniously devises a plan that frees both herself and Lotario from the labyrinth that Lotario's madness has gotten them into. In this way, she becomes the 'Mistress of the Labyrinth,' identifying herself with Ariadne, and her association with mirrors only serves to strengthen this identification. Further reinforcing Camila's role as goddess is the fact that the god with whom Ariadne is associated is Dionysus (Bacchus), one of her names being 'Wife of Dionysos' (Kerényi 1976, 109). Therefore, Anselmo's identification with Bacchus further links Camila to Ariadne. Camila's resourceful stratagem is a plan whereby the unsuspecting Anselmo, from his hiding place behind some tapestries, will observe a scene enacted by Camila, her maid Leonela, and Lotario. This scene, staged to deceive Anselmo is an artfully crafted theatrical production. Dionysus/Bacchus, we will remember, is also the god associated with theatre, most especially with tragedy: 'In tragedy, his own art form,

Dionysus connects inward damage with outer damage. Damage of mind, damage to fortune ... Dionysus and madness: both are rare in Homer, and found all over tragedy' (Padel 1995, 29).

The *Curioso* makes explicit the theatrical and tragically ironic aspect of Camila's subterfuge, once it has been executed, by declaring that, 'atentísimo había estado Anselmo a escuchar y a ver representar la tragedia de la muerte de su honra; la cual con tan estraños y eficaces afectos la representaron los personajes della, que pareció que se habían transformado en la misma verdad de lo que fingían' [Anselmo had been very attentive as he heard and watched the performance of the tragedy of the death of his honor, which had been performed with such unusual and convincing effects by the actors that they seemed to have been transformed into the very parts they were playing] (1978, 1.35.436; 2003, 304). This passage implicitly attributes a number of Dionysian elements to Camila's ruse: 1) it is tragic theatre; 2) it possesses that strangeness associated with madness which we have found in Narcissus, Anselmo, and Lotario; and 3) it expresses the transformation of those involved, for Dionysus was a god of transformation (Otto 1965, 95). Indeed, Camila becomes so transformed by the part she is playing, that she, like a Dionysian reveller, a bacchante, appears to have gone mad: 'se paseaba por la sala con la daga desenvainada, dando tan desconcertados y desaforados pasos y haciendo tales ademanes, que no parecía sino que le faltaba el juicio, y que no era mujer delicada, sino un rufián desesperado' [she paced the room with the dagger unsheathed, making such disordered and extravagant movements and gestures that she appeared to have lost her mind and seemed not a fragile woman but a desperate ruffian] (1978, 1.34.432; 2003, 300). Just as Anselmo's initial madness had previously spread to Lotario, it now seems to take possession of Camila.

When Lotario, who knows that Camila is staging some kind of performance to confound Anselmo, comes into the room, Camila begins a harangue in which she accuses Lotario of being a false friend. It is at this point that she uses the metaphor of the mirror to drive home her point: '¿con qué rostro osas parecer ante quien sabes que es el espejo donde se mira aquel en quien tú te debieras mirar para que vieras con cuán poca ocasión le agravias?' [how do you dare appear before the one who, as you know, is the mirror that reflects him (Anselmo)? If you looked in it carefully, you would see how little justification you have for offending him] (1978, 1.34.433; 2003, 301–2). In the metaphor used by Camila, she herself is a mirror that reflects Anselmo. By the use of this metaphor, Camila suggests that she has, in the fashion of a mirror, captured Anselmo's semblance, that she is a copy of Anselmo, and we have already seen that she duplicates Anselmo's Dionysian madness. If Camila is identified with Ariadne, her mirroring of Anselmo reinforces Anselmo as Bacchus, husband of Ariadne. Furthermore, because Camila mirrors Anselmo, and because Anselmo is truly in love with Camila, we are brought back to the story of Narcissus, who falls in love with a reflection of himself.

However, it is Lotario whom Camila urges to look into this particular mirror, and if he does so, he will see himself, Anselmo's double. At this point, the mirror would seem to have captured all three – Camila, Anselmo, and Lotario – within its shimmering surface, and to be projecting them out into the world, a phenomenon that would be in keeping with the idea of mirror as creative source: 'an invisible "elsewhere" in the heart of the visible. Form without substance, subtle and impalpable, the mirror image manifests a diaphanous purity, a revelation of the divine source, from which all likeness emanates' (Melchior-Bonnet 2001, 102). The mirror, then, symbolically expresses the 'divine source' of creation. The fact that Camila *is* the mirror, in all three of its appearances in *El curioso impertinente*, suggests that Camila is being identified with the Magna Mater, the great goddess of antiquity, the mother of all creation.

We have seen that Anselmo may be identified with Bacchus and Camila with Ariadne or the Magna Mater. Ovid, in his story of Narcissus, suggests a possibility for placing Lotario too among the gods. In the story of Narcissus in the *Metamorphoses*, we read of Narcissus: 'stretched out along the ground, he stares again, / again at the twin stars that are his eyes; / at his fair hair, which can compare with Bacchus' or with Apollo's' (1993, 94). Bacchus and Apollo, mirror images of one another, are doubles. These two gods, half-brothers, shared the rule of the Delphic oracle (March 2001, 267). To some extent, Narcissus both exemplifies and parodies the Delphic principle of knowing oneself and, in this sense, he is also connected to both gods. Ovid's Narcissus story places these mirror images, Bacchus and Apollo, within the mirror into which Narcissus gazes, the reflecting pool, the essential element at the centre of Ovid's tale and the stories that frame it. We have seen that *El curioso impertinente* reflects elements of the stories of Bacchus, Tiresias, and Narcissus; it will not be surprising if we discover that Bacchus and his mirror image, Apollo, located within Narcissus's mirror, at the centre of this series of Ovid's stories, reflect Anselmo and his double Lotario.

Probably no one has had a greater influence on our perception of what Dionysus (Bacchus) and Apollo represented to the Greek mind than

Friedrich Nietzsche, who characterized the two gods in *The Birth of Tragedy*. Walter Kaufman points out that, 'far from depreciating what he [Nietzsche] called "the Apollinian" [*sic*], he argued that one could not appreciate it sufficiently until one became aware of another side of Greek culture that was barbarous by comparison and found expression in the Dionysian festivals ... Nietzsche claimed that the same boundless and cruel longing to exceed all norms is also occasionally encountered in the *Iliad* and in subsequent Greek poetry' (2000, 9–10). Nonetheless, Nietzsche did at times seem to favour the Dionysian. At the beginning of *The Birth of Tragedy*, he states: 'There are those who, from obtuseness or lack of experience, turn away from such phenomena as from "folk-diseases," with contempt or pity born of the consciousness of their own "healthy-mindedness." But of course such poor wretches have no idea how corpselike and ghostly their so-called "healthy-mindedness" looks when the glowing life of the Dionysian revelers roars past them' (2000, 36–7).[20] Anselmo, Lotario, and Camila, even though ensnared by a tragic fate, may be considered as representative of the sort of 'Dionysian revelers' alluded to by Nietzsche. Indeed, the theatrical performance orchestrated by Camila, with herself, Lotario, and Leonela as players and Anselmo as audience, may be understood, as already suggested, as a work of Dionysian dramatic art. As such, that theatrical episode may be interpreted as a miniature version of the novella embedded within the novella, just as the novella itself, to some extent, is a miniature of *Don Quijote* embedded within the novel.

Anselmo, with his 'boundless and cruel longing to exceed all norms' – to use Nietzsche's phrase – has been identified with Dionysus. Lotario, with his reasonable entreaties and his attempts to logically convince Anselmo of the latter's madness, is a mirror image of Anselmo, in the sense that a mirror turns everything seen in it completely around, as right is left and left is right; we have already mentioned that Lotario is Anselmo's double, just as Freud's image in the mirror was Freud's double. Lotario may, as we have previously noted, be identified with Apollo. The text also strengthens Lotario's connection with Apollo in other ways. Lotario, like Apollo, is linked to the muses. When Anselmo offers to compose the poetry he wants Lotario to recite to Camila, Lotario replies that that will not be necessary, because he is in contact with the muses (1978, 1.34.421; 2003, 291). Thus, Apollo, god of poets and close associate of the muses, finds a counterpart in Lotario, who recites two poems and composes and recites two sonnets in the *Curioso*. This is all the more striking, because the only other poetry in the novella is an admonitory poem addressed to Anselmo by the narrator.

Another example of Lotario's likeness to Apollo is that the text links him to oracular utterances, Apollo being the god most associated with prophecy: 'Contentísimo quedó Anselmo de las razones de Lotario, y así se las creyó como si fueran dichas por algún oráculo' [Anselmo was made happy by Lotario's words, and he believed them as if they had been spoken by an oracle] (1978, 1.34.421; 2003, 291).[21] Although Lotario may be associated with Apollo in the first part of the *Curioso*, as events progress, both he and Camila are transformed into Dionysian figures; as we have seen above, it is as though Anselmo's madness begins to affect them, in a manner similar to that in which Don Quijote's madness progressively affects Sancho.

Anselmo, on the other hand, initially a Dionysian personality who sets in motion the events that comprise the novella, is transformed into a more Apollonian figure as the novella progresses. This transformation is suggested by Anselmo's likeness to Pentheus. In Ovid's story, Pentheus represents the civic and moral order of society and, because of this, he is an essentially Apollonian figure. He stands in opposition to the Bacchic festivities that have raucously broken out within his city. Like Pentheus, Anselmo hides to secretly observe a Bacchic/Dionysian spectacle; in the *Curioso*, Camila, Lotario, and Leonela enact a sort of theatrical bacchanal while Anselmo watches. And, like Pentheus, who is torn to pieces by the bacchantes, Anselmo is subsequently destroyed by a Dionysian transgression against the Apollonian order of society, a transgression that he himself, unlike Pentheus, has initiated.

In the *Curioso*, the three protagonists end badly, and this is justified in terms of the moralizing comments scattered throughout their story. But, one cannot help wondering if Cervantes did not place such moralizing in a text so rich in pagan allusions in order to appease those who, to use Nietzsche's words again, 'from obtuseness or lack of experience, turn away from such phenomena … with contempt or pity born of the consciousness of their own "healthy-mindedness"' (2000, 36–7). When considering the identification of Anselmo and Camila with Bacchus and Ariadne, of Camila with the Magna Mater, and of Lotario with Apollo, we cannot help but conclude that they are not depicted as the vital, mysterious, deeply powerful forces they must have been in the remote time of greatest antiquity. They represent at best desacralized and displaced versions of the primordial god and goddess.[22] The sense of not belonging conveyed by the word *impertinente*, therefore, may be extended to god and goddess as they are represented in the novella. As portrayed in the *Curioso*, they recall the title of Heinrich Heine's essay *The Gods in Exile*. Just as Anselmo, Camila, and Lotario lose their identities during the course of the story, the gods of antiquity, who maintain at least a vestige of their divine nature in Ovid, had by Cervantes' time completely lost their primordial identities.

This displacement of the gods is not, of course, unique to the *Curioso*; we also find it in depictions of the gods and goddesses in early modern painting and literature. Malcolm Bull observes that, 'the return of the gods did not lead to their acceptance as deities, or to the rejuvenation of pagan religion, but rather to a steady increase in the fictive and the false. By the eighteenth century, classical mythology had so expanded these categories that it furnished the stock example of the unreal' (2005, 394). Bull's observation brings to mind the priest's criticism of *El curioso impertinente* as unrealistic, containing events that do not seem real, events that could not happen in the real world (1978, 1.35.446; 2003, 312–13).

The gods were not taken seriously by the rational mind during the early modern period, but they remained active in the realm of the imagination (Bull 2005, 395). In the hierarchy of mental faculties, in Cervantes' day as in ours, reason is considered superior to imagination. Because it suggests the survival, albeit in a demeaned form, of the gods, *El curioso impertinente* challenges the superiority of reason over imagination and the disparagement of the gods that this superiority entails. By its representation of the gods, disguised as caricatures of themselves, the *Curioso* draws attention to the generative as well as destructive power of the imagination, the Dionysian, the impossible, that from time to time erupts within the rational, Apollonian, world. Indeed, this is the dominant theme of the novella, the events of which are heralded by the outburst of Anselmo's Dionysian imagination, his desire to break the well-ordered, clearly delineated norms of society, a desire that ends in the tragic, equally Dionysian, destruction of the three protagonists. In this way, the *Curioso* suggests that the imagination is as valid as reason as a means for knowing, if not *the world*, at least *a world*. This theme links Cervantes' masterpiece to the novella embedded within it.

NOTES

1 For Cervantes' use of Herodotus's tale of Giges and the story of Cupid and Psyche found in Apuleius in *El curioso impertinente*, see de Armas (1992 and

2006, 191–3) and de Armas Wilson (1987 and 1994, 89 and 94). De Armas Wilson (1987) also discusses Cervantes' use of Ariosto's *Orlando furioso* and the tale of the two friends as models used by Cervantes in the *Curioso*.

2 The presence in the *Curioso* of elements found in Ovid would not be surprising, because Cervantes explicitly refers to Ovid at several times in the *Quijote*. In one of the sonnets that precede the novel, Cervantes alludes to himself as 'nuestro español Ovidio' [Ovid of our Spain] (1978, 64; 2003, 15). The humanist university student that Don Quijote meets in chapter 22 of part 2 tells the knight that one of the books he is composing is a burlesque version of Ovid's *Metamorphoses*, which has as its subtitle '*Ovidio español*' [the Spanish Ovid] (1978, 2.22.206; 2003, 600). In chapter 18 of part 2, Don Lorenzo recites a sonnet that is an ingeniously compact retelling of the story of Pyramus and Thisbe found in book 4 of the *Metamorphoses* (1978, 2.18.175; 2003, 574). And, chapters 19–21 of part 2, the story of Quiteria, Camacho, and Basilio is also based on Ovid's story of Pyramus and Thisbe (1978, 2.19–21.178–202; 2003, 577–96). All references to Cervantes' novel are from the edition by Luis Andrés Murillo (1978), followed by the English translation by Edith Grossman (2003) in parenthesis. A parenthetical reference then provides the part, chapter, and page number of the Murillo edition; after a semicolon, the page number of the Grossman translation is provided.

3 All references to the *Metamorphoses* refer to the Allen Mandelbaum translation (Ovid 1993).

4 'On earth, things followed all of Fate's decrees, / and even twice-born Bacchus' infancy was passing tranquilly. The story goes / that meanwhile, in his home on high, great Jove, / his spirits warmed by nectar' (1993, 89). In this manner, Ovid uses Bacchus's birth and childhood as a background against which he then goes on to tell the story of Jupiter's dispute with Juno about whether a man or a woman experiences greater enjoyment in love-making, a dispute they decide to settle by consulting Tiresias, because the latter had been both man and woman. Tiresias's role as arbiter in this argument leads to his blindness as well as to his gift of prophecy (1993, 89–90).

5 The Latin I am citing, 'novitasque furoris,' comes from Miller in the Loeb Classical Library edition of books 1–8) of the *Metamorphoses* (book 3, line 350) (1977, 148).

6 In *Whom the Gods Destroy: Elements of Greek and Tragic Madness*, Ruth Padel elaborates upon Dionysus's association with madness (1995, 24–9). 'So we might take it further and call Dionysus god of the verb in tragic madness. Especially of the first verb to label him in Western literature, *mainomai*. But other verbs speak of him even more acutely: like bacchao, baccheuo ("I rave" or, causative, "I madden"')' (Padel 1995, 28).

7 Although they are different stories with different protagonists, the story of Echo, like the story of Narcissus, involves the element of mirroring, because Echo's strange affliction is that she can only 'mirror' the sounds she hears. Mirroring, then, in the case of Echo is a mirroring of the sense of hearing, rather than of the sense of sight. However, it is the sense of sight – a sense that holds a place of central importance in the *Curioso* – that inflames Echo's love for Narcissus (1993, 92). Echo may be likened to the pool into which Narcissus gazes, since her voice 'reflects' Narcissus's voice; her voice cannot reach him with her own thoughts, just as the pool cannot provide Narcissus with the embrace of the body he beholds.

8 In Ovid, the destruction of Pentheus signals the supremacy of a pagan god, while in the *Curioso* Anselmo's undoing would seem to result from his breaking the religious, moral code of sixteenth-century Spain. My essay, to some degree, questions this way of understanding the *Curioso*.

9 Allen Mandelbaum's remark that, 'Ovid's fictions form a bacchanalian narrative revel' (1993, 558), suggests that Bacchus presides not only over this series of stories, but also over the entire *Metamorphoses*. The present essay implies the possibility that Bacchus also presides over the novel in which the *Curioso* is embedded.

10 Not only is the *Curioso* the centrepiece of the interpolated stories that surround it, but it also lies at the centre of *Don Quijote*, part 1, thus emphasizing the novella's importance: 'Thus, it seems as if the whole novel is an elaborate frame that contains this curious tale' (de Armas 2006, 190).

11 This definition of 'pertain' has been taken from *The American Heritage Dictionary*, 4th ed. (2000, 1312).

12 Although I am associating Freud's story of the mirror with Ovid's story of Narcissus, Freud himself does not locate his thoughts about the 'uncanny' or the phenomenon of the double within the context of his theory of narcissism.

13 Narcissus finds his image attractive, not repellent as in Freud's case. Freud observes that the double can both attract and repel (2003, 142).

14 Freud consults a dictionary to explore the meanings of *heimlich* and its antonym *unheimlich* (2003, 125–32).

15 Historian Carlo Ginzburg, quoted in Melchior-Bonnet (2001, 158).

16 Seneca, quoted in Maurizio Bettini (1999, 228).

17 Quoted in Bettini (1999, 229).

18 Anselmo initially declares that if Camila succumbs to Lotario, he will experience 'el gusto de ver que acerté en mi opinión' [the pleasure of seeing that I was correct in my opinion] (1978, 1.33.403; 2003, 275). Here, *ver* (seeing) may be metaphorical, but Anselmo's voyeurism suggests that the meaning is literal.

19 For a detailed exploration of Ariadne as the Cretan 'Mistress of the Laby-
    rinth,' the 'Great Moon Goddess of the Aegean world,' and more, see
    Kerényi (1976, 89–125).
20 Nietzsche might have placed the priest who criticizes *El curioso imperti-
    nente*, because it contains impossible events that could not happen in real-
    ity, within this category of 'healthy-minded' individuals.
21 The fact that what Anselmo takes to be an oracular statement is a lie un-
    derscores the diminution of the gods in *El curioso impertinente*.
22 In *El curioso impertinente*, this devaluation of the gods is taken to the point
    of debasement, farce, or parody. The *Metamorphoses* expresses 'irreverent
    playfulness' (Graf 2002, 108). If Cervantes had Ovid in mind, it would not
    be surprising to find the gods parodied in the *Curioso*.

WORKS CITED

Bataille, Georges. 1991. *The Impossible*. San Francisco: City Lights Press.
Bettini, Maurizio. 1999. *The Portrait of the Lover*. Trans. Laura Gibbs. Berkeley:
    University of California Press.
Bull, Malcolm. 2005. *The Mirror of the Gods*. Oxford: Oxford University Press.
Cervantes, Miguel de. 1978. *El ingenioso hidalgo don Quijote de la Mancha*. Ed.
    Luis Murillo. 2 vols. Madrid: Castalia.
– 2003. *Don Quixote*. Trans. Edith Grossman. New York: HarperCollins.
De Armas, Frederick A.1992. 'Interpolation and Invisibility: From Herodotus
    to Cervantes's *Don Quixote*.' *Journal of the Fantastic in the Arts* 4:8–28.
– 2006. *Quixotic Frescoes: Cervantes and Italian Renaissance Art*. Toronto: Uni-
    versity of Toronto Press.
De Armas Wilson, Diana. 1987. '"Passing the Love of Women": The Intertextu-
    ality of *El curioso impertinente*.' *Cervantes* 7: 9–28.
– 1994. 'Homage to Apuleius: Cervantes' Avenging Psyche.' In *The Search for
    the Ancient Novel*, ed. James Tatum, 88–100. Baltimore: Johns Hopkins Uni-
    versity Press.
Freud, Sigmund. 2003. *The Uncanny*. London: Penguin.
Graf, Fritz. 2002. 'Myth in Ovid.' In *The Cambridge Companion to Ovid*, ed.
    Philip Hardie, 108–21. Cambridge: Cambridge University Press.
Immerwahr, Raymond. 1958. 'Structural Symmetry in the Episodic Narratives
    of *Don Quijote, Part One*.' *Comparative Literature* 10:121–35.
Kaufmann, Walter. 2000. 'Translator's Introduction.' In *Basic Writings of
    Nietzsche*, ed. and trans. Walter Kaufmann, 3–13. New York: The Modern
    Library.

Kerényi, Carl. 1976. *Dionysus: Archetypal Image of Indestructible Life*. Princeton: Princeton University Press.

Mandelbaum, Allen. 1993. Afterword. In *The Metamorphoses of Ovid*. Trans. Allen Mandelbaum, 551–9. New York: Harcourt Brace.

March, Jennifer R., ed. 2001. *Cassell's Dictionary of Classical Mythology*. London: Cassell.

Melchior-Bonnet, Sabine. 2001. *The Mirror: A History*. London: Routledge.

Nietzsche, Friedrich. 2000. *The Birth of Tragedy*. In *Basic Writings of Nietzsche*. Trans. and ed. Walter Kaufmann, 15–144. New York: The Modern Library.

Otto, Walter F. 1965. *Dionysus: Myth and Cult*. Trans. Robert B. Palmer. Bloomington: Indiana University Press.

Ovid. 1977. *Metamorphoses*. Trans. Frank Justus Miller. 2 vols. Cambridge, MA: Harvard University Press.

– 1993. *Metamorphoses*. Trans. Allen Mandelbaum. New York: Harcourt Brace.

– 2002. *The Art of Love*. Trans. James Michie. New York: The Modern Library.

– 2004. *Fasti*. Trans. A.J. Boyle and R.D. Woodard. London: Penguin.

Padel, Ruth. 1995. *Whom Gods Destroy: Elements of Greek and Tragic Madness*. Princeton: Princeton University Press.

Salzman-Mitchell, Patricia B. 2005. *A Web of Fantasies: Gaze, Image, and Gender in Ovid's Metamorphoses*. Columbus: Ohio State University Press.

The American Heritage Dictionary of the English Language. 4th ed. 2000. New York: Houghton Mifflin.

6 Forging Modernity: Vulcan and the Iron Age in Cervantes, Ovid, and Vico

KEITH BUDNER

In some regards, examining Cervantes in relation to any classical author, in this case Ovid, represents a paradox of sorts. On the one hand, Cervantes is considered to be the author who penned the first modern novel, who overturned past aesthetic paradigms and embarked on groundbreaking literary themes and styles that set the model for much, if not all, writing that followed. And yet, on the other hand, there is Cervantes himself, who in the opening sonnets of this modern novel, *Don Quijote*, refers to himself as the 'Spanish Ovid' / 'español Ovidio' (2004, Prologue 29; 2005, 15)[1]. This complex relationship between the ancient and the modern is reflected in the *Quijote* itself. It is a work at once said to be the beginning of the modern novel, and yet it is at its heart the story of a man who longs for the past and an older way of life.

Through loss of sanity our protagonist, Don Quijote, does eventually come to see his own world of early modern Spain as one filled with chivalric noblemen from the Middle Ages and mythic heroes from an even more distant time. And through Cervantes' own evocation of past writers, this world often feels less like the drab seventeenth-century Spain in which knights no longer exist and more like the worlds of Homer, Virgil, and Ovid (not to mention the various authors of chivalric romances whom he also evokes). But if we are to take seriously this notion that *Don Quijote* is the world's first modern novel, we should perhaps ask ourselves – to put it simply – what business the first modern novelist has in referring to himself as the Spanish incarnation of a classical poet when he calls himself the 'español Ovidio' – or a bit more formally – what new significance would the appropriation of classical sources take on when incorporated into the genre of the modern novel.

The topic of Cervantes and modernity has been the focus of several scholars in the last few decades. Carroll Johnson (1990 and 2000), David Quint (2003), Anthony Cascardi (1992 and 1997), and Eric Graf (2007), have all provided us with rigorous treatments from various perspectives that demonstrate how an attuned reading of Cervantes will indeed reveal an author who was deeply preoccupied with a society at the crossroads of modernity. It would seem from reading these works that if Cervantes were able to live up to his title of 'español Ovidio' it was by dealing with metamorphoses of a far different kind than Ovid's 'transforming bodies.' And likewise, that when dealing with societal transformations such as the shift from a feudal to market-based economy (discussed in Johnson), or the changes relating to the institution of marriage in regards to this new economic world (Quint), or the theological and political shifts of the Enlightenment (Graf), or the altered notion of the individual in relation to desire and the secularizing world (Cascardi) – that when dealing with changes of this nature – Ovid's classical poems that tell the tales of gods and mythic heroes would have been of little service.

Though it is my belief that Cervantes' *Quijote* provides us with an enormous amount of room for extended treatment on the clash between the ancient and the modern, and within this discussion much room to analyse the specific role that Ovid plays, in this essay I am going to focus on a rather short portion of the text, the episode of the fulling hammers in chapter 20, part I. In this crucial moment of the text Cervantes not only presents the reader with an image of modernity in the industrial mechanism of the fulling hammers, he also calls upon two important myths that stem from Ovid. Furthermore, these elements of the ancient and modern worlds are juxtaposed in such a way that the reader can see more than the mere mismatch of two different worlds within one text. Within this chapter the ancient and the modern interact in such a way that they become crucial to understanding each other in Cervantes' own literary world; that in a sense, beneath the shell of mythic figures lies Cervantes' early-modern Spain, and that the material appropriated from writers such as Ovid is not only central to his commentary to the modern world, but it also by its very nature raises larger issues surrounding the ancient and the modern, and the role of the former within the latter. To aid this discussion I will frequently draw on several principles of the eighteenth-century Italian philosopher Giambattista Vico, who in his principal work, *The New Science*, laid down what many consider to be the first systematic philosophy of history (a study that would go on to influence such philosophers as Hegel, Nietzsche, and Marx and writers such as Dostoevsky and Joyce). But what is perhaps most crucial about Vico for this essay is that his philosophy of history developed from a careful reading of classical myths, which in turn resulted in his offering profoundly insightful observations as to how myths could themselves be interpreted as statements of historical change. Though I do not propose any connection of influence between Cervantes and Vico, I do hope to show that through turning to such theories of history and myth we can further understand the complex role of influence that existed between Ovid and his myths and Cervantes and his novel.

With a chapter title that begins 'De la jamás vista ni oída aventura' [Of the never before seen nor heard adventure] Cervantes begins the episode of the fulling hammers by setting a tone of high expectation for the reader. It would seem that all we have just read in the previous chapters (such as the episode of the windmills or the first encounter in the inn, to name a few) is about to be outdone. This mood is heightened all the more with Quijote's initial response to hearing the horrific noise of the fulling hammers; it is here that he evokes classical myth. Upon first hearing the clanging noise of the hammers, he declares his intent to carry out what is quite literally a mythic feat: to bring back the Age of Gold (2004, 1.227). And a bit later, he compares the bravery he will need in this encounter to that of Mars (2004, 228). And yet despite the title and this allusion to classical myth, it is hard to say that anything at all really happens by the end of the episode. Upon finally encountering these fulling hammers, there is no display of quixotic madness, no attacking of giants, and no blaming of anything on the 'encantadores' we so often hear; indeed the very heroic task Quijote proposes, the reviving of the Age of Gold, is mocked by Sancho when the fulling hammers are eventually revealed to be what they are. Even Quijote himself does not know how to react. As Robert Brody points out, '[f]or the first time in the novel, Don Quijote is at a loss for words' (1975, 372). All of this for Brody results in the fulling hammers being a 'surprise-episode' that 'seems to strike a discordant note in the consistent scheme, up till now, established by Cervantes' (1975, 372). The question is thus an obvious one: why break at all with the established formula, and especially why here? Furthermore, why establish a connection between two notable mythic images – that of the Golden Age and that of Mars – in an episode where nothing at all happens?

Our understanding of the episode begins with a closer look at Cervantes' treatment of these two myths, beginning with the Age of

Gold. As mentioned earlier, it is the frightening sound of the fulling hammers which leads to Quijote's evocation of the Age of Gold: 'Sancho amigo, has de saber que yo nací por querer del cielo en esta nuestra edad de hierro para resucitar en ella la de oro, o la dorada, come suele llamarse' [Sancho, my friend, know that I was born, by the will of heaven, in this our age of iron, to revive the one of gold, or the Golden Age, as it is called] (2004, 1.227–8; 2005, 142). Perhaps even more important than this passage's drawing upon the notion of the metallic ages (a common trope in classical literature that dates back to Hesiod and found its ways into the writings of figures as diverse as Seneca, Virgil, and, of course, Ovid) is the fact that with this declaration to revive the Age of Gold Quijote echoes a far more extended discussion of the Golden Age/Iron Age theme that he offered only chapters before in chapter 11.

As many studies have pointed out, Quijote's chapter 11 discourse on the Age of Gold owes much to Ovid, and more so to the Ovidian image of the Golden Age than any other classical author who likewise presented his own respective image of these utopian times. Everything from the centrality of the acorns (which in Ovid symbolize the eternal sustenance of the earth and in Cervantes bring the very image of the Golden Age to Quijote's mind), to the lack of private property and absence of greed, and the pure state of an earth untouched by man or his technology all point to Ovid as a definite influence and source of material for Cervantes' crafting of his own Age of Gold. Geoffrey Stagg, whose study examines several possible sources for this discourse of the Age of Gold goes as far as to say that 'no other author's treatment is as close to Cervantes's as Ovid's,' proposing that 'evidence suggests that Cervantes studied Ovid in the original with great care, perhaps as a school text' (1985, 82).

Despite the attention that Stagg, as well as others, have directed toward Quijote's discourse on the myth of the Golden Age and its classical antecedents, a crucial detail has gone unobserved: that in declaring his intent to revive the Age of Gold when later returning to the topic upon encountering the fulling hammers, Quijote breaks from Ovid's framework. As the historian Henry Kamen noted when examining characterizations of the Golden/Iron Age across Europe, 'To look forward was an important departure from the Ovidian model, which had only looked backwards' (1993, 138). Kamen's assertion rests on the understanding that Ovid used the Golden and Iron Ages (and those ages in between) to present an image of man's origins, his history not his future; the concept of a return to the Age of Gold (let alone the idea that this could be brought about by human will) is completely absent from Ovid. Of course what is most striking for the reader of Cervantes is not that this signifies a break between Cervantes and Ovid, but that it signifies a break between Cervantes and himself, between his earlier treatment of the two ages as presented in Quijote's original discourse and this new concept that the Golden Age can be restored, and that this restoring can be accomplished by Quijote himself. Rather than attribute this discord to carelessness on Cervantes' part, or even a mere change of heart and disinclination to mend such inconsistencies, I believe it was a profoundly meaningful departure that reveals Quijote's very conception of history. A closer examination of the two passages will not only further underscore differences between these two treatments of the Golden Age/Iron Age, but also allow us to understand why such differences are meaningful and why the departure between the two understandings of the Age of Gold occurs as it does.

For the purposes of this essay, what is most meaningful is not Cervantes' characterization of the Age of Gold but rather that of Iron. Though the majority of Stagg's study of Cervantes' treatment of the golden age discourse focuses on the Golden Age itself, it is worth noting that a large portion of Quijote's discourse is devoted to the Age of Iron. The parts that Stagg examines in relation to this later age, and much of what he does not examine, reveal a relationship between Cervantes and Ovid as close as that which was established in Cervantes' treatment of the Age of Gold. In their respective dystopian visions of post-golden-age-humanity, greed and avarice guide all human motivation, the earth is pillaged for her resources, and war is a constant part of life. Humanity has abandoned communal ways of living, learning instead the meaning of private property, and even family members are no longer able to trust one another.[2]

But by the end of Quijote's discourse Cervantes enters a poetic territory that would have been entirely anachronistic for Ovid; he discusses the role of the knight errant within the Age of Iron:

Y agora, en estos nuestros detestables siglos, no está segura ninguna ...
Para cuya seguridad, andando más los tiempos y creciendo más la malicia,
se instituyó la orden de los caballeros andantes, para defender las doncellas, amparar las viudas y socorrer a los huérfanos y a los menesterosos.
Desta orden soy yo ...

[But now, in these our detestable times, no maiden is safe ... It was for their protection, as time passed and wickedness spread, that the order of knights errant was instituted: to defend maidens, protect widows, and come to the aid of orphans and those in need. This is the order to which I belong ...] (2004, 1.135; 2005, 77)

The world of chivalry has now found a home within Ovid's conception of history and human decline. Cervantes' ability to extend the Ovidian model to encompass that which is most important to his own literary world – the order of knighthood – is noteworthy on several accounts. For one, it illustrates that Cervantes was not only looking to borrow source material from the Latin poet to add stylistic flourishing to his own novel, but that he was at least a little interested in attempting to make the poetic world of Ovid compatible with his own literary world. And indeed, scholars of Ovid have noted the central importance of the Iron Age in *The Metamorphoses* as a whole. While many poets of both antiquity and modernity have fixated on the idyllic image of the Golden Age, as Richard McKim points out in his study of Ovid's account of creation, it is the fallen state of human nature found in the Age of Iron that allows the poet to over and over again tell the tales of warriors and hunters, conquests and expeditions. McKim writes:

Humanity in the *Met.* resembles the men of the Iron Age and of Giants' blood far more than it does those of the Golden Age ... But the poet is no admirer of the Golden Age any more than of the philosophers' God. To the poet, both are not only unreal but unattractive, the higher nature's cosmos being the negation of the metamorphic world of mythical imagination, and the Golden Age being likewise a world of negatives where nothing of interest can ever happen. (1985, 105)

Though Cervantes himself may not have made such a connection between the wicked nature of men that arises in the Age of Iron and the following images of men as violent adventurers, warriors, hunters, murderers, and so forth, which encompass nearly all subsequent tales told in *The Metamorphoses*, by situating chivalry within his own Age of Iron he establishes a similar bond. Due to the fundamental role that the world of chivalry has in Quijote's life (more or less a model which guides his very means of existence) and by extension the novel as a whole, Cervantes' choice to situate the world of chivalry within the Age of Iron creates a necessary relationship between the inherent consequences of this wicked age and the fundamental ingredient of his own poetic imagination and Quijote's very reason for being, that being the world of knighthood. Without the evils of the Iron Age, chivalry itself would have no purpose and no means of existence. Like the classical heroes of Ovid who need a world of violence and human wickedness, Quijote's task as a knight is likewise only made possible by a world of human evil; and like Ovid himself, whose poetry as a whole requires such wickedness on the part of men, Cervantes' world of fiction requires the violence – even if it comes in satirized form – of a fallen age.

This connection extends beyond the conceptual. In purely practical terms the order of knighthood is also unable to exist in any age beside that of the iron because it is not until the Iron Age that mankind sees the advent of weaponry and warfare: 'come forth, war comes forth, which fights with both, / and with its bloody hand strikes together the clashing arms.' (Ovid 2004, 1.142–3). Quijote's embrace of weaponry, which begins within the very first chapters and continues throughout the book, is only possible in the age that bears the apt distinction of iron, connoting not only a metal baser than gold, but also the primary material used to create armour and weapons. Knights become in a sense an almost necessary evil in this Age of Iron, willing to take up the wicked invention of arms and the use of violent force, but only to stave off even greater evils and protect the innocent. Of course, the relationship of the knight and more weaponry is almost paradoxical since knights used swords instead of gun powder.[3] Consequently, while Cervantes amended Ovid's image of the Iron Age in order to incorporate the order of knighthood within this poetic framework of human history, and in doing so brought an entirely anachronistic theme to what had up till then been a remarkably faithful appropriation of Ovid, this emendation is still entirely in keeping with Ovid's central concept of temporal progress as human decline.

All of this makes it all the more perplexing as to why Cervantes would then break with the Ovidian model only chapters later when he has Quijote declare his intent to revive the Age of Gold upon his coming across the fulling hammers. Kamen goes on to identify a likely source for this new framework: 'But this too was classical in origin. The chief source was Virgil, whose cyclical theory of history catered for the reappearance of the age of gold. This would come in the reign of a future ruler (Augustus) or through the birth of a heavenly child' (1993, 138). Though it might appear at first glance that Cervantes is doing nothing more than engaging in a bit of poetic heterodoxy, appropriating various classical sources regardless of contradictions, I believe something far more meaningful is occurring. Let us look further at Quijote's words when making this declaration:

> Sancho amigo, has de saber que yo nací por querer del cielo en esta nuestra edad de hierro para resucitar en ella la de oro, o la dorada, come suele llamarse. Yo soy aquel para quien están guardados los peligros, las grandes hazañas, los valerosos hechos. Yo soy, digo otra vez, quien ha de resucitar los de la Tabla Redonda, los Doce de Francia y los Nueve de la Fama, y del que ha de poner en olvido los Platires, los Tablantes, Olivantes y Tirantes, los Febos y Belianises, con toda la caterva de famosos caballeros andantes del pasado tiempo, haciendo en este en que me hallo tales grandezas, estrañezas y fechos de armas, que escurezcan las más claras que ellos ficieron.

> [Sancho, my friend, know that I was born, by the will of heaven, in this our age of iron, to revive the one of gold, or the Golden Age, as it is called. I am he for whom are reserved great dangers, great deeds, valiant feats. I am, I repeat, he who is to revive the Knights of the Round Table, the Twelve Peers of France, the Nine Worthies, he who is to make the world forget the Platirs, Tablatants Olivants, and Tirants, the Phoebuses and Belianises, and the entire horde of famous knights errant of a bygone age, by performing in this time in which I find myself such great and extraordinary deeds and feats of arms that they will overshadow the brightest they ever achieved.] (2004, 1.227–8; 2005, 142)

Given our recent discussion as to how Cervantes amended the Ovidian framework in order to incorporate knights into the Age of Iron, we should wonder why 'the entire horde of famous knights errant' that Quijote hopes to revive are now placed in the 'bygone age' of gold. In shifting from an Ovidian framework to one Virgilian, Cervantes is doing more than merely demonstrating his wide knowledge of classical poetry; he is completely disrupting the very parallel between knights and the Age of Iron that he himself established. Of course, in doing this Cervantes has also entirely recast the image of the Golden Age from what was earlier a time of idyllic primitivism, pre-war and pre-technology, to one that is now typified by heroic knights and 'great feats of arms.' As Kamen points out this too was part of the overall Virgilian model: 'Taken however as part of a cyclic view, it [the progress of time] presented the possibility of recurrence and therefore renewed vigor' (1993, 152). Renewed vigour certainly seems to be guiding Quijote's thoughts when he cites the 'great dangers, great deeds, valiant feats' he must confront in bringing about this revival of the Golden Age.

Earlier I mentioned that the ideas of the eighteenth-century Italian philosopher Giambattista Vico would play a role in this interpretation of Ovid and Cervantes. Considered by many to be the first philosopher of history, Vico proposed a framework of human history in his principal work, *The New Science*, very much based on the Virgilian understanding of history as a cyclical phenomenon. Likewise, for Vico, the recurrence of past ages signified the reemergence of heroic valour. This last point was especially significant to Vico's philosophy as it lead to his being identified not only as the first philosopher of history, but as the first philosopher of the counter-enlightenment. Witness to the philosophical, social, and political changes that had occurred in the seventeenth century under the banner of enlightenment and progress, Vico worried that such 'advances' were also diminishing the basic values (and valour) that had guided humanity up till then. For Vico history moved in three ages: the divine, the heroic, and the human, and while the last age, the human age, did result in equality, it also created an atmosphere in which the piety that guided the divine age and the boldness that guided the heroic age were overtaken by a decadence and softness of the human spirit that was steered by meaningless philosophical thought – what he called the *'barbarism of reflection.'* In his book, *G.B. Vico: The Making of an Anti-Modern*, Mark Lilla proposes that the entire treatise of *The New Science* can be read as an attack on modernity and an exaltation of the Roman Empire as an idealized alternative (1993, 9). Vico's decadent human age is thus in many regards a stand-in for modern times and his heroic age its climax, a time, as Lilla writes, when humans are 'at their most vigorous and virtuous' (1993, 154).

Though obviously neither Cervantes' amended Ovidian model of history nor his version of the Virgilian model is exactly like that of Vico, I do believe that we can apply certain concepts of Vico's understanding of history to our reading of Cervantes. In Quijote's latter declaration to revive the Golden Age, this idealized time bears a striking resemblance to the heroism of Vico's heroic age. Both are characterized by valour and bravery and viewed as a return away from a less grand era. There are still some questions that must be asked and gaps that must be filled: namely, what brought about this shift from Quijote seeing the Age of Iron as one of chivalry to seeing it as a time void of heroes? The answer to this question lies, I believe, in the very objects Quijote encounters, the fulling hammers.

In the beginning moments of the episode the darkness of the night prevents anything from being seen; Quijote and Sancho are guided by the sounds they hear. Lured by what sounds like water 'hurtling over large cliffs' [un grande ruido de agua, come que de algunos grandes y levantados riscos ded depañaba], the thirsty wanderers are made happy by the sound – 'Alegroles el ruido en gran manera ...' [The sound made them very happy ...] (2004, 227; 2005, 141). But what at first sounds like water crashing on the rocks of a cliff soon takes on a far different, less pleasant nature as 'oyeron que daban unos golpes a compás, con un cierto crujir de hierros y cadenas, que, acompañados del furioso estruendo de agua, que pusieron pavor a cualquier otro corazón que no fuera el de don Quijote' [they heard the sound of rhythmic pounding, along with a certain clanking of irons and chains that, accompanied by the clamorous fury of the water, would have put terror in any heart other than Don Quixote's] (2004, 1.227; 2005, 141).

That their happiness quickly turns to terror is significant. Equally significant, and I believe connected, is that the noise of the falling water has gone from one associated with nature (water crashing on cliffs) to one of a more mechanical presence (the clanking of iron and chains and rhythmic pounding). The strange sound of machinery, it would appear, is the source of Quijote and Sancho's anxiety. But perhaps we can go even further and conclude that Cervantes has provided us a material connection between the iron of the chains and the Age of Iron. As Harry Levin notes in his book-length study on the Golden Age in Renaissance literature, the Age of Iron carries with it the symbol of technological progress: 'Iron has connotations which are harsher and harder; yet, since it indicates a crucial step on the way to civilization as we know it, with all its potentialities for construction and destruction, it should connote the plow as well as the sword' (1969, 13). Though Levin sees the 'plow' as symbolic of the peaceful technology that arose from the Age of Iron (in contrast to the more destructive militant technology of the 'sword'), I am not so sure that Quijote would see things quite the same way; regardless though, the plow/sword duality serves as a useful metaphor for understanding the complexities and consequences of this age.

Though in the chapter 11 discourse on the Golden Age Quijote decries the progress of both industrial and military technology, both the plow and the sword, (albeit leaving some room for virtuous use of the sword), by later associating the machinery of the fulling hammers with the Age of Iron and the valour of knighthood with the Age of Gold,

Quijote denies the more standard view that Levin points out in which military and industrial progress go hand in hand. Furthermore, whereas Levin sees the sword as harmful and the 'plow' as a beneficial advance of civilization, for Quijote it is quite the opposite: it is the machinery that strikes fear and the sword which must be revived.

The notion of machinery and technological progress as characteristic of a time inhospitable to heroic knights is echoed later by Quijote in his arms versus letters discourse;

> Bien hayan aquellos benditos siglos que carecieron de la espantable furia de aquestos endemoniados instrumentos de la artillería ... con la cual dio causa que un infame y cobarde brazo quite la vida a un valeroso caballero ... Y así considerando esto, estoy por decir que en el alma me pesa de haber tomado este ejercicio de caballero andante en edad tan detestable como es esta en que ahora vivimos.

> [Happy were those blessed times that lacked the horrifying fury of the diabolical instruments of artillery ... which allows an ignoble and cowardly hand to take the life of a valiant knight ... When I consider this, I am prepared to say that it grieves my very soul that I have taken up the profession of knight errant in an age as despicable as the one we live in now.] (2004, 1.491; 2005, 332–3)

Once again depicting his own time as a despicable age in which the nobility of knights has given way to the rise of vulgar industry, Quijote furthers the notion of the Iron Age as modernity itself, a time which is literally coming to be filled with the iron of machinery and artillery. Iván Jaksic, whose study on technology in the *Quijote* provides a wonderful survey of the many instances technology enters Don Quijote's world, does himself recognize the unique effect that the technology of the fulling hammers has on Quijote. In regards to this episode Jaksic writes: 'Don Quijote begins to show signs of deep distress which ultimately undermine the very foundations of his adopted life' (1994, 80). And indeed it certainly does appear that the sound and sight of the fulling hammers has caused a radical rethinking on Quijote's part as to what exactly the Iron Age would signify for his very way of living. Times that would produce such machinery can no longer be home to the heroic valour of knights; in fact, such times evoke for Quijote the very notion that he is living in a time inhospitable to such chivalric valour and that it is his duty to resuscitate the past age of heroes.

I would now like to set aside this discussion of Quijote's two characterizations of the Ages of Gold and Iron and move onto another portion of the fulling hammer episode that will allow us to see that while Cervantes may have abandoned the Ovidian framework of history in order to illustrate the unheroic nature of the modern era, he did not abandon Ovid altogether. As I mentioned in the beginning of this essay, the fulling hammers episode evokes two mythic images from Ovid, that of the metallic ages and one having to do with the figure of Mars, to whom Quijote compares himself when coming upon the fulling hammers:

> Bien notas, escudero fiel y legal, las tinieblas desta noche, su estraño silencio, el sordo y confuso estruendo destos árboles, el temeroso ruido de aquella agua en cuya busca venimos, que parece que se despeña y derrumba desde los altos montes de la Luna, y aquel incesable golpear que nos hiere y lastima los oídos; las cuales cosas, todas juntas y cada una por sí, son bastantes a infundir miedo, temor y espanto en el pecho del mesmo Marte.

> [Note well, my faithful and loyal Squire, the darkness of this night, its strange silence, the indistinct and confused sound of these trees, the fearful clamor of the water we came seeking, which seems to be falling and crashing from the high mountains of the moon, and the unceasing noise of pounding that wounds and pains our ears; all these things, taken together and separately, are enough to instill fear, terror and dread in the bosom of Mars himself.] (2004, 1.228; 2005, 142)

In stating that Mars himself would experience fear upon encountering the darkness, the silence, and especially 'the fearful clamor of water,' Quijote establishes a clear parallel between his own valour and that of the heroic god of war, this time even going so far as to state that Mars's courage is wanting in comparison to Quijote's own. And the parallel between Quijote and Mars does not end here; in the very next episode, when receiving the helmet of Mambrino, he states that this helmet is comparable to that of Mars, 'que hizo y forjo el dios de las herrarías para el dios de las batallas' [the one made and forged by the god of the smithies for the god of war] – meaning specifically the one Vulcan made for Mars [2004, 1.247; 2005, 155]. We should begin by taking note of the fact that despite Quijote's allusion to a helmet made for Mars by Vulcan, no such helmet exists within the entire canon of mythology, Greek or Roman. However, while Vulcan may have never crafted a helmet for Mars, he did build a chain net in which to ensnare the god of war upon hearing of Mars's adulterous affair with Venus, Vulcan's wife, which takes us back to Ovid, *The Metamorphoses* IV: 'At once he [Vulcan] perfected graceful chains of bronze ... and nets and snares to deceive the eyes' (2004, 4.176–81).

By carefully placing an allusion to Mars within the episode of the fulling hammers and then continuing this allusion only a chapter later, Cervantes provides us with a way of understanding these two episodes in unison. Since Vulcan's net is composed of chains, it would seem that perhaps we could see a relationship between the helmet of Mambrino and the frightening sound of clanging chains that provokes Quijote to compare himself to Mars – were it not for the fact that Ovid explicitly states that the chains are composed of bronze – 'aere catenas' – not iron, the crucial metal which symbolizes all to which Quijote stands in opposition (1994, 190). It is here though where we can return to Vico's theories and examine a crucial component to his philosophy of history: the role of myth across the ages.

Central to Vico's attack on modernity's philosophy of the Enlightenment was the idea that myth was essential to understanding humanity; that myth stemmed, as Vico writes, from man's 'natural need to create poetic characters' in order to express 'imaginative class concepts or universals' (1948, section 74). Myth was in effect the most expressive of all human communication because it was through myth that humans in each of Vico's three ages expressed and understood the values of their respective times. As Laurence Coupe writes in his study of myth, 'In his *The New Science* he [Vico] argued that the only "science" of humanity which could be of use was one that comprehended what lay behind *logos*. Not reason but imagination was the key to myth. Myth was not a failed attempt to articulate rational truth but a creative impulse underlying human history' (1997, 119).

According to Vico, as the ages changed from divine to heroic, heroic to human – and as these temporal changes brought about shifts in societal values – so too would the myths themselves change. What was most vital and of interest to Vico was not how new myths were invented or new heroes added, but rather how the very same mythic figures who stood for certain values in one age were appropriated by later ages and underwent a metamorphosis to represent entirely opposing values. As such, a certain god in the human age would maintain the same shell as he did in the age of heroes but would come to represent entirely different and often contradictory values – a phenomenon Vico terms: 'double fables or characters' (1948, 581). And as it happens, one of the myths central to Vico's theory of 'double characters' is the very Venus, Vulcan, Mars myth found in Ovid. Vico writes: 'Returning now to the three [poetic] characters, Vulcan, Mars and Venus, it must be noted here (and this must be considered an important canon of our mythology) that there were three divine characters signifying the heroes, distinguished from three others signifying the plebeians' (1948, 579).

In one of the most widely published translations of Ovid in Renaissance and early-modern Spain, that of Jorge Bustamante (1577), Vulcan's net is said to be described as made of iron: 'una red de hierro tan degada y sutil' (1577, 74). Such a discrepancy between Ovid's original Latin and Bustamente's Spanish rendering could certainly have spurred Cervantes to connect the net of Vulcan, and thus Vulcan himself, to the iron chains that characterize the noise of the fulling hammers and through them to larger concepts of the Age of Iron as an age of industry.

Bustamante's translation was by no means the only existent rendering of Ovid into Spanish during the Renaissance and Golden Age; others such as Antonio Perez (1580), Felipe Mey (1586), and Pedro Sánchez de Viana (1589) all provided their own editions of Ovid's poem. Nor, however, were translations alone the definitive sources of mythical accounts during this time, as many scholars (such as Spain's Juan Pérez de Moya) who possessed knowledge of the classical tongues drew on various accounts, Greek and Roman, and assembled their own encyclopedic volumes that not only told how the mythic adventures unfolded but also elaborated with commentary and/or allegory on the possible meaning (or meanings) contained within the stories. Each and every one of the translations and commentaries mentioned above will take us closer to seeing how the figure of Vulcan was understood in early modern Spain and thus further allow us to appreciate Cervantes' own complex interpretation.

It is clear that throughout the episode of the fulling hammers and in the following episode of the helmet of Mambrino, Mars is Quijote's archetypal hero. As a god of war who stood in opposition to Vulcan, Mars represents for Quijote the triumph of valour over modern industry. But if we actually recall what occurred in the myth, we should realize that the comparison to Mars is a rather odd one. Mars is of course trapped by the god of the forge (perhaps we may even at this point take the liberty of saying the god of industry). Furthermore, though Ovid's account contains nothing to suggest that Vulcan was anything other than a god as divine and as heroic as Mars, within the Spanish accounts of the myth, Vulcan's more unheroic elements are underscored; the god is, after all, crippled and known for his ugliness.

Like Vico, the Spanish scholar Juan Pérez de Moya believed there was a form of wisdom expressed beneath the myths, going so far as to title his work the *Philosophía Secreta*, a study which contains a chapter-by-chapter analysis of all the different figures that come to us from mythology. The accounts of Vulcan he discusses early on reveal a heroic Vulcan who was esteemed as a god, 'es de creer que fue varón excelente, pues los de su tiempo lo tuvieron por dios' [it is to be believed that he was an excellent man, as those of his time took him for a god] (1995, 220). However, further along in his discussion, the tone shifts and he begins to discuss Vulcan in relation to depictions of an ugly and crippled god, unwanted by his fellow gods: 'Pintaban a Vulcano, según Alberico, de figura de un herrero lleno de tizne, y ahumado, y *muy feo, y cojo de una pierna*, con un martillo en la mano, y la pintura mostrando como que los dioses con impetus le echaban del cielo' [They painted Vulcan, according to Alberico, as the figure of a blacksmith covered with soot and smoke, *and very ugly, and crippled in one leg*, with a hammer in his hand, and the painting shows how the other gods violently threw him from the heavens] (1995, 222). After establishing this divergent image of an ugly, crippled Vulcan he transitions into a discussion of the myth, recounting Mars's affair with Venus, frequently contrasting the beauty of Venus with the ugliness of Vulcan. 'En lo del adulterio de Martes y Venus es historia, porque como Vulcano fuese muy feo y Venus muy Hermosa ...' [Regarding the adultery between Mars and Venus, it's a story, because as Vulcan was very ugly and Venus very beautiful ...'] (1995, 230).

Pérez de Moya's last comment is especially noteworthy for it seems to imply that the myth can only make sense when one takes into account the stark contrast between Venus's beauty and Vulcan's ugliness, despite the fact that Ovid's account offers nothing at all regarding Vulcan as either ugly or even crippled, actually referring to him only as 'Iunonigenaeque marito' [son of Juno, her (Venus's) husband] (1994, 190). Moya though is not alone in deviating from Ovid in supplying his own image of Vulcan's less heroic attributes. In Antonio Perez's 1580 translation, Vulcan's lameness is his defining nature, as he is regarded as 'el Dios coxo' [the crippled god] (1580, 82). This label is echoed in the 1586 translation of Felipe Mey, titling him 'coxo herrero' [the crippled blacksmith] (1586, 200). In a similar manner, in Sánchez de Viana's 1589 translation the god is also titled according to his unwanted nature, referred to as 'feo Vulcano, dios de la herrería' [ugly Vulcan, god of the forge] (1990, 1.321).

This consortium of views surrounding Vulcan points in the direction of Vico's theory that heroic figures could be appropriated and given plebeian or unheroic characteristics during certain times. The Vulcan of Cervantes, and perhaps all of sixteenth-century Spain, was an unheroic figure, ugly and lame. Furthermore, such unheroic physical attributes combined with his affiliation with metallurgy (and by extension the industry that was making chivalry obsolete) made Vulcan the perfect archetype for an Age of Iron in which, as Quijote tells us, any coward could take the life of a valiant knight through the advent of technology and industry. In connecting Vulcan to not only industry but a broader idea of anti-heroic modernism, we can now begin to complete our overall reading of the episode of the fulling hammers. Coming across these objects of industry forced Quijote to realize a frightening truth of his age: that while his age may be one of iron it is an iron far closer to that of Vulcan than Mars, more of industry than warfare. It is for this reason that he broke with his early Ovidian conception of history that housed chivalry within the Age of Iron, and for this reason that he enjoys seeing himself as the god of war confronting the god of the forge.

We should remember though that our analysis is not fully complete; we still must take into full account the continuation of the Mars/Vulcan theme in the next episode, that of the helmet of Mambrino. If as Brody stated, the episode of the fulling hammers represents a departure from the predictable quixotic episode, that of the helmet of Mambrino represents its quick return. Here we once again see the typical quixotic formula: Quijote sees an object (the barber with a shaving basin on his head), mistakes it for something it is not (a golden helmet), and Sancho corrects him (telling him that what he mistakes as a golden helmet is nothing more than a shiny object). Given our recent exploration into the connection between the literal, material iron of the fulling hammers and the symbolic, conceptual iron of the Iron Age, it is tempting to extend this focus on the metallic quality of objects to the helmet itself. Quijote's mistaking the basin as one of gold represents not only his return to the standard modus operandi of his chivalric self, but also his desire to see the possibility of gold where no such possibility exists – a concept we can extend beyond simply the helmet to his whole conception of the Golden Age itself. As Kamen aptly points out, in visions of the Golden Age often 'gold is illusory' and it is not so easy 'to differentiate adequately between the glitter and the dross' (1993, 135).

It is my belief though that all that Quijote misunderstands and confuses is well understood by Cervantes. In having his hero mistake the helmet to be of gold, Cervantes underscores Quijote's delusional thoughts in believing that reviving a past time is within his reach, and in having Quijote claim that this new-found helmet is made by Vulcan, Cervantes places Quijote in the very iron chains of modernity that he sought to escape. The helmet is a continued symbol of Vulcan's – and thus modernity's – ability to ensnare even the most heroic spirits who would prefer to live in another time. Though Quijote might believe he can stop the movement of historical progress and usher in an idyllic time of valour and heroism, I am not so sure Cervantes was as naive. And here once again we see a possible similarity to Vico who did not share the Virgilian (and quixotic) view that great men, even great world-leaders, could have any effect on the cycle of history. For Vico, the course of history was set by divine providence and any attempt to alter the fate of human society would be somewhat like that all too well-known image of Quijote attacking windmills, nothing more than the absurd attempt of a lone individual to try and stop an unchangeable cycle, expending all his strength and energy in vain.

NOTES

1 Cervantes writes this opening sonnet as if it were by Gandalín (the squire of Amadis) and dedicated to Sancho. Cervantes writes: 'Salve otra vez, ¡Oh Sancho!, tan buen hombre, / que a solo tú nuestro español Ovidio / con buzcorona te hace reverencia' [Hail once again, O Sancho! So good a man, / that only you, when the Ovid of our Spain / bows to kiss your hand, smack him on the head] (2004, Prologue 29; 2005, 15). A footnote addresses a possible explanation as to why such reference would be made to Cervantes as Ovid: 'No está claro por qué Gandalín trata al autor de la obra de *nuestra español Ovidio*: quizá por narrar la metamorphosis de Sancho, de labrador en escudero' [It is not clear why Gandalin addresses the author of this work as the *Ovid of our Spain*: perhaps because he narrates the metamorphosis of Sancho, from peasant into squire] (2004, Prologue 29; 2005, 15). All translations of *Don Quijote* are taken from the 2005 Edith Grossman edition. Unless otherwise referenced, other translations are by the author.
2 On the opposition between the utopian Golden Age and a dystopian world replete with harmful inventions, see Maravall.
3 The technology of war was well developed during the reign of Philip II. As David C. Goodman states: 'There's clear evidence in the 1590s that existing artillery schools were failing to produce gunners in the required numbers

... In May 1595, the King granted gunners qualifying at Seville some of the privileges associated with the nobility' (2002, 125). Thus we can see how chivalry/nobility and technology were coming together.

WORKS CITED

Brody, Robert. 1975. 'Don Quijote's Emotive Adventures: Fulling Hammers and Lions.' *Neophilologus* 59.3:372–81.

Cascardi, Anthony J. 1992. *Subject of Modernity*. Cambridge: Cambridge University Press.

– 1997. *Ideologies of History in the Spanish Golden Age*. University Park: Pennsylvania State University Press.

Cervantes, Miguel de. 2004. *Don Quijote de la Mancha*. Edición del Instituto Cervantes, dirigida por Francisco Rico. Barcelona: Galaxia Gutenburg.

– 2005. *Don Quixote*. Translated by Edith Grossman. London: Vintage.

Coleman, Robert. 1967. 'Ovid and the Anti-Epic.' *The Classical Review* 17.1:46–51.

Coupe, Laurence. 1997. *Myth*. London: Routledge.

De Armas, Frederick. 1986. *The Return of Astraea: An Astral-Imperial Myth in Calderón*. Lexington: University of Kentucky Press.

Goodman, David C. 2002. *Power and Penury: Government, Technology and Science in Philip II's Spain*. Cambridge: Cambridge University Press.

Graf, E.C. 2007. *Cervantes and Modernity: Four Essays on Don Quijote*. Lewisburg: Bucknell University Press.

Jaksic, Iván. 1994. 'Don Quijote's Encounter with Technology.' *Bulletin of the Cervantes Society of America* 14.1:75–95.

Johnson, Carroll. 1990. *Don Quixote: The Quest for Modern Fiction*. Prospect Heights: Waveland Press.

– 2000. *Cervantes and the Material World*. Urbana: University of Illinois Press.

Kamen, Henry, ed. 1993. 'Golden Age, Iron Age: A Conflict of Concepts in the Renaissance.' In *Crisis and Change in Early Modern Spain*, 135–55. Brookfield, VT: Variorum.

Levin, Harry. 1969. *Myth of the Golden Age in the Renaissance*. Oxford: Oxford University Press.

Lilla, Mark. 1993. *G.B. Vico: The Making of an Anti-Modern*. Cambridge, MA: Harvard University Press.

Maravall, José Antonio. 1991. *Utopia and Counterutopia in the Quixote*. Trans. Robert W. Felkel. Detroit: Wayne State University Press.

McKim, Richard. 1985. 'Myth against Philosophy in Ovid's Account of Creation.' *The Classical Journal* 80.2:97–108.

Ovid. 1577. *Las Metamorphoses, o Transformaciones del excelente Poeta Ovidio, en quinze libros buelto en Castellano*. Trans. Jorge Bustamante. Toledo.

– 1580. *Los Quinze Libros de los Metamorphoseos de el excellente Poeta Latino Ovidio Traduzidos en verso suelto y octava rima por Antonio Perez, con sus alegorias al fin de cada libro*. Salamanca.

– 1586. *Del Metamorfoseos de Ovidio en otava rima traduzido por Felipe Mey, Siete Libros con otras cosas del mismo*. Tarragona.

– 1990. *Las Metamorphosis*. Ed. Juan Francisco Alcina. Trans. Pedro Sánchez de Viana. Barcelona: Planeta.

– 1994. *Metamorphoses, Books I–VIII (Volume III of VI)*. Translated by Frank. J. Miller. Loeb Classical Library. Cambridge, MA: Harvard University Press.

– 2004. *Metamorphoses*. Trans. Z. Philip Ambrose. Newburyport, MA: Focus Publishing.

Pérez de Moya, Juan. 1995. *Philosofía secreta de la gentilidad*. Ed. Carlos Clavería. Madrid: Cátedra.

Stagg, Geoffrey. 1985. '*Illo tempore*: Don Quixote's Discourse on the Golden Age, and Its Antecedents.' In *La Galatea de Cervantes, 400 anos después*, ed. Juan Bautista Avalle-Arce, 70–90. Newark: Juan de la Cuesta.

Quint, David. 2003. *Cervantes's Novel of Modern Times*. Princeton: Princeton University Press.

Vico, Giambattista. 1948. *The New Science*. Trans. Thomas Goddard Bergin and Max Horld Fisch. Ithaca: Cornell University Press.

Weiner, Jack. 2008. 'Cervantes y Don Quijote ante el ocaso de España.' *Annali dell'Universita degli Studio di Napoli 'L'Orientale'* 50.1:107–44.

7 Cervantes Transforms Ovid: The Dubious Metamorphoses in *Don Quijote*

WILLIAM WORDEN

The fifteen books that comprise Ovid's *Metamorphoses* first describe the creation of the world and then portray both gods and mortals undergoing an array of mutations that change them into trees, flowers, rivers, constellations, and animals, as well as an assortment of other beings. The work not only recounts multiple mythological tales, but it also highlights the author's familiarity with the literature of his time, which is apparent in the wide variety of genres incorporated into the epic poem.[1] Beyond simply recounting tales of transformation, the narrative of the *Metamorphoses* foregrounds the act of storytelling itself, adding a strikingly self-reflective dimension to the poem.[2] Writing sixteen centuries after Ovid, Cervantes also chooses to include diverse genres in his most famous work.[3] As is the case with Ovid's poem, *Don Quijote* time and again thematizes the nature of narrative and the ways in which stories are told. And like the *Metamorphoses*, Cervantes' novel depicts transformations of all kinds, including – among many other metamorphoses – a country gentleman who becomes a knight, a labourer who becomes a squire, and a woman dressed as a man who becomes a princess. Beyond their mutual interest in both transformation and generic diversity, Ovid and Cervantes – the former a major author of the Golden Age of Latin literature, the latter a major author of the Golden Age of Spanish literature – create works that share a similar literary afterlife: both the *Metamorphoses* and *Don Quijote* are still being read with interest centuries after their first publication, and each has inspired numerous adaptations in a variety of artistic genres, ranging from illustrations, engravings, paintings, and sculptures to musical works and theatrical productions.

For a number of reasons, the relationship between these two influential writers has not passed unnoticed by literary critics. In addition to resembling his forebear both generically and thematically, Cervantes includes in his texts numerous references to Ovid and his works. Considering just the case of *Don Quijote*, the Prologue of the first part of the novel quotes from *Tristia* and mentions Ovid's tale of the cruel Medea while the sonnet from Gandalín to Sancho Panza that appears soon after the Prologue refers to Cervantes himself as 'nuestro español Ovidio' [our Spanish Ovid] (1998b, 28). Discussions of Ovid and his poetry continue in the second part of the novel, as when Don Quijote explains to Don Diego that the Roman poet was exiled for writing *Ars amatoria*. In another conversation focused on literature, this time on the way to the Cave of Montesinos, the cousin of a *licenciado*, known for his swordsmanship, asserts that one of the many books he is writing is *Metamorfóseos, o Ovidio español* [*Metamorphoses, or the Spanish Ovid*] (1998b, 2.22.812; 1995, 465). In his monograph titled *Ovid and the Renascence in Spain*, Rudolph Schevill analyses the degree to which Cervantes knew the work of the Roman poet and concludes: 'After gathering all the evidence, it is apparent that Cervantes was intimately acquainted with the tales of Ovid's *Metamorphoses*; he carried them in his memory and referred to them as we refer nowadays to well-known writers and their works' (1913, 174).[4] Beyond direct references to Ovid and his writings, other passages in Cervantes' texts point to a detailed knowledge of the Roman author's work. In a study examining the sources Cervantes may have used in composing Don Quijote's discourse on the Golden Age, for example, Geoffrey Stagg asserts with reference to the *Metamorphoses*: 'The evidence suggests that Cervantes studied Ovid in the original with great care, perhaps as a school text. No other author's treatment [of the Golden Age] is as close to Cervantes's as Ovid's' (1985, 82).

This essay will examine the nature of the metamorphoses that occur in *Don Quijote* in light of those presented in Ovid's poem, focusing especially on the differences between the novelistic and poetic transformations. Others have analysed particular episodes of Cervantes' novel in order to compare metamorphoses that take place in the work with corresponding ones that occur in the *Metamorphoses*.[5] My interest here addresses a more general question: How do Ovid and Cervantes introduce the idea of metamorphoses in their texts and, consequently, in what ways do readers respond to transformations in the two works? Put another way, I am interested in analysing how Cervantes transforms Ovidian transformations. In choosing to examine a Cervantine text in the light of Ovid's *Metamorphoses*, I am in fact following in a tradition established by the Spanish author himself. Cervantes was the first to suggest the possibility of comparing the metamorphoses that characters experience in his own work with those that occur in Ovid's epic poem.[6] We will see in this study that the transformations that take place in *Don Quijote* are, as I suggest in my title, 'dubious' when compared to Ovidian metamorphoses. Doubt is both fundamental and necessary in considering the transformations that occur in Cervantes' novel while it is incidental and peripheral to the metamorphoses presented in Ovid's poem.

Transformative Texts

The *Metamorphoses* maintains a constant focus on acts of transformation; throughout the work 'about two hundred fifty metamorphoses are narrated or mentioned' (Solodow 1988, 15). Though not nearly so numerous in Cervantes' text, transformations do indeed constitute an important aspect of *Don Quijote,* from the very first chapter of the 1605 novel – in which Alonso Quijano becomes Don Quijote de la Mancha – to the last chapter of its 1615 continuation – which recounts the protagonist's renunciation of his chivalric identity and his concomitant acceptance of his former name and station in life. A brief list of some of the metamorphoses that occur in *Don Quijote* would include the following:

1 Alonso Quijano → Don Quijote de la Mancha → Alonso Quijano the Good[7]
2 Sancho the labourer → Sancho the squire → Sancho the governor → Sancho the squire → Sancho the labourer
3 Aldonza Lorenzo → Dulcinea del Toboso → Dulcinea the coarse peasant girl
4 The rejected Dorotea (dressed as a man) in search of Fernando → Princess Micomicona → Dorotea the accepted wife of Fernando
5 Sansón Carrasco → The Knight of the Forest / The Knight of the Mirrors → The Knight of the White Moon → Sansón Carrasco
6 Ginés de Pasamonte → Maese Pedro

There are, of course, others that could be added to the list, including any number of metamorphoses that take place at the ducal palace as part of the elaborate hoaxes played on Don Quijote and Sancho.[8] Still, the six transformations shown above are the ones that produce the most far-reaching consequences in the novel.

Both Ovid's poem and Cervantes' novel recount metamorphoses of all kinds. How should we as readers make sense of the transformations that we encounter in the two texts? Alonso Quijano decides to call himself Don Quijote de la Mancha, but does that actually make him a knight errant? Surely not, a reader of the work would argue, and almost all of the characters in *Don Quijote* would agree. But the issue is not quite resolved. We might wonder, for example, whether the protagonist himself believes in his chivalric identity.[9] And what does Sancho really think about his master's profession? We could ask similar questions regarding all of the above metamorphoses, for none of them is easily deciphered. While pondering these points, it seems logical to pose similar queries regarding the *Metamorphoses*. Does Ovid expect his reader simply to accept unquestioningly the numerous transformations in his poem? Or are there specific problematic transformations that provoke doubts on the part of a reader of the work? In order to arrive at some answers to these questions, let us begin our analysis by comparing the first book of the *Metamorphoses* to the initial chapters of *Don Quijote*. I contend that from the very beginning of their works, both Ovid and Cervantes offer readers clues about how their texts should be read, insights which in great measure help clarify the differences between Ovidian and Cervantine metamorphoses.

Making Sense of the Initial Transformations

Ovid begins the *Metamorphoses* by announcing: 'My intention is to tell of bodies changed / To different forms; the gods, who made the changes, / Will help me – or I hope so – with a poem / That runs from the world's beginning to our own days' (1983, 3). The poem then proceeds to describe the creation of the world in a manner consistent with Roman beliefs of the time.[10] After the world has been created, Jove summons a council of the gods; in fact, the first narrative voice that speaks in the *Metamorphoses* other than the poet's is that of Jove, whose status as the greatest of all the gods would seem to recommend him as credible narrator. The metamorphoses that occur in the first book of the poem – the creation of the world, humanity passing from a Gold to Silver to Bronze to Iron Age, Lycaon becoming a wolf, and Daphne transforming into a laurel tree (to name just a few) – are neither questioned nor presented as particularly problematic within the poem. They are quite simply the work of the gods, those powerful beings invoked in the poem's opening verses. The *Metamorphoses* has begun with discrete, generally accepted transformations, one following the other. A reader of the work is inclined to focus on the stories being told, the chain of metamorphoses that constitute the poem, rather than to question each transformation that occurs.

It must be noted that there are moments of doubt that creep into the *Metamorphoses*.[11] Even in the poem's first book, when Deucalion and Pyrrha throw stones behind them which are transformed into humans, a momentary question arises regarding whether this metamorphosis is plausible: 'The stones – who would believe it, had we not / The unimpeachable witness of Tradition? – / Began to lose their hardness, to soften slowly, / To take on form, to grow in size, a little, / Become less rough, to look like human beings' (1983, 15). In later sections of the poem further doubts and questions arise from time to time. At certain moments characters do not believe what they are told, while at other moments the narrator himself seems unsure of what is happening.[12] In book 8, for example, Pirithous responds to a transformational story by saying: 'These are fairy tales; / The gods have no such powers, Achelous, / To give and take away the shape of things' (1983, 200). Nevertheless, these moments of possible doubt are fleeting instances that are relatively few in number in the poem.[13] From the beginning of the *Metamorphoses* and throughout almost the entirety of the work, Ovid conditions his reader to accept, rather than question, the many transformations portrayed in the poem.

While for Ovid the initial transmutation – on which all subsequent transformations depend – is the separation of earth, water, and land, the original metamorphosis in Cervantes' novel is less far-reaching but no less influential within the world of the literary work: Alonso Quijano, a mere country gentleman, becomes a knight errant known as Don Quijote de la Mancha. If in Ovid's poem a seemingly reliable narrator and then Jove himself supply the work's initial narrative voices, in *Don Quijote* the first voice we encounter appears in the prologue and announces: 'aunque parezco padre, soy padrastro de don Quijote' [though I may seem to be Don Quijote's parent, I'm only his stepfather] (1998b, 10; 1995, 3), a gesture that distances the writer from his text while seeming to call into question the truthfulness of the words on the page. A reader of *Don Quijote* learns in the novel's first chapter that Alonso Quijano goes mad and that his supposed transformation into Don Quijote de la Mancha occurs (for the protagonist if not for others) not because of divine will, but rather simply because he decides that it has happened.[14] Other characters, and in fact the first narrator himself, repeatedly mock or pity the supposed knight errant and refuse to accept his chivalric identity as true (with Sancho being the obvious exception to this rule).[15] Given this confluence of circumstances, readers of the novel cannot avoid confronting later transformations presented in the work with an eye toward evaluating their truthfulness and deciding for themselves how to interpret what is presented in Cervantes' text. In other words, from the very first chapter of the work, doubt regarding supposed metamorphoses is a fundamental aspect of the experience of reading *Don Quijote*.

Both authors, then, deliver on their promise made to readers early in their works. Given the way in which we have been guided toward a non-questioning reading of the transformations in the *Metamorphoses*, what follows Ovid's opening matches the presumed plausibility of the changes in form that he describes. Cervantes, on the other hand, presents one problematic metamorphosis after another, starting with a mad protagonist whose supposed transformation serves as the main narrative thread that spans the entire novel. Ovid does in fact touch on the notion of disbelief in his poem, but Cervantes creates gaping holes of doubt from the very inception of his work. Any reader of *Don Quijote* must confront and continually wrestle with the uncertainty of transformations from the earliest episodes of the novel. The nature of reality, storytelling, and belief in general, is much more precarious in Cervantes' work than in Ovid's. After comparing the beginning of the poem with the start of the novel, it is clear that Ovid does not depend on uncertainty the way that Cervantes does, and that the role of doubt for the latter is part of the very fabric of his generic experiment which so often questions the nature of reality. Unlike Ovid, Cervantes openly invites his readers to decide for themselves the plausibility of the transformations to come.

Now it is time to turn our attention to the transformations that take place within *Don Quijote* and to consider the ways in which both the characters in the work and the reader make sense of the changing forms in the novel. The six transformations listed earlier in this essay could be categorized as follows: 1) Questionable Transformations: Alonso Quijano, Sancho Panza, and Aldonza Lorenzo; 2) Pretended Metamorphoses: Dorotea, Sansón Carrasco, and Ginés de Pasamonte. I term this latter group 'Pretended Metamorphoses' because these three characters pretend to be someone they are not in order to fool Don Quijote and Sancho.[16] In all three cases the characters know their true identity and are aware that their supposed transformation into someone new (be it Princess Micomicona, the Knight of the White Moon, or Maese Pedro) is simply a ruse. Though studying in detail their supposed transformations could most certainly produce interesting findings,[17] space considerations limit my analysis to what I have termed the 'Questionable Transformations.' In the pages that follow I will examine the three most important transformations in the work: Alonso Quijano becoming Don Quijote de la Mancha, Sancho Panza becoming a squire, and Aldonza Lorenzo being transformed into Dulcinea del Toboso. For each of these three I will analyse key textual moments in *Don Quijote* which force the reader to decide whether a metamorphosis has occurred and, if so, for whom.

Don Quijote, Sancho the Squire, and Dulcinea del Toboso: Questionable Metamorphoses

The very existences of Don Quijote as knight, Sancho as squire, and Dulcinea as a beautiful princess are questioned repeatedly both by other characters and the reader throughout *Don Quijote*. Not long after Alonso Quijano transforms himself into Don Quijote, he succeeds in persuading Sancho to serve him as squire, but throughout the rest of the novel he struggles to convince others that he truly is a knight errant (though most often he remains unaware of their doubts). Hardly any character who gets to know Don Quijote and Sancho well believes that they truly are knight and squire.[18] Granting, then, that others refuse to accept the country gentleman's transformation into knight errant, let us consider the cases of master and squire and attempt to determine whether they themselves believe in their own metamorphoses and whether they truly accept the existence of Dulcinea as a princess.

Given the clarity with which Alonso Quijano's madness is presented at the opening of the novel, it is quite reasonable to judge that he really does consider himself a knight errant. According to this assessment, he has lost his mind and for that reason he now truly believes that he is Don Quijote de la Mancha, follower of Amadís de Gaula. Such an interpretation, however, is challenged by a description of Don Quijote's thoughts when he first arrives at the ducal estate in the second part of the novel. Seeing himself treated so well by the Duke and Duchess – who are, of course, simply enjoying themselves at the expense of a madman whose story they have read – Don Quijote turns introspective. The novel's narration explains the protagonist's entrance into the palace: 'aquel fue el primer día que de todo en todo conoció y creyó ser caballero andante verdadero, y no fantástico, viéndose tratar del mesmo modo que él había leído se trataban los tales caballeros en los pasados siglos' [finding himself treated exactly as he had always read that knights were treated, in ancient times, it was the first time he was ever fully convinced that he was a real rather than, somehow, an imaginary knight errant] (1998b, 2.31.880; 1995, 510). How exactly should we interpret this passage and what does it tell us about the transformation of Alonso Quijano into Don Quijote de la Mancha? Has the protagonist simply been playing a role up to this point, and only now suspects that he might, in fact, be a knight errant? Or is this the moment in the text when the metamorphosis actually takes place and the country gentleman finally does become Don Quijote de la Mancha? Or are we to suspect, reading this passage, that the self-consciousness displayed here by the character – who quite obviously has been questioning his identity – indicates that he will never really believe himself a knight errant and will instead always be aware that he is simply Alonso Quijano?

Similar issues are raised when considering Sancho's relationship with his master. For the majority of the work Sancho accompanies Don Quijote, believes what his master tells him, and carries out, to the best of his abilities, his duties as a squire. Yet in the second part of the novel, when he is on the way to Dulcinea's palace, Sancho says to himself: 'Este mi amo por mil señales he visto que es un loco de atar, y aun también yo no le quedo en zaga, pues soy más mentecato que él, pues le sigo y le sirvo' [Now this master of mine has proved a thousand times over he's a raving lunatic, and me, I'm not much better – in fact, when I follow along after him, and I serve him, I'm a worse fool than he is] (1998b, 2.10.703; 1995, 397). Similar concerns are evident in Sancho's discussion with the Duchess, to whom he confides: 'yo tengo a mi señor don Quijote por loco rematado' [in my opinion, my lord Don Quijote's hopelessly out of his head] (1998b, 2.33.905; 1995, 526). Neither master nor squire seems to fully accept as true the very transformations that motivate their adventures in the novel.

From the first chapter of the first part of the work, the narrator and the reader have doubted that Alonso Quijano truly becomes a knight. From the following chapter – when the knight interacts with the prostitutes and the innkeeper – other characters have doubted Don Quijote's chivalric claims. These moments just mentioned from the second part of the novel imply that even knight and squire do not believe that they are really and truly knight and squire. Perhaps Cervantes is showing us the strong similarities between characters and readers, between life as portrayed in the pages of a book and life as lived outside of it. *Don Quijote* is a work of fiction to those of us reading the text; we know it is not true, but enjoy reading the novel anyway. Likewise it would seem that Don Quijote is a fictional knight to all of the characters within the text (including, at least at times, Don Quijote and Sancho themselves); all are aware that he is not truly a knight, but they all enjoy playing their roles anyway.

With regard to the transformation of Aldonza Lorenzo into Dulcinea del Toboso, after choosing his own new name and that of his horse, Don Quijote 'se dio a entender que no le faltaba otra cosa sino buscar una dama de quien enamorarse, porque el caballero andante sin amores era árbol sin hojas y sin fruto y cuerpo sin alma' [realized that all he needed and had to hunt for was a lady to be in love with, since a knight errant without love entanglements would be like a tree without leaves or fruit, or a body without a soul] (1998b, 1.1.43; 1995, 12). He then decides that his beloved will be Aldonza Lorenzo, a 'moza labradora de muy buen parecer' [very pretty peasant girl] (1998b, 1.1.44; 1995, 12) whose name he changes to Dulcinea del Toboso. Unlike the metamorphoses of Alonso Quijano into a knight errant and Sancho into a squire – which, though questionable, are at least tangible to some degree given that other characters interact with them – in this case there is no physical metamorphosis that can be examined. The woman's transformation occurs only in the imagination of Don Quijote, who now believes that a fundamental aspect of his chivalric mission is to serve Dulcinea. And like his own metamorphosis into a knight, the change from peasant girl to princess occurs in the very first chapter of the novel. But does Don Quijote, in fact, really accept as true the existence of Dulcinea or, as some suggest regarding his own chivalric identity, is he merely pretending that she exists?

There are two moments in the text which suggest that Don Quijote himself has doubts regarding the existence of his beloved. When Sancho learns that Dulcinea is really Aldonza Lorenzo, he admits a misunderstanding to his master, explaining that he had been under the impression that Dulcinea was a princess. Don Quijote responds to Sancho by saying: 'por lo que yo quiero a Dulcinea del Toboso, tanto vale como la más alta princesa de la Tierra. Sí, que no todos los poetas que alaban damas debajo de un nombre que ellos a su albedrío les ponen, es verdad que las tienen … Y, así, bástame a mí pensar y creer que la buena de Aldonza Lorenzo es hermosa y honesta, y en lo del linaje, importa poco, que no han de ir a hacer la información dél para darle algún hábito, y yo me hago cuenta que es la más alta princesa del mundo' [for what I want of Dulcinea del Toboso, she's every bit as good as the noblest princess on earth. Indeed, none of the poets who sang so exaltedly of their ladies (using the names they felt like giving them) ever actually had such mistresses … For me, in the same way, it's enough to think and believe that your good Aldonza Lorenzo is beautiful and modest, and her ancestry doesn't make much difference either, because no one's going to come searching out her pedigree, in order to confer any titles on her, while as far as I'm concerned she's the loftiest princess in the whole world] (1998b, 1.25.285; 1995, 149). In a later conversation with the Duchess the knight once again reveals his uncertainty regarding Dulcinea, whose ontological status, like much in the novel, defies easy explanation.[19]

Once Sancho understands that Don Quijote himself transformed Aldonza Lorenzo into Dulcinea, he decides that he too can play this game. As a result he performs his own metamorphosis on Dulcinea in chapter 10 of the novel's second part, transforming what had been a beautiful princess (according to his master) into a coarse peasant girl.[20] His master's reaction to what he sees – 'Yo no veo, Sancho – dijo don Quijote – sino a tres labradoras sobre tres borricos' ['All I can see, Sancho,' said Don Quijote, 'is three village girls on three donkeys'] (1998b, 2.10.706; 1995, 399)[21] – offers evidence that his own imaginative transformational powers have begun to wane. In fact, Sancho's metamorphosis of Dulcinea shows the extent to which Cervantine metamorphosis can reach. While in Ovid's poem the gods themselves are responsible for the work's many metamorphoses, and both gods and humans accept the many changes with rarely a question, in Cervantes' novel the very nature of the transformational act is constantly questioned, doubted, even contradicted. Not gods, but a madman who has read too many books starts the transformational sequence presented in *Don Quijote*. And the squire's enchantment of Dulcinea shows that in the world of Cervantes' fiction even an illiterate peasant is granted the power to transform reality. Should Don Quijote believe Sancho's transformational account? Should the reader? It would seem that when faced with a metamorphosis in *Don Quijote*, one should always keep in mind Cide Hamete's words of advice: 'Tú, letor, pues eres prudente, juzga lo que te pareciere' [You, reader, as a sensible man, are perfectly capable of making up your own mind] (1998b, 2.24.829; 1995, 476).

Adaptations of the *Metamorphoses* and *Don Quijote*: Literature Transformed

Characterized by content that focuses on transformation, form that includes diverse genres, and exerting a profound influence on later generations of writers, the *Metamorphoses* and *Don Quijote* stand as canonical works that both broke with the established literary traditions of their time and assured their authors an enduring fame.[22] The sonnet from Amadís de Gaula to Don Quijote, which precedes the first part of Cervantes' novel, ends by praising the Manchegan knight with the following verses: 'tendrás claro renombre de valiente; / tu patria será en todas la primera; / tu sabio autor, al mundo único y solo' [In thy renown thou shalt remain secure, / Thy country's name in story shall endure, / And thy sage author stand without a peer] (1998b, 25; Ormsby trans. 1899, 132). This last verse could refer to either Cervantes or Ovid, both peerless creators of texts that were immediate literary sensations in their lifetime and that remain widely read and appreciated all these many years later.[23]

As he does at the beginning of the *Metamorphoses*, at poem's end Ovid turns his attention to his own role in the creative process. He writes in the epilogue: 'Now I have done my work. / It will endure, / I trust, beyond Jove's anger, fire and sword, / Beyond Time's hunger ... / ... my name will be remembered / Wherever Roman power rules conquered lands, / I shall be read, and through all centuries, / If prophecies of bards are ever truthful, / I shall be living, always' (1983, 392). The poet's words here have proved prophetic in a number of ways: his poem has been read throughout the many centuries since the work's initial appearance; moreover, the *Metamorphoses* lives on in a myriad of adaptations that have transformed the poem's content into a wide variety of other art forms.[24] Of the work's importance for later writers and artists, Elaine Fantham explains: 'Ovid was famous and successful before he began the *Metamorphoses*, but it is probable that in the two millennia after his death his epic of transformation not only transformed epic but exercised a greater influence over the shaping of art and literature than any other Latin work' (2004, 133). For its own part, *Don Quijote* has likewise inspired painters and illustrators (including Picasso, Doré, Dalí, and numerous others), sculptors, choreographers, and composers, and has consequently been transformed into an array of forms across the artistic landscape, ranging from opera, ballet, and symphony to film and theatrical presentation.[25]

Though it is true that other literary works have likewise been reworked by later artists, both Ovid's magnum opus and Cervantes' have generated countless adaptations in a variety of art forms to a degree that other canonical texts from centuries past have not. Perhaps this is due to the timeless qualities inherent in the notion of metamorphosis as well as the pathos and conflict that so often accompany the act of transformation. Among the more recent metamorphoses of these two texts into new artistic forms, both *Don Quijote* and the *Metamorphoses* have been adapted as theatrical works that enjoyed successful runs on Broadway. *Man of La Mancha*, the musical based on Cervantes' novel, first appeared on Broadway in 1965 and won five Tony Awards in 1966 including Best Musical, Best Director of a Musical, Best Actor in a Musical, Best Composer and Lyricist, and Best Scenic Designer. Mary Zimmerman adapted Ovid's *Metamorphoses* into a play that likewise had an extended run on Broadway and for which she won the 2002 Tony Award for Best Director of a Play. In fact, in December of 2002 and January of 2003 both a revival of *Man of La Mancha* and Zimmerman's *Metamorphoses* were on Broadway at the same time, a curious moment in which Ovid and Cervantes met in New York. The form-changing endeavours begun by the Roman poet and later transformed by the Spanish novelist continue to inspire other writers and artists to create their own versions of the *Metamorphoses* and *Don Quijote*, two influential texts still charged with the power to delight readers even as they continue generating new transformations.

NOTES

1 'In addition to epic, virtually every significant ancient genre is somehow made part of the poem' (Feeney 2004, xxvi). In his study titled 'Ovid and Genre: Evolutions of an Elegist,' Stephen Harrison explains: 'The incorporation of other genres was of course not foreign to the epic tradition: the model of the *Aeneid* here is clear. But the sheer range of other genres which are in some sense included in the *Metamorphoses*, and its occasional stress on this process of inclusion, suggests that generic multiplicity within a formally epic framework is particularly fundamental to the poem' (2002, 89).

2 'The *Metamorphoses* is as much a web of narratives, acts of story-telling, as it is of stories. The act of story-telling is basic to the whole plot ... A genre consisting in telling stories about actions becomes increasingly interested in the action of storytelling' (Barchiesi 2002, 181).

3 Genres that make an appearance in *Don Quijote* include the book of chivalry, the pastoral novel, the exemplary tale, the sentimental romance, the Moorish novel, and various forms of poetry. Of the wide-ranging nature of the work's generic interplay, Carroll Johnson writes: 'the *Quixote* simultaneously incorporates into itself and carries on a dialogue with all the forms of imaginative literature current in late sixteenth-century Spain' (1990, 71).

4 A chapter in the book titled 'Classical Mythology, Ovid and Cervantes' offers a detailed listing of the many references to Ovid and his works found in Cervantine texts. Though published almost a century ago, Schevill's study remains the most comprehensive examination of the many points of contact between the Roman poet and the Spanish author.

5 A recent example is R. John McCaw's insightful article titled 'Transforming Phaethon: Cervantes, Ovid, and Sancho Panza's Wild Ride,' which shows how 'Don Quijote and Sancho's adventure on the wooden Clavileño both reflects and distorts the Phaethon myth' (2007, 245).

6 As Schevill notes (1913, 175), the 'Ilustre Fregona' – one of Cervantes' *Novelas ejemplares* – begins by describing the work's protagonists, Don Diego de Carriazo and Don Juan de Avendaño, as 'caballeros principales y ricos' [eminent and wealthy gentlemen] (2001, 371; 1998a, 185). Later in the story, after these two have established themselves firmly in a picaresque world, the text explains: 'tenemos ya – en buen hora se cuente – a Avendaño hecho mozo del mesón con nombre de Tomás Pedro, que así dijo que se llamaba, y a Carriazo, con el de Lope Asturiano, hecho aguador; transformaciones dignas de anteponerse a las del narigudo poeta' [Let it be happily recorded that Avendaño was thus transformed into a stable boy calling himself Tomás Pedro, and Carriazo, taking the name Lope Asturiano, into a water carrier; metamorphoses impressive enough to eclipse the examples narrated by the big-nosed poet] (2001, 393; 1998a, 199). The term 'narigudo poeta' is a pun on Ovid's full name in Spanish – Publio Ovidio Nasón.

7 When he is a knight errant, it could be argued that Don Quijote undergoes even further metamorphoses, acquiring new names and reaching higher stages of development. With regard to the moment when the duke refers to Don Quijote as 'el gran Caballero de la Triste Figura' [the great Knight of the Sad Face], only to be corrected by Sancho – who explains that his master is now called 'el Caballero de los Leones' [the Knight of the Lions] – Leo Spitzer writes: 'The importance of the *name* for the Middle Ages appears here most clearly; any knight of romance, Amadis or Perceval or Yvain, is presented as undergoing an inner evolution, whose outward manifestations are the different "adventures" which mark his career; and it is by virtue of these adventures that he acquires different names, each of which is revelatory of the particular stage attained; in this way, the evolution is clearly labeled for the reader. Ivain acquires a new dignity, so to speak, when he becomes the "Chevalier au Lion"; "Orlando inamorato" is a different person from "Orlando furioso"' (1988, 228, emphasis in original).

8 It should be added that at times Don Quijote meets characters who have previously undergone a transformation (such as Marcela, who has already

become a shepherdess), while at other moments future metamorphoses are hinted at (as occurs, for example, when Sancho suggests the possibility that Teresa Panza might become a countess).

9   The majority of critics accept the madness of Alonso Quijano as a sufficient explanation for the protagonist's belief that he is indeed a knight errant. There is, however, no consensus on this point. Mark Van Doren's *Don Quixote's Profession*, to cite just one contrary opinion, argues that throughout the work Alonso Quijano is aware that he is playing a role and for this reason his profession is most aptly characterized as 'actor.'

10 'Philosophically speaking, Ovid does not surprise his readership with a controversial new doctrine about the nature of the universe. He does not set out to correct erroneous beliefs and introduce philosophical enlightenment. Rather he invites his readers to share the assumptions of a popular philosophical view of the world that has gained normative status in Augustan Rome: namely, that a divine intelligence directed the creation of natural order for the benefit of mankind' (Wheeler 1999, 30).

11 Two excellent studies on the topic of belief and disbelief as presented in the *Metamorphoses* are Joseph B. Solodow's chapter titled 'The Narrator' in *The World of Ovid's 'Metamorphoses'* and Stephen M. Wheeler's chapter titled 'The Danger of Disbelief' in *A Discourse of Wonders: Audience and Performance in Ovid's 'Metamorphoses.'* Wheeler writes: 'In the *Metamorphoses*, the Ovidian narrator is clearly aware of the delicate balance between belief and disbelief when entertaining fictions' (1999, 169).

12 Here are three examples: in book 4: 'That was Leuconoe's story, and the others / Listened, spell-bound, and some did not believe it,' (1983, 90); in book 5: 'Polydectes, / The king of little Seriphos, stood hard / In hate and unrelenting, unjust anger, / Against the hero; neither manliness / Nor trials had power to move him, and, he added, / It was all a lie, this fiction of Medusa' (1983, 114); in book 11 when Ceyx is kissed by his wife (already transformed into a bird), the text explains: 'No one could say / Whether Ceyx felt those kisses and responded, / Or whether it was the lift of the waves alone / That made him raise his face. But he had felt them, / And through the pity of the gods, the husband / Became a bird, and joined his wife' (1983, 282).

13 My own reading of the fifteen books of the *Metamorphoses* uncovers only nine instances of doubt in the entire poem, most of which are expressed in just a verse or two.

14 His madness and its consequences are described as follows: 'del poco dormir y del mucho leer, se le secó el celebro de manera que vino a perder el juicio' [with virtually no sleep and so much reading he dried out his

brain and lost his sanity] (1998b, 1.1.39; 1995, 10); 'le pareció convenible y necesario, así para el aumento de su honra como para el servicio de su república, hacerse caballero andante y irse por todo el mundo con sus armas y caballo a buscar las aventuras y a ejercitarse en todo aquello que él había leído que los caballeros andantes se ejercitaban' [he decided to turn himself into a knight errant, travelling all over the world with his horse and his weapons, seeking adventures and doing everything that, according to his books, earlier knights had done, righting every manner of wrong, giving himself the opportunity to experience every sort of danger, so that, surmounting them all, he would cover himself with eternal fame and glory] (1998b, 1.1.40–1; 1995, 10).

15 Even in the first chapter the narrator is already pointing out the pathetic nature of the crazed character: 'Imaginábase el pobre ya coronado por el valor de su brazo, por lo menos del imperio de Trapisonda' [The poor fellow already fancied that his courage and his mighty sword-arm had earned him, at the least, the crown of the Emperor of Trebizond] (1998b, 1.1.41; 1995, 10–11).

16 A distinction should be made at this point. Both Dorotea and Sansón Carrasco transform themselves in order to deceive Don Quijote and Sancho and with the intent of forcing the two of them to return to their village and abandon their chivalric adventures. As Maese Pedro, Ginés de Pasamonte does indeed trick knight and squire (who are unaware of his true identity), but he also fools others who watch the puppet show as well. This transformation, then, is not put in place by Ginés de Pasamonte solely for knight and squire, but rather as a means for him to earn money while staying out of jail.

17 One point of interest would be the reactions of Don Quijote and Sancho to the three characters. Knight and squire discuss Princess Micomicona's identity on several occasions and are at first unable to understand how Sansón Carrasco could be the Knight of the Forest (at least until Don Quijote decides that evil enchanters are responsible for the entire situation). Another topic worth pursuing in another study would be reader reaction to these three transformations. In the case of Princess Micomicona, the reader knows from the outset that she is really Dorotea. Such is not the case with the metamorphoses of Sansón Carrasco and Ginés de Pasamonte, which are only explained in the text after the appearance of the Knight of the Forest and Maese Pedro.

18 Doña Rodríguez, who asks Don Quijote to fight in order to restore her daughter's honour, may be the one character who does believe that the knight is who he says he is.

19 Don Quijote explains: 'Dios sabe si hay Dulcinea o no en el mundo, o si es
    fantástica o no es fantástica' [God only knows if the world does or does
    not contain anyone like Dulcinea, or whether she is or is not a mere phan-
    tom] (1998b, 2.32.897; 1995, 521).

20 'Until now it had been Don Quijote who, encountering everyday phenom-
    ena, spontaneously saw and transformed them in terms of the romances of
    chivalry, while Sancho was generally in doubt and often tried to contradict
    and prevent his master's absurdities. Now it is the other way round. San-
    cho improvises a scene after the fashion of the romances of chivalry, while
    Don Quijote's ability to transform events to harmonize with his illusion
    breaks down before the crude vulgarity of the sight of the peasant women'
    (Auerbach 1987, 42).

21 'Cervantes's masterful division of Don Quijote's words in this sentence, so
    that the first section can stand as an independent clause, indicates that
    Don Quijote does not see at all, or rather that he sees only what is really
    before him: he is no longer the visionary – and delusional – seer of Part
    One' (Quint 2003, 105).

22 In terms of the originality of the writers' texts, Carolyn Nadeau explains: 'In
    contrast to Virgil, Ovid turned away from epic poetry and valorizing the glo-
    ries of the past to substantiate further the glories of the present. Instead, he
    chose to challenge concepts of unity, foundation, and patriarchy that under-
    line the Augustan epic, the *Aeneid*, and to celebrate change (*Metamorphoses*),
    subjectivity, and multiplicity (*Heroides*), decisions that inevitably led to his ex-
    ile. And while Cervantes was not exiled from his *patria*, the lack of recogni-
    tion after achieving the status of military hero and being held captive five
    years in Algiers, and his failure to secure royal preferment at court, led to a
    similar disillusion about the state of affairs in Spain. And like Ovid, Cer-
    vantes turned away from established writing practices, in this case, of imita-
    tion, and explored new literary venues as he formulated his novel' (2002, 84).

23 There is still work to be done in analysing the multifaceted ways in which
    Ovid and Cervantes recount the many tales included in the *Metamorphoses*
    and *Don Quijote*. Alessandro Barchiesi hints at a need for such studies in
    his examination of Ovid's narrative technique, asserting: 'The poet who
    minted Latin words like *narratus* "narrative" and *narrabilis* "narratable" is
    no passive participant in the modern debate about story-telling and its
    techniques, and the *Metamorphoses* is one of the indispensable readings for
    a theory of narrative, along with texts by authors like Cervantes, Sterne,
    Proust, James and Borges' (2002, 180).

24 During the Renaissance, for example, Ovid's poem served as a necessary
    point of reference for artists with an interest in mythological subjects. In

an essay titled 'Ovid and Art' Christopher Allen writes: 'Ovid was the most important literary source for mythological subjects in the art of the Renaissance and the subsequent centuries' (2002, 336). Allen also offers numerous examples of artists who created paintings, illustrations, frescoes, engravings, and sculptures based on the *Metamorphoses* including (among many others) Botticelli, Carracci, Titian, Poussin, Rubens, and Bernini.

25 Eduardo Urbina points out that reworkings of Cervantes' novel have in fact become more well known than the original text itself. He writes: 'In spite of its fame and canonical status, most people know about the *Quixote* through some derivative representation, from some image or icon and its cultural associations. One could affirm indeed, without fear of exaggeration, that the *Quixote* is an often seen, talked-about, but seldom-read book' (2005, 15).

WORKS CITED

Allen, Christopher. 2002. 'Ovid and Art.' In *The Cambridge Companion to Ovid*, ed. Philip Hardie, 336–67. Cambridge: Cambridge University Press.

Auerbach, Erich. 1987. 'The Enchanted Dulcinea.' In *Miguel de Cervantes*, ed. Harold Bloom, 37–60. Philadelphia: Chelsea House.

Barchiesi, Alessandro. 2002. 'Narrative Technique and Narratology in the *Metamorphoses*.' In *The Cambridge Companion to Ovid*, ed. Philip Hardie, 180–99. Cambridge: Cambridge University Press.

Cervantes, Miguel de. 1899. *The Ingenious Gentleman Don Quixote of la Mancha*. Trans. John Ormsby. New York: Dodd, Mead and Company.

– 1995. *Don Quijote*. Trans. Burton Raffel. New York: W.W. Norton.

– 1998a. *Exemplary Stories*. Trans. Lesley Lipson. Oxford: Oxford University Press.

– 1998b. *El ingenioso hidalgo don Quijote de la Mancha*. Ed. Francisco Rico. 2 vols. Barcelona: Instituto Cervantes-Crítica.

– 2001. *Novelas ejemplares*. Ed. Jorge García López. Barcelona: Crítica.

Fantham, Elaine. 2004. *Ovid's 'Metamorphoses.'* Oxford: Oxford University Press.

Harrison, Stephen. 2002. 'Ovid and Genre: Evolutions of an Elegist.' In *The Cambridge Companion to Ovid*, ed. Philip Hardie, 79–94. Cambridge: Cambridge University Press.

Johnson, Carroll B. 1990. *'Don Quixote': The Quest for Modern Fiction*. Boston: Twayne.

McCaw, R. John. 2007. 'Transforming Phaethon: Cervantes, Ovid, and Sancho Panza's Wild Ride.' In *The Changing Face of Ovid's 'Metamorphoses' in Medieval and Early Modern Europe*, ed. Alison Keith, 236–52. Toronto: Centre for Reformation and Renaissance Studies.

Nadeau, Carolyn A. 2002. *Women of the Prologue: Imitation, Myth, and Magic in 'Don Quixote I.'* Lewisburg: Bucknell University Press.

Ovid. 1983. *Metamorphoses*. Trans. Rolfe Humphries. Bloomington: Indiana University Press.

– 2004. *Metamorphoses*. Intro. Denis Feeney. Trans. David Raeburn. London: Penguin.

Quint, David. 2003. *Cervantes's Novel of Modern Times*. Princeton: Princeton University Press.

Schevill, Rudolph. 1913. *Ovid and the Renascence in Spain*. Berkeley: University of California Press.

Solodow, Joseph B. 1988. *The World of Ovid's 'Metamorphoses.'* Chapel Hill: University of North Carolina Press.

Spitzer, Leo. 1988. 'Linguistic Perspectivism in the *Don Quijote*.' In *Leo Spitzer: Representative Essays*, ed. Alban K. Forcione, Herbert Lindenberger, and Madeline Sutherland, 223–71. Stanford, CA: Stanford University Press.

Stagg, Geoffrey L. 1985. '*Illo tempore*: Don Quixote's Discourse on the Golden Age, and Its Antecedents.' In *'La Galatea' de Cervantes – cuatrocientos años después*, ed. Juan Bautista Avalle-Arce, 71–90. Newark, DE: Juan de la Cuesta.

Urbina, Eduardo. 2005. 'Visual Knowledge: Textual Iconography of the *Quixote*.' In *'Don Quixote' Illustrated: Textual Images and Visual Readings: Iconografía del 'Quijote,'* ed. Eduardo Urbina and Jesús G. Maestro, 15–37. Pontevedra: Mirabel Editorial.

Van Doren, Mark. 1958. *Don Quixote's Profession*. New York: Columbia University Press.

Wheeler, Stephen M. 1999. *A Discourse of Wonders: Audience and Performance in Ovid's 'Metamorphoses.'* Philadelphia: University of Pennsylvania Press.

PART THREE

Poetic Fables

8 The Mirror of Narcissus: Imaging the Self in Garcilaso de la Vega's Second Eclogue

MARY E. BARNARD

Within the highly charged visual culture of the early modern period, the newly invented flat mirror became an ideal instrument – and metaphor – for self-imaging. Developed in Venice at the beginning of the sixteenth century, the flat-surface tin-amalgam mirror gradually superseded the medieval mirror, convex and circular in shape.[1] This novel cultural arte-fact became an agent of modernity, at once abetting and encouraging a fascination with specular images and, by extension, with introspection and the construction of an interiorized model of selfhood. For Leonardo da Vinci, the flat mirror was 'the master of painters,' 'the secret accom-plice' no self-portraitist could do without (Woods-Marsden 1998, 31).[2] Leonardo also understood, as did Leon Battista Alberti, that the mirror was the site where reality and illusion, truth and appearance, are most intricately intertwined, which made for ingenious experiments in self-portraiture by painters and poets alike. For the poet, moreover, the text as mirror was a powerful discursive device, a master model to be copied, alternately appropriated and modified for acts of figuration.

One especially fruitful exercise involving the mirror was the reexami-nation of the Ovidian myth of Narcissus, the beautiful young man, be-loved of Echo, who looks into the waters of a pool only to fall in love with his own reflection (1984, 3.344–510).[3] Narcissus's encounter with the pool offered early modern poets an intriguing exemplar of mirror recognition: What did it mean to look at one's reflection in a mirror and to locate the self within? What type of knowledge was received and what type of im-age was constructed? Garcilaso engages these questions in his Second Eclogue, where he recasts the myth of Narcissus to map the complex workings of the psyche, in the process constructing internal landscapes like those Petrarch had rehearsed so influentially in his *Rime sparse*.[4] For

Garcilaso the mirroring pool is a dynamic site where illusion and reality, self-knowledge and self-deception, image and simulacrum actively converge. In this essay I examine how the solitary shepherd Albanio of the eclogue figures himself in his sense of loss and melancholia as a new Narcissus, one who shares the reflecting waters with his companion, the huntress Camila, whom he invites to look into his mirror. By introducing a female counterpart, in essence an anti-Narcissus, Garcilaso considerably enlarges the role of the mirror as mediator of self-revelation and self-definition. Yet the mirror as the site of epistemological discovery and the locus of a gendered look ultimately calls into question the act of self-knowledge, challenging and complicating the very act of defining the self. I consider the twin mapping of the self – male and female – against the background of the trope of self-portraiture in contemporary paintings of women looking at themselves in mirrors and in Parmigianino's audacious *Self-Portrait in a Convex Mirror*.

The Mirror of Melancholia

The poem opens with Albanio's apostrophe to the clear spring acting as mirror at the centre of the pastoral enclosure. The waters serve as a specular screen, where Albanio's visual memory of losing Camila for the first time is projected onto its reflecting surface:

¡Oh claras ondas, cómo veo presente,
　en viéndoos, la memoria d'aquel día
de que el alma temblar y arder se siente!
En vuestra claridad vi mi alegría
　escurecerse toda y enturbiarse;
cuando os cobré, perdí mi compañía.   (1995, 4–9)[5]

[O clear waters, how I see now, in seeing you, the memory of that day which makes my soul tremble and burn! In your brightness I saw my happiness darken and cloud over; when I recovered you, I lost my companion.]

What Albanio sees in his vulnerable introspection are traces of a wounding recollection, where happiness is transformed into something dark and blurry. The shepherd obliquely imports Ovidian Narcissus's presence into his text, engaging fragments of a troubled mythic fiction to construct his melancholic identity. In Ovid's story the blind seer Tiresias, when asked if the beautiful Narcissus would live to a ripe old age, replied:

'If he never learns to know himself' [si se non noverit] (1984, 3.348).
Tiresias's prophecy comes true and Narcissus's crisis of self-knowledge
is revealed in the realization that he and his beloved, the reflected image
in the mirror, are one and the same, 'I am he ... I know now my own image' [iste ego sum ... nec me mea fallit imago] (1984, 3.463), and that he
can love only himself. As Narcissus laments his fate, Ovid's narrator
meditates on the watery image both obscured and magnified by the rip-
ples made by fallen tears: 'et lacrimis turbavit aquas, obscuraque moto /
reddita forma lacu est ' [His tears ruffled the water, and dimly the image
came back from the troubled pool] (1984, 3.475–6). Even though Albanio's
own lament is not a moment of self-knowledge or self-love, the water's
reflecting surface is the locus of grief, dislocation, and irreparable sorrow
for him as it is for Narcissus: 'turbavit' and 'obscura' become Albanio's
'enturbiarse' and 'escurecerse.' In a discursive reversal, however, the
shepherd interiorizes Narcissus's reflection ('obscura forma'), shifting
from a dimly reflected image to a bleakness within, in a melancholic
mood that overpowers the self and its fiction.

Sigmund Freud's definition of melancholia in his *Mourning and
Melancholia* applies to Albanio more profoundly than to any other subject
in Garcilaso's poems. 'The melancholic,' writes Freud, 'displays an extraordinary diminution in his self-regard, an impoverishment of his ego on
a grand scale' (1978, 14:246), yet manifests an obsessive need to speak his
loss in exhibitionistic performances. As his soliloquy unfolds by the
fountain, the lovesick Albanio – somber and brooding in his pain but
eloquently meticulous in depicting it – once again adapts Narcissus's
language to his private personal history. Narcissus reveals his impoverishment while lamenting unexpected erotic riches, his 'beloved' being so
strangely an intimate part of him. But that abundance ironically makes
him poor ['inopem me copia fecit'] (1984, 3.466) and grief saps his strength
['dolor vires adimit'] (1984, 3.469). The diminishment of Narcissus is emblematic of Albanio's inner poverty after the loss of his own riches:

¿Cómo puede ora ser que'n triste lloro
    se convertiese tan alegre vida
y en tal *pobreza* todo mi *tesoro*?
Quiero mudar lugar y a la partida
    quizá me dejará parte del daño
que tiene el *alma* casi *consumida* ...
¡Ay miembros fatigados, y cuán firme
    es el *dolor* que os *cansa* y *enflaquece*!   (1995, 22–8, 31–2; my emphasis)

[How could it be that in sadness was converted such happy life and in such *poverty* all my wealth? I want to move away and upon my leaving perhaps part of this illness that has my *spirit* almost *consumed* will leave me as well ... Oh tired limbs, how firm is the *grief* that *weakens* and diminishes you!]

Narcissus's text serves as Albanio's linguistic mirror into which the shepherd 'looks' to construct a self profoundly different from that of the Ovidian youth. The scene of loss, which is fashioned as a scene of discovery, reveals the distance between the early modern figure and his ancient counterpart. Consumed by desire, Narcissus's body dissolves, the text offering gentle images of the fragile boy melting like yellow wax near a flame or like frost before the morning sun (1984, 3.487–90). While in the world of the dead he still gazes at his image in the Stygian pool, his body, conforming to Ovid's typically ambiguous endings, finds a new, albeit tenuous, life in the form of a delicate flower, the narcissus (1984, 3.509–10). Albanio dissolves in quite a different way, unravelling into madness. The blurring of boundaries between body and image, so central to the Narcissus myth, induces ontological catastrophe in a different mode, for Albanio descends into schizophrenia, blankly unaware of his own self. This troubled act of figuration logically occurs at the mirror, Albanio's 'secret accomplice,' where he paints his self-portrait. But before discussing the shepherd's figuration, I turn to chaste Camila, who constructs her own self-portrait, both in relation to Albanio and, most significantly, in relation to the reflecting surface of the fountain.

Mirroring Camila

Transforming bits from a self-obsessed Narcissus for a self-destructive Albanio consumed with melancholia is only part of Garcilaso's reworking of the Ovidian myth. Equally innovative is the introduction of Virgilian Camila, an active female counterpart to the new Narcissus. Albanio explains to Salicio, a former unhappy lover-turned-*magister* in the art of love, 'de bien acuchillado a ser maestro' [from deeply slashed to teacher] (1995, 355), that the origin of his affliction is the body of unavailable Camila, who is unaware of the pleasurable look he fixes upon her: 'El placer de miralla con terrible / y fiero desear sentí mesclarse' [the pleasure of looking at her mingled with a fierce desire] (1995, 320–1). 'Lust of the eyes' in contemplating corporeal beauty is well documented in Plato's *Phaedrus*, where sight is the active agent of *eros* (1972, 251 A). In Marsilio Ficino's *De amore* (1469), it appears as visual pleasure tinged with lycanthropic feelings, a kind of bestial love that carries a measure of insanity ['amor ferino'] (1987, 7.3), which here fuels Albanio's desire. Innocently detecting the shepherd's erotic feelings in his blushing face ['rostro y color'] (1995, 427), Camila wants to know the cause. Albanio urges her to peer into the clear fountain to see fully the beautiful face of the one he loves: 'le dije que en aquella fuente clara / veria de aquella que yo tanto amaba / abiertamente la hermosa cara' (1995, 470–2):

a la pura fontana fue corriendo,
  y en viendo el agua, toda fue alterada,
en ella su figura sola viendo.
Y no de otra manera, arrebatada,
  del agua rehuyó que si estuviera
de la rabiosa enfermedad tocada,
y sin mirarme, desdeñosa y fiera,
  no sé qué allá entre dientes murmurando,
me dejó aquí, y aquí quiere que muera.   (1995, 476–84)

[She went running to the pure fountain, and looking at the water, was all disturbed, seeing in it only her face. And crazed, she fled from the water as if she were touched by rabies, and without looking at me, disdainful and fierce, mumbling inaudibly, she left me here, and here she wants me to die.]

Having stepped into Albanio's mirror world, Camila sees her reflected self as the shepherd's construct, the lovely object of his misplaced desire. Her implicit 'I am she,' a recognition that she and the 'figura' in the waters are one and the same, parallels Narcissus's moment of discovery. But whereas Narcissus's eyes offer him the unintended knowledge that he is his own beloved, Camila's offer her a different kind of knowledge, an awareness of the other in her, Albanio's beloved. This recognition pushes the text into the politics of gender, which is intimately connected with the dynamics of vision. Camila rebels against the visual entrapment implicit in the sexual allure of her mirrored image. Repelled at seeing herself through Albanio's projection – and the role he has prescribed for her – she angrily averts her eyes from the reflecting waters and from the shepherd. Camila's rejection reminds us of the disdain of unruly Laura, the 'aspra fera' of the *Rime sparse* that both fascinates and dislocates her male creator. Yet Camila is as distant from the self-reflexive world of idolatrous obsession of Petrarch's subject, which famously prefigures early modern lovers like Albanio, as from the world of Ovid's Narcissus. Her true model lies in the non-introspective realm of Virgilian epic, in the Volscian warrior-maiden of the *Aeneid*, a follower of Diana who joins with Turnus against the Trojan intruder, Aeneas, and is killed by the Etruscan Arruns (1998, 11.532–895). Virgil tells the story:

> But in the heart of the slaughter, like an Amazon, one breast bared for the fray, and quiver-girt, rages Camilla; and now tough javelins she showers thick from her hand, now a stout battle-axe she snatches with unwearied grasp; the golden bow, armour of Diana, clangs from her shoulders. And even if, back pressed, she withdraws, she turns her bow and aims darts in her flight. (1998, 11.648–54)

Garcilaso's reimagined Camila rages against a new intruder, the alien image 'inscribed' in the mirror. In this furious act, the chaste huntress sets herself against one of the period's cultural icons, the woman who looks at herself in a mirror to celebrate her physical beauty. Women contemplating their reflection in mirrors became a popular theme in the iconography of the female figure in contemporary paintings, as in Giovanni Bellini's *Young Woman with a Mirror* (1515) and Titian's *Woman with Two Mirrors* (ca. 1512–17), which, by adding a second mirror to the specular act, capture the excesses of self-contemplation. Both paintings focus our attention on the physical beauty of the women and their fixed gazes, which invite the viewers to enter the sensual spectacle, implicating them in a voyeuristic experience. In Bellini's painting (fig. 1), a young nude woman looks into a small flat mirror she holds in her right hand; a larger mirror on the wall reflects the back of her head and the *reticella* – the brocade hair covering – she is presumably arranging. Rona Goffen notes that this self-referential picture is at once a representation of beauty itself and a novel commentary on the sense of sight: 'while we look at the woman and at her mirror reflection, she looks at herself and into the mirror on the wall – into which she gazes indirectly, through the intermediation of her hand mirror' (1989, 255). For Goffen, she may be a type of Venus, evoked by two of the goddesses' attributes, the mirror and the pearls embroidered on the woman's Venetian *reticella*.[6] Titian's woman strikes a similar pose (fig. 2). Partially undressed, a detail that expresses her sexuality, she employs the two types of mirrors then available, both held by a male attendant: a convex mirror that

1 Giovanni Bellini, *Young Woman with a Mirror*, 1515. Kunsthistorisches
Museum, Vienna. Erich Lessing/Art Resource, NY.

reflects her image from the back and a small flat rectangular mirror from the front. If Bellini's female may be a married woman, identified as such by her *reticella*, Titian's may be a courtesan. Her gaze, locked on her reflection in the hand-held mirror, evokes simultaneously an image of feminine pride and self-love, and an allegory of vanity, 'a melancholy memento mori' (Phillippy 2006, 168).[7] Camila, by refusing to fix her eyes on her image in the fountain, implicitly rejects the mirror's dangerous lure, with the implications it carries of both female narcissism and male voyeurism, the latter represented in the text by the shepherd's lusty eyes. She subscribes instead to an alternate model, one resembling the unblemished *speculum sine macula*, which symbolizes the purity of the Virgin Mary (Goldberg 1985, 121–2; Schwarz 1952, 98–100), popular in Europe among the Carmelites and the Franciscans.[8] But Camila's Virgilian origin offers her another virgin to emulate, Diana, chaste goddess of the hunt and the moon.

Contesting the Mirror

Having told his tale of inner discord, Albanio leaves the fountain in the company of Salicio. Camila, alone and outside Albanio's narrative, returns to the bucolic site to claim the mirror as her own. She appropriates it in order to 'paint' her own portrait, but not by looking into it, for she refuses to play Albanio's game of visual self-reflection. Instead, she transforms Albanio's tainted mirror into an unreflecting and unblemished surface:

> ¡Ay dulce fuente mía, y de cuán alto
> con solo un sobresalto m'arrojaste!
> ¿Sabes que me quitaste, fuente clara,
> los ojos de la cara, que no quiero
> menos un compañero que yo amaba,
> mas no como él pensaba? ...   (1995, 744–9)

> [Oh my sweet fountain, and from how high, with a slight jolt, you hurled me down! Do you know that you took away from me, clear fountain, the eyes of my face? Do you know that I do not cherish less a companion whom I loved, but not as he thought? ...]

Camila's lament ('me quitaste, fuente clara, los ojos de la cara') registers a common expression signifying the loss of a friend, here her companion

2 Titian, *Woman with Two Mirrors*. Louvre, Paris, Réunion des Musées Nationaux/Art Resource, NY.

Albanio. But that loss also liberates her from an imposed seeing, an imposed 'reading' of her reflection implicit in those very words ('me quitaste … los ojos'): she saw her image through *his* eyes not her own. Freed from Albanio's representational trap, she reaffirms her singularity as virgin huntress, alluding to Diana's banishment of Callisto from her train after the nymph is seduced by Jupiter (Ovid 1984, 2.417–65):

> … ¡Dios ya quiera
> que antes Camila muera que padezca
> culpa por do merezca ser echada
> de la selva sagrada de Dïana!   (1995, 749–52)

> [God grant that Camila die before she commits an offence that will banish her from Diana's sacred woods!]

Albanio, returning to the fountain and finding Camila asleep, again makes her the source of his visual delight and embraces her. After a long, angry struggle, she escapes his grasp, the bower, and the text for good.

Madness and the Poet

Denied Camila, the lovesick Albanio slips into schizophrenia, the manic phase of melancholia that is accompanied by delusions. Ovidian Narcissus's crisis of self-knowledge is carried one step further to pose a more troubling epistemological crisis for the new Narcissus of the eclogue: the impossibility of knowing the self at all. Earlier in the text, Albanio's dealings with the mirror signal moments of interiorization that go hand in hand with what melancholia provokes in the afflicted: a deep self-awareness often manifested by 'opening' the body to display the spreading disease as spectacle.[9] In a particularly telling instant, Albanio aligns his self-diagnosis with humoral theory, making mental states and bodily matter pass through permeable boundaries: 'el mal … ha penetrado hasta el hueso' [my sickness has penetrated to the bone] (1995, 144–5). Now in his madness he turns his attention outward, away from the inner self to an obsession with the body, which he perceives as stolen. He remains but naked spirit:

> Espirtu soy, de carne ya desnudo,
>   que busco el cuerpo mío, que m'ha hurtado
> algún ladrón malvado, injusto y crudo.   (1995, 919–21)

[I am all spirit, naked of flesh, searching for my body, which has been stolen by an evil, unjust, and cruel thief.]

Seeing not his image reflected in the mirror but his detached body frame, he begs it to return to give him back his human form: 'a darme verdadera forma d' hombre' (1995, 935). In his drama of misrecognition, Albanio takes over fragments of Narcissus's speech from the *Metamorphoses* (1984, 3.448–68) to woo his body, only to conclude with a delusional 'discovery,' that a 'thief' has dressed himself up with his flesh ['revestido de mi carne'] (1995, 990).[10] This scene recasts for another agenda Ovidian Narcissus's belief that his reflection is a 'living form,' luring him 'from the bottom of a pool' (Melchior-Bonnet 2002, 102). In the *Metamorphoses*, as Shadi Bartsch points out, Ovid engages philosophical notions of Socrates's teachings in the *Phaedrus* about eros, reflection, and self-knowledge (2006, 84). All three are evoked in Narcissus's story of 'reflection gone awry,' a tale of self-love that came to stand 'for an entire pathology of the self' (2006, 84). The process of discovery at the reflecting pool does not lead to higher things as in the specular mirroring of the *Phaedrus*, but instead follows a Lucretian model of deceptive, vain imaging: it is 'mired in a circularity that – far from providing the impetus for change (the 'social' mirror) or for progress toward the Forms (the 'Platonic' mirror) – cannot escape beyond two pairs of mirroring eyes, one by the water and one in it' (2006, 88).[11] Caught in the realm of *simulacra*, the illusory, fleeting images that he loves and that are brought into focus by the warning of Ovid's narrating voice ['that which you behold is but the shadow of a reflected form and has no substance of its own'] (1984, 3.434–5), Narcissus dies, as Tiresias had prophesized, dissolving by the side of the pool.

Albanio embodies a pathology of a different kind. Certain of his 'invisibility' and oblivious to the reflecting nature of his mirror, the shepherd materializes his specular double. Seeing his image as an alien body that has assumed his flesh ultimately reveals his own act of dissolution as an interior event. Removing the mirror's mediating function erases epistemological certainty: it calls attention to his psychic rupture, the self's internal exile from itself. The splitting of the self, the disjunction between the observing subject and the perceived object of Narcissus at the mirror, reworked as a symptom of Albanio's melancholia, yields his fragmented interiorized selfhood. Albanio's mirror scene is the opposite of Lacan's 'mirror stage,' a moment of plenitude when the infant sees his reflected image as a whole, coherent entity, which is paradigmatic of the formation of the ego-ideal (Lacan 1977, 1–7). Albanio's disjunctive specular projection gives the lie to this imaginary, deceptive wholeness, marked – like Lacan's signifying subject – by the unhinging web of his unmet desire.

With the erasure of the pool as a reflecting surface, the shepherd's self-figuration is displaced into another myth of loss and absence, with death at its centre: the tale of Orpheus, the *vates* and enchanter who cast a spell on the inhabitants of Hades to recover his lost Eurydice. Invoking the Thracian's voice, Albanio obsessively fixes his attention on the recovery of his body, hoping to cross over and find it in the dark kingdom of the dead:

> convocaré el infierno y reino escuro
> y romperé su muro de diamante,
> como hizo el amante blandamente
> por la consorte ausente que cantando
> estuvo halagando las culebras
> de las hermanas negras, mal peinadas.   (1995, 940–5)

[I will convene the dark reign of hell and I will break its diamond wall, like the lover did for his absent consort, singing sweetly and enchanting the snakes of the black, badly combed sisters.]

The mirroring surface of the fountain not recognized as such is transformed into a 'muro de diamante' [diamond wall], the entrance to the Underworld, as in the *Aeneid*, where a 'huge gate' is flanked by 'pillars of solid adamant' (1998, 6.552). In appropriating Orpheus's magical song to 'break' the unyielding surface, Albanio displays a characteristic detected by Freud in narcissism and shared by children and schizophrenics, an omnipotence of thought linked to the belief in the magic of words. Freud describes this condition as 'an overestimation of the power of their wishes and mental acts ... [and] a belief in the thaumaturgic force of words' (1978, 14:75). If Albanio lacks Orpheus's verbal magic, his association with this Logos figure is highly significant, for it allusively represents the shepherd as poet.[12]

Even more relevant in defining Albanio as poet is Ovidian Echo, the nymph whose speech is curtailed by Juno as punishment for distracting the goddess with her chatter from Jove's erotic dalliance with other nymphs. Fated to repeat another's speech, her seductive messages to Narcissus are revealed only through her unintended echoes of his words (1984, 3.379–92).[13] In the eclogue, this discursive mirroring is borrowed for a new act of figuration, one that parallels the play with Narcissus's mirror reflections in Albanio's intimate self-disclosure. Echo appears in the shepherd's apostrophe to the creatures of the woods as he seeks consolation after Camila's first rejection. Albanio establishes a special bond with Echo, who shares his unhappy fate in love and shows some pity, answering his plaint ['respondiéndome'] (1995, 599), though she denies her presence ('mas no quiere mostrarse' [refuses to show herself]) (1995, 601). Albanio welcomes Echo's verbal presence, but it is his own words, echoing in the woods, that the invisible nymph repeats, just as Narcissus's words had rebounded back to him from Echo's voice. Echo, meaning 'image of the voice' in Latin, is recognized as such in Ovid's text when Narcissus is deceived by the nymph's verbal repetitions: 'alternae deceptus imagine vocis' [deceived by the answering voice] (1984, 3.385). Albanio, by mirroring himself through Echo's voice as image, is an 'echoed sound,' much like Narcissus. But the 'disembodied' Albanio, reduced to a name in his imagination –'agora solo el nombre m'ha quedado' [now I am but a name] (1995, 936), his voice implicit in the lament – resembles more precisely and evocatively the nymph, who spurned by Narcissus wastes away to a bodiless voice that bears only a name (1984, 3.399–401). Mieke Bal writes that 'Ovid exploits to the full the literary potential of the auditive mirroring through the figure of Echo, as a sonoric embodiment of the visual mirroring [of Narcissus]' (2001, 255, note 3). The acoustic mirroring opens the way for Echo as an emblem of poetic voice, even if she can speak only when spoken to, abridging Narcissus's statements by repeating his final words.

Ann Rosalind Jones writes about the figure of Echo as the alter ego of the Italian poet Gaspara Stampa, Garcilaso's contemporary, in Sonnet 152 (written in the 1540s), which reads in part: 'an image almost identical to Echo, of woman I retain only the voice and name' [quasi ad Eco imagine simìle, / Di Donna serbo sol la voce e 'l nome']. Jones notes that Stampa's disembodiment 'still leaves her with the two attributes of a poet: a voice and a name, discursive power and literary renown' (1991, 268). Speaking as Echo ['I ... answer to his final words'], Jones adds, 'she reactivates the nymph's relation to language. No longer merely listening to Narcissus and abbreviating his words, Stampa's Echo becomes a speaker of her own desires ...' (1991, 269). Similarly Echo-like, Albanio ascribes name and voice to himself and, like Stampa, goes one step further, activating his own words as the eloquent melancholic that he has become. If

Albanio, of all the melancholics in Garcilaso's poems, suffers the most extreme case of inner impoverishment, he also is the most verbally exuberant. He is an ideal example of a cultural prototype, the exceptional individual who suffers from melancholia as an 'accredited pathology,' an 'eloquent form of mental disturbance' that Freud finds in Hamlet, the visionary and 'speaker of truths,' and that Ficino regarded as the special gift of the superior man of letters (Schiesari 1992, 8–9).[14] Albanio's gifted eloquence is attested to by a copious discourse: 460 lines in *terza rima* to describe the hunting scenes and dalliance with Camila, and 81 lines of lament in *rimalmezzo* over his lost body. This impassioned storyteller in the lyric mode figures himself metatextually as a poet. Unable to recognize himself in the fountain, he sees instead a young man who looks like him: 'Allá dentro en el fondo está un mancebo, / de laurel coronado y en la mano / un palo, propio como yo, d'acebo' [Down there at the bottom is a youth, crowned with laurel and in his hand a stick of holly, just like me] (1995, 913–15). In ancient texts, both madmen and poets were crowned with laurel.

Albanio may be unaware that the reflection in the water is his own, but in this specular moment the text self-consciously reflects on the shepherd's double identity: the mirror informs the reader about the troubled nature of the melancholic and his fractured psyche – his distorted visual perception conspiring with the mirror to prevent self-knowledge or escape – but it also announces his status as one of the most eloquent, albeit self-absorbed, poetic voices in Garcilaso's fiction. But if Albanio seems to be rescued from his imagined immateriality by the letter – his abundant discourse – in another interpretive register something unsettling and even dangerous is brewing in the shepherd's figuration through Echo. The nymph stands for an act of precarious voicing, like Orpheus, whose 'voice and death-cold tongue' mournfully call out from a decapitated head, rolling down the Hebrus river, repeating his lost Eurydice's name (Virgil, *Georgics* 1998, 4.523–7). Echo's own truncated, limited speech is not devoid of its power to communicate, for in answering Narcissus's cries with partial echoes, she supplies loving phrases that he understands and rebukes (Brenkman 1976, 300–4). Yet her speech unfolds without agency of its own, her fragmented words being mere repetitions. And this uncontrolled verbal performance may serve as a foreshadowing of Albanio's own by the end of his story, where his speech, fragmentary and dispersed, prevents coherent communication with his shepherd friends, Salicio and Nemoroso.

Slapstick accompanies the swift, broken dialogue (1995, 984–1031) as the shepherds keep Albanio from throwing himself into the fountain, and then proceed to tie him up.

Painting in the Mirror

Albanio the poet, craftsman of verbal illusions, is also a painter like Narcissus. Leon Battista Alberti in his treatise on painting, *De pictura* (1435), declares Narcissus to be the inventor of painting, in effect the first painter. 'What is painting,' Alberti asks, 'but the act of embracing by means of art the surface of the pool?' (1972, 63). Alberti animates in his own way Narcissus's attempt to embrace the beloved in the pool, that is, his own reflection, by expressing the double calling of painting as a form of truth and a form of deception, advocated by contemporary painters and theorists. As Paula Carabell puts it: 'Alberti's account of the origins of painting compares image making to the natural phenomenon of reflection; it responds to the fact that both the surface of water and that of pictorial space have the potential faithfully to reproduce reality. His parallel also establishes, however, that like its prototype, painting creates a mimetic equivalent that is illusory in nature' (1998, 53). Looking into the watery mirror before the moment of recognition, Narcissus 'paints' his own work of art, his self-portrait, which is, as Paul Barolski notes, 'a double illusion,' for the viewer in his self-deception is fooled into believing the reflection is at once a real person and someone 'other than himself' (1995, 255).

Standing motionless, looking 'in speechless wonder' at his reflection, Ovidian Narcissus seemed 'like a statue sculpted in Parian marble' [ut e Pario formatum marmore signum] (1984, 3.419). Ovid's 'ut ... signum' [like a statue] may also mean in its multivalence, like a mark, like an image, like a sign. Albanio at his mirror seems an equally illusory construct, a flimsy presence 'painting' itself through signs, so revealing in the very verbal performance its inherent fragility. Like Narcissus at first, Albanio does not recognize himself nor does he recognize the mirror for what it truly is, 'a boundary between reality and fiction,' a site of illusion that is as well a site of creation and artifice.[15]

Parmigianino's *Self-Portrait in a Convex Mirror* (1524, fig 3) offers an intriguing comparison with the eclogue, for this *maniera* painter, like his contemporary Garcilaso, explored the confusion of boundaries at the mirror as the site of illusion and artifice. The self-portrait was a gift to

3 Parmigianino, *Self-Portrait in a Convex Mirror*. Kunsthistorisches Museum, Vienna. Foto Marburg/Art Resource, NY.

the Medici pope Clement VII, a discerning collector of antiquities and paintings, and may well have been hanging in the papal residence, acclaimed in its own time, when Garcilaso passed through Rome in 1532 on his way to Naples with newly appointed Viceroy Pedro de Toledo. Vasari deemed the painting a 'cosa rara.' As he points out in his *Lives of the Artists*:

> In order to investigate the subtleties of illusion, he set himself one day to make his own portrait, looking at himself in a convex barber's mirror. And in doing this, perceiving the bizarre effects produced by the roundness of the mirror ... the idea came to him to amuse himself by counterfeiting everything ... (1912–15, 5:245)

Parmigianino painted his reflection on a wooden panel shaped like a convex mirror (according to Vasari this was made by dividing a ball of wood in half). What is most compelling in this painting is not the reflected self but the distortions, most prominently, the outsized scale of the hand relative to the head and the discordant planes of the eyes. The hand, the craftsman's tool, calls attention in particular to the mirror as the site for creating illusions, for what the viewer sees as the right hand is actually Parmigianino's left hand. The hand also seems to transgress the painting's frame, spilling over from the bounded world of reflection into the viewer's own world. As Joanna Woods-Marsden writes, the painting is a 'capriccio,' an 'amusing conceit,' to demonstrate the artist's *ingegno*, a display of art at its most deceptive (1998, 137). David Ekserdjian points to a remarkable detail, omitted by Vasari, that further focuses on the ingenious play of reality and fiction: the gold-frame form to Parmigianino's extreme left, which is 'the portrait the viewer is admiring set up on the artist's easel' (2006, 130).

In our eclogue, Albanio's misreading – the projection of his ruptured psyche, the illusory images of his inner chaos – call attention to the deception of self-imaging. The *magister* Salicio, listening to Albanio's mad ravings before the mirror, captures best the artifice of the performance. Praising the gifted shepherd-poet-painter, Salicio remarks: 'El curso acostumbrado del ingenio, / aunque le falte el genio que lo mueva ... corre un poco' [he is using his natural talent (ingenio) even though he lacks the disposition (genio) to control it] (1995, 948–50). Like Parmigianino, Garcilaso – through Albanio as a new Narcissus – plays with the mirror to present his exceptional performance within the liminal spaces between fantasy and reality.

NOTES

1   On mirrors, see, especially, Bialostocki (1977), Goldberg (1985), Grabes (1982), and Melchior-Bonnet (2002). The convex mirror was more popular in northern European painting of this period than in Italy. One notable exception was Parmigianino's self-portrait, which I examine below.

2   Leonardo writes on this notion in his *Treatise on Painting* (1436) under a heading that reads 'How the Mirror is the Master and Guide of Painters.' For Leonardo's treatise, see Kemp (1989).

3   The following studies from the abundant scholarship on Narcissus have been particularly useful: Bartsch (2006, 84–96), Bettini (1999, 94–108, 228–36), Brenkman (1976), Hardie (1988), Knoespel (1985), and Vinge (1967).

4   On this influential practice in Petrarch, see Barkan (1980, 1986, 206–15), Vickers (1982), and Enterline (2000).

5   Quotations from Garcilaso's text come from Morros's edition (1995). Translations are mine.

6   On Bellini's painting, see also Goffen (1991), Hills (1999, 130–1), and Phillippy (2006, 165–6). Quintero (2004) examines paintings of women looking into mirrors, notably Titian's *Venus with a Mirror* (ca. 1555) and Velázquez's *The Rokeby Venus* (ca. 1647–51), and Golden Age literary analogues,

pointing to the 'specular staging' in terms of male mastery. Quintero comments on the period's production of this type of painting for private male viewing, revealed in the secret galleries at the Prado and Philip II's private chamber in the Escorial, with pertinent bibliography, in particular, Civil (1990) and Portús (1999).

7 On Titian's painting, see also Bialostocki (1977, 70) and Goffen (1997, 66–7, 70–1).

8 For a Neoplatonic reading of Camila, see Rivers (1973), and compare with Lumsden, who offers an interpretation along the lines of a moral taboo (1947, 268–9).

9 On the relation between interiority and melancholia, see Schoenfeldt (1999).

10 Parts of Albanio's apostrophe to his body are a reworking of Narcissus's own. Albanio, however, weaves fragments from Narcissus's refined seduction into a *frottola*, a poetic form in *rimalmezzo*, often used by Italian poets 'to portray highly emotional states of mind or the disconnected language of rustics' (Fernández-Morera 1982, 59). Albanio, like Narcissus, tells his body that the barrier separating them is not the sea, not even city walls or mountains, but a thin layer of water (1995, 958–62). Also like Narcissus, the shepherd tells his image that its gaze – Narcissus's 'friendly looks' become Albanio's eager 'nunca te hartas de mirarme' [you never tire of looking at me] – its movements, and gestures show its desire for union (1995, 965–9).

11 Bartsch bases her interpretation on Hardie, who writes on Ovid's use of Lucretius's *De Rerum Natura*: 'Narcissus is condemned to the insatiable gazing of the Lucretian lover (cf. Lucr. 4.1102), who can never get past the surface, lured on by the *simulacra* that stream from the superficies of the body' (1988, 84).

12 The main models for the Orpheus myth are Virgil's *Georgics* 4 and Ovid's *Metamorphoses* 10–11. For another appropriation of Orpheus for Garcilaso's representation of the poetic voice (featured in the first tapestry of the Third Eclogue), see Barnard (1987).

13 On Echo, see Hollander (1981), Loewenstein (1984), and Spivak (1994).

14 On melancholia, in addition to Schiesari, see, especially, the now classic study by Klibansky, Panofsky, and Saxl (1964), as well as Enterline (1995) and Wittkower (1963). Albanio also displays clinical symptoms of melancholia familiar from contemporary medical treatises: a sad, suicidal figure, fearful and paralysed with grief, he goes for days without sleep or food. For a catalogue of Albanio's clinical symptoms, see Soufas (1990, 69–70).

15 The phrase cited is from Bal (2001, 240), for whom the Narcissus story is 'about the denial of the true, natural body' (2001, 241).

WORKS CITED

Alberti, Leon Battista. 1972. *On Painting and On Sculpture*. Ed. and trans. Cecil Grayson. London: Phaidon.

Bal, Mieke. 2001. *Looking In: The Art of Viewing*. London: Routledge.

Barkan, Leonard. 1980. 'Diana and Actaeon: The Myth as Synthesis.' *English Literary Renaissance* 10:317–59.

– 1986. *The Gods Made Flesh: Metamorphosis and the Pursuit of Paganism*. New Haven: Yale University Press.

Barnard, Mary E. 1987. 'Garcilaso's Poetics of Subversion and the Orpheus Tapestry.' *PMLA* 102:316–25.

Barolski, Paul. 1995. 'A Very Brief History of Art from Narcissus to Picasso.' *Classical Journal* 90:255–9.

Bartsch, Shadi. 2006. *The Mirror of the Self: Sexuality, Self-Knowledge, and the Gaze in the Early Roman Empire*. Chicago: University of Chicago Press.

Bettini, Maurizio. 1999. *The Portrait of the Lover*. Trans. Laura Gibbs. Berkeley: University of California Press.

Bialostocki, Jan. 1977. 'Man and Mirror in Painting: Reality and Transience.' In *Studies in Late Medieval and Renaissance Painting in Honor of Millard Meiss*, ed. Irving Lavin and John Plummer, 1:61–72. New York: New York University Press.

Brenkman, John. 1976. 'Narcissus in the Text.' *The Georgia Review* 30:293–327.

Carabell, Paula. 1998. 'Painting, Paradox, and the Dialectics of Narcissism in Alberti's *De pictura* and in the Renaissance Theory of Art.' *Medievalia et Humanistica* 25:53–74.

Civil, Pierre. 1990. 'Erotismo y pintura mitológica en la España del Siglo de Oro.' *Edad de Oro* 9:39–49.

Ekserdjian, David. 2006. *Parmigianino*. New Haven: Yale University Press.

Enterline, Lynn. 1995. *The Tears of Narcissus: Melancholia and Masculinity in Early Modern Writing*. Stanford: Stanford University Press.

– 2000. 'Embodied Voices: Petrarch Reading (Himself Reading) Ovid.' In *Desire in the Renaissance: Psychoanalysis and Literature*, ed. Valeria Finucci and Regina Schwartz, 120–45. Princeton: Princeton University Press, 1994. Revised version in *The Rhetoric of the Body from Ovid to Shakespeare*, 91–124. Cambridge Studies in Renaissance Literature and Culture 35. Cambridge: Cambridge University Press.

Fernández-Morera, Darío. 1982. *The Lyre and the Oaten Flute: Garcilaso and the Pastoral*. London: Tamesis.

Ficino, Marsilio. 1987. *El libro dell'Amore*. Ed. Sandra Niccoli. Florence: Olschki.

Freud, Sigmund. 1978. *Mourning and Melancholia*. The Standard Edition. Trans.

James Strachey. 14 vols. London: Hogarth.

Garcilaso de la Vega. 1995. *Obra poética y textos en prosa*. Ed. Bienvenido Morros. Barcelona: Crítica.

Goffen, Rona. 1989. *Giovanni Bellini*. New Haven: Yale University Press.

– 1991. 'Bellini's Nude with Mirror.' *Venezia Cinquecento* 2:185–99.

– 1997. *Titian's Women*. New Haven: Yale University Press.

Goldberg, Benjamin. 1985. *The Mirror and Man*. Charlottesville: University Press of Virginia.

Grabes, Herbert. 1982. *The Mutable Glass: Mirror-Imagery in Titles and Texts of the Middle Ages and English Renaissance*. Trans. Gordon Collier. Cambridge: Cambridge University Press.

Hardie, Philip. 1988. 'Lucretius and the Delusions of Narcissus.' *Materiali e discussioni per l'analisi dei testi classici* 20–1:71–89.

Hills, Paul. 1999. *Venetian Colour: Marble, Mosaic, Painting and Glass 1250–1550*. New Haven: Yale University Press.

Hollander, John. 1981. *The Figure of Echo: A Mode of Allusion in Milton and After*. Berkeley: University of California Press.

Jones, Ann Rosalind. 1991. 'New Songs for the Swallow: Ovid's Philomela in Tullia d'Aragona and Gaspara Stampa'. In *Refiguring Woman: Perspectives on Gender and the Italian Renaissance*, ed. Marilyn Migiel and Juliana Schiesari, 263–77. Ithaca: Cornell University Press.

Kemp, Martin, ed. 1989. *Leonardo on Painting*. New Haven: Yale University Press.

Klibansky, Raymond, Erwin Panofsky, and Fritz Saxl. 1964. *Saturn and Melancholy: Studies in the History of Natural Philosophy, Religion and Art*. New York: Basic Books.

Knoespel, Kenneth J. 1985. *Narcissus and the Invention of Personal History*. New York: Garland.

Lacan, Jacques. 1977. *Écrits: A Selection*. Trans. Alan Sheridan. New York: Norton.

Loewenstein, Joseph. 1984. *Responsive Readings: Versions of Echo in Pastoral, Epic, and the Jonsonian Masque*. Yale Studies in English 192. New Haven: Yale University Press.

Lumsden, Audrey. 1947. 'Problems Connected with the Second Eclogue of Garcilaso de la Vega.' *Hispanic Review* 15:251–71.

Melchior-Bonnet, Sabine. 2002. *The Mirror: A History*. Trans. Katharine H. Jewett. New York: Routledge.

Ovid. 1984. *Metamorphoses*. Ed. and trans. Frank Justus Miller. 2 vols. Loeb Classical Library. Cambridge, MA: Harvard University Press.

Phillippy, Patricia. 2006. *Painting Women: Cosmetics, Canvasses, and Early*

Modern Culture. Baltimore: Johns Hopkins University Press.

Plato. 1972. *Phaedrus*. Trans. R. Hackforth. Cambridge: Cambridge University Press.

Portús, Javier. 1999. 'Los cuadros secretos del Prado.' *Descubrir el Arte* 1:73–80.

Quintero, María Cristina. 2004. 'Mirroring Desire in Early Modern Spanish Poetry: Some Lessons from Painting.' In *Writing for the Eyes in the Spanish Golden Age*, ed. Frederick de Armas, 87–108. Lewisburg: Bucknell University Press.

Rivers, Elias. 1973. 'Albanio as Narcissus in Garcilaso's Second Eclogue.' *Hispanic Review* 41:297–304.

Schiesari, Juliana. 1992. *The Gendering of Melancholia: Feminism, Psychoanalysis, and the Symbolics of Loss in Renaissance Literature*. Ithaca: Cornell University Press.

Schoenfeldt, Michael C. 1999. *Bodies and Selves in Early Modern England: Physiology and Inwardness in Spenser, Shakespeare, Herbert, and Milton*. Cambridge Studies in Renaissance Literature and Culture 34. Cambridge: Cambridge University Press.

Schwarz, Heinrich. 1952. 'The Mirror in Art.' *The Art Quarterly* 15:97–118.

Soufas, Teresa Scott. 1990. *Melancholy and the Secular Mind in Spanish Golden Age Literature*. Columbia: University of Missouri Press.

Spivak, Gayatri Chakravorty. 1994. 'Echo.' *New Literary History* 24:17–43.

Vasari, Giorgio. 1912–15. *Lives of the Most Eminent Painters, Sculptors and Architects*. Trans. Gaston du C. de Vere. 10 vols. London: Macmillan and The Medici Society.

Vickers, Nancy. 1982. 'Diana Described: Scattered Woman and Scattered Rhyme.' *Critical Inquiry* (1981) 8:265–79. Reprinted in *Writing and Sexual Difference*, ed. Elizabeth Abel, 95–109. Chicago: University of Chicago Press.

Vinge, Louise. 1967. *The Narcissus Theme in Western European Literature up to the Early 19th Century*. Lund: Gleerups.

Virgil. 1998. *Eclogues. Georgics. Aeneid. The Minor Poems*. Ed. and trans. H. Rushton Fairclough. Rev. G.P. Goold. 2 vols. Loeb Classical Library. Cambridge, MA: Harvard University Press.

Wittkower, Rudolf, and Margot Wittkower. 1963. *Born under Saturn: The Character and Conduct of Artists: A Documented History from Antiquity to the French Revolution*. London: Weidenfeld and Nicolson.

Woods-Marsden, Joanna. 1998. *Renaissance Self-Portraiture: The Visual Construction of Identity and the Social Status of the Artist*. New Haven and London: Yale University Press.

9 Circe's Swan: The Poet, the Patron, and the Power of Bewitchment

KERRY WILKS

As the articles in this collection show, there is no shortage of authors who turned to Ovid for inspiration during the Age of Cervantes. Ovid's influence comes from a variety of sources, yet it is the myths contained within the *Metamorphoses* that serve as an impetus or even the foundation for a plethora of works in this period.[1] This is the case of the myths found at the end of book 13 and in book 14 that Lope de Vega developed in his poem 'La Circe' (1624).[2] Lope's imitation of Ovid can be found in both the structure of the poem and in its thematic content. By combining the myths that featured Ulysses, Lope recreated Ovid's storytelling technique, as these accounts, like their characters, engage in their own metamorphosis from one tale to the next in a seamless fashion. It is worth noting, though, that several early critics of the poem believed that Homer was the sole or primary source for the creation of *La Circe*, among them George Ticknor, who called the work an 'unfortunate amplification' of Homer (1965, 217).[3] Both Ernest Martineche and Rudolph Schevill began the debate in the early part of the twentieth century, with their analyses of *La Circe*. When speaking of the poem, Schevill not only compares the writers' styles, but he also speculates on the similarities between the authors' lives: 'careful scrutiny of both poets suggests the conclusion that Lope was a kindred spirit of Ovid: his facile pen, his lavish poetic endowment, his pagan morals, even episodes of his life, such as his exile, recall the Latin poet' (1913, 223). While Schevill and Martineche offer proof as to the inclusion of Ovid as a primary source for the poem, Emmanuel Hatzantonis carries the debate further with his article, offering detailed proof to exclude Homer as a possible source through the construct of antithetical parallels, proving Lope's poem is 'in strident contrast to Homer's *Odyssey*' (1965, 475).

More recent studies, such as those by Antonio Carreño, editor of the 2004 edition, and Antonio Sánchez Jiménez, offer fresh insight to the work, going beyond source identification or poem description to explore the psychology underlying Lope's poem.[4] For example, Sánchez's *Lope pintando a sí mismo* offers a political reading of *La Circe* when he posits that the transformation of the goddess, combined with similar themes from other works within the published collection, work together to promote a vision of the poet that coincides with the changing political tides and 'neo-stoic fury' that characterized the first years of Olivares's regime.[5] Lope's recounting of the myth is unique since it is Circe, rather than the men who stumble upon her island, who undergoes a metamorphosis, forcing the enchantress to become the enchanted through Neoplatonic love.[6] Sánchez's thesis is reinforced by the liberally sprinkled laudatory verses and dedication of the poem to Don Gaspar de Guzmán, Count of Olivares.[7] While it is not my intention to deny that Lope included these praises for the king's powerful favourite, I would like to suggest that 'La Circe' often exhibits a dichotomy that reflects Lope's praise and criticism of the powerful man who controlled the Spanish empire. Lope uses images of Circe, the lascivious Ovidian witch and his new Neoplatonic woman, to promote an ambiguous message for and about the favourite.[8]

Before the poem 'La Circe' even begins, the reader is attuned to the fact that Lope is courting Olivares's favour within the frontal materials. The elaborate frontispiece of the collection features the Olivares family shield in the middle of a triumphant arch (Vega Carpio, Carreño ed. 2004, xxix). A ribbon streams across the width of the drawing and around the shield proclaiming: 'Adversa cedunt Principi magnanimo' [Opposition yield to a magnanimous prince/ruler] (ibid.).[9] The pillars of the arch contain two statues depicting the goddess of war offering a crown to the triumphant goddess of peace (ibid.). The base of the first column with the goddess of war states 'Optimo tutelari' [To the best defender] while we find the motto 'Musarum instauratori' [To the restorer of the Muses] underneath that of the second column with the goddess of peace. Clearly the visual images and written words contained within this opening illustration are designed to portray the new favourite in a positive light.

The *aprobaciones* for the collection are found next, followed by a sonnet entitled 'A Circe' (To Circe).[10] In this poem, Lope addresses the goddess directly and asks Circe to surrender her knowledge and to admire the greatness of the Guzmanes: 'Rinde tu ciencia, y con temor retira /

de los Guzmanes rayos los febeos' [Surrender your knowledge and only with fear take away the Guzmanes's Phoebean rays] (2004, 357).[11] Circe may be the daughter of the sun, but Lope reminds her that she must respect the light from the Guzmán family: 'hija del sol, humilla tus trofeos, / su luz respeta, su grandeza admira' [Daughter of the sun, be humble, put aside your trophies, honour their light, admire their greatness] (2004, 357). After the sonnet we find a short prose dedication to the favourite, in which the poet asks Olivares to consider the poem's Castilian verses as children ['hijos'], who though not born into the illustrious Guzmán household, will hopefully be raised there (2004, 358). This laudatory paragraph is followed by a second sonnet dedicated to the favourite's daughter, Doña María de Guzmán (2004, 359).[12] The poet then includes a narrative prologue that briefly explains the content of the poem and the dedications from the compilation, after which, he describes Ulysses's virtue, citing Horace's second epistle: 'A Ulises nos dio Homero por ejemplo / de lo que puede la virtud difícil / y el ser los hombres sabios' [With Ulysses, Homer gave us an example of what the difficulties of virtue and the wisdom of men can bring] (2004, 360). Lope deliberately uses a citation that references Homer, even though several of the poem's episodes are obviously taken from other sources since they are not found within *The Odyssey*. It is easy to understand why Homer has been cited as the primary source for the poem, since he is the first author mentioned from the poet's own pen. Why would Lope introduce his work with a reference to the Greek epic writer, rather than to Ovid? To cite both Homer and Horace, in addition to the fourth-century poet Ausonio, sets the framework for an epic that can educate and entertain the reader ['dulce et utile'] while simultaneously demonstrating the breadth of Lope's classical knowledge. However, the exclusion of Ovid in the dedication may be deliberate, for as Schevill reminds us, Ovid is the 'champion of the love of mundane beauty in women' (1913, 100). Thus, it is not antithetical to posit that Ovid is indeed one of Lope's primary sources for the work, even though the author's name is mysteriously absent from the introductory pieces. For, following Sánchez's thesis, we would not expect Lope to begin his work with a reference to the 'racy' Latin poet as he was forging a new identity to conform to the ideals of the new regime. We will see, though, that the careful laudatory remarks found in this frontal material are challenged by the opening stanzas of the poem.

The first canto begins with a new direct invocation to Circe and unlike the sonnet 'A Circe' from the frontal material, Lope does not chastise the goddess, but instead he uses the informal address ('tú') in the first four strophes to exalt Circe, while imploring her to serve as his muse. In the first stanza the poet compares her to Jupiter and to the fount of poetic inspiration:

> Circe, que al blanco cisne, al rubio toro,
> en variedad de formas excediste,
> de la excelencia del castalio coro
> la humilde musa de mis versos viste;
> harás que las corrientes del Leteo
> presuman otra vez que canta Orfeo.

[Circe! You who exceeded in variety of forms, the white swan and the crimson bull; you who saw my verses' humble Muse in the excellence of the Castalian chorus; you'll make the currents of Lethe presume that Orpheus sings again.] (2004, 1.1)[13]

Not only will her magic inspire the poet's verses, but she is even more powerful than the king of the gods, Jupiter, who turns himself into animals, such as the swan and bull (and other objects) to achieve his sexual conquests. The swan metaphor is expanded in the second stanza when Lope asks the goddess to transform him with her new artifice into a Platonic swan: 'con nueva forma / en platónica cisne me transforma' (2004, 1.2). Circe, who has the power to transform men into beasts, can transform Lope, the poetic voice, into a Platonic swan to sing her praises.[14] However, the solely Platonic qualities of the swan image may be questioned, since the animal encompassed several meanings. Swans are a symbol of the muses and Apollo's sacred animal, and yet they are also associated with the erotic, serving as 'horses' for Venus's chariot or as metamorphic body for Jupiter's seduction of Leda.

In the third stanza Lope describes Circe's origin from the 'humor del Oceano' [humour/moisture of the Ocean] and the 'calor del sol' [heat of the sun]. The description of the goddess's parentage reflects the fact that Circe was considered to be the daughter of the Sun and the Ocean, yet the specific words that Lope employs echo Pérez de Moya's description of her in the 'sentido natural' section of the *Philosophía secreta*: 'Ser Circe hija del Sol y de Perseides, hija de Océano, es que las inclinaciones y apetitos se engendran en los animales del *humor* y *calor*' [Circe being the daughter of the Sun and of Perse, daughter of the Ocean, comes from the fact that inclinations and appetites in animals are engendered from humours and heat] (1996, 843; emphasis mine). [15] The moralist then stresses the importance of the combination of these two elements for the creation of life, with the humours of water ['humidad de Océano'] functioning as the feminine and the sun ['Sol'] the masculine. Thus, Circe is the emblem of creation and functions as metaphor for 'generación.' This power of creation allows Circe to transform the poet into the Platonic swan, who will sing of her deceit and her beauty with a Pythagoran, Ovidian soul ['Yo cantaré tu engaño y tu hermosura / con alma pitagórica ovidiana'] (2004, 1.4).[16] Thus, in the last stanza of Lope's invocation to Circe, the author directly references the Ovidian source, rather than the Homeric one found in the frontal material of the collection. The poet is careful to couch the Ovidian references to the goddess with the philosopher Pythagoras and with a 'Platonic' swan. We must remember, though, that readers would typically associate Circe with a very different set of attributes, primarily that of the enchantress who lures men away from their duty and/or changes them into animals. Lope himself recognizes that Circe is already 'typecast' for his readers as he states in the 1602 edition of the *Rimas*: 'usar lugares comunes, como engaños de Ulises, salamandra, Circe y otros, ¿por qué ha de ser prohibido, pues ya son como adagios y términos comunes, y el canto llano sobre que se fundan varios conceptos?' [Using commonplaces, like Ulysses's deceits, salamanders, Circe, and others, why should this be prohibited since they are already like adagios and well-worn terms, the plainsong upon which various concepts are created?] (cited in De Armas 1986, 147). Therefore, no matter how many neutral descriptors the poet adds to Circe's name, readers are naturally reminded of the more commonplace vision of the sorceress, that of seductive witch.[17] With this, we see a series of contrasts emerging from the invocation section: Circe who represents the creative power of nature; Circe as creator of beasts (through the destruction of men); Circe who creates poets; and Circe who is greater than Jupiter, king of the gods. These creative powers can be tied to Pérez de Moya's definition of the goddess, who associates this ability with her lascivious nature, which could also explain the stress on Jupiter's amorous adventures for the comparison of the goddess to him.[18]

The opening section of the poem is followed by seven stanzas in which Lope directly addresses Olivares ['vos']. At first glance, the verses appear to continue the laudatory tone from the frontal material as Lope describes the *privado*'s relationship to the king: 'vos, ya del sol resplandeciente luna' [You, already the resplendent moon of the sun]

(2004, 1.5). As many critics have already shown, Olivares actively promoted the image of Phillip IV as the 'rey planeta' [planet king], with the young monarch ushering in the new golden age to Spain.[19] As the king's moon, Olivares's light bathes the elements with clarity and happiness: 'que con su misma luz los elementos / bañáis de claridad y alegría' (2004, 1.5). Moreover, this moon can also substitute for the light of the sun when it sleeps: 'que mientras duerme el sol, velando puede / sustituir su luz vuestro cuidado' [While the sun sleeps, by keeping vigil you can substitute for its light with your dedication] (2004, 1.6). The moon's light is not 'borrowed,' but is instead compared to a 'paraelio,' or an image of the sun reflected in the sky creating a halo effect.[20] The verses seem to praise Olivares, since he is shown to be a worthy replacement of the sun, and not a poor reflection of it. These metaphors, though, could provoke the question as to whether Olivares (moon) should attempt to substitute for the king (sleeping sun). Olivares's predecessor, the Duque de Lerma, was removed from power in 1618 amid the fury of a call to reform and moderation. In order to gain political power, and then later to separate and distance himself from the former regime, Olivares advocated the idea that an all-powerful favourite was not needed and he was careful to promote the image of a 'disinterested' servant, selflessly serving his monarch.[21] Lope's description of the favourite as a replacement for the king was therefore antithetical to the ideals endorsed in the early 1620s, but perhaps more accurately reflects the reality of the political situation.

The ambiguity that is ever so slight in the fifth and sixth stanzas increases during the eight verses of the seventh stanza as the sun analogy is made more explicit with a direct reference to Olivares's relationship with the king: 'vos, que por bien universal tuvistes / con el planeta cuarto aspecto trino' [You, who for universal good had a trine aspect with the fourth planet] (2004, 1.7). Once again, we see that Lope praises Olivares, who has taken on the trine, or positive aspect, of the sun, the king. Olivares's capabilities as political leader are then finally mentioned: 'a método político trujistes / la descompuesta edad; alto destino / sólo digno de vos, en quien el cielo / iguales hizo entendimiento y celo' [To political method you brought the age of chaos; a high destiny worthy only of you, in whom heaven equally created insight and zeal] (2004, 1.7). Using hyperbaton, an initial reading of these four verses shows the idea that with his knowledge and zeal, Olivares brings a new beginning to the 'descompuesta edad,' as represented by Lerma's regime. However, there is another possibility, if the reader does not invert the two nouns; the implication is that Olivares himself has brought about the 'descompuesta edad.' With this, Lope's description of the age as the favourite's great destiny would be ironic. This reading is reinforced in the last verse of the stanza, which states that heaven has given Olivares both 'entendimiento' [knowledge] and 'celo' [zeal]. While the word 'entendimiento' has a plethora of meanings, all of which are complimentary, 'celo' is much more open for interpretation. The 1739 dictionary of the Real Academia Española lists three definitions of the word under 'zelo' with the first two encompassing positive attributes. The third entry for the word is more curious as it is associated with sexual impulse: 'significa tambien el apetito a la generacion en los irracionales: y asi se dice, que están o andan en zelo' [it also signifies an appetite to breed in the irrationals (animals) and thus it is said that they are or they roam in rut]. One may even be tempted to compare the noun 'generacion' to the same word that Pérez de Moya used when describing Circe in the *Philosophía secreta*. Is it only a coincidence that Lope chose to use this noun? Are there any other indications that would support the reading of this verse as sexual appetite?

The poem was written during the beginning years of the Olivares regime and many scholars have made reference to what would become the infamous nightly sorties of the young king under Olivares's tutelage.[22] The archbishop of Granada felt compelled to write Olivares during the first year of the new king's reign (August 1621) to warn the *privado* about the gossip that was ensuing related to these excursions. He advised Olivares to avoid as much as possible the king's outings at night, since they implicated the favourite himself and implied a greater culpability. Moreover, he claimed that these actions were destroying the hope that people had in Olivares at the beginning of his reign:

Suplícole cuanto me es posible que evite las salidas del Rey de noche, y que mire la mucha parte de culpa que le dan las gentes en ellas, pues publican que le acompaña y que se las aconseja; de lo cual se afligen con razón, por parecerles que vuecencia malogra las esperanzas que hubo al principio de su gobierno.

[I urge you, as much as possible, to avoid the king's evening outings, and consider that people have given you a large portion of blame in this matter, since it is said that you accompany him and advise him about this; with this, they are rightly distressed, since it seems that Your Excellency is wasting the hope that existed at the beginning of your reign.] (1926, 61)[23]

The archbishop then chastises Olivares concerning his forgotten res-
ponsibilities as favourite and tutor of the young monarch: 'Son muchas las circunstancias que deben concurrir en quien tiene a su cargo la
dirección de un príncipe. Vuecencia las sabe, pero las olvida ...' [There
are many specifics that those who are advising a prince need to attend
to. Your Excellency knows them, but has forgotten them ...] (1926, 61). It
is then suggested that Olivares 'improve' the situation before any permanent damage is done: '... y por esto estoy precisado a recordárselas
para que aplique el remedio antes que experimente el castigo' [... because of this I need to remind you of them so that you may apply the remedy before punishment is suffered] (1926, 61). Olivares's response to
the archbishop (September of 1621) does not deny the outings, but he
does explain that they were designed to educate the new king and to
encourage him to have a more 'hands-on' approach to government
than that practised by his father. He also states that the king should
'informarse con los ojos de muchas cosas que, si no las viera, tal vez
llegarían torcidas a sus oídos' [learn through his eyes of the many
things that, if he might not see them, could come to his ears in a
distorted manner] (1926, 61). It is interesting to note that Olivares's
opening line to the archbishop includes a reference to the previously
discussed word *celo* as the *privado* thanks the archbishop for the good
zeal shown in the letter ['El buen celo que usía ilustrísima muestra en su
carta, estimo mucho ...'] (1926, 61). Given the context of the letter, the
double entendre of the word, with its more 'passionate' meaning, could
be implied in this sentence. While this reading is more unlikely than the
double entendre encompassing Lope's poem, the coincidence bears
pointing out. With this, Olivares would gently chastise the archbishop's
subtle criticisms by insinuating that the man's interests are a result of his
more lascivious nature rather than flaws in Olivares's character.

Whether or not Olivares's response pleased the archbishop is unknown, but we do know that the rumours surrounding Phillip IV's
amorous adventures did not end during the first year of his reign and
Olivares continued to be tied to this gossip.[24] Moreover these letters appear to have been heavily circulated, lending stronger credence to the
idea that these rumours were well known throughout the court. A cursory glance at the indexes for the manuscripts housed in the Sala
Cervantes of Madrid's National Library indicates that there are copies
of the archbishop's letter, as well as Olivares's response, in various
volumes. There are at least eleven separate volumes that contain the
letter, yet they are not identical copies.[25] For example, one immediately

notices the differences with respect to the dates of the letters as MS 290 says that the letter is signed in Granada on 24 August 1621, yet MS 1390 lists 28 August 1621 as the date. There are also copy errors contained within the documents that one would expect from a document that was copied by hand on multiple occasions. The first citation from the preceding paragraph, when the archbishop warns Olivares that he should stop accompanying the king on the evening excursions, illustrates these differences:[26]

Suplícole cuanto me es posible que evite las salidas del Rey de noche, y que mire la mucha parte de culpa que le dan las gentes en ellas, pues publican que le acompaña y que se las aconseja; de lo cual se afligen con razón, por parecerles que vuecencia malogra las esperanzas que hubo al principio de su gobierno, porque al fin siempre se está con grande observación de las menores acciones de quien se espera mucho. En realidad, ese gusto no es bueno ... (modern edition cited above).

Suplícole cuanto pueda desvie las salidas del Rey de noche, y mire cuanta parte de culpa que le dan en esto las gentes, publicando todos que es su compañero, afligiendoles, el parezerles, que se mal logran las esperanzas que hubo luego al principio de su govierno, porque del fin siempre se esta con recelo, de que en se espera mucho y en realidad de verdad que esse gusto no es bueno ... (MS 11,045).

Suplícole cuanto pueda desvie las salidas del Rey de noche, y mire cuanta parte de culpa le dan en esto las gentes, publicando todos que es su compañero, afligiendose que se mal logran las esperanzas que hubo luego al principio de su govierno, porque del fin siempre se esta con gran recelo, de que se espera mucho y en él realidad ese gusto no es bueno ... (MS 11,262, 15).

Suplícole cuanto puedo [sic] desvie las salidas del Rey de noche, y mire cuanta parte de culpa le dan en esto las gentes, publicando que es su compañero, y afligiendose de parecerles que se malogran las esperanzas que hubo luego al principio de su govierno, que al fin siempre se esta con gran recelo, de que se espera mucho y en realidad ese gusto no es bueno ... (MS 13,684).

Whether or not these documents were actually written by the archbishop and Olivares does not alter the fact that this knowledge was presented as factual during the seventeenth century. The plethora of letters housed in Madrid's library, combined with the copy errors that indicate a substantial number of rewritings of the document, suggest that this information was widely circulated throughout the peninsula at the beginning of the new regime. It seems unlikely, then, that Lope would not be familiar with this scandal since it occurred only two years prior to the placement of the book in the censor's hands, making it possible that the gossip circulated contemporaneously with Lope's writing of 'La Circe.'

In light of this background, Lope's choice of words with the 'descompuesta edad' and 'celo' casts a shadow over the surface meaning of the verses and could be seen as a criticism of the favourite in this supposed 'morally superior' regime. Olivares is not tutoring the young monarch, but instead the favourite substitutes for him, bringing with him a dubious moral character that spreads to the king. The double entendre with the words is not the only ambiguous meaning that can be found in these three stanzas. Similar to the king's nightly excursions, critics have also noted the gossip surrounding Olivares's undue influence over the king. Rumours circulated that the *privado* achieved this influence through witchcraft, the first notice of which comes from 1622 (September), one year before the *aprobaciones* of 'La Circe' were processed.[27] The basis of these rumours is found in the case of the 'filtros de Leonerilla,' when a woman testified that in an attempt to prove the efficacy of her spells, Leonerilla offers the fact that her spells ensure that Olivares is able to maintain his power: 'estaban probados en su eficacia y en su inocencia, ya que eran los mismos [hechizos] que el Conde de Olivares daba al Rey para conservar su privanza' [both their innocence and efficacy were proven since they (spells) were the same as those that the Count of Olivares gave the king in order to maintain his position of favourite] (Marañón 1965, 196). Olivares's association with spells and the description of him as moon, connects the favourite to Circe, who is also related to the moon and witchcraft. Therefore, by linking Olivares to Circe, Lope's poem may serve as one of the first literary artefacts to document what would become a common criticism of the *privado*. Olivares, then, takes on the Ovidian Circean attributes with his connection to the king. There is no Neoplatonic influence with the relationship since the witch's lascivious nature and her enchantments are stressed.[28] With these ambiguous references, Lope is able to offer praise to Olivares, which he would want to do since he had not yet given up on his hope of receiving a court position, but at the same time, this praise is muted, if not contradicted by the ambiguity contained within the references.[29]

The fact that Lope intended for his reader to view or at least consider Circe as a witch rather than a benefic figure can be seen in one of Lope's plays that was published only one year before Lope submitted 'La Circe' to the censors, *El premio de la hermosura* (1621). Phillip III's queen (Margarita) commissioned Lope to create a court drama from his epic *La hermosura de Angélica*. Unfortunately, the queen died in childbirth before the play could be staged and it was not until 1614 that the work was performed at Lerma's palace.[30] Even though the play was first performed in 1614, Lope waited several years to publish the piece in his 'decimasexta parte de las comedias' [sixteenth part of the plays]. During this time, Lope had made a habit of dusting off plays from the past, while he individually dedicated them to prominent personages (Wright 2002, 106). Since Lerma fell from power in 1618, there was no need to dedicate the play to the former favourite who hosted the debut of the work and he turned his attention to the new favourite, Olivares, for the dedication of the play that leads off the collection. Using Greer's terminology, Wright shows that *El premio* had become a 'power play' since Lope literally handed it over as a prize to the winner of the battle between Lerma and Olivares for government control (2001, 121). Before turning the play over, though, Lope made a few curious changes to this spectacle that used the ladies-in-waiting and young prince and princess as actors. First, he inserted the frequently cited scene in which a gardener complains about the fact that he was not given the position of royal chronicler. This gardener, of course, is seen as the poetic voice of Lope in his frustration to receive the title in 1620 (Wright 2001, 122). It is the ending, though, that directly concerns this study since Lope changed his *comedia* to a *tragicomedia*, eliminating the multiple marriages that characterized the first version of the play. Instead, Lope inserts a mother figure into the comedia, Circea, who represents Circe.[31] Circea is the mother of one of the young women from the play who is caught up in the typical *enredos* one would expect from a *comedia*. When it appears that the girl will not be able to obtain the object of her affection, she calls upon her mother to assist her. Circea uses her magical powers to frustrate the plans that the other couples have made, but when this is not successful Circea herself arrives to resolve the plot. However, this is not done in stereotypical deus ex machina formula with weddings. Instead, Circea declares that no one will find happiness with his/her partner since she will enchant them all and they will languor in forgetfulness forever. Ferrer believes that Lope made these changes to fit the needs of a new production in the *corrales* (1991, 183). Wright, though, has pointed out that one could eliminate the stage machinery used in the court play and still end with multiple weddings in the corral. She posits that the new ending indicates a 'resonancia política' [political impact] due to the failed marriage that the original play was created to celebrate (2002, 111). It seems logical to extend the idea of Lope's disappointment at not receiving the court position, as evidenced in the gardener's monologue, to the ending of the play, since as Wright has pointed out, the garden often served as emblem for the 'fracaso cortesano' [failure at court] (2002, 110). We see then that while critics have often cited *El premio* as one of the first examples of Lope's desire to flatter the new favourite by dedicating works to him, the changes the author employed makes it difficult to view this piece as simple flattery.

In the gardener's monologue Lope clearly expressed his disappointment with 'the powers that be' or more specifically, with Olivares, in not being formally recognized and more importantly, rewarded, by the court. He then uses Circea with her powers of enchantment, to 'disappoint' the ending of the play. One short year later, Lope tries again, and dedicates a second work to the favourite, 'La Circe,' whose title character in the opening segments would seem to more accurately reflect the image from *El premio* than the Neoplatonic woman described in the subsequent story of Ulysses and Circe. Lope does not leave us an easy trail to uncover with his ambiguous references to Circe and Olivares. This very ambiguity, though, may stem from his first failed attempt to flatter the favourite with *El premio*. The poet becomes more careful with his criticism and more verbose with his praise as he attempts to finally win the prize of one of Olivares's court poets or chroniclers. The fact that Olivares withheld his praise, in the form of economic recompense or a court position, could be an indication that Lope's obvert flattery could not cover the ambiguities inherent within the ultimately Ovidian Circe.

NOTES

1 Schevill's seminal study of Ovid maintains that the Latin author represents a 'great repository of classical legends' and that *The Metamorphoses* takes 'first rank because of the wealth of material which they contain' (1913, 145).
2 The three-canto poem 'La Circe' was published in the collection *La Circe con otras rimas y prosas* in 1624. Charles Aubrun and Manuel Muñoz Cortés edited the poem 'La Circe' apart from the collection, each providing a thorough critical study of the work for the introduction (Vega Carpio 1962). Carreño's more recent edition (Vega Carpio 2004) includes all of the works published

in Lope's original collection. The volume includes an introduction and the Spanish is modernized. When referring to the collection of poems *La Circe* will be italicized but the poem itself will be in quotation marks.

3 Cossío's study also references Homer as Lope's primary source calling *The Odyssey* the 'armazón' of the poem (1952, 340). Bonnet recognizes Homer's influences, but adds that there are touches ['algunos detalles'] of Virgil and Ovid (1953, 123).

4 Carreño offers a detailed study of the poem, placing it within the literary battles of the epoch with Lope's attempt to compete with Góngora's *Polifemo* (Vega Carpio 2004). Sánchez includes the work in his monograph on Lope's poetry (2006) as well as in his article focusing on ekphrastic food descriptions in two of Lope's poems, 'La Circe' and *El Isidro* (2003).

5 See especially his chapter 'El poeta enamorado.'

6 For an alternative point of view, see Aubrun who believes that the ideas found in the poem more accurately reflect seventeenth-century Thomist philosophy rather than the Neoplatonism from fifteenth-century Italy (1963, 224, 231). The article cited is a Spanish translation of his introduction in French to the poem he coedited with Muñoz.

7 He received the title Duke of San Lúcar el Mayor in January of 1625 and shortly thereafter began to sign his letters as the Count-Duke, the title by which he is commonly referred to today (Elliot 1986, 166).

8 This line of criticism follows those who explore the hidden political messages contained within Spanish literature ['decir sin decir']. Stern brought Lope's writings to the foreground of the debate in her 1982 article and McKendrick's more recent publication, *Playing the King* (2000), also focuses on Lopean literature. De Armas (1986), Blue (1989), and Greer (1991), among others, have applied this technique to the study of Calderón's plays. To my knowledge, this approach has not been applied to 'La Circe,' as critics have focused on the overtly laudatory aspects of the work.

9 The motto is modelled on a famous aphorism of Cicero (de Officiis 1.77), 'cedant arma togae' [let arms yield to the toga], i.e., military force should yield to political rule. Special thanks to classicist Dr Gregg Schwendner for his assistance with the reference and Latin translations in this paragraph. The frontispiece can be viewed online within the Biblioteca Augustana's collection at the following website: http://www.hs-augsburg .de/~harsch/hispanica/Cronologia/siglo17/Lope/lop_circ.html.

10 This page dates from 1623 and includes El licenciado Murcia de la Llana, Fray Alonso Ramón, and Don Antonio Hurtado de Mendoza.

11 This and all subsequent citations to the frontal material are from Carreño's edition (2004). I would like to thank Dr Wilson Baldridge and Dr Maria

Akrabova, Wichita State University's translators extraordinaire, for their generous assistance with the translations of the Spanish passages. Any errors, though, are of course my own.

12 The collection contains a second poem, 'La rosa blanca,' which is also dedicated to the favourite's daughter. For more information, see Carreño's introduction (2004, xxxix).

13 This and all future references to the poem are from Carreño's edition. I have cited the canto and stanza, rather than the page numbers, to facilitate verse location.

14 The swan, with plume in beak, is also seen in the shield of the frontispiece of the collection.

15 I would like to thank Frederick de Armas, who kindly pointed out these references in Pérez de Moya's work. It is also possible that Lope was basing his allusions of 'humor' and 'calor' on Ovid's text rather than that of Pérez de Moya. Sánchez de Viana appears to have borrowed Pérez de Moya's description of Circe for the commentaries that accompany his translation of Ovid's work, including these specific references (1589, 248). If Lope used this source for his Ovidian borrowings, then they would have come from his copy of *The Metamorphoses* rather than the mythographer's manual. Of course Lope may also have used one of the other translations available at the time (i.e., Pérez Sigler, Bustamante, Mey). See Cossío (1952) or Schevill (1913) for a detailed description of these translations. An additional thank you goes to John Parrack who sent me a copy of Harvard's Sánchez de Viana edition. Please see his article in this book for a detailed description of this translation and commentary of Ovid's work.

16 Pythagoras appears in the last book of *The Metamorphoses*, when Ovid expounds upon the Samian's philosophical viewpoints.

17 See Yarnell (1994) for an excellent overview of the various representations of Circe throughout history, especially chapters 4 and 5 ('The Legacy of Allegory' and 'Renaissance Circes'). Leocardio Garasa's article (1964) is especially useful for studies of the goddess during the Age of Cervantes.

18 This could be extended to include the ekphrastic description of Circe's palace in the latter half of the first canto, where the paintings feature scenes from *The Metamorphoses*, including Jupiter's adventures with Leda and Danae. See Wilks 2005 for more information on the passage.

19 For example, see Brown and Elliot for a frequently cited source (2003, 33).

20 Paraelio can be found under parhelio in the Real Academia Española's dictionary.

21 See the first section of Elliot's biography of the Count-Duke for a description of the government during the period (1986).

22   Brown and Elliot are often cited for their description of the king's activities
     that were mimicked on stage (2003, 33).
23   This and subsequent citations to the letters (unless otherwise specified),
     with modernized Spanish, are from those published in the *Biblioteca de
     Autores Españoles* volume *Epistolario español*, edited by Ochoa.
24   See de Armas's description of the king's neglectful relationship with the
     queen in the early 1630s (1986, 148).
25   The following manuscripts contain the letters: MS 290, 98v–9 (Papeles de
     diferentes materias políticas y de buen gobierno sacadas de la real librería
     de la octava maravilla de S. Lorenzo de el Escorial); MS 1,390, 4–5 (Papeles
     varios en italiano y español); MS 2,341, 17 (Papeles varios, historias, fabu-
     las, avisos, cartas y relaciones); MS 7,371, 1–4 (Papeles tocantes al Conde-
     Duque de Olivares); MS 7,968, 13v–16 (Papeles curiosos de la vida y
     ministerio del Conde-Duque de Olivares); MS 9,163, 16–17 (Papeles va-
     rios); MS 10,659, 33–5 (Papeles referentes al Conde-Duque de Olivares);
     MS 11,045, 25v–7 (Papeles varios); MS 11,262, 15 (Papeles referentes al
     Conde-Duque de Olivares); MS 12,875, 2–5 (Papeles varios curiosos); MS
     13,684, 17v–23 (Papeles curiosos de la vida y ministerio del Conde-Duque
     de Olivares, privado del Sr. Rey Phelipe IV).
26   The slight, yet constant word changes in these citations have not been
     translated since the differences do not affect the meaning of the passage.
27   See de Armas for a description of how other Spanish authors alluded to
     Olivares's connection with the occult to influence the king (1986, 144).
28   It is also ironic that Olivares's court-appointed 'favourites' were given the
     label 'hechuras,' just like Circe made or turned Ulysses's men into pigs.
29   This ambiguity is similar to the strategy McKendrick outlines when she de-
     scribes how Lope makes 'self-protective gestures of obeisance' in his plays
     before contradicting this with 'home truths' from the dialogue (2000, 78).
30   Elizabeth Wright underlines the irony of this when she states that the queen
     asked Lope to write the play as an 'arma' for the fight between her and the
     privado. Lerma, though, was able to use the play after the queen's death to
     promote his own agenda and show off the gardens of his palace (2002, 99).
31   Not only is Circea's name and character close in structure and personality
     to Circe, but two different mythographers, Juan Pérez de Moya (1996) and
     Baltasar Vitoria (1620) mention the word Circeo in their descriptions of
     Circe. Both claimed that the goddess moved to Italy at the end of her life
     and the island where she resided, Circeo, was eventually named after her
     (1996, 841; 1620, 884, respectively). While both manuals were extremely
     popular during the Age of Cervantes, we can be certain that Lope was fa-
     miliar with one of these, Vitoria's *Theatro de los dioses de la gentilidad*, since
     he signed the *aprobaciones* for this volume in 1619.

WORKS CITED

Aubrun, Charles. 1963. '"La Circe": Estudio de estructura.' *Cuadernos hispanoamericanos* 161/2:213–45.

Blue, William. 1989. *Comedia: Art and History*. New York: Peter Lang.

Bonnet, Julio Palli. 1953. *Homero en España*. Barcelona: Elzeviriana and Lib. Cami.

Brown, Jonathon, and John H. Elliot. 2003 (1980). *A Palace for a King: The Buen Retiro and the Court of Phillip IV*. New Haven: Yale University Press.

Cossío, José María de. 1952. *Fábulas mitológicas en España*. Madrid: Espasa Calpe.

De Armas, Frederick A. 1986. *The Return of Astraea: An Astral-Imperial Myth in Calderón*. Lexington: University Press of Kentucky.

Elliot, J.H. 1986. *The Count-Duke of Olivares: The Statesman in an Age of Decline*. New Haven: Yale University Press.

Ferrer Valls, Teresa. 1991. *La práctica escénica cortesana: de la época del emperador a la de Felipe III*. London: Tamesis.

Greer, Margaret Rich. 1991. *The Play of Power: Mythological Court Dramas of Calderón de la Barca*. Princeton: Princeton University Press.

Hatzantonis, Emmanuel. 1965. 'Lope de Vega's Non-Homeric Treatment of a Homeric Theme.' *Hispania* 48.3:475–80.

Leocardio Garasa, Delfín. 1964. 'Circe en la literatura española del siglo de oro.' *Boletín de la Academia Argentina de Letras* 29:227–71.

Marañón, Gregorio. 1965. *El Conde-Duque de Olivares (La pasión de mandar)*. Madrid: Espasa Calpe.

Martineche, Ernest. 1922. '*La Circe* y los poemas mitológicos de Lope.' *Humanidades* 4:59–66.

McKendrick, Melveena. 2000. *Playing the King*. London: Tamesis.

Ochoa, Eugenio, ed. 1926. *Epistolario español: Colección de cartas de españoles ilustres antiguos y modernos*. Biblioteca de Autores Españoles 62. Madrid: Hernando.

Papeles curiosos de la vida y ministerio del Conde-Duque de Olivares. MSS 7,968. BN, Madrid.

Papeles curiosos de la vida y ministerio del Conde-Duque de Olivares, privado del Sr. Rey Phelipe IV. MSS 13,684. BN, Madrid.

Papeles de diferentes materias políticas y de buen gobierno sacadas de la real librería de la octava maravilla de S. Lorenzo de el Escorial. MSS 290. BN, Madrid.

Papeles referentes al Conde-Duque de Olivares. MSS 10,659. BN, Madrid.

Papeles referentes al Conde-Duque de Olivares. MSS 11,262/15. BN, Madrid.

Papeles tocantes al Conde-Duque de Olivares. MSS 7,371. BN, Madrid.

Papeles varios. MSS 9,163. BN, Madrid.

Papeles varios. MSS 11,045. BN, Madrid.

Papeles varios curiosos. MSS 12,875. BN, Madrid.

Papeles varios en italiano y español. MSS 1,390. BN, Madrid.

Papeles varios, historias, fabulas, avisos, cartas y relaciones. MSS 2,341. BN, Madrid.

Pérez de Moya, Juan. 1996 (1585). *Comparaciones o símiles para los vicios y virtudes. Philosophía secreta.* Ed. Consolación Baranda. Madrid: Biblioteca Castro.

Sánchez Jiménez, Antonio. 2003. 'Manjar de héroes, manjar de santos: La comida en el *Isidro* y "La Circe" de Lope de Vega Carpio.' In *En gustos se come géneros, III: Congreso internacional comida y literatura*, ed. Sara Poot Herrera, 185–96. Mérida, Mexico: Instituto de cultura de Yucatán.

– 2006. *Lope pintando a sí mismo: Mito e imagen del autor en la poesía de Lope de Vega Carpio.* London: Tamesis.

Sánchez de Viana, Pedro. 1589. *Anotaciones sobre los quinze libros de las Transformaciones de Ovidio, con la mithología de las fabulas y otras cosas.* Valladolid: Fernández de Córdova.

Schevill, Rudolph. 1913. *Ovid and the Renascence in Spain.* University of California Publications in Modern Philology 4.1. Berkeley: University of California Press.

Stern, Charlotte. 1982. 'Lope de Vega, Propagandist?' *Bulletin of the Comediantes* 34.1:1–36.

Ticknor, George. 1965 (1891). *History of Spanish Literature.* New York: Gordian Press.

Vega Carpio, Lope de. 1962. *'La Circe.'* Ed. Charles Aubrun and Manuel Muñoz Cortés. Paris: Centre de Recherches de l'Institut d'Estudes Hispaniques.

– 2004. *Poesía IV: La Filomena. La Circe.* Ed. Antonio Carreño. Madrid: Biblioteca Castro.

Vitoria, Baltasar. 1620. *Theatro de los dioses de la gentilidad.* R/19,013. Madrid: Biblioteca Nacional.

Wilks, Kerry. 2005. 'Ekphrasis and Enchantment: Images of Circe in Italy and Spain during the Renaissance.' *Cahiers Parisiens/Parisian Notebooks* 1:138–48.

Wright, Elizabeth. 2001. *Pilgrimage to Patronage.* Lewisburg: Bucknell University Press.

– 2002. 'Recepción en el palacio y decepción en la imprenta: *El premio de la hermosura* de Lope de Vega.' In *El teatro del Siglo de Oro ante los espacios de la crítica: encuentros y revisiones*, ed. Enrique García Santo Tomás, 97–114. Madrid, Frankfurt: Iberoamericana, Vervuet.

Yarnell, Judith. 1994. *Transformations of Circe: The History of an Enchantress.* Urbana: University of Illinois Press.

'Zelo.' Def. 1–3. Diccionario de la Real Academia Española 1739. www.rae.es.

10 Ovid Transformed: Cristóbal de Castillejo as Conflicted Cosmopolitan

STEVEN WAGSCHAL

In *Cosmopolitanism: Ethics in a World of Strangers* American philosopher Kwame Anthony Appiah describes and prescribes the phenomenon cast as his title. Appiah resuscitates this concept, which he traces back to its fourth-century BCE origins in the Greek Cynics, for a particular kind of contemporary global ethics, one that is concerned primarily with the universality of humankind while celebrating differences among cultures. As Appiah explains, the Cynics coined the term 'cosmopolitan' – citizen of the cosmos, or rather the universe – in contradistinction to 'polites' – a citizen who belonged to a 'polis' – to question the widely held belief that 'every civilized person belonged to a community among communities' 2004, xiv). This appeal to universality over locality became central to Stoic ideas on the oneness of humanity and particularly to Marcus Aurelius's formulation of this idea. Glossing over medieval and early modern times, Appiah finds cosmopolitanism at the heart of the Enlightenment, and specifically in the French revolution's Declaration of the Rights of Man, Kant's plan for a 'league of nations,' and the thought of both Wieland and Voltaire. From this long and colourful history, cosmopolitanism, for Appiah, has two intertwining strands:

> One is the idea that we have obligations to others, obligations that stretch beyond those to whom we are related by the ties of kith and kind, or even the more formal ties of a shared citizenship. The other is that we take seriously the value not just of human life but of particular human lives, which means taking an interest in the practices and beliefs that lend them significance. People are different, the cosmopolitan knows, and there is much to learn from our differences. (2004, xv)

Among such differences, what Appiah calls 'receptiveness to art and literature from other places' plays a key role (2004, 4). Writers who incorporate insights, texts, and ideas from other cultures into their work figure prominently among cosmopolitans; thus it is no surprise to find Terence or Goethe among Appiah's cosmopolitans, the former who incorporated multiple Greek plays into a single Latin drama, and the latter whose work was punctuated with the *West-Eastern Divan* 'inspired by the oeuvre of the fourteenth-century Persian poet Hafiz' (2004, 5). Appiah's reader also comes across the likes of David Hume and Montesquieu, whose writings openly reflected their wide reading of travel literature, and Sir Richard Burton, who had a deep knowledge of other languages, religions, and literatures of the world, and as Appiah points out, who nineteenth-century English readers often suspected had more sympathy for Muslims than Christians. More recently, Salman Rushdie exemplifies cosmopolitanism, having himself written about his fatwa-inspiring novel that 'it celebrates hybridity, impurity, intermingling, the transformation that comes of new and unexpected combinations of human beings, cultures, ideas, politics, movies, songs. It rejoices in mongrelization and fears the absolutism of the Pure' (quoted in Appiah 2004, 112).

The notion of cosmopolitanism versus 'the absolutism of the Pure' is an interesting prism through which to examine that moment of rapid cultural change amid integration of foreign elements, alongside the countervailing tendencies of absolutism, religious fanaticism, and other forms of intolerance that was the early modern Hispanic world. In particular, cosmopolitanism provides an illuminating concept for viewing poetic innovation versus traditionalism in the early sixteenth century, a period of time when expanded interest in the cosmos was spreading. As Elias Rivers recalls, *Las obras de Boscan y algunas de Garcilaso de la Vega* [The Works of Boscan and Some by Garcilaso de La Vega] was published in 1543, simultaneously with the publication of works dealing with the macro- and microcosmoses respectively: Copernicus's astronomical treatise – on the macrocosmic heavens – and Vesalius's anatomical treatise on the microcosmic human body.[1]

As poets who cultivated the incorporation of Italian influences into Spanish literature, the cosmopolitanism of Juan Boscán and Garcilaso de la Vega can hardly be doubted. Like many of Appiah's exemplary cosmopolitans, the two Spanish poets were travellers who learned much about other communities directly and brought this knowledge home to Spain. Founding a school of poetry that became the norm for over a hundred years, in its incipient moment Boscán and Garcilaso celebrated the hybridity of cultural contamination, while incorporating Italian and classical themes, verse forms, metres, cadences, rhyme schemes, and tropes into Spanish letters, forever transforming them, in what Navarrete has called 'a radical plan for the rehabilitation of Spanish letters through the adoption of Italian verse forms' (1994, 73) akin to Appiah's example of Terence who hybridized Greek and Latin genres. Indeed, while Boscán was the innovator, the initial idea to write Italianate sonnets in the Spanish language was not even a Spanish one at all, but the suggestion of a foreigner, Andrea Navagero, the Venetian ambassador at the Granadine court of Charles V.[2] While in hindsight, these tendencies of incorporating Italian and other influences into Spanish letters might not seem 'mongrelizing' in Rushdie's sense – given the cultural prestige of Italy and classical antiquity during the European Renaissance – it was, as Navarrete phrases it, a 'radical' move. Indeed, the fact that a reactionary element in Spain opposed such innovations in exactly the terms of 'pure' versus 'other' – in the manner that will be delineated as follows – speaks to the question of hybridity.

In stark contrast to these early modern poets of mongrelization – celebrators of impure innovations – the sixteenth-century Spanish poet Cristóbal de Castillejo (ca. 1489–1550) is generally considered to be a traditionalist. Rightfully so, he is singled out in histories of literature as the principal representative of a reaction against the innovations of Boscán and Garcilaso.[3] Indeed, at a thematic level, many of Castillejo's compositions are openly hostile to cultural contamination and thus, in the Appiahn history of cosmopolitanism, he seemingly would fall into the anti-cosmopolitan camp. Castillejo typically composed his poetry in metres that were considered autochthonous rather than foreign; while he sometimes dabbled in hendecasyllables, he had a noted preference for rhyming octosyllabic verse, in the *cancionero* tradition of Juan de Encina. However, reading Castillejo's complex relationship to Ovid's *Metamorphoses* through Appiah's notion, I demonstrate that the Spanish poet is more of a cosmopolitan than common sense would seem to dictate. In what follows I will analyse some of Castillejo's writings against the backdrop of Boscán and Garcilaso, casting him as a conflicted cosmopolitan.

In the first quarter of the sixteenth century, when Boscán and Garcilaso were introducing Italianate forms and themes into Spain, Castillejo explicitly deplored the importation of these elements in a series of poems. 'Musas italïanas y latinas' [Italian and Latin Muses] is a sonnet in which he explicitly condemns these importations and the poets who propagated them. Drawing on an analogy between nature and poetry, Castillejo ponders how strange such foreign poetic elements appear amid the geographical features, such as the Tagus River, and autochthonous flora of 'nuestra España' [our Spain] (1998, 269 v. 3). He thus promotes an us-versus-them vision of Spanish purity in peril of contamination. In the closing tercet, Castillejo rejoices in the deaths of Garcilaso, Boscán, and Luis de Haro, lamenting that one of their ilk, Diego de Mendoza, still survives: 'Los dos llevó la muerte paso a paso / Solimán el uno y por amparo / Nos queda don Diego, y basta solo' [Death took two of them little by little / Mercury sublimate the other, and for protection / We are left with Don Diego, and he's enough on his own] (1998, vv. 12–14). Following a similar but more vicious line of poetic argument, the poem 'Pues la sancta Inquisición' [Since the Holy Inquisition] creates an analogy not with Spanish nature but religion. Here, Castillejo ties literary miscegenation – the use of foreign elements in autochthonous literature – to religious heresy, one that should be punished as Lutherans should be by the Inquisition. The innovative poets are 'secta ... muy nueva y extraña' [a new and strange ... sect] comparable to 'anabaptistas' [Anabaptists], 'infieles' [infidels] who have been newly baptized as 'petrarquistas' [Petrarchists] (1998, 263 v. 4, v. 9, v. 12, v. 29, v. 15). The poem repeatedly emphasizes their strangeness: they are from 'tierra ajena' [a strange land] (1998, v. 45), not of 'patria natural' [native country] (1998, v. 24), followers of 'Lutero / en las partes de Alemania' [Luther / in parts of Germany] (1998, vv. 9–10). Likewise, in the sonnet, 'Garcilasso y Boscán, siendo llegados,' [Garcilaso and Boscán, Having Arrived] explores yet another metaphorical analogy, that between contamination by foreign literary elements and political treason. For Castillejo, these poets – who had served in war on behalf of Spain against the Turks – are traitors who conspire against Spain, 'Espías o enemigos desmandados' [Spies or renegade enemies] (1998, 264 v. 8). In a strong anti-cosmopolitan vein, their very hybridity is what makes them suspect as spies or double agents. Sartorially, they seem like Spaniards: 'Y juzgando primero por el traje, / Paresciéronles ser, cómo debía, / Gentiles españoles caballeros' [And judging them first by their clothes / they seemed to be, as would be expected / Genteel Spanish knights] (1998, vv. 9–11). But their manner of speaking gives them away as strangers: 'Y oyéndoles hablar nuevo lenguaje / Mezclado de estranjera poesía, / Con ojos los miraban de estranjeros' [But hearing them speak a new language / Mixed with foreign poetry / They looked at them with the eyes of foreigners] (1998, vv. 12–14); he emphasizes this seemingly paradoxical incongruence, pairing the words 'traje' [clothes]

(1998, v. 9) and 'lenguaje' [language] (1998, v. 12) through rhyme. Relying in these poems on three analogies of otherness – nature (race), religion, and politics – Castillejo would seem to be a xenophobic reactionary resisting all foreign literary elements, one who would apparently tend to the opposite pole of Rushdie's appeal to cultural mongrelization. At the same time, this anti-cosmopolitan stance would seem to ally Castillejo with the nationalistic and conservative elements of the Spanish power elite, who sought to diminish racial mixing and religious heterodoxy in Spain through the Inquisition.

But Castillejo was at home not in a small monolingual Castilian city – he left his birthplace of Ciudad Rodrigo at the age of fourteen and according to the historical record never seems to have returned – but at court in Spain and Vienna, where he served first as a page and later as secretary. He was a traveller who had the opportunity to engage deeply with other cultures. In 1522, he served on an ambassadorial mission to England alongside the bishop of Astorga, where he most likely met Henry VIII and Catherine of Aragon (Beccaria Lago 1997, 185). He served as a secretary at the court of Ferdinand the Catholic, and in 1525 moved to the Austrian court with Charles V's brother Ferdinand (the archduke of Austria and, after Charles V's abdication, Holy Roman Emperor). In Vienna, Castillejo would apparently fall in love with a German lady. A series of additional travels, while not documented, is attested to in his poem 'A la cortesía' [To Courtesy], where he describes his search for the ideal woman: 'Hela buscado en España / Francia, Ytalia, Esclauonía, / Flandes, Polonia y Vngría, / Inglaterra y Alemaña' [I have looked for her in Spain / France, Italy, Slavonia, / Flanders, Poland, and Hungary / England and Germany] (quoted in Beccaria Lago 1997, 183 vv. 10–13). And he would ultimately die and be buried in Vienna, making him something of a citizen – if not of the cosmos, then at least – of Europe.

Like many of the cosmopolitans in Appiah's book, then, Castillejo was a 'traveller of the world' who learned about other cultures firsthand. For the U.S. philosopher, travel is thought to be one of the constitutive elements of cosmopolitanism, whatever the motive for travel may be: 'The urge to migrate is no less natural than the urge to settle. At the same time, most of those who have learned the languages and customs of other places haven't done so out of mere curiosity. A few were looking for food for thought; most were looking for food' (2004, xviii). In more personal sections of *Cosmopolitanism*, Appiah draws on his own mixed cultural and educational experiences of growing up in Ghana with a mother from England and a father with ties to the Asante royal family of Ghana. His book is dedicated to his mother, whom he calls 'citizen of one world, and many' and points out that she continues to live in Ghana and intends to be buried there (despite the fact that her Ghanan spouse died years ago). But foreign travel does not seem to have always agreed with Castillejo. In his 'Respuesta del Autor a un caballero que le preguntó qué era la causa de hallarse tan bien en Viena' [Reply of the Author to a Gentleman Who Asked Him the Cause of Finding Himself Well in Vienna], evidently written after 1525, he suggests that he might have preferred to end up back in Spain, rather than one day dying in Germany, complaining that 'Quién t'engañó, Castillejo, / estando bien en España / a venirte a Alemaña / para dexar tu pellexo / en tierra agena y extraña?' [Who tricked you, Castillejo / doing well in Spain / to come to Germany / to leave your skin / in a strange and foreign land?] (quoted in Beccaria Lago 1997, 198 vv. 101–5).

More than his travels and biographical sketch, Castillejo's proto-cosmopolitanism is laid out in his own rewritings of Ovid. In fact, it might seem ironic that it was the self-proclaimed purist Castillejo who, before Navagero, Boscán, or Garcilaso, betrayed his alleged desire to keep Spain pure from the 'musas latinas' [Latin muses]. As both Cossío and Beccaria Lago have noted, following the highly moralizing versions of Ovid that were produced during the Middle Ages, Castillejo was the first poet to faithfully translate parts of Ovid's *Metamorphoses* into Spanish. In fact, Cossío singles out Castillejo's 'Píramo y Tisbe' [Pyramus and Thisbe] for demonstrating his 'understanding of its full meaning, without moralizings or allegories' (quoted in Beccaria Lago 1997, 377–8). With Cossío, Beccaria Lago agrees that 'Píramo y Tisbe' was probably the first such attempt in Spanish to write a non-moralizing mythological *fábula*. And it is important to note that Castillejo did so at least nine years before Boscán finished his lengthy and ambitious 'Leandro' based on the classical myth of Hero and Leander. In contrast, his version of the Acteon myth is highly moralizing.

Thus, Castillejo's predilection for Roman poetry can be appreciated in his own admirable translations of it into Castilian, demonstrating at least some degree of 'receptiveness to art and literature from other places' in the cosmopolitan vein. At a time when non-moralizing adaptations of Ovidian stories were just beginning, Castillejo produced innovative adaptations of a past culture. Against the backdrop of anti-cosmopolitan sentiments in his original poetry, hostile toward Boscán and Garcilaso in particular, such receptiveness might seem to neutralize his anti-cosmopolitanism. Could it be that Castillejo was merely against the mixture of foreign or past elements with literature in Spanish but that he did not conceive of a translation as anything but an aide to make a foreign literature more accessible to those who could not read the original? That is, he may not have been opposed to foreign elements per se, but only insofar as these seemed to invade the alleged 'purity' of Castilian literature. No matter how the problem is addressed, Castillejo's engagement with Ovid's poetry, even if only a good translation, demonstrates a receptiveness toward another culture, one that Castilian speakers evidently had something to learn from (otherwise, why the need for a good translation)?

It is in the light of his problematized cosmopolitanism that I now move to a closer reading of another of Castillejo's original poems, one that has not been widely studied by critics. Through this analysis, I find that his alleged antipathy to cultural contamination – his traditionalism – finds significant disjuncture. Exploring the cosmopolitan tensions in one of his octosyllabic poems, 'La transfiguración de un vizcaíno' [The Transfiguration of a Vizcayan], I read this poem not as a mocking parody of Ovid – a foreign poet who wrote in a strange tongue – but as a more complex transformative imitation showing a deeper appreciation of the *Metamorphoses* and of its possibilities for Spanish letters. And yet, even in this poem, there remain elements of anti-cosmopolitanism, more subdued than in his attacks on Boscán and Garcilaso, but present nonetheless. In this way, Castillejo at once staves off what he sees as foreign contagion while also, in a limited manner, perhaps unwittingly he helps make the Spain of his day just slightly more cosmopolitan.

Ovid's tremendous importance in the Iberian Peninsula had been appreciated by scholars of early modern literature even before Rudolf Schevill devoted his 1913 monograph, *Ovid in the Renascence in Spain*, to the topic. Ovid's works were held in high esteem, and his mythological narratives became the basis for countless imitations. Indeed, some of the greatest poems of the sixteenth and seventeenth centuries are serious reworkings of myths based on Ovid, like Garcilaso's sonnet 'A Daphne ya los braços le crecían' [Daphne's Arms Were Already Growing] and Góngora's *Fábula de Polifemo y Galatea* [The Fable of Polyphemus and Galathea].

Despite his prestige, however, Ovid was at times treated less than seriously by prominent Spanish writers. In the seventeenth century, in *Don Quijote*, for instance, Cervantes depicts a risible counterpart to Ovid in the character of the Humanist Cousin, author of *Las transformaciones* [The

Transformations]. The Humanist Cousin shares Don Quijote's penchant for confusing fact with fiction as he says that he will use the information from Don Quijote's vision of the Cave of Montesinos, as if it were fact, happy to have learned 'lo que se encierra en esta cueva de Montesinos, con las mutaciones de Guadiana y de las lagunas de Ruidera, que me servirán para el *Ovidio español* que traigo entre manos' [that which is enclosed in this Cave of Montesinos, with the transformations of the Guadiana and the lakes of Ruidera, which will serve me for my *Spanish Ovid* which I hold in my hands] (1978, 2.24). Similarly, Góngora and Quevedo among others, wrote burlesque versions of Ovidian myths as well, such as Góngora's 'Romance de Píramo y Tisbe' [Ballad of Pyramus and Thisbe], treating these characters and stories with somewhat less empathy than did the Latin poet, in what Alberto Sánchez has called the 'burlesque degradation of mythological themes in the Baroque period' (1998, 10). Góngora's satire is directed not only at the characters in that poem, but also at the Latin poet himself, whom the Cordoban poet introduces into the poem punning on his name, place of origin, and nose-shape: 'el licenciado Nasón / (bien romo o narigudo)' [the licenciate Nasón / whether big- or snub-nosed] (1998, vv. 19–20).

The historical literary moment of Castillejo's poem is much earlier than the burlesque treatments of Góngora and Quevedo, who perhaps in those poems were signalling a certain exhaustion with the *Metamorphoses* after a hundred or so years of Spanish Ovidian adulation. I would argue that the less-than-serious reworking of Ovid in Castillejo's 'Transfiguración de un vizcaíno' is not so much a degradation of Ovid, given that it is not closely based on a particular Ovidian narrative, but rather that it is a transformative imitation in George W. Pigman's well-known sense of that term.[4]

Castillejo's 'La transfiguración de un vizcaíno, gran bebedor de vino' [Transfiguration of a Vizacayan, Heavy Wine Drinker] is obviously jocose in its intention, and the transformation it entails seems quite ridiculous, at first glance, perhaps even akin to an Ovidian metamorphosis. Written in ten nine-verse stanzas of rhyming octosyllabic verse, the poem highlights how a drunken Basque drinks himself into absolute poverty because of his love of alcohol, and is ultimately transformed into an insect through Bacchus's intercession.[5] As the poem relates, as soon as the Basque drank, he would already be thirsty again, for as the poet puts it, 'pero junto al paladar / tuvo una esponja por vena, / que, acabada de mojar, / se le tornaba a secar / como el agua en el arena' [but next to his palate / he had a sponge as a vein, / that, as soon as it got wet, / would become dry / like water in the sand] (1998, vv. 24–8). This image of eternally frustrated thirst may be an allusion to Tantalus, who, in book 4 of the *Metamorphoses*, suffers irreparable thirst and hunger: 'Tántalo está las aguas deseando / que a la boca le llegan, y desea / el árbol cuya fruta está tocando' [Tantalus desires that the waters / reach his mouth, and desires / the tree whose fruit is touching] (1990, 4.790–2). In order to fund his addiction, Castillejo's Vizcayan sells off everything he owns, little by little, from his undergarments, to his swords, to his footwear – 'las botas y cuero' [his boots and leather] (1998, v. 45) – until, ultimately he sells his own skin, as Castillejo puns on 'cuero' [skin]. He was left with nothing to drink but his soul (1998, v. 54). Finally, in another allusion to classical culture, Castillejo's character asks for the intercession not of Jesus or the Virgin Mary, but of Bacchus. Thus, having prayed that he not die of thirst, the god converts him into a 'mosquito,' while preserving his 'inclination and appetite.' In this light, the evocation of 'Malvasia' (1998, v. 13) – referring to the Malevizi region of Crete, the origin of some of the wines he prefers – may also serve Castillejo's purpose of providing a more direct link to the Hellenic god of wine.

While I have pointed out a few possible connections to Ovid's *Metamorphoses*, one potential pitfall of this reading might be that among the many Ovidian transformations – from nymph to tree, from boy into flower – there are none about mosquitoes. Indeed, *sensu stricto*, there are no insectival metamorphoses at all. The choice of mosquito seems quite strange, conjuring up the image of a winged creature that sucks blood. One way to explain Castillejo's selected transformation would be to take it metaphorically, drawing on the time-honoured relationship between blood and wine; so the blood that the mosquito will draw is akin to the drunkard's beloved red wine. But the image can be read more literally as well. According to the early eighteenth-century *Diccionario de Autoridades*, 'mosquito' was the term used for various small flies. It referred not only to what in modern Spanish is called a mosquito ('hinchan la parte que pican' [they inflame the part they bite]), but also the common fruit fly ('se crian en el vino ù vinagre' [they breed in wine or vinegar]):

Insecto pequeñissimo, especie de mosca, de que hai varias especies. Unos hai con zancas muy largas, que llaman zancúdos ù de trompetilla, por el sonido u zumbido que hacen: otros hai mui pequeñitos y cortos de alas y piernas, pero muy molestos y venenosos, porque hinchan la parte que pican, y otros que se crian en el vino ù vinagre, y en la humedad de las cuevas, que no hacen mal alguno.

[Tiny insect, a species of fly, of which there are various species. Some have very long legs, that are called 'leggy' or 'little trumpet mosquitoes,' for the sound or buzz that they make; there are others with very small legs and wings, which are very bothersome and venomous, because they inflame the part they bite, and others that breed in wine or vinegar, and in the humidity of caves, that do not cause any harm at all.]

Thus, rather than the story of a small vampire, Castillejo's transformation depicts a completely innocuous insect that 'breed[s] in wine or vinegar' and, metaphorically, a person with a penchant for wine, as the *Diccionario*'s next entry continues: 'Por alusion llaman al que acude frequentemente à la taberna' [By allusion, it refers to a man who regularly frequents the tavern].

As I mentioned above, none of Ovid's stories portray a fruit fly, mosquito, or other insect in metamorphosis. The closest transformation within the animal kingdom between Castillejo's 'mosquito' and one of Ovid's creatures would be the story of Arachne, involving the transformation of a woman into a spider. Of course, a spider is not technically an insect according to modern entomology, but rather an arachnid. However, in the sixteenth and seventeenth centuries, no such distinction between insect and arachnid was made, and in his 1611 *Tesoro*, Covarrubias defined 'araña' [spider] as 'un animalejo de especie de insectos' [a little animal of the species of insects]. In the story of Arachne from book 6 of the *Metamorphoses*, made famous by Velazquez's painting *The Weavers*, the admiration of the weaver's skill by her companions leads to her boastful challenge to Athena. The goddess then reduces her to a spider, and as such, one who will keep on subtly spinning silk in her amazing manner. Arachne is paradigmatic of Ovidian transformations, in that, in general, the thing or animal into which a character is transfigured often has a metonymical connection with the ontological entity that preceded it. For instance, in another illustrative example, from book 3 of the *Metamorphoses*, Narcissus is transformed into a flower whose image will be reflected in water, just as it was when he gazed adoringly upon his own reflected beauty as a boy. A second paradigmatic element of Arachne's tale is the intercession of a supernatural being in the transformation. In her case, the goddess Athena causes the change; in the case of Narcissus, it is Nemesis. Frequently, however, it is Bacchus, the god of wine.

In a footnote on this poem in her book on the life and works of Castillejo, Beccaria Lago suggests that the Ovidian transformation most like the Basque's may be that of the daughters of Minaues in book 4.[6] Indeed, both are transformations into winged creatures – the Mineides are turned into bats – and in both cases the change is sudden and described concisely in parts. For the Basque, 'el corpezuelo se troca, / aunque antes era bien chico, / en otra cosa mas poca, / y la cara con la boca se hicieron un rostrico' [His little body changes / even though it was quite small before, / into another even smaller thing / and his face with his mouth became a tiny mug] (1998, vv. 77–81). Similarly, for Ovid's Mineides, 'los brazos se hacen alas y se extiende / un cuero por sus miembros delicado / (...) Cada una de ellas vuela y bien lo siente / mas no son plumas causa de este vuelo / sino alas de pellejo transparente' [their arms became wings and a film extended itself upon their delicate limbs ... Each one of them flies and suffers this fate, but feathers are not the cause of this flight, but rather wings of transparent skin] (1990, 4.698–9; 4.704–6).

The transformed state of affairs usually contains a relationship of contiguity with the former state of affairs. Thus, as Arachne was punished by Athena to do that which she did so well but reduced to a spider, the Mineides, as Ovid explains, are forced to live in darkness, because that is how they lived beforehand, in metaphorical darkness, refusing to acknowledge that the young god Bacchus was indeed a god, and ignoring his rites and rituals. Likewise, the mosquito-fruit fly, in its new ontological state, will above all else continue to obsessively drink wine as did its precursor entity, the Basque. Since he was about to die of alcohol thirst before the conversion (so the poem tells us), it is hard to think of this metamorphosis as a punishment, unlike those of Arachne and the Mineides. Rather, it may be more of a reward, for now the Basque will not have to worry about purchasing the liquor he loves and needs.

Castillejo's narrative poem can also be read as following the pattern of desire set up by Ovid. Indeed, a common thread among most of the *Metamorphoses* is the involvement of love. While sometimes it is the love of a god for a mortal that leads to the mortal's transformation – for instance, the myth of Daphne and Apollo – in other stories, it is a mortal's love of something that leads to the conversion. Thus, Narcissus's self-love leads to his transformation. In the Basque's case, it is his love of Bacchus's libation.

While Castillejo is generally thought to be, quite separately, on the one hand a translator of Ovid, and on the other, the traditionalist writer of Castilian verse in the *cancioneril* style, this reading of the 'Transfiguración' posits Castillejo as something of an innovative poet. The 'Transfiguración,'

I would argue, is better read as a transformative imitation in octo-syllables, with thematics and tropes from a Latin author. It is neither a translation, nor a disrespectful burlesque degradation. Rather it is a metamorphosis in the vein of Ovid's, but different in the ways adduced above. Despite his virulent attacks on the Italianate innovators, always tinged with at least a small degree of explicit xenophobia, Castillejo is himself an innovator, transforming the Latin tradition into something new, with the transformation of a man into a mosquito. Cultures are always hybrid to some extent, or, as Appiah puts it, 'cultural purity is an oxymoron.' Well before Garcilaso and Boscán, Castillejo's Castilian tradition had already inherited many strands from other lands, includ-ing his allegedly despised Tuscany.

It is difficult to provide sufficient explanations of Castillejo's various attitudes toward the incorporation of non-Spanish elements into his writing, that is, to glean from his poetic writings his views on cosmo-politan mongrelization. Against the backdrop of his explicitly anti-cosmopolitan critiques of Boscán and Garcilaso – where he demonstrated a kind of xenophobia, specifically with respect to poetic innovations drawing on Latin and Italian authors, and likened the essentialized transgressors who hybridize Spanish poetry to Lutherans, foreign spies, and enemies of the Inquisition and the nation – his 'Transfiguración de un vizcaíno' demonstrates Castillejo's readiness to have a laugh at the expense of an Iberian non-Castilian – the Basque – in a very non-cosmopolitan way. In two of his other poems about Basques, Castillejo is similarly disparaging.[7] Castillejo – who in fact visited Bilbao en route to England in 1522 – would not be alone in this ridicule of Basques in Spanish letters. Indeed, the tradition of mocking Basques continues throughout the century and into the next. But it certainly does not make Castillejo a proponent of increasing understanding of others.[8] Furthermore, his poem may even suggest that *Wanderlust* – one of the most important elements for Appiah of the cosmopolitan who seeks to learn from other cultures – is deleterious, confirming the negative ap-praisal of travel associated with his lengthy stay in Germany attested to in his 'Respuesta del Autor a un caballero.' After all, the Vizcayan drinks wines not only from Spain, but also from the Rhone in Germany and Malevizi in Greece. He would have acquired a taste for such wines presumably from peregrinations in those regions. While Appiah's cases and arguments for the impact of travel on cosmopolitan sympathies are compelling, travel itself seems insufficient in leading to personal cosmo-politanism. Despite his considerable time abroad, Castillejo is indeed a case in point of a traveller who seems to remain somewhat intolerant of other nationalities and continues to prefer strongly his own Castilian people and land over everyone and everywhere else. Perhaps Appiah's category is overly optimistic about the impact that foreign travel can have on an individual whether in the past or in the present. For instance, most travel of Southern Europeans during Castillejo's adulthood – almost perfectly synchronic with the reign of Charles V – would have been in the crusade against the Turks, in an attempt to stop the advance of Islam and maintain Catholic hegemony in Europe, hardly an openness to other nations and ideas.

Complicating his proto-cosmopolitan status, however, is Castillejo's deep knowledge of Ovid's *Metamorphoses*. Translation alone might not necessarily be inconsistent with a view that cultures should maintain their alleged purity, for he might still analyse the Latin and the Spanish traditions as distinct. Nonetheless, the 'Transfiguración de un vizcaíno' demonstrates true hybridization of Spanish and classical Roman culture, as the poet incorporates the use of his proud, autochthonous octosyllabic metre to write a poem with echoes of Ovid's *Metamorphoses*. Indeed, the very term used in sixteenth-century Spain for Ovid's metamorphoses, his *Transformaciones*, is the one used by Salman Rushdie to talk about cosmopolitanism itself, which is 'the *transformation* that comes of new and unexpected combinations of human beings, cultures, ideas, politics, movies, songs' (Rushdie quoted in Appiah 2004, emphasis mine). While such a transformation does not seem to have happened in Castillejo himself, it does occur to a limited extent within the 'Transfiguración de un vizcaíno.'

Thus Castillejo is a complex voice in the incipient cosmospolity of Renaissance Spain, one whose lauded version of 'Pyramus and Thisbe' – predating Boscan's 'Leander' by several years – may have inspired the cosmopolitan and innovative Barcelonan poet whose advances he later rejected. Additionally, Castillejo is also a forebear to seventeenth-century poets like Cervantes who continued to write in traditional metres but with complex thematics and rhetoric (what some critics have called Cervantes's 'retrograde' tendencies in poetry, in octosyllabic works like 'Romance de los celos' [Ballad of Jealousy], a poem that, I have argued elsewhere, mediates a complex dialogue between the Spanish present and the classical past).[9] Strangely enough, Castillejo is also a precursor of the most cosmopolitan of baroque poets, Góngora, whose own romance, 'Pyramus and Thisbe,' is a jocose Ovidian parody written in octosyllables. An analysis and contextualization of Castillejo's poetry through the lens of Appiah's *Cosmopolitanism* helps us see that 'traditionalism' and 'innovation' are not isolated concepts in the history of literature and art, but categories with larger socio-cultural ramifications.

NOTES

1 See Rivers, in the Introduction to *Renaissance and Baroque Poetry of Spain*.
2 Boscán describes this influential conversation with Navagero in his well-known 'Carta a la Duquesa de Soma' which serves as preface to book II of his works, where he writes 'Por que estando un día en Granada con el Navagero (al qual, por haver sido varon tan celebrado en nuestros días, he querido aquí nombralle a vuestra señoría) tratando con él en cosas de ingenio y de letras, y especialmente en las variedades de muchas lenguas, me dixo: porque no provava en lengua castellana sonetos y otras artes de trobas usadas por los buenos authores de Italia; y no solamente me lo dixo así livianamente, más aun me rogó, que lo hiziesse' [While in Granada one day with Navagero (whom I wanted to name for Your Lordship, for his having been such a celebrated man in our times) discussing with him intellectual and literary matters, and especially the variations between languages, he said to me: 'why not try to write in Castilian the sonnets and other kinds of poems composed by the good authors of Italy?' And he didn't say it t o me lightly but begged me to do it] [fol. XXr–XXv]; I have modernized the orthography following common practice, where it does not affect pronunciation); the meeting between Boscán and Navagero is mentioned by several critics including Navarrete (1994, 60). All translations from the Spanish are mine.
3 For instance, Navarrete calls Castillejo a 'reactionary' writer (1994, 127).
4 Pigman distinguishes transformative imitation from other varieties (emulation or eristic imitation). For Pigman, transformative imitation is 'grounded in an awareness of the historical distance between past and present,' and involves the latter poet's 'critical reflection on or correction of the model' (1980, 32).
5 Having 'fun' at the expense of the Basque was common in early modern Castilian works, and even Cervantes was not immune to the impulse; for instance, in *Don Quijote* 1. 8–9, the author pokes fun at the way Sancho de Azpetia speaks Spanish. For a more complete treatment of the topic, see P. Anselmo de Legarda.
6 The tale of Pyramus and Thisbe – which Castillejo translated – is one of the tales told within the story of the Mineides in book 4.

7 See 'A un vizcaíno,' which begins 'Servido no ge lo tienes' (He is not pleased).
8 Other signs of his ethnic or nationalist intolerance can be seen in *Diálogo entre Adulación y Verdad*, where he negatively stereotypes various nations: 'a Movscovia la grossera, / y a Polonia y a Rusía / donde la glotonería / tiene puesta la vandera, / ... a Alemaña populosa / pero ingrata y codiciosa / sobre quantas oy hallamos; / y baxemos / a Flandes, donde veremos / la miseria y la avaricia. / A Inglaterra y su malicia' [to Moscow the rude, and to Poland and Russia, where gluttony has raised its flag ... And Germany, populous yet ungrateful and covetous above all others; and let's descend to Flanders, where we'll see misery and avarice. And England and her malice] (quoted in Beccaria Lago 1997, 259, vv. 1516–19; vv. 1522–30).
9 See Wagschal.

WORKS CITED

Appiah, Kwame Anthony. 2004. *Cosmopolitanism: Ethics in a World of Strangers*. New York: Norton.
Anselmo de Legarda, P. 1953. *Lo 'Vizcaíno' en la literatura castellana*. San Sebastián: Biblioetca Vascongada de los Amigos del País.
Beccaria Lago, María Dolores. 1997. *Vida y obra de Cristóbal de Castillejo*. Madrid: Añejos del Boletín de la Real Academia Española.
Boscán, Juan. 1543. *Las obras de Boscan y algunas de Garcilasso de la Vega repartidas en quatro libros*. Barcelona: Carles Amorós.
Castillejo, Cristóbal de. 1998. *Obra completa*. Ed. Rogelio Reyes Cano. Madrid: Fundación José Antonio de Castro.
Cervantes, Miguel de. 1978. *El ingenioso hidalgo don Quijote de la Mancha*. Ed. Luis Murillo. 5th ed. 2 vols. Madrid: Castalia.
Cossío, José María de. 1952. *Fábulas mitológicas en España*. Madrid: Espasa-Calpe, S.A.
Covarrubias, Sebastián de. 1994. *Tesoro de la lengua española o castellana*. Ed. Felipe C.R. Maldonado. Madrid: Castalia.
Diccionario de Autoridades. 1976. Facs. ed. 3 vols. Madrid: Real Academia Española.
Garrison, David. 1994. *Góngora and the 'Pyramus and Thisbe' Myth from Ovid to Shakespeare*. Newark, DE: Juan de la Cuesta.
Góngora y Argote, Luis de. 1998. 'La fábula de Píramo y Tisbe.' In *Romances II de Luis de Góngora*, ed. Antonio Carreira, 355–420. Barcelona: Quaderns Crema.
Moya del Baño, F. 1966. *El tema de Hero y Leandro en la literatura española*. Murcia, Spain: Publicaciones de la Universidad de Murcia.

Navarrete, Ignacio. 1994. *Orphans of Petrarch: Poetry and Theory in the Spanish Renaissance*. Berkeley: University of California Press.

Ovid. 1990. *Las metamorfosis*. Trans. Pedro Sánchez de Viana. Ed. Juan Francisco Alcina. Barcelona: Planeta.

Pigman III, G.W. 1980. 'Versions of Imitation in the Renaissance.' *Renaissance Quarterly* 33.1:1–32.

Rivers, Elías L. 1966. *Renaissance and Baroque Poetry of Spain*. Prospect Heights, IL: Waveland.

Sánchez, Alberto. 1998. 'Historia y poesía: La historia de Piramo y Tisbe en el *Quijote*.' *Anales Cervantinos* 34:9–22.

Wagschal, Steven. 2007. 'Digging up the Past: The Archeology of Emotion in Cervantes's "Romance de los celos."' *Cervantes: Bulletin of the Cervantes Society of America* 27.2:213–28.

11 Ovid's 'Hermaphroditus' and Intersexuality in Early Modern Spain

PABLO RESTREPO-GAUTIER

In chapter 1 of *Guzmán de Alfarache* (1599–1604) by Mateo Alemán, the narrator describes a hermaphrodite monster purportedly born in Ravenna, Italy, in 1512: 'Tenía de la cintura para arriba todo su cuerpo, cabeza y rostro de criatura humana; pero un cuerno en la frente. Faltábanle los brazos y dióle naturaleza por ellos en su lugar dos alas de murciélago. Tenía en el pecho figurado la Y pitagórica y en el estómago hacia el vientre una cruz ... bien formada. Era hermafrodito y muy formados los dos naturales sexos. No tenía más de un muslo en él una pierna con su pie de milano y las garras de la misma forma. En el ñudo de la rodilla tenía un ojo solo' [From the waist up it was fully human; however, it had a horn on its forehead. It had no arms and nature gave it two bat wings. It had a Pythagoric Y on its chest and on its stomach, a clearly marked cross ... It was a hermaphrodite and had both sets of genitals clearly defined. It only had one thigh with one leg and a hawk's claw for a foot. On the knee it had one eye] (1962, 70).[1] The Ravenna monster became a popular creature in European culture, appearing not only in literary works but also in scientific pieces such as *Aristotle's Master-Piece* (London, 1684), a manual of gynaecology and obstetrics. The manual presents an illustration of the monster, and describes it providing details similar to those presented in *Guzmán*: 'A Monster was Born in Ravenna, having a Horn upon the Crown on his Head, and besides, two Wings, and one Foot alone, most like the Feet of Birds of Prey, and in the Knee thereof an Eye, the Privities of Male and Female, the rest of the body like a Man, as you may see by this figure' (1962, 1.4). The Ravenna monster, an imaginary composite of animal, human, and mystical features, possesses male and female genitalia, revealing both fascination and abhorrence toward intersexuality.

Attitudes toward intersexed individuals ranged from fear, abhorrence, and rejection to an ambivalent acceptance of hermaphrodites as God's creatures. Spanish authors of the period found Ovid's 'Hermaphroditus' to be a useful tool to express their own varied and ambivalent attitudes toward intersexuality.[2] Their choice of this Ovidian myth is not surprising given their subject matter, and neither is their preference for classical sources since, as Gayle Bradbury argues, 'almost inevitably the overlap between Christian morality and classical culture produced ambivalence and contradiction in seventeenth-century attitudes towards irregular sexuality' (1981, 570).

Taking a moral approach to intersexuality, Sebastián de Covarrubias metamorphoses Ovid's 'Hermaphroditus' tale in Emblem 64 of *Emblemas morales* (Madrid, 1610). In contrast to Covarrubias, his father, Sebastián de Horozco takes a scientific approach to the matter in poems 257 and 258 of his *Cancionero*. Their contradictory conclusions about intersexuality are corroborated by Juan Pérez de Moya and Fray Baltasar de Vitoria's commentaries on hermaphrodites and give us valuable insight into the anxiety the two authors and their contemporaries felt about the binary gender system.

Rudolph Schevill's seminal study, *Ovid in Renascence Spain* (1913), confirms the popularity of Ovid's *Metamorphoses* in the Iberian Peninsula. Chapter 3 focuses on two translations of the *Metamorphoses* and on Cervantes' use of Ovid's work. Schevill states that 'particularly in Spain the vogue of this mythological poem steadily grows in the course of the fifteenth and sixteenth centuries. The evidence of this is frequent mention of the *Metamorphoses* by writers of all kinds, as well as numerous allusions to the tales therein contained' (1913, 146). As Schevill points out, the success of the translations into Spanish is evidence that Ovid's popularity 'extends far beyond the academic atmosphere' and that the *Metamorphoses* 'became known among all readers of fiction' (1971, 146).

Further evidence that Ovid's mythological poem was well known beyond academic circles is its frequent use in books of emblems, popular educational tools that circulated widely and were used for didactic or recreational purposes. The 'Índice de fuentes de los lemas' [Index to the Sources of the Mottoes] of the outstanding *Enciclopedia de emblemas españoles ilustrados* by Antonio Bernat Vistarini and John T. Cull lists sixty-seven references to the *Metamorphoses* in Spanish emblem books, far more than the references to all other Ovidian works combined (1999, 882).

Ovid's tale, 'Hermaphroditus ' has a rich and complex mythographic tradition in medieval and early modern Europe, as Lauren Silberman shows in her article 'Mythographic Transformations of Ovid's Herma-phrodite.' According to Silberman, 'mythographic interpretations tend to focus either on the physiological or the moral aspects of Ovid's story' (1988, 645). Silberman does not include any Spanish adaptations of Ovid's 'Hermaphroditus' but her conclusions apply to the treatment of the tale in Spain. Silberman points out that 'one of the more widely dif-fused interpretations finds in Ovid's myth a scientific explanation of her-maphrodites. According to this account, the fountain of Salmacis represents the womb, which is said to comprise seven chambers' (1988, 645). This scientific approach reaches great popularity in Spain. The defi-nition of 'andrógeno' in Covarrubias's *Tesoro de la lengua castellana* [Treasure of the Spanish Language] states that 'en la matriz de la muger ay tres senos a la parte derecha y tres a la izquierda y uno en medio; los unos engendran varones, los otros hembras, el del medio hermafrodito' [there are three chambers in the right side of the womb and three on the left and one in the middle; one set produces males, the other set females, and the middle one a hermaphrodite] (1977, 119). In his *Philosophía secreta* (1595), Pérez de Moya uses the scientific explanation to interpret Ovid's 'Hermaphroditus': 'La significación desto es que por la fuente Salmacis se entiende el lugar medio entre los seis susodichos, y cuando en aquel lugar deciende la viril simiente, y de la hembra ... hácese una cosa que ambas virtudes parecen, señalándose en un solo cuerpo vaso de mujer y de varón' [Its meaning is that the fountain of Salmacis signifies the mid-dle space in between the six chambers, and when a male and a female seed join there, a thing is created that resembles both, creating in one body both man and woman] (1928, 240).[3]

In Emblem 64 of *Emblemas morales*, Covarrubias metamporphoses Ovid's 'Hermaphroditus' poem into a baroque emblem, a hybrid of im-age and word, of verse and prose. He also turns it into an 'Ovidio mor-alizado,' aligning his emblem with the hermeneutic tradition that extracts moral lessons from classical myths. Covarrubias develops his metamorphosis within the most purely emblematic tradition: he frag-ments the Ovidian tale, chooses some elements from the fragments, modifies them, and combines them with material from other sources to produce a new meaning.

Emblem 64 has the basic tripartite emblematic structure: a Latin motto, an illustration or *pictura*, and a Spanish-language epigram or *subscriptio*. To these three elements, Covarrubias adds a fourth: a prose explanation on a separate page. The *pictura* in Emblem 64 shows an individual dressed in female garb, bearded, arms crossed over the chest, standing in front of an idealized rural landscape with church spires in the background. The motto, from Ovid's *Metamorphoses*, hovers over the woman's head, and reads 'Neutrumque et utrumque' [Neither and both] (1973, 164r). The unusual combination of male and female elements points to the outside of the binary gender system: judging by her dress, she is a woman, but judging by his beard he is a man. The motto gives us another piece of the puzzle: 'neither and both' (1973, 164r). For readers familiar with Ovid's 'Hermaphroditus' tale, the moral meaning of this image/word combination becomes clear. In case the reader misinterprets the *pictura*/motto riddle, the *subscriptio* and the prose explanation reiterate that Emblem 64 is a warning against confusing gender lines.

A close reading of the eight lines of the epigram sheds light on attitudes toward intersexuality in seventeenth-century Spain, which often demonize those who do not fit within traditional categories. The first four lines of the epigram emphasize that the individual in the engraving does not fit within any contemporary gender categories. Using masculine grammatical forms through the poem, the speaker claims that he is 'hic, y hac, y hoc' [him, her, and it] (1973, 164r), both male and female, but neither one nor the other. As traditional gender identities do not apply to him, he classifies himself as a 'tercero' [outsider], a lonely individual, an 'horrendo monstro y raro' [frightful and strange monster] (1973, 164r), and a 'mal agüero' [bad omen] (1973, 164r). He ends with a warning that if a man were to act in an effeminate manner, he would become like him ['que es otro yo'] (1973, 164r). Standing outside the gender system, the speaker's conclusions express sheer uncertainty about his gender identity.

The prose explanation (1973, 164v) retells Ovid's 'Hermaphroditus' and makes a few interpretative remarks about it: according to the fable, reads the explanation, Hermaphroditus, son of Mercury and Venus, as seen by his name, went to bathe in a fountain whose goddess was a nymph called Salmacis. She fell in love with the beauty of the youth, plunged into the water, and embraced him so tightly that he could not get rid of her. She asked the gods to make the embrace eternal and they became grafted onto each other. The author explains that this fable has much of natural and moral history, because among some of the wonders of nature occasionally a baby is born with both sexes. The author explains that he has already presented his moral interpretation in the *Tesoro de la lengua castellana* [Treasure of the Spanish Language]. He then points out that he borrows the last line of the epigram, 'Que es otro yo, si vive afeminado' [That he becomes like me, if he lives effeminately] (1973, 164v), from Cicero, and the motto, 'Neutrumque et utrumque' [Neither and both] (1973, 164v), from the fourth book of Ovid's *Metamorphoses*. The last sentence claims that the image is a portrait of the real-life bearded woman from Peñaranda.

Covarrubias, then, metamorphoses Ovid's androgynous and delicate youth into a real-life Spanish woman: Brígida de los Ríos, known as 'la Barbuda de Peñaranda,' a masculine bearded female that was the subject of a portrait by Juan Sánchez de Cotán (1560–1627). Covarrubias characterizes his Spanish Hermaphroditus as a monster, a frightful creature, which fascinates and repels at the same time. Emblem 64 constitutes a warning to men who adopt female characteristics, qualities, or manners, and indeed, to anybody who crosses and breaks down gender categories.

Covarrubias's characterization of Hermaphroditus as a monstrous individual is already foreshadowed in Ovid's text: the mythical hermaphrodite, fusion of Salmacis and Hermaphroditus, although fascinating and delicate, is unclassifiable and, consequently, fearsome and disturbing. The outcome of the youth's metamorphosis is so undesirable that Hermaphroditus himself asks his parents to metamorphose every man who touches the fountain's waters in the same manner as a punishment.

Elena del Río Parra points out in her excellent study, *Una era de monstruos: Representaciones de lo deforme en el Siglo de Oro español* [An Era of Monsters: Representations of Deformity in the Spanish Golden Age], 'lo monstruoso es, por definición, lo no natural, lo que está fuera de la taxonomía y es ajeno a cualquier otro orden' [the monstrous is, by definition, that which is not natural, that which stands outside taxonomies, and is foreign to the order of things] (2003, 16). That is precisely Covarrubias's strategy: placing the bearded woman from Peñaranda outside the gender system to signify that intersexuality is dangerous and must be feared.

Underscoring the monstrous and unclassifiable elements of Ovid's intersexed youth reveals much more than the simple moral warning. Del Río Parra points out that a monster can be presented in three different ways: 'Se puede presentar como asombro o prodigio que anuncia males y alimenta la superstición. Segundo, como documento científico que anima la curiosidad por descifrar a esta criatura escapada de las reglas de la creación. Tercero, como problema de los signos y de su capacidad para nombrar lo diferente, raro o insólito' [It can be presented as a thing of wonder that is a bad omen and feeds superstition. Second, as a scientific document which entices us to decipher this creature that escapes the rules of creation. Third, as a problem of signifiers and their ability to name things that are different, strange, or extremely unusual] (2003, 18).

All these three elements are present in Covarrubias's transformation of Hermaphroditus into the bearded woman from Peñaranda. First, there is an element of 'asombro' [fascination] toward this unclassifiable individual. The society of the period was intrigued by 'mujeres varoniles' [manly women], including 'barbudas' [bearded women], who appear in countless Spanish works of literature and art, such as numerous *comedias*, Cervantes' *Don Quijote*, Cotán's portrait, and Ribera's famous painting of Magdalena Ventura of the Abruzzi. Second, there is a desire in Covarrubias's emblem to find the reasons for the existence of such unusual individuals. Finally, and most interestingly, the emblem's *subscriptio* reveals that assigning a label to an individual who does not fit within an existing sign system is problematic. Neither the term 'hermafrodito' nor its contemporary synonym 'andrógeno' is used in the poem, as if assigning a label to the bearded man/woman would grant him/her a rightful place within the gender system. Placing hermaphrodites within the gender system would be counter to Covarrubias's desire to protect existing social categories. The epigram does mention, however, the two accepted gender categories: 'mujer' [woman] and 'hombre' [man]. In contrast, the Spanish Hermaphroditus receives a generic term that is not part of the gender discourse: 'tercero' [outsider].[4]

If Emblem 64 takes a moral approach and depicts Hermaphroditus as a monster, Horozco's *Cancionero* poems do nearly the opposite. According to Covarrubias's own definition of *monstro*, the androgynous youth would be the result of a 'parto contra la regla y orden natural' [a birth against the rule and the natural order] (1977, 812). Not so in poems 257 and 258 of Horozco's *Cancionero*, where hermaphrodites are 'cosa natural' [something natural] (1975, 139). Poem 257 poses the question of whether the birth of a hermaphrodite is 'natural / o monstruo contra natura' [natural / or monster 'contra natura'] (1975, 139). The answer given in poem 258 is based on the widely held belief described by Covarrubias and Pérez de Moya that the womb has seven chambers:

Los tres están contendiendo
Para concebir mugger,
Los otros contradiziendo,
Procurando y entendiendo
En que varón ha de ser.

El de en medio a sus anchuras
De todos quiere atraer,
Donde él las criaturas
Toman dentrambas naturas
Y todo lo quieren ser.

[The three chambers are battling
To conceive a woman
The other three are attacking
Trying to make sure
A man is conceived.
The middle one, feeling good,
Wants to attract them all,
And in it, all creatures
Take on both natures
And want to become it all.]   (1975, 139)

Based on this incorrect idea of the anatomy of the womb, Horozco concludes that a hermaphrodite 'mas es cosa natural / que monstruo contra natura' [is a thing of nature / rather than a monster 'contra natura'] (1975, 139). Furthermore, nature being part of divine creation implies that 'nacer hermafrodito [es] ... sobre toda razón, / voluntad y operación / del alto Dios infinito' [being born a hermaphrodite is, above all, / the will and work / of God] (1975, 139). Horozco is not alone among his contemporaries in considering hermaphrodites a natural phenomenon that should not be interpreted as an omen of bad things to come. Juan Pérez de Moya, in his *Philosophía secreta* (Alcalá de Henares, 1611), refers to the Ovidian tale to introduce his discussion on hermaphrodites and, like Horozco, concludes: 'porque se entienda que los hermafroditos no son por via de monstruosidad ... mas de natural ayuntamiento de varón y hembra' [so that we understand that hermaphrodites don't come into being from a monstrous pairing ... but rather from the union of male and female] (1928, 238). Pérez de Moya is arguing against the belief that hermaphrodites are conceived when the mother is impregnated by an animal or a monstrous creature. Fray Baltasar de Vitoria in the second part of *Teatro de los dioses de la gentilidad* (Salamanca, 1620–3) agrees with both Horozco and Moya and, using the language of 'conceptista' theorists, presents hermaphrodites as 'un artificio grande de naturaleza' [a great device of Nature] (1722, 60): 'dice el grande español Quintiliano, es la naturaleza muy amiga de la variedad, y así con ella parece que se adorna y hermosea, y aunque al parecer de los ignorantes produce, y cria algunas cosas imeprfectas, y monstruosas, con ellas se muestra ella mas bella y Hermosa. Tal es el caso presente del hermafrodito' [Quintilian, the great Spaniard, says that Nature likes variety, and adorns itself with it. Although some ignorant people think Nature creates imperfect and monstrous things, with these very things, Nature becomes more beautiful] (1722, 60).

Although seemingly arguing for an acceptance and even admiration of hermaphrodites, Vitoria requires them to make a behavioural choice to adjust to the gender system: 'a los que así son, los llaman hermafroditos, porque pueden usar de entrambos miembros, y aunque es esto en la potencia, en el hecho no les es permitido en ley de Christiandad, sino que hagan elección de la pieça que han de usar, y de esa se aprovechen' [those who are this way are called hermaphrodites because they can use both sets of genitals. However, this is only in theory, for in actual life Christian law does not allow them to act that way and forces them to choose which piece to use, and use it well] (1722, 63).

In spite of their fascination with intersexuality, Vitoria and his contemporaries find it problematic to accept hermaphrodites as God's creatures as opposed to 'monstros' [monsters] because such acceptance can lead to the inclusion of a third category within a strictly dualistic gender system. Although the authors seem to agree with Horozco that hermaphrodites are created by 'voluntad y operación / del alto Dios infinito' [the will and work / of God] (1975, 139), they find intersexuality acceptable only as a biological phenomenon and not as part of the constructed gender system.

Legends such as the birth of the Ravenna monster, as it appears in *Guzmán de Alfarache,* and paintings such as the bearded women by Ribera and Sánchez de Cotán are evidence of the interest intersexed individuals exerted on early modern Spaniards. Authors such as Covarrubias and Moya use Ovid's 'Hermaphroditus' tale to give moral or scientific interpretations of intersexuality. Faced with individuals created by God who nonetheless defy classification within the binary gender system, the four authors arrive at widely differing interpretations of intersexuality. While Horozco, Moya, and Victoria indicate that intersexed individuals are a normal part of nature, Covarrubias, in his *Tesoro de la lengua castellana,* argues that their birth is *contra natura.* All four authors do agree, nonetheless, that finding a place for them in their society is problematic. While accepting the birth of intersexed individuals as natural, Horozco, Moya, and Vitoria do reveal a profound uneasiness with intersexuality. Covarrubias, on the other hand, presents intersexed individuals in a fully negative light. Such uneasiness and, in Covarrubias's case, outright condemnation, may arise from the fear that if individuals who have both male and female genitals are a normal part of creation then the binary gender system, based on two sexes, may have to be questioned and indeed modified. The authors avoid the potential for subversion innate in a 'third sex' by understanding intersexuality in ways which confirm the validity of the binary gender system, such as in Covarrubias's treatment of the issue in Emblem 64 where he metamorphoses Ovid's Hermaphroditus into the Barbuda de Peñaranda as a warning against effeminate male behaviour.

NOTES

1 All translations are by the author unless otherwise referenced.
2 Ovid tells the tale of Hermaphroditus in book 4, lines 274 to 316, of the *Metamorphoses*. The Naiads in the caves of Mount Ida raise Hermaphroditus, son of Hermes and Aphrodite. At the age of fifteen, he leaves his native mountains and travels the world, reaching the Carians. The youth finds a clear pool of water, home to the nymph Salmacis. For Salmacis, it is love at first sight but Hermaphroditus is a true 'hombre esquivo.' She tries to seduce the beautiful youth but he threatens to leave if she continues her pursuit. She agrees to stop, lets him stay, and hides behind some branches. Hermaphroditus undresses and jumps into the clear waters. Salmacis follows him and, during a tight embrace, asks the gods to join them. The gods join them into one being, half male, half female. Hermaphroditus, metamorphosed, comes out of the water and asks his parents to poison the pool so that any male who bathes in its waters is transformed in the same manner. Hermes and Aphrodite grant their son his wish.
3 There are other early modern explanations for the birth of hermaphrodites. For instance, in his *Examen de ingenios para las ciencias* (1594), Juan Huarte de San Juan explains that 'especially in this case, where we see by experience, that if man's seed is of evil substance, and enjoy not a temperature convenient, the vegetative soul runs into a thousand disorders: for if the same be cold and moist more than it requisit, Hippocrates sayth, that men prove Eunuches, or Hermofrodites' (1959, 34).
4 In the prose explanation, the word 'Hermafrodito' (1973, 164v) does appear but only as a proper noun referring to Ovid's youth.

WORKS CITED

Alemán, Mateo. 1962. *Guzmán de Alfarache*. Ed. Samuel Gili y Gaya. Madrid: Espasa-Calpe.

Aristotle's Master-Piece, or the Secrets of Generation Displayed in All the Parts Thereof. 1684. London: J. How.

Bernat Vistarini, Antonio, and John. T. Cull. 1999. *Enciclopedia de emblemas españoles ilustrados*. Madrid: Akal Ediciones.

Bradbury, Gail. 1981. 'Irregular Sexuality in the Spanish "Comedia."' *Modern Language Review* 76:566–80.

Covarrubias Orozco, Sebastián de. 1973. *Emblemas morales 1610*. Ed. John Horden. Menston, Yorkshire: The Scolar Press.

– 1977. *Tesoro de la lengua castellana o española*. Madrid: Ediciones Turner.

Horozco, Sebastián de. 1975. *El Cancionero*. Ed. Jack Weiner. Bern: Herebert Lang.

Huarte de San Juan, Juan. *Examen de ingenios. The Examination of Mens Wits (1594)*. 1959. Trans. Richard Carew. Ed. Carmen Rogers. Gainesville, FL: Scholar's Facsimiles & Reprints.

Ovid, *Metamorphoses*. 1987. Trans. A.D. Melville. Ed. E.J. Kenney. Oxford: Oxford University Press.

Pérez de Moya, Juan. 1928. *Philosophía secreta*. Ed. Eduardo Gomez de Baquero. Madrid: Compañía iberoamericana de publicaciones.

Rio Parra, Elena del. 2003. *Una era de monstrous: Representaciones de lo deforme en el Siglo de Oro*. Pamplona: Universidad de Navarra.

Schevill, Rudolph. 1913. *Ovid and the Renascence in Spain*. Berkeley: University of California Press.

Silberman, Lauren. 1988. 'Mythographic Transformations of Ovid's Hermaphrodite.' *Sixteenth Century Journal* 19:643–52.

Vitoria, Fray Baltasar de. 1722. *Teatro de los dioses de la gentilidad*. Barcelona: Imprenta de J.P. Martí.

PART FOUR

Ovidian Fame

12 Ovidian Fame: Garcilaso de la Vega and Jorge de Montemayor as Orphic Voices in Early Modern Spain and the *Contamino* of the Orpheus and Eurydice Myth

BENJAMIN J. NELSON

Basing one's fame on classical writers was not uncommon during Spain's early modern period. In addition to the omnipresent *rota Virgilii*, writers were turning to other celebrated Romans, like Publius Ovidius Naso, or simply Ovid. Within a fictional space, Miguel de Cervantes' *Don Quijote*, for example, illustrates the popularity of imitating Ovid with the adventure involving the Cave of Montesinos.[1] The knight-errant and his squire Sancho Panza are led to the famous cave by a guide who is a 'famoso estudiante y muy aficionado a leer libros de caballerías' [a famous scholar and very fond of reading books of chivalry] (1978, 2.22.205; 2003, 632).[2] Inspired by Ovid's *Metamorphoses*, this self-described humanist is engaged with a *translatio studii* by recording Spain's own metamorphoses, including the origins of the 'lagunas de Ruidera' that are rumoured to be found within this cavernous landmark. The scholar describes to his travelling companions the status of his ongoing book project:

> Otro libro tengo también, a quien he de llamar *Metamorfoseos, o Ovidio español*, de invención nueva y rara; porque en él, imitando a Ovidio a lo burlesco, pinto quién fue la Giralda de Sevilla y el Ángel de la Madalena, quién el Caño de Vecinguerra, de Córdoba, quiénes los Toros de Guisando, la Sierra Morena, las fuentes de Leganitos y Lavapiés, en Madrid, no olvidándome de la del Piojo, de la del Caño Dorado y de la Priora; y esto, con sus alegorías, metáforas y translaciones, de modo que alegran, suspenden y enseñan a un mismo punto.

> [I've written another book which I'm going to call *Metamorfoseos, or the Spanish Ovid*, and its contents are most novel and unusual, because in it I

imitate Ovid in a burlesque style and describe the Giralda in Seville and the Angel Weather-Vane on St Mary Magdalene Church in Salamanca, the Vecinguerra Sewer in Cordova, the Bulls of Guisando, the Sierra Morena, the Fountains of Leganitos and Lavapiés in Madrid, not forgetting the Fountain of the Louse, the Fountain of the Gilt Tap and the Fountain of the Prioress, complete with allegories, metaphors and similes to delight, amaze and instruct all at once.] (1978, 2.22.206; 2003, 633)

By replacing classical metamorphoses with Iberia's own, this humanist directly engages Ovid in an *imitatio* that, he hopes, will garner him fame.

Over half a century before the publication of Cervantes' masterpiece, two distinct writers – one a posthumously celebrated poet, the other the first known contributor to the Spanish *libros de pastores* – attempted to achieve the same. Instead of presenting legendary transformations found on Spanish soil, however, they incorporated the figure of Orpheus, popularized by Ovid, to announce their emerging role as Spain's Orphic poets. As numerous Renaissance and early modern writers throughout Europe closely followed the *rota Virgilii* to become famous, others, as I will discuss shortly, chose different classical authors to imitate. In his third, and final, eclogue, the soldier-poet Garcilaso de la Vega decrees that his own myth (established by the preceding two eclogues) is tantamount to Ovid's, while, decades later, the courtier Jorge de Montemayor presents himself as an Orphic voice with the epic-like 'Canto de Orfeo' situated in the middle of his pastoral *La Diana* (1559).

In his study of Edmund Spenser's literary career, Patrick Cheney discusses how poets of Renaissance England were trying to fashion themselves as the 'new Orphic voice': 'the New Poet is to be the new national poet, heir to a long line of poets extending back to his native medieval heir, Chaucer, to his Continental classical heir, Virgil, and eventually to the legendary founder of poetry himself, Orpheus' (1993, 3). Cheney recognizes that poets during the sixteenth and seventeenth centuries imitated not only Virgil's literary career, but others – primarily Ovid's and St Augustine's:

> The Ovidian model traces a pattern of interrupted cyclic closure – the breaking of the Virgilian circle – by showing how the love lyric sabotages the poet's epic career ... Like the Virgilian, [the Ovidian model] is classical, triadic, semicircular, and political. Unlike the Virgilian, it locates love poetry at its centre, albeit in what looks to Ovid, reflecting on his blighted career, as a decidedly disastrous centre. (1993, 56–7)

Although Cheney focuses his study on Spenser's career, I would like to extend this Ovidian model to the idea of Garcilaso de la Vega and Jorge de Montemayor as Spain's new Orphic poets. For this latter pastoralist, I additionally argue that, similar to Edmund Spenser during his literary career, Montemayor attempted to follow not just the Ovidian model, but the Virgilian one also. Yet, who is the classical author of Orpheus – Virgil or Ovid?[3]

Since antiquity, the myth of Orpheus was transmitted through various texts, primarily Virgil's *Georgics* and Ovid's *Metamorphoses*. Confusion between these two, at times contradictory, texts ultimately equated this particular myth with the pastoral. In book 4 of Virgil's *Georgics*, Proteus, enraged at the divine Aristaeus, decries how the latter, chasing after Eurydice, led her to her death: 'She [Eurydice], in headlong flight along the river, if only she might escape you, saw not, doomed maiden, amid the deep grass the monstrous serpent at her feet that guarded the banks' (1999, 251). In book 10 of Ovid's text, which appeared chronologically after Virgil's, Eurydice is simply bitten by a poisonous serpent that she accidentally treads upon while in the company of nymphs: 'The new-wed bride, / Roaming with her gay Naiads through the grass. / Fell dying when a serpent struck her heel' (1986, 225).[4] Comparing these two versions of the myth, C.M. Bowra argues that Virgil's addition of Aristaeus is 'flimsy and uncanonical, and Virgil may perhaps have based it on the legend that Aristaeus was born of a nymph on a Mount Orpheus' (1952, 114). Bowra also adds that Ovid's spin of the tale is more faithful to the original. Additionally, Richard Tarrant states that 'Ovid's distanced account in *Metamorphoses* 10 of Orpheus' descent to the Underworld and his almost matter-of-fact description of the loss of Eurydice can make the emotively charged narrative in the *Georgics* seem overwrought and melodramatic' (2002, 26–7).[5]

Yet, at some point Virgil's distinct portrayal of Eurydice's demise became incorporated into Ovid's, creating a *contamino*. A sixteenth-century Spanish prose translation of the *Metamorphoses*, for example, places the blame on the shepherd Aristaeus (Aristeo) and his undying love for Eurydice.[6] After marrying her beloved Orpheus, Eurydice, on a stroll with her parents, encounters the shepherd Aristeo, who still pines for her: 'andando muerto por ella y no pudiendo alcanzar nada por ruegos, [Aristeo] se determinó a gozarla por fuerza, y a esta causa yendo tras ella por aquellos verdes prados, por donde ella con el temor huya, pisando una culebra que entre las yerbas estaba, fue muerta' [Walking dead for her and not being able to attain anything with begging, (Aristaeus) made up his mind to enjoy her by force, and pursued her with this cause through the green fields, through which she fled with fear; she died stepping on a snake that was hidden in the grass] (Ovid 1577, 180A). In his synopsis of the myth, Juan Pérez de Moya confirms the shepherd's pursuit of the nymph: 'A esta Eurídice, por su gran beldad amó el pastor Aristeo, el cual no pudiendo ya por ruegos efetuar su deseo, quiso usar de fuerzas' [Eurydice was loved due to her great beauty by the shepherd Aristaeus, who not being able to achieve his desire by begging, wanted to use force] (1995, 514–15).[7] Due to this confusion between Virgil's and Ovid's texts, the pastoral became intertwined with the myth of Orpheus and Eurydice during the early modern period, and this same *contamino* entered sixteenth-century texts.

With the pastoral omnipresent within the Iberian Peninsula (Juan de Encina's bucolic dramatic eclogues) and throughout Europe (Jacopo Sannazaro's *L'Arcadia*) during the beginning of the sixteenth century, other writers absorbed this mode into their works. One of the most notable was soldier-turned-poet Garcilaso de la Vega, who composed during his lifetime, among other works, three *églogas*.[8] Unlike Virgil's ten eclogues, Garcilaso contributes only three during his poetic career. Instead of focusing on the oft-studied *Égloga I* and the polemical second one, I turn to his last one to demonstrate how Garcilaso, within the space of pastoral poetry, establishes his presence as Spain's (future) celebrated poet via Ovid's and Virgil's portrayal of Orpheus.[9]

Before the third eclogue is discussed, it is imperative to demonstrate Garcilaso's acquaintance with Ovid's works. As countless studies (including those found within this collection) demonstrate, the numerous translations and extensive circulation of Ovid's *Metamorphoses*, and other works, like the *Heroides*, have also influenced Spanish writers. Rudolph Schevill has cataloged the many translations of this collection of letters into the Spanish language, titled *Epístolas (de Ovidio)* (1913, 244). In addition, Marina Brownlee (1990) has analysed the relationship between this collection of letters and the development of the *novela sentimental*. Garcilaso himself was quite familiar with this genre. In one of Garcilaso's *coplas*, the narrator, assuming a morbid tone, relates translating the last lines of Dido's letter to Aeneas and expressing his personal desire of having his own death described as Ovid has done for the Carthaginian queen's:

Pues este nombre perdí
'Dido, mujer of Siqueo,'
en mi muerte esto deseo
que se escriba sobre mí:

'El peor de los troyanos
dio la causa y el espada;
Dido, a tal punto llegada,
no puso más de las manos.'

[Thus I lost this name / 'Dido, wife of Sychaeus,' / in my death I desire
this / that about me it may be written: / 'The villain of the Trojans / gave
cause and sword; / Dido, arrived at such a point, / did not place more
than her hands.'] (1996, 39)[10]

In his analysis of Ovid's literary career, Tarrant remarks that '*Heroides 7*
(Dido to Aeneas), a pre-suicide letter of some 200 lines, constitutes one
of the earliest surviving reactions to the *Aeneid*, and one of the boldest'
(2002, 25). Thus, this epistle may be viewed as Ovid's rewriting of
Virgil's celebrated epic, for the former makes the queen of Carthage
'more loving even at the end, but also more scathing about Aeneas'
(2002, 25). Garcilaso's *copla*, in turn, becomes his rewriting of Ovid's, for
he (or the lyric speaker) desires a death comparable to Dido's. Through
this *contamino*, Garcilaso demonstrates his ability to control both of
these classical texts.

Turning from fame through death to fame through verse, Garcilaso, in
his third and final eclogue, honours himself as the poet of Spain's nascent
empire, under the reign of Charles V.[11] With only 376 verses, *Égloga III*
depicts, for the majority of its length, a friendly competition between
four nymphs of the Tagus River. Emerging from the depths of the river,
these nymphs (Filódoce, Dinámene, Climene, and Nise) display the delicate tapestries that they have finely woven. Each tapestry, in turn, presents a well-known myth. The arrival of these four nymphs approximates
the entourage of Cyrene, Aristaeus's mother, that appears in the *Georgics*,
especially Phyllodoce and Clymene. Garcilaso appears to be borrowing
directly from Virgil's text, but at the same time announces his textual
authority by having these nymphs rise to the surface of the Spanish
Tagus on his command and display his subjects.[12] Initiating the competition, Filódoce's craft retells the myth of Orpheus and Eurydice:

Estaba figurada la hermosa
Eurídice en el blanco pie mordida
de la pequeña sierpe ponzoñosa,
. . . .
Figurado se vía estensamente
el osado marido, que bajaba

al triste reino de la escura gente
y la mujer perdida recobraba;
y cómo, después desto, él impaciente
por mirarla de nuevo, la tornaba
a perder otra vez, y del tirano
se queja al monte solitario en vano.

[Was depicted the beautiful / Eurydice bitten on her white foot / by the small venomous serpent, / … / Depicted is extensively seen / the daring husband, who descended / into the sad kingdom of the dark people / and recovered the lost wife; / and how, afterwards, he impatient / to see her again, he / lòst her once more, and of the tyrant / complains in vain on the solitary mountain.] (1996, 215; 129–31, 137–44)[13]

Before the narrator even starts describing this nymph's entry, however, he begins to demonstrate his own Orphic-like powers through his verses. In the *exordium*, the narrator through *captatio benevolantiae* attempts to free his voice to honour the 'ilustre y hermosísima María [Osorio Pimentel]' [illustrious and very beautiful María]:

mas con la lengua muerta y fria [*sic*] en la boca
pienso mover la voz a ti debida;
libre mi alma de su estrecha roca,
por el Estigio lago conducida,
celebrando t'irá, y aquel sonido
hará parar las aguas del olvido.

[But with the cold and dead tongue in my mouth / I plan to move the voice owed to you; / free my soul from its narrow rock, / lead by the Stygian lake, / it will go to you celebrating and that sound / will make the waters of forgetfulness.] (1996, 209; 11–16)

Through these cited verses, the narrator insinuates the power of his voice over the soul and inanimate objects, in this case a rock (*roca*). This harkens to Ovid's description of Orpheus's powers over the living and nature: 'While Orpheus sang his minstrel's songs and charmed / The rocks and woods and creatures of the wild' (1986, 249). Reference to the Stygian lake metonymically reminds, although paradoxically due to the water's inherent power of forgetfulness, the reader of Hades and Orpheus's failed *catabasis* to the underworld.[14]

Yet, Garcilaso is not satisfied with only being a sixteenth-century Orpheus. After Filódoce's entry in this artistic competition, Dinámene and, afterwards, Climene display their tapestries, depicting other well-known Ovidian myths – Apollo's hapless pursuit of the nymph Daphne and Venus's unrequited love for the doomed Adonis, respectively.[15] Before the final nymph, Nise, proceeds with her entry, however, the narrator of *Égloga III* announces that her handicraft will be an interesting departure from the previous themes:

> La blanca Nise no tomó a destajo
> de los pasados casos la memoria,
> y en la labor de su sotil trabajo
> no quiso entretejer antigua historia;
> antes, mostrando de su claro Tajo
> en su labor la celebrada gloria,
> la figuró en la parte dond' él baña
> la más felice tierra de la España.

> [The fair Nise did not take diligently / the memory of past events, / and in the labour of her subtle task / she did not want to weave an ancient story; / before, displaying from her clear Tagus / the celebrated glory in her labour, / she depicted it in the part where it bathes / the happiest land of Spain.] (1996, 218; 193–200)

As announced by the narrator, the topic of Nise's tapestry will not be one from Greco-Roman mythology, but rather a more contemporary legend from her native Spain. Nise, like the previous three nymphs, will depict some manifestation of lost love (Orpheus losing Eurydice to the underworld, Daphne escaping Apollo's amorous pursuit, and Venus lamenting over Adonis's tragic death). In this case, the tapestry portrays the tragic death of a beautiful nymph:

> Todas, con el cabello desparcido,
> lloraban una ninfa delicada
> cuya vida mostraba que habia [*sic*] sido
> antes de tiémpo y casi en flor cortada;
> cerca del agua, en un lugar florido,
> estaba entre las hierbas degollada
> cual queda el blanco cisne cuando pierde
> la dulce vida entre la hierba verde.

[All of them, with their hair dispersed, / were crying over a delicate nymph / whose life (the tapestry) showed had been / cut before its time and almost in flower / close by the water, in a flowery place, / beheaded she was among the grass / as the white swan remains when it looses / its sweet life among the green grass.] (1996, 219; 225–32)

This nymph, beheaded and found dead along a water source, reminds the reader of the aforementioned myth of Orpheus and Eurydice. As cited earlier, Filódoce's tapestry depicts Eurydice, after being bitten by the serpent, found 'entre la hierba y flores' [among the grass and flowers], suggesting that the importance of Nise's subject is tantamount to classical writers. The poor nymph's decapitation (suggested by 'degollada') also refers back to Orpheus in the *Georgics*.[16] After reunion with his beloved being denied to him, Orpheus finds death by being torn apart with his head brutally severed from his body and then tossed away: 'And even when Oeagrian Hebrus rolled in mid-current that head, severed from its marble neck, the disembodied voice and the tongue, now cold as ever, called with departing breath on Eurydice – ah, poor Eurydice' (1999, 257). Mentioning the headless nymph metonymically reminds the reader of decapitated Orpheus and reinforces the idea that the previous poet-singer is deceased and that the (at the time) living Garcilaso is ready and willing to fill the vacated position.

For Nise's tapestry, the narrator reads through ekphrasis an inscription that is carved into the bark of an elm tree, revealing that this nymph is no other than Elisa, the shepherd Nemoroso's deceased beloved:

Elisa soy, en cuyo nombre suena
y se lamenta el monte cavernoso,
testigo del dolor y grave pena
en que por mí se aflige Nemoroso
y llama 'Elisa'; 'Elisa' a boca llena
responde el Tajo, y lleva presuroso
al mar de Lusitania el nombre mío,
donde será escuchado, yo lo fío.

[Elisa I am, in whose name sounds / and laments the cavernous mountain, / witness of pain and grave sorrow / in which for me Nemoroso is distressed / and calls 'Elisa'; 'Elisa' in full voice / responds the Tagus, and carries hastily / to the Lusitanian sea my name, / where it will be heard, I entrust it.] (1996, 220, 241–8)

Faithful readers of Garcilaso's trilogy of eclogues will remember the first mention of Elisa and Nemoroso's bereavement over her death in *Égloga I*.[17] Since the second eclogue briefly mentions how the sage Severio ameliorates Nemoroso's amorous anguish, I argue that, although critics speculate that *Égloga II* may have been written first, it was purposely composed to follow *Égloga I* so that there would be narrative continuity throughout all three of Garcilaso's poetic pieces.[18] By having the fourth nymph display his own literary creation as tantamount to three well-known Ovidian myths, Garcilaso transforms and elevates his own creation into a legend, or even into a myth, and, consequently, fashions himself into Spain's next Ovid/Orphic poet.

Through the guise of pastoral poetry, Garcilaso pays homage to Spain's emerging empire and the principal architects of this imperial expansion. Garcilaso de la Vega provided the literary means for Spain to produce a literature adequate for its emergence from a fractured nation-state to an empire – a topic that later writers, like Jorge de Montemayor, picked up.

Born in the early 1520s in Montemor-o-Velho, from which his surname is derived, Montemayor, as Bruno M. Damiani infers, was raised in a poor, silversmith family (*Jorge* 1984, 17). To a lesser degree of certainty, Damiani speculates that a young Montemayor 'served in the Portuguese army in the rank of a common soldier' (ibid., 19). After his military service, Montemayor may have taken advantage of the fluidity between the Portuguese and Spanish courts by accompanying King João III's daughter María to Castile for her marriage to the soon-to-be King Philip II. Although short-lived, this royal union, as Tanner explains, 'was perceived to have joined the East to the West. The marriage enhanced Spanish claims on the Portuguese territories; these were consolidated in 1580 when Philip gained sovereignty over Portugal' (1993, 139). Later, the courtier Montemayor distinguished himself by becoming the chapel singer for Doña María, the eldest daughter of Charles V, in 1548. Afterwards, he became a groomsman for Doña María's sister Juana when she transferred to the Portuguese court after having contracted marriage with Prince João of Portugal in 1552. With Don João's untimely death in 1554, however, Montemayor returned to Castile along with the now widowed Juana. After his return to Spanish realms, the biography of this Hispanized Portuguese courtier becomes unclear. Some critics, including Damiani, have suggested that Montemayor may have accompanied Philip II during his 1554 voyage to England after the king married Queen Mary Tudor. During this journey, Montemayor may have become acquainted with various nobles whom he would later visit either in Spain or in Italy after his return from England. Between 1558 and 1560, however, Montemayor situated himself in Valencia, where he composed, among other literary works, his pastoral masterpiece. Although cursory, this biographical sketch reveals how Montemayor maintained an intimate relationship with both royalty and the noble classes of Spain, Portugal, and even Italy – a relationship which may have influenced his reasons for writing *La Diana*. Due to the unprecedented accomplishments of Spain during this timeframe, this pastoral novel may be considered Montemayor's overt praise for the members of royalty, especially Emperor Charles V, who constructed the vast empire that allowed Spain to be transformed, in this author's eyes, into a *locus amoenus*.

As the genre dictates, *La Diana* is replete with shepherds (Sireno, Sylvano, Selvagia, Diana, etc.) but, additionally, contains two other social classes – villagers and courtiers. Although joining the pastoral cohort in its *peregrinatio amoris* to the Temple of Diana, Belisa identifies herself through her narration more as an *aldeana* than *pastora*: 'No muy lejos deste valle, hacia la parte donde el sol se pone, está un [*sic*] aldea en medio de una floresta' [Not far from this valley, near where the sun sets, there is a town in the middle of a forest] (1999, 232; 1989, 129)[19] and, later, 'adelante con otras doncellas, mis vecinas, me fue forzado ir a un bosque espeso … adonde las más de las siestas llevábamos las vacas, así porque allí paciesen como para que … cogiésemos la leche de aquel día siguiente, con que las mantecas, natas y quesos se habían de hacer' [I had to go with other maidens, my friends, to a thick wood … where we took our cattle to pasture most afternoons; when the cool and delicious evening came, we would take the milk with which we would make butter, cheese, and cream the next day] (1999, 244; 1989, 138). Populated with shepherds and the farmers Belisa, Arsenio, Arsileo, and others, *La Diana* presents another social class – the courtier, who appears to occupy a more prevalent position. Recently returned from his lengthy sojourn at court, Sireno, who cannot refrain from thinking about his beloved Diana, struggles so that his amorous thoughts are not contaminated by the courtier lifestyle that he had seen and experienced: 'No se metía el pastor en la consideración de los malos o buenos sucesos de la fortuna, ni en la mudanza y variación de los tiempos, no le pasaba por el pensamiento la diligencia y codicias del ambicioso cortesano, ni la confianza y presumpción [*sic*] de la dama celebrada por sólo el voto y parecer de sus apasionados' [The shepherd never thought about the bad or good quirks of Fortune, nor of change or mutability. Nor did the cares and greed of the ambitious courtier cross his mind, nor the vanity and presumption of the lady celebrated only by the vows and opinions of her suitors] (1999, 110–11; 1989, 51). Although the shepherd Sireno dominates the opening pages of *La Diana*, the life of a particular courtier, however, receives special attention.

Disguised as a shepherdess, Felismena is actually a *dama* who belongs to the courtier class. While narrating her amorous torment, Felismena mentions how Don Felis, the object of her affection, is sent away in service of a monarch, leaving her behind: 'Quiso, pues, mi desventura que al tiempo en que nuestros amores más encendidos andaban, su padre lo supiese, y quien se lo dijo se lo supo encarecer de manera que, temiendo no se casase conmigo, lo envió a *la corte de la gran princesa Augusta Cesarina*' [My misfortune would have it that at the time when our love burned at its brightest, his father discovered it, and whoever told him, revealed it so that fearing his son would marry me, he sent him to *the court of the great Princess Augusta Cesarina*] (1999, 201; 1989, 110; my emphasis). Although identified by critics as Juana, sister of Philip II, 'Augusta Cesarina' resembles the feminized construct of the famed Emperor Augustus Caesar, to whom Virgil dedicated his poetic works. By presenting shepherds, farmers, and even courtiers, and mentioning this great Roman ruler, Montemayor accomplishes via Virgil's literary *cursus*, as I shall argue, praise for himself as a poet/prose writer and for the Spanish monarchy and empire.

At first glance, one would deem Sireno to be the leader of the shepherds who represent the bucolic (*Eclogues*). Although this love-lost shepherd does receive special attention from Felicia during their residency in her temple (albeit near the end of his stay), I would argue that Selvagia justly represents the *Eclogues*. As we will see later, this shepherdess is favoured over Sireno not only by Felicia but also by the living statue of Orpheus. If Selvagia portrays the bucolic and Belisa's dairy chores make her more of a farmer (*Georgics*),[20] the courtier Felismena fulfils the role of soldier (*Aeneid*), since she demonstrates her remarkable marksmanship by slaying the three menacing *salvajes* in book 2 and the unknown knights in book 7. This triad of female characters (Selvagia, Belisa, and Felismena), who represent three distinct social classes and, therefore, Virgil's three major masterpieces (*Eclogues*, *Georgics*, and the *Aeneid*) suggests an approximation of the *rota Virgilii*. Instead of adhering to the strict classical guidelines concerning one's literary career, however, Montemayor single-handedly transforms this *cursus* from being overtly male-dominated into a more feminine one.[21]

This feminized *rota Virgilii*, as we will see, will be played out fully within book 4, but, at the same time, the same *cursus* places higher demands on the poetic content of *La Diana*.

Having the courtier Felismena represent the epic raises the reader's expectation for an epic poem in the novel. The reader detects the possibility of the upcoming inclusion of one due to the ekphrastic descriptions of the portraits of famed soldiers/warriors ornamenting the halls of Felicia's fantastic temple. Appropriately starting with Mars, the pagan progenitor of battle, the narrative guides the reader through a metonymic history of warfare: 'En este padrón ... estaba el bravo Aníbal, y del otro el valeroso Scipión Africano ... A la otra parte, estaba el gran Marco Furio Camilo ... Horacio, Mucio Scévola, el venturoso Cónsul Marco Varrón, César, Pompeyo, con el magno Alexandro y todos aquellos que por las armas acabaron grandes hechos' [On one side of this pillar ... stood the courageous Hannibal, and on the other the brave Scipius Africanus ... On another side was the Great Marcus Furious Camillus ... Horace, Mutius Scevola, the happy consul Marcus Varro, Caesar, Pompeii, and Alexander the Great and all who accomplished mighty feats in arms] (1999, 270–1; 1989, 151). This guided tour passes to a nationalistic homage of celebrated legendary heroes of Spanish history: El Cid, Fernán González, Bernardo del Carpio, etc. The group of shepherds and nymphs then move from the valorous men to chaste women: 'las paredes de alabastro y en ellas esculpidas muchas historias antiguas, tan al natural que verdaderamente parecía que Lucrecia acababa allí de darse la muerte, y que la cautelosa Medea deshacía su tela en la isla de Íthaca' [the carved alabaster depicted many ancient historical representations, so realistic it seemed that Lucrecia had just killed herself, the crafty Medea was undoing her web on the island of Ithaca] (1999, 274; 1989, 153). As Lucretia's death led to the establishment of the Roman Republic (and later Imperial Rome) and Penelope (not Medea) plays an important role in Homer's epic *Odyssey*, these women figure justly with their male counterparts in metonymic representations of the building of empire.[22] Thus, the only substantial poem that could possibly satiate this demand for an epic is the forty-three octaval 'Canto de Orpheo [or Orfeo]' [Song of Orpheus] sung by a living statue of Orpheus situated in the center of the Temple of Diana. Montemayor, in his description of Orpheus, seems, at first, to be borrowing from the *Georgics* with the mention of Aristaeus: 'junto a la fuente sentado el celebrado Orpheo, encantado de la edad que era al tiempo que su Eurídice fue del importuno Aristeo requerida' [and the famous Orpheus was seated next to the fountain, singing of the time when his Euridyce was sought after by the troublesome Aristaeus] (1999, 276; 1989, 154). Afterward, while foreshadowing Orpheus's impending death by the Ciconians, however, Montemayor, in the same proverbial breath, combines Virgil with Ovid: 'De la misma manera estaban todos oyendo al celebrado Orpheo, que al tiempo que en la tierra de los Ciconios cantaba, cuando Cipariso fue convertido en ciprés, y Atis en pino' [In this way they all heard the famous Orpheus as he sang of the time of the land of the Cyconians, when Cyparissus was turned into a cypress and Atis into a pine] (1999, 277; 1989, 154). Although both Ovid and Virgil both describe Orpheus's death, the latter two metamorphoses (Cyparissus and Attis) are Ovidian myths found in book 10 of the *Metamorphoses* (the same book section that contains the Orpheus and Eurydice myth). In his commentary of Ovid's text, E.J. Kenney mentions that 'only Ovid mentions this metamorphosis' of Attis into a pine tree and 'the story of Cyparissus makes its first appearance here' (Ovid 1986, 432).

With the attention of the entire cohort of shepherds and nymphs, the living statue of Orpheus begins plucking his harp and singing the *exordium* of his rather lengthy song:[23]

Escucha, oh Felismena, 'l dulce canto
    d'Orpheo, cuyo amor tan alto ha sido;
    suspende tu dolor, Selvagia, en tanto
    que cant'un amador d'amor vencido,
Olvida ya, Belisa'l triste llanto;
    oíd a un triste, ¡oh ninfas!, qu'ha perdido
    sus ojos por mirar, y vos pastores
    dejad un poco'star el mal d'amores.

[Hear, oh Felismena, Orpheus' sweet song, / Whose love was so noble; / Suspend your grief, Selvagia, while / A lover conquered by love sings. / Forget Belisa, your sad weeping; / Hear a wretch, oh nymphs, who has lost / His sight for looking, and you, shepherds, / Cease your sad sighings.] (1999, 278; 1989, 154)

Returning to Cheney's study, one could identify Montemayor's attempt to present himself as a celebrated poet by having Orpheus, who inhabits Felicia's temple, sing his (Montemayor's) own crafted poetry – making both of them one and the same.[24]

On first inspection, however, the 'Canto de Orpheo' fails to fulfil the classical definition of 'epic,' for it celebrates only famous historical women, not any particular battle or soldier/warrior. If we follow the trajectory of epic poetry from Homer to the Italian Ludovico Ariosto, however, we discover an interesting development that Montemayor achieves. In the *Iliad*, Homer proclaims that he will sing of arms while glorifying a man in the *Odyssey*. In his *translatio studii*, Virgil furthers Homer's masterpieces by singing of a man and arms in the *Aeneid*. Early Renaissance Italy witnesses an interesting transformation when Ariosto includes women in the first canto of his *Orlando furioso*: 'Le donne, i cavallier, l'arme, gli amori, / le cortesie, l'audaci imprese io canto' [Of ladies, cavaliers, of love and war, / Of courtesies and of brave deeds I sing] (1975, 1.1–2).[25] Montemayor may have incorporated women into his epic vision due to *Orlando furioso*'s widespread success. By imitating models spanning from antiquity to contemporary poets and, at the same time, adding his own originality, Montemayor may have employed what Thomas Greene would label heuristic *imitatio*. Out of the four types of *imitatio* presented in his seminal *The Light of Troy*, Greene theorizes this third type as 'imitations [that] come to us advertising their derivation from the subtexts they carry with them, but having done that, they proceed to distance themselves from the subtexts and force us to recognize the poetic distance traversed' (1982, 40). Thus, Montemayor respectfully recognizes this long-standing poetic tradition but, at the same time, distances himself by transforming these once androcentric themed-epics into a gynocentric one, to praise contemporary, primarily Spanish, women. Consequently, the 'Canto de Orpheo' doubly praises Imperial Spain by making this nation part of the aforementioned poetic tradition and by immortalizing certain historical figures who contributed to the expansion of the empire.

In the *exordium* of his musical piece, Orpheus declares that he will refrain from singing about his ill-fated attempt to rescue his beloved Eurydice from the pits of Hades:

No quiero yo cantar, ni Dios lo quiera,
aquel proceso largo de mis males,
ni cuando yo cantaba de manera
qu'a mí traía las plantas y animales
Ni cuando a Plutón vi, que no debiera,
y suspendí las penas infernales,
ni cómo volví'l rostro a mi señora,
cuyo tormento aún vive hast'agora.

[I do not want to sing, nor would God grant, / The long story of my misfortune, / Or when I sang so that / I moved the plants and animals; / Or
when I saw Pluto, and should not have, / And I suspended infernal griefs,
/ Or how I turned my head to see my lady; / The torment lives to this
day.] (1999, 278; 1989, 155)

Although his denial of narrating his tragic past actually reminds his
audience of what transpired, the mere presence of this mythical being,
in fact, serves as a metonymic reminder of his *catabasis*. A central element to Virgil's *Aeneid* is Aeneas's own *catabasis* through Hades. As the
'Canto de Orpheo' is situated in the centre of *La Diana*, Aeneas's journey to the underworld is found in the sixth book of this twelve-book
epic. Upon arriving on the shores of Hesperia (Italy), Aeneas and his
men disembark and journey to the prophetic Sibyl's abode, which bears
certain common characteristics of Felicia's Temple of Diana: 'Now they
pass under the grove of Trivia and the roof of gold' (1999, 533).[26]
Although the Sibyl resides within a grotto, its association with the goddess Diana and its golden roof parallels the interior decorations of
Montemayor's architectural construct: 'Y trabados de las manos se en-
traron en el aposento de la sabia Felicia, que muy ricamente estaba ade-
rezado de *paños de oro* y seda de grandísimo valor' [And holding hands,
they entered the sage Felicia's chamber, which was very richly hung
with valuable *gold and silk tapestries*] (1999, 261; 1989, 147, my emphasis). In fact, Virgil's epic hero compares his impending descent into
Hades with Orpheus's failed rescue: 'Orpheus availed to summon his
wife's shade, strong in his Thracian lyre and tuneful strings' (1999,
541). By alluding to Orpheus and Eurydice's tragic separation, Aeneas
also references his own poignant separation with Dido, the queen of
Carthage, and foreshadows what will occur during his supernatural
adventure.

   Although a meticulous examination of the entire cohort of women presented in the 'Canto de Orpheo' would exceed the confines of this study,
the praise of Doña María and Doña Juana merits closer inspection, since
these two particular women aided the establishment and government of
the Spanish Empire. Although the halls of Felicia's temple honour the
valour of arms – an essential element for the growth and expansion of an
empire, the same halls recognize the more peaceful process of obtaining
territories – marriage. As Kamen cites in his study, Juan de Mariana, a
Jesuit historian, noted the indispensable importance of royal matrimony:
'Empires grow and extend themselves through marriages. It is well
known that if Spain has come to be such a vast empire, she owes it both

to the valor of her arms and to the marriages of her rulers, marriages which have brought with them the addition of many provinces and even of very extensive states' (2003, 37). Initiating his ekphrastic description, Orpheus pays homage to the woman who maintained Montemayor in the Castilian court (as chapel singer) after the untimely death of the Portuguese Doña María – the Spanish Doña María de Austria:

> Los ojos levantad mirando aquella
>   qu'en la suprema sill'está sentada,
>   el cetro y la corona junto a ella,
>   y d'otra parta la fortun'airada.
> Ést'es la luz d'España y clar'estrella,
>   con cuy'absenci'está tan eclipsada;
>   su nombre, ¡oh ninfas!, es doña María,
>   gran reina de Bohemia, d'Austria, Ungría.

> [Lift up your eyes, upon seeing her / Who sits upon the highest throne, / Her scepter and crown beside her / On her other side, angry Fortune. / She is the light of Spain, and her bright star / In whose absence she is eclipsed. / Her name, oh nymphs, is Doña María, / Great Queen of Bohemia, Austria, and Hungary.] (1999, 278–9; 1989, 155)

By merely hearing Doña María's name, Orpheus's listeners would immediately recall her association with the Spanish monarchy, being the sister of Philip II and firstborn of the great Emperor Charles V. In addition to metonymically reminding the listeners/reader about the military conquests of these two Spanish monarchs, her presence also praises her contributions to the growth and support of the empire by marriage. After reaching an acceptable age for marriage, Charles V's daughter became a political asset for the redrawing of Europe, the Spanish Empire, and the Holy Roman Empire. Plagued by uprisings in his native Low Countries, the emperor, as Parker explains, strategically planned the role for María:

> The possibility of severing the link between Spain and the Netherlands had already been considered in 1544, when Charles promised to marry his daughter María to Francis I's younger son, the duke of Orléans, as a means of securing a more lasting peace between Habsburg and Valois, with either Lombardy or the Low Countries serving as María's dowry. Only the sudden death of Orléans solved the dilemma. (1998, 89)[27]

In 1548, Doña María married her cousin Maximilian II, who would become later in 1551 the emperor of Bohemia, therefore invoking the image of 'el cetro y la corona junto a ella' (1999, 278). Doña María's fortuitous marriage, however, did not involve the Spanish Empire engulfing the realms of Bohemia. Instead, this alliance, via marriage, established closer ties between these two European powers (Kamen 2003, 165).

Similar to her sister, Doña Juana strengthened political ties by marrying not into the East, but the West with Prince João III of Portugal: 'L'otra junta a ella es doña Joana [Juana] / de Portugal Princes', y de Castilla / Infanta, a quien quitó fortun'insana / el cetro, la corona y alta silla' [The other, near her, is Doña Joana, / Princess of Portugal and of Castille [*sic*]. / Angry Fortune stole the scepter, crown, / And mighty throne from this Infanta] (1999, 279; 1989, 155). Due to her marriage to Don João, Doña Juana transferred to Portugal, accompanied by Montemayor himself. Although royal marriage with Portugal would have been fortuitous for these two neighbouring (and imposing) powers, this alliance crumbled when Prince João III passed away in 1554, leaving Juana widowed and the future (newly born) heir to the Portuguese throne – Don Sebastian: 'Y a quien la muerte fue tan inhumana / qu'aun ell'así s'espanta y maravilla / de ver cuán presto'nsangrentó sus manos, / en quien fu'espejo y luz de lusitanos' [Death was so inhuman to her, / That even he marvels and is awed / To see how quickly he bloodied the hands / Of she on who was the mirror and light of the Lusitanians] (1999, 279; 1989, 155).[28] After her return to Castile, Doña Juana served as regent for both her father and brother during their absence: '[ella] volvió a Castilla a hacerse cargo del gobierno del resto de la Península durante la ausencia de su padre y hermano, que aquel año pasó a Inglaterra. Gobernó en nombre del Emperador y de Felipe II después (1556) hasta 1559' [(she) returned to Castile to take charge of the governing of the rest of the Peninsula during the absence of her father and brother, who that year went to England. She governed in the name of the Emperor and of Philip II afterwards (1556) until 1559] (Montemayor 1999, 279, note 56).

After honouring Charles V's daughters, Orpheus/Montemayor turns to other notable Spanish *damas* and, later, to celebrated *valencianas*, which ends his 'Canto.'[29] Although the novel does not conclude when Orpheus finishes singing his verses, the 'Canto de Orpheo' (and the fourth book) marks the apogee with the remaining three books serving as the denouement of the principal plot threads.

As we have seen, basing one's fame on classical writers was not a rarity during the early modern period of Spain. As poets scrambled to become the next inheritor of Virgil's legacy, others attempted to garner popularity via other famed Roman authors, especially Ovid. Incorporating the figure of Orpheus into his *Égloga III*, the soldier-poet Garcilaso de la Vega aptly presents the Orpheus and Eurydice myth to announce his role as Spain's Orphic poet and, at the same time, Spain's next Ovid, as the fourth nymph displays his now legendary tale of Nemoroso and Elisa. In the Spanish court, Jorge de Montemayor uses his assumed voice as Orpheus to praise the women who have kept him in his privileged position. As studies often focus on the importance of Virgil in early modern works, this essay demonstrates how writers were turning to other celebrated authors of antiquity to garner their own fame and prestige to metamorphose themselves via Ovid and the myth of Orpheus.

NOTES

1 Gloria Fry discusses how, parallel to the transformations encountered in Ovid's *Metamorphoses*, the adventure of Montesinos is a series of dualities (or transformations) for the knight-errant. She equates, for example, Don Quijote's descent into the cave 'as a rebirth into the world of reality, or normalcy, the world of the barber, of the Canon of Toledo and of Sansón Carrasco, where each man has his own appointed place' (1965, 469).
2 All translations of *Don Quijote* are Rutherford's. When I cite the original, I first include the part, then the chapter and finally the page number. For the English translation, only the page number is used. Unless stated, all other translations are mine.
3 In this essay, I am not ignoring the Renaissance treatment of the myth of Orpheus but rather highlighting the importance of Ovid in the works of Garcilaso and Montemayor. For a succinct but comprehensive discussion of Orpheus, see Cain, who states the importance of this mythical poet during the sixteenth century: 'But it is the Renaissance humanists who make Orpheus prototype of the compellingly articulate orator or poet. It is the humanists who promote the idea of a primarily literary culture; who shift the emphasis in the trivium from logic to rhetoric; who make the formal oration the goal of education; who equate eloquence and civilization. And it is the humanists who find in Orpheus a convenient culture hero' (1978, 11).
4 In his *Tristia*, written during his period of exile, Ovid mentions his distanced relationship with Virgil: 'Virgil I only saw' (1992, 88).
5 Tanner posits this final thought about Ovid's 'reworking' of Virgil: 'One might also ask whether by defining himself in opposition to Virgil in matters

relating to Augustus Ovid did not help to create the image of Virgil the pure "Augustan" that much recent criticism has been at pains to complicate' (2002, 27).

6 In the *Georgics,* Aristaeus is labelled as an 'Arcadian Master' (1999, 239) and a 'shepherd' (1999, 241).

7 In the 'Declaración moral,' Pérez de Moya interprets the allegorical significance of Aristeo's pursuit of Eurydice: 'Enamorarse Aristeo pastor, de Eurídice, significa la virtud, porque Aristeo quiere decir cosa que tiene virtud, y la virtud ama a Eurídice, porque la virtud quiere atraer los naturales deseos a orden y regla, apartándolos de los carnales deseos. Huir Eurídice de Aristeo es que los naturales deseos o concupiscencias huyen de la virtud, pensando ser bueno aquello que ellos cubdician' [The shepherd Aristaeus falling in love with Eurydice means virtue because Aristaeus means a thing that has virtue, and virtue loves Eurydice, because virtue wants to attract natural desires to order and rule, separating them from carnal desires. Eurydice fleeing from Aristaeus is the natural desires or concupiscences fleeing from virtue, thinking to be good that one whom they desire] (1995, 519).

8 In his seminal study Curtius explains how Spain exemplified this combination of *armas y letras* with soldiers-turned-poets: '[n]owhere else has the combination of the life of the Muses and the life of the warrior ever been so brilliantly realized as in Spain's period of florescence in the sixteenth and seventeenth centuries. It is the glory of the Spanish Empire that there the ideal of *armas y letras* is most highly esteemed' (1990, 178). In *Égloga III,* in fact, Garcilaso poetically writes about his change in careers: 'tomando ora la espada, ora la pluma' (1996, 210; 40) [taking now the sword, now the quill]. When citing Garcilaso's poetry, I give first the page number then the verse number.

9 Elías Rivers calls the third eclogue 'a firmly controlled synthesis of classical conventions and of Toledan landscape, or art and nature' (1962, 131).

10 In a modern translation of Ovid's epistle, the last lines read: 'When I have been consumed by the flames, / do not write, "Elissa, wife of Sychaeus," / but in the marble of my tomb, carve: / "From Aeneas came a knife and the cause of death, / from Dido herself came the blow that left her dead"' (1990, 64–5).

11 In a sense, Garcilaso's portrayal of himself parallels Stephen Greenblatt's (2005) concept of 'self-fashioning' during the Renaissance. In her essay, Anne J. Cruz offers a meticulous study of this soldier-poet's self-fashioning by comparing his biography with his poetry. Yet, she dismisses the three eclogues as having nothing to do with his present reality or self-fashioning by stating: 'Although the three eclogues written during this last period

attest to Garcilaso's compulsion to displace real concerns by means of the pastoral, his two elegies obsessively reinscribe the conflicts that originate from his opposing roles of brother, soldier, lover, and courtier' (1992, 532). A decade later, Cruz (2002) revisits her discussion of the literary career of Garcilaso, focusing more on the balance between soldier and poet ('armas y letras').

12 Paterson flatly denies any possibility that Garcilaso consulted Ovid's rendering of the Orpheus myth: 'There is no question that the major model for the first ecphrasis is to be found in the so-called "Aristaeus epyllion" that concludes the fourth book of Virgil's *Georgics*. El Brocense and Herrera rightly fixed upon Virgil's account of Orpheus's loss and of the singer's retreat to Strymon as Garcilaso's model, ignoring Ovid's memorable but inappropriate version, with its malicious reference to Orpheus's paederasty and its robust, farm-yard violence' (1977, 76). Paterson proceeds to offer Sannazaro's treatment of the same myth in his pastoral *L'Arcadia* and other contemporary humanistic texts. For another account of the classical and contemporary models of the Orpheus myth that Garcilaso had available to consult, see Barnard ('Garcilaso's Poetics' 1987). I, however, refuse to believe that Garcilaso did not consult Ovid's *Metamorphoses*, especially since the next two nymphs' tapestries display popular myths found in Ovid's text. To a limited extent, Elías Rivers agrees by stating that 'for the Orpheus one Garcilaso draws on Virgil's version as well as on Ovid's' (1962, 137).

13 For a detailed analysis of how Garcilaso reworks the Orpheus myth, see Barnard ('Garcilaso's Poetics' 1987).

14 The mention of the Stygian is another reference to the *Georgics*. Virgil describes Eurydice's return to Hades after Orpheus commits his mistake – 'She indeed, already death-cold, was afloat in the Stygian barque' (1999, 255).

15 The myth of Apollo and Daphne is found in book 1 of Ovid's *Metamorphoses* while the myth of Venus and Adonis is present in book 10. Since these two latter nymphs' tapestries depict myths found in Ovid's *Metamorphoses* and not in Virgil's *Georgics* and since there is no mention of the shepherd Aristaeus, I argue that Garcilaso is also drawing upon Ovid's account of Orpheus and Eurydice. For a detailed study of Garcilaso's treatment of Ovid's myth of Apollo and Daphne, see Barnard (*The Myth* 1987), although she discusses more the poet-soldier's sonnet than his third eclogue.

16 For the decapitated nymph, see Barnard ('Garcilaso's Poetics,' 1987) and Martínez-López (1972), who both argue that 'degollada' signifies 'decapitated.'

17 In *Égloga I*, Nemoroso laments:

y en este mismo valle, donde agora
me entristezco y me canso en el reposo,
estuve ya contento y descansado.
¡Oh bien caduco, vano y presuroso!
Acuérdome, durmiendo aquí algún hora,
que, despertando, a Elisa vi a mi lado.
    ¡Oh miserable hado!
    ¡Oh tela delicada,
    antes de tiempo dada
a los agudos filos de la muerte!
Más convenible fuera aquesta suerte
a los cansados años de mi vida,
    que's más que'l hierro fuerte,
pues no la ha quebrantado tu partida.   (1996, 139, 253–66)

[And in this same valley, where now / I become saddened and tire in the repose, / I was already happy and rested. / Oh so feeble, vain and hasty! / I remember, sleeping here some hour, / that, waking, Elisa I saw at my side. / Oh miserable fate! / Oh delicate web! / before your time given / to the sharp blades of death! / More accommodating would be this luck / to the weary years of my life, / which is stronger than iron, / since your departure has not broken it.]

18 In the second eclogue, Nemoroso tells his shepherd audience about his magical cure:

No te sabré decir, Salicio hermano,
la orden de mi cura y la manera,
mas sé que me partí d'él libre y sano.
. . . .
Como cerca me vido, adevinando
la causa y la razón de mi venida,
suspenso un rato 'stuvo así calando,
. . . .
No sé decir sino que'n fin de modo
aplicó a mi dolor la medicina
qu'el mal desarraigó de todo en todo.   (183–5; 1095–7, 1101–3, 1110–13)

[I don't know how to tell you, brother Salicio, / the means and the way of my cure, / but I know that I left him free and sound. / ... / As he saw me close, guessing / the cause and the reason of my arrival, / suspenseful a while he was thus quiet, / ... / I don't know what to say that at the end / he applied to my pain the medicine / that completely removed the illness.]

19 All translations of *La Diana* are Mueller's.

20 In book 3 of his *Georgics*, Virgil discusses the importance of milking cattle and making milk products (like cheese) and infers the relationship between farmer and shepherd: 'But let him who longs for milk bring with his own hand lucerne and lotus in plenty and salted herbage to the stalls. Thus they love streams the more, and the more distend their udders, while their milk recalls a lurking savour of salt. Many bar the kids from the dams as soon as born, and from the first front their mouths with iron-bound muzzles. What milk they drew at sunrise or in the hours of day, they press into cheese at night; what they drew at night or sunset, they press at dawn: they ship it in baskets which a shepherd takes to town, or else they salt it sparingly and put it by for the winter' (1999, 205).

21 Having three female characters represent the *rota Virgilii* corresponds with presenting the character Augusta Cesarina, a feminized construct of the Emperor Augustus Caesar.

22 Asunción Rallo, in his edition, suggests that Montemayor erroneously confuses Medea with Penelope (Montemayor 1999, 274, note 46).

23 Concerning the importance of Orpheus in *La Diana*, Bruno Damiani states: 'Significantly, Orpheus avoids the use of a wind instrument, traditionally seen as appealing to the baser parts of the soul ... and plays instead the harp, the "noble" instrument by which David, God's helper, gave aid and comfort to Saul, thereby softening his evil spirit' (*La Diana* 1984, 89).

24 In his verses, Orpheus alludes to the need for the poet to compose what he is about to sing: 'qu'allí'stá el fin, allí veréis la suma / de lo que contar puede lengua y pluma' ['For there lies the sum and total / That pen or tongue can describe' (1999, 278; 1989, 155)].

25 All translations of Ariosto's *Orlando furioso* are those of Barbara Reynolds.

26 'Trivia' was another name for Hecate, which is one of the three names of the goddess Diana.

27 With Doña María as an invaluable commodity for political ties, marriage was proposed in 1547 between her and Emanuel Philibert of Savoy – causing them to be joint rulers of the Netherlands and permit Philip II to receive Piedmont from his brother-in-law. The marriage details between Maximilian II and María, however, were already arranged (Parker 1998, 329, note 55).

28 Although Doña Juana vacated the Portuguese realm, she, literally and figuratively, planted the seed for the future acquisition of Portugal, for her son

later became the king of Portugal. As his father perished early in life, so did he: 'When young Sebastián perished in the battle of al-Qasr al-Kabir in the North African desert in August 1578, Philip emerged as the candidate with the firmest dynastic claims to the vacant throne' (Kamen 2003, 301).

29 Although I have argued that Montemayor, through the voice of Orpheus, praises Spanish women, primarily Doña María and Doña Juana, other critics, like Hernández-Pecoraro, take an opposing stance: 'First, they [the stanzas of the 'Canto de Orpheo'] are clearly meant to remind the reader of Montemayor's own privileged connections to members of the Hapsburg court. Second, they reveal a veiled anxiety ... about the constantly changing web of relations and fortunes that dictate an individual's place at court ... La Diana thus produces a fictional space where all women, even two powerful royal women, perfectly fit an emptied and unproblematic ideal as beautiful, chaste, and appropriately subdued' (2006, 73–4).

WORKS CITED

Ariosto, Ludovico. 1975. *Orlando furioso*. Trans. Barbara Reynolds. 2 vols. New York: Penguin.

Barnard, Mary E. 1987. 'Garcilaso's Poetics of Subversion and the Orpheus Tapestry.' *PMLA* 102.3:316–25.

– 1987. *The Myth of Apollo and Daphne from Ovid to Quevedo: Love, Agon, and the Grotesque*. Duke Monographs in Medieval and Renaissance Studies. Durham: Duke University Press.

Bowra, C.M. 1952. 'Orpheus and Eurydice.' *The Classical Quarterly* 2.3/4:113–26.

Brownlee, Marina Scordilis. 1990. *The Severed Word: Ovid's Heroides and the novela sentimental*. Princeton, NJ: Princeton University Press.

Cain, Thomas H. 1978. *Praise in* The Faerie Queene. Lincoln: University of Nebraska Press.

Cervantes Saavedra, Miguel de. 1978. *El ingenioso hidalgo don Quijote de la Mancha II*. Ed. Luis Andrés Murillo. Madrid: Castalia.

– 2001. *The Ingenious Hidalgo Don Quixote de la Mancha*. Trans. John Rutherford. New York: Penguin.

Cheney, Patrick Gerard. 1993. *Spenser's Famous Flight: A Renaissance Idea of a Literary Career*. Toronto: University of Toronto Press.

Cruz, Anne J. 1992. 'Self-Fashioning in Spain: Garcilaso de la Vega.' *Romanic Review* 83.4:517–38.

– 2002. 'Arms versus Letters: The Poetics of War and the Career of the Poet in Early Modern Spain.' In *European Literary Careers: The Author from Antiquity to the Renaissance,* ed. Patrick Cheney and Frederick A. de Armas, 186–205. Toronto: University of Toronto Press.

Curtius, Ernst Robert. 1990. *European Literature and the Latin Middle Ages.* Trans. Willard R. Trask. Princeton, NJ: Princeton University Press.

Damiani, Bruno Mario. 1984. *Jorge de Montemayor.* Rome: Bulzoni.

– 1984. *La Diana of Montemayor as Social & Religious Teaching.* Lexington: University Press of Kentucky.

Fry, Gloria M. 1965. 'Symbolic Action in the Episode of the Cave of Montesinos from "Don Quijote."' *Hispania* 48.3:468–74.

Garcilaso de la Vega. 1996. *Poesías castellanas completas.* Ed. Elias L. Rivers. Madrid: Castalia.

Greenblatt, Stephen. 2005. *Renaissance Self-fashioning: From More to Shakespeare.* Chicago: University of Chicago Press.

Greene, Thomas M. 1982. *The Light in Troy: Imitation and Discovery in Renaissance Poetry.* New Haven: Yale University Press.

Hernández-Pecoraro, Rosalie. 2006. *Bucolic Metaphors: History, Subjectivity, and Gender in the Early Modern Spanish Pastoral.* North Carolina Studies in the Romance Languages and Literatures. Chapel Hill: University of North Carolina Press.

Kamen, Henry Arthur Francis. 2003. *Empire: How Spain Became a World Power, 1492–1763.* New York: HarperCollins.

Martínez-López, Enrique. 1972. 'Sobre "aquella bestialidad" de Garcilaso (égl. III.230).' *PMLA* 87.1:12–25.

Montemayor, Jorge de. 1989. *The Diana.* Trans. RoseAnna M. Mueller. Lewiston, NY: E. Mellen Press.

– 1999. *La Diana.* Ed. Asunción Rallo. Madrid: Cátedra.

Ovid. 1577. *Las Metamorphoses, o Transformaciones del excelente Poeta Ouidio, en quinze libros buelto en Castellano.* Toledo: Francisco de Guzmán.

– 1986. *Metamorphoses.* Trans. A.D. Melville. Ed. E.J. Kenney. New York: Oxford University Press.

– 1990. *Heroides.* Trans. Harold Isbell. New York: Penguin.

– 1992. *Sorrows of an Exile: Tristia.* Trans. A.D. Melville. Oxford: Clarendon Press.

Parker, Geoffrey. 1998. *The Grand Strategy of Philip II.* New Haven: Yale University Press.

Paterson, Alan K.G. 1977. 'Ecphrasis in Garcilaso's "Egloga Tercera."' *Modern Language Review* 72.1:73–92.

Pérez de Moya, Juan. 1995. *Philosofía secreta de la gentilidad.* Ed. Carlos Clavería. Madrid: Cátedra.

Rivers, Elías L. 1962. 'The Pastoral Paradox of Natural Art.' *Modern Language Notes* 77.2:130–44.

Schevill, Rudolph. 1913. *Ovid and the Renascence in Spain*. 1913. Berkeley: University of California Press.

Tanner, Marie. 1993. *The Last Descendant of Aeneas: The Habsburgs and the Mythic Image of the Emperor*. New Haven: Yale University Press.

Tarrant, Richard. 2002. 'Ovid and Ancient Literary History.' In *The Cambridge Companion to Ovid*, ed. Philip Hardie, 13–33. Cambridge: Cambridge University Press.

Virgil. 1999. *Eclogues, Georgics, Aeneid I–VI*. Trans. H. Rushton Fairclough. Loeb Classical Library Cambridge: Harvard University Press.

13 Eros, *Vates*, *Imperium*: Metamorphosing the *Metamorphoses* in Mythological Court Theatre (Lope de Vega's *El Amor enamorado* and Calderón's *Laurel de Apolo*)[1]

JULIO VÉLEZ-SAINZ

Hapsburg imperial propaganda showed a remarkable penchant for the myth of Apollo and Daphne. By the early 1630s Philip IV was already identified as the *Rey Planeta* (planet king), an obvious reference to the astral representation of the Greek god. The correlation between Apollo/Sol and the monarchy is promoted since in Copernican and Ptolemaic theories the sun serves as the point of inflection of the cosmos.[2] If the sun orders and hierarchizes the universe, the sun king is the centre that illuminates the social orbs or hierarchies. Even though we tend to think of the sun king as the *Roi Soleil* Louis XIV of France, Spain's Hapsburg monarchs amply utilized the motif. Philip II selected Apollo (the Greek mythological sun god) as his favourite emblem. In the kingdom of the sun, Apollo's subjects depend on his divine light just as shepherds and harvests depend on the actual heavenly body. The motif can be traced back to the first festivity designed for the Catholic monarchs in Naples in 1493. Charles V also was able to see the myth depicted upon the columns of a triumphal arch in 1547 Valencia (Checa Cremades 1999, 107). Philip IV's solar image is so prominent that it contaminates other political icons. A 1660 *Relación verdadera* (True Account) declares: 'Este [Plutón], pues, le combatian quatro hermosas galeras, que exalauan de si brillantes bombas, siendo artificiales cometas de aquel cielo, a quienes regian Remeros, y Capitanes rica- ménte vestidos. Y despues de auer esto durado hasta las nueve de la noche, diò su Magestad la buelta a Palacio, siendo los pretiles de la Puente montañas de luminarias, y todo el lugar globo de respland- ecientes rayos' [Pluto was being attacked by four handsome galleys which exhaled bright bombs, that became artificial comets of the sky. These were ruled by rowers and captains richly clad. This battle having lasted until nine at night His Highness walked around the palace, with the bridge's columns being shiny mountains and the whole place, a globe of resplendent rays of light] (1660, folio 1v).[3] One can easily observe the designers' intention of dazzling attendants while at the same time uniting the monarch with the luminary's light. The mythological context can be seen as reflecting a sense of marvel that encrypts a readable message: each galley represents one of the four parts of the world while the globe-sun illuminates the scene. The scenography seems upheld by the greatness of King Philip. But the motif expands beyond the confines of laudatory spectacles. The Austrians included the sun god in their art collections. For instance, Francisco Camilo painted fourteen scenes from the *Metamorphoses* in frescoes at the Buen Retiro palace (Morán Turina and Checa Cremades 1986, 159, note 48). Moreover, the same motif connected all decorations at the Pardo Palace and the Parada Tower, including Rubens's *Apollo and the Python* (Morán Turina and Checa Cremades 1986, 156–7). Among many other courtly writers, Lope de Vega and Calderón de la Barca were inclined to feature Phoebus as protagonist of their mythological court plays. Lope's *El Amor enamorado* and Calderón's *El Laurel de Apolo* were staged for the planet king Philip IV at the Buen Retiro Palace.[4] It therefore seems advisable to explore the possible propagandistic significance of the motif, especially given that this symbol has been a highly problematic representation of rulers since Ovid. Both Lope's and Calderon's plays are baroque metamorphoses of the Apollo and Daphne myth, which present interesting permutations of the same famous passages from the *Metamorphoses* dealing with love, empire, and the courtly poet.

8 BC: Eros (Ovid, *Metamorphoses* 1.452–567)

Ovid utilizes the oldest extant version of the myth, which stems from Thessalian mythography. Though ancient, it is far from a simple etiology of Apollo's attribute as a tree (Barnard 1998, 19–43). The poetics of the *Metamorphoses* is anchored in the Pythagorean formulation of constant transformation of beings (Segal 1969, 284–8). The author further emphasizes the instability of the world through the appearance of the philosopher Pythagoras, who in a famous speech declares: 'Devouring Time, and you, jealous Age, consume everything, and slowly gnawing at them, with your teeth, little by little, consign all things to eternal death!' (Ovid 1960, 15.234–6). Arguably this image of horror and pathos imbues every page of the book, impacting the Apollonian myth.

William S. Anderson in his edition (1977) has shown that Ovid breaks away from literary conventions (epic *decorum*, *maiestas*, *virtus*) in order to create distance from readers so that they can focus on the multiple grotesque passages surrounding the main scene such as the animalization of the characters and the arborification of Daphne, the metamorphosis itself. Book 1 of Ovid's *Metamorphoses* begins with a triumphant Apollo who, having defeated the python, encounters Cupid, who is mocked because of his figure and childish arrows: 'Impudent boy, what are you doing with a man's weapons?' (1960, 1.456).[5] Phoebus arrogantly reminds Cupid of his role in the pantheon: 'You should be intent on stirring the concealed fires of love with your burning brand, not laying claim to my glories!' (1960, 1.461–2).[6] The hurting Cupid replies: 'You may hit every other thing Phoebus, but my bow will strike you: to the degree that all living creatures are less than gods, by that degree is your glory less than mine' (1960, 1.463–5).[7] Cupid places himself above Apollo and draws a distinction between the animal world (*animalia*) and the divine (*deum*) through their recognition of Love. Gods must be knowledgeable in the arts of love. Cupid enters Apollo's temple, and shoots two arrows that provoke contrary effects in their victims: 'one kindles love, the other dispels it' (1960, 1.470).[8] Apollo is wounded with the former, triggering an irrepressible love, while Daphne is pierced with the latter, making her flee from Phoebus. Eros runs rampant through the race, in an episode brimming with latent phallic symbolism.[9] Ovid juxtaposes Phebe, the maiden, to Phoebus, the gentleman, while the racing and excitement feeds Apollo's adoration. Ovid utilizes a series of natural images as *paragon* to the two characters: the wolf and the lamb, the lion and the reindeer, which accentuate the *venatio amoris*. In his quest for romantic fulfilment, Phoebus behaves much like an unknowing youth with little experience: he tries to impress Daphne with his high ascendancy and ingenuity, his invention of the lyre, his clout in medicinal matters, and his relation to Jupiter. Apollo is then described 'like a hound which has seen a hare in an open field' (1960, 1.533).[10] Mary E. Barnard explains 'Apollo's animalization is part of a larger picture in Ovid's work, the theme of "monstrous" and forbidden love ... which Ovid often elaborates to reveal foolish eroticism' (1998, 25). Apollo's becoming an animal signals the fact that he will lose the bet, while his subjection to the lower passions reveals that he belongs more in the animal world than in the divine.

At the end of the love race, Daphne begs her father Peneus to save her by converting her into a laurel tree. However, Phoebus still loves her under this disguise ('Hanc quoque Phoebus amat') (1960, 1.553): the dog ends adoring the bush. However, Ovid remarks that Phoebus's desire does not stem from carnal appetite and stresses new and more transcendent meanings to Apollo's lust:

> Since you cannot be my bride, you must be my tree! Laurel, with you my hair will be wreathed, with you my lyre, with you my quiver. You will go with the Roman generals when joyful voices acclaim their triumph, and the Capitol witnesses their long processions. You will stand outside Augustus's doorposts, a faithful guardian, and keep watch over the crown of oak between them. (1960, 1.557–63)

The story climaxes with an allusion to Rome and its politics, which serves as colophon to an adventure that borders on the absurd. What are we to make of a story that starts with lust and ends with an elegy to Augustus Caesar? Multiple answers can be offered, all of which are articulated around the trinomial eros, *imperium*, and *vates*.

Ovid turns a short poem of love into a political laudation of the emperor. As Barnard points out 'The laurel of victory becomes, paradoxically, a symbol of his amorous defeat' (1998, 42). The power (*imperium*) of weaponry is beaten by Apollo's failure in a love affair, which ultimately proves Cupid right. This passage can thus be read as a contrastive opposition between empire and eros. On the one hand, it could be argued that this is nothing more than simple praise for Augustus. The connection between Apollo and the emperor would then work as a topos to eternalize the latter in the same fashion as the last of the metamorphoses represents Julius Caesar's catasterization (the transformation of an earthly body into a celestial one) and apotheosis as *divus Iulius* (Julius, the divine) (1960, 15.483–52). The symbol of the laurel tree would, then, represent fame in two of its main aspects: political, since it is bestowed upon Augustus as it was upon triumphant generals; and poetic, for Apollo is after all the god of musicians and poets. Finally, the defeat of Apollo lifts him up as emperor of both realms: arms and letters. The problems arise when we understand how ultimately problematic such representation of imperial greatness really is. A somewhat veiled criticism of the *Princeps* was noted at the time. Ovid was expelled from the court for something related to one of his poems in 8 BC. E.J. Kenney has described this poem in the *Tristia* as a 'campaign of psychological warfare – for it was nothing less – against

Augustus' (1992, xix). In Ovid, for all his greatness, Apollo, who has become a clear image of Augustus by the end of the poem, is subdued by eros. This would help Augustus's imperial *maiestas* very little.

To complicate matters further, there is a noticeable self-laudation running through the episode. Ovid places himself between the Lucretian and Hesiodic tradition of the poet as philosopher and the Virgilian tradition of the poet as a *vates* – a vessel for divine inspiration and prophecy. Ovid emphasizes his role as a prophet: 'Wherever Rome's influence extends, over the lands it has civilized, I will be spoken, on people's lips: and, famous through all the ages, if there is truth in poet's prophecies – vivam – I shall live' (1960, 15.875–9). Ovid links his immortality to the Roman imperial project. The *Metamorphoses* works through these three pivotal motives of love, politics, and poetry. When metamorphosing the *Metamorphoses*, Lope and Calderón will articulate their works through the same topoi. However, Lope's play centres upon the figure of the poet while Calderón prefers to explore the possibilities of the myth as a mirror of the prince.

1635: *Vates* (Lope de Vega's *El Amor enamorado*)

For I.P. Rothberg, *El Amor enamorado* 'no sólo refunda Lope el mito de Dafne y Apolo sino que también lo junta con una seudomitología de su propia invención: la intriga irónica y conceptista pregonada por el propio título de la obra' [not only does Lope reset the myth of Daphne and Apollo but he also joins it to a pseudomythology of his own invention: the ironic and witty intrigue heralded by the title] (1983, 95). The plot of the entire play circulates metonymically around its title. Lope surrounds the two lovers with numerous secondary characters: Aristeo, a prince deeply smitten by Daphne; Bato the *gracioso*; Sirena the nymph who worships Diana along with Daphne; Venus, who forces Cupid to avenge her; and the goddess Diana. These new characters infuse the play with greater formal complication and dramatic tension. Ovid's story of Apollo's amorous defeat and ultimate triumph covers only the first *jornada*, leaving the second and third acts to develop the paradox implied in the title: Amor (Cupid) tries his own medicine and falls in love. *El Amor enamorado*'s plot distances itself from Ovid's. In fact, it combines Ovid's Thessalian version of the myth with later Arcadian reconstructions. However, Lope's play attempts to rewrite the same three main topics present in the Ovidian text: eros, *imperium*, and *vates*, while centring on the second of the three.

Lope begins this story of love affairs with the nymph Sirena's cry for help: a monster not shown on the stage (presumably the defeated Python) threatens her. Alcino, the shepherd, hears the scared nymph and rescues her. The first scene refashions Ovid's main motif of the love-race in a gallant and courteous manner. Bato and Silvia, comic figures, boast of having seen the monster, which Bato describes in grotesque detail, thus metamorphosing the beast into a 'rinoceronte' (rhino), 'una mujer con celos' [jealous woman], or a 'suegra enojada' [annoyed mother-in-law]. After these jokes, which serve to balance the scene after the first dramatic encounter, Alcino tells Daphne and Sirena of the creation of the world in a clear reconstruction of Ovid's *Metamorphoses* (1960, 1.5–88). When Apollo finally makes it to the stage, Alcino has already assumed his role as protagonist of the story. Although Lope's Phoebus is much more a courtier than Ovid's, Bato consistently pokes fun at the sun:

Señor Pollo, el que nos hunde
a rayos en el verano
y en el invierno se escurre;
por acá los labradores
se quejan que no madure
las cosas cuando es sazón
que unas cría y otras pudre.

[Mister Rooster (Pollo), you are the one who / Drowns us with your summer rays / And who flees away during winter; / Around here ploughmen / Complain that you do not make things ripen appropriately / some you rot and some you grow.] (1965, 247)

At a time of rampant famine – to the point that heavy restrictions were placed on begging – Bato, a shepherd, makes a mild joke about the scarcity of food.[11] Bato's remark goes hand in hand with a witty pun on Apollo's name, who becomes a rooster (Apolo/Pollo), underscoring the comedy in the scene. Ovid's animalization of Apollo as a hound seems laudatory in comparison. This highly parodic use of the mythical figure contrasts heavily with the abstract, idealized heliotropic iconifications of the king present at court. As Mikhail Bakhtin reminds us, carnivalesque laughter is ambivalent: 'it is gay and triumphant, yet mocking and derisive. It asserts and denies, it buries and revives' (1984,

12). Later representations at court would intensify the carnivalesque parodying of kingly figures to the point of converting them almost into buffoonesque figures (see Huerta Calvo 1984).

By making Apollo a risible figure, the play lowers the pantheon of deities to the material and the prosaic. Lope burlesquely stresses Phoebus's attributes as god of doctors and musician: 'Si estás herido, yo soy / el primero que compuse / aforismos medicables' [If you are wounded, I was the first to ever compose medical aphorisms] (1965, 246). But Apollo knows how to poke fun at the rest of the gods in *entremés*-like fashion. In the Ovidian version Apollo derides Cupid. In Lope's, Phoebus serves to desecrate every deity (much like Velázquez's *La fragua de Vulcano*): he makes fun of Vulcan and Mercury, calling the former a lowly ironsmith and the latter a simple court courier (1965, 255). These deities will ultimately help Cupid in his revenge. Amor overcomes the strength of this courteous and all-powerful Apollo. Before Cupid pierces Apollo, he is described as a lord of all the world: 'desde el [reino] indio al español, / y del alemán al scita' (from the Indian to the Spanish [kingdom], from the German to the Scithian' (1965, 262).[12] After the arrow, he becomes an apprentice of courtly manners who must learn the rules of the game of love. His *imperium* is subdued to eros. Significantly, in his final speech Apollo recognizes that, even though he governs over the globe, he adores Daphne and is subordinate to her 'Dafne, yo te adoro; yo [que] / soy el que tengo el gobierno / del mundo' (1965, 265). Apollo's identification with King Philip is explicit at the end of the play. Bato, the *vates*, calls Apollo and the Moon: 'divino planeta cuarto, / Luna, madre de otro sol ... dé fin en vuestro servicio / Amor' [divine fourth planet / Moon, mother of the sun / ... be *Amor* at your service] (1965, 284). The fourth planet was a very appropriate emblem for the fourth Philip (Elliott 1990, 210). Víctor Mínguez points out that 'el rey español que adquiere una imagen más "solar" es sin lugar a dudas Felipe IV' [the Spanish king who best acquires a 'solar' image is, without a doubt, Philip IV] (1994, 210). John H. Elliott goes as far to call him 'the original Sun-King' (1989, 156; see also Tanner 1993, 223-48).[13] An emblem celebrating Philip II's wedding develops the stellar analogy of Philip II and Isabel of Valois as the sun king and the moon queen (Tanner 1993, 245). Both lighten the firmament: Philip with his own beam of light and Isabel as the moon who reflects the rays of the sun. The image is also present in the Count of Villamediana's *La Gloria de Niquea* and Feliciana Enríquez de Guzmán's *La tragicomedia de los campos y jardines sabeos*. Lope had indeed used the motif before, in his *El vellocino de oro* and in the poem he read at Philip IV's birth, a poem still extant in a 1605 *Relación de las fiestas* [Account of the Festivities] where he requests a royal patronage for poets from Philip Vélez-Sainz 2006, 159–93).

Lope repeatedly points toward patronage in the play. If Apollo is clearly Philip IV, Bato can be easily identified with Lope himself. Lope had performed a similar transformation in 1599 when he disguised himself as the Italian comic Bottarga as an allegory of Carnival and utilized his position to speak directly to the king (Carreño 1995, 55; Wright 2001, 61–2).[14] Bato works similarly as a burlesque *vates* who talks to Apollo (image of King Philip) and complains about the poetic scene. After Phoebus defeats the snake Fitón, he sponsors a poetic joust, aptly labelled 'fitones' (games), involving several poets. He claims: 'Daré premio a los que fueren / ya en la lucha los mejores, / ya en hacer versos, / o en otras gracias conformes / a la fiesta de aquél día' [I will reward the best at this competition either in the art of versification or in the art of making puns for this festive occasion] (1965, 254). However, Bato explains that Apollo's judgment is greatly misdirected: 'lo peor se premia' [only the worst is prized] (1965, 258). So Bato, the *vates*, decides to make 'perverse verses' [versos perversos]. The arrogant and youthful Apollo is not ready to judge proper poetry until his final defeat, signalled by Daphne's transformation. After learning to situate himself below the god of love, Lope's Phoebus rejects the oak-tree and accepts the laurel-tree as his symbol. At this moment he claims:

Tú serás la verde insignia
De Césares imperiales
Tú aureola de ingenios
En las científicas artes,
Tú de poetas honor
Que de siglo a siglo nacen.

[You will be the symbol of imperial caesars / you will be the halo of inventors in the arts of sciences/ you will be the honour of poets / who are born once in every century.] (1965, 268)

Lope expands the Ovidian version to include references to scientists and poets. Ovid's Apollo learns and betters himself in an educational process directed by love and decides to make the laurel tree his personal symbol. Lope's version undervalues the god-poet until he goes through the same sentimental education. The message is clear: Apollo/ King Philip needs to learn to value and reward his poets. Lope's age-old ambition for the position of royal chronicler can easily be glimpsed. While Lope favours *vates* inside the triad, eros, *vates, imperium,* Calderón will mostly focus on the last one: empire.

1657: *Imperium* (Calderón's *El laurel de Apolo*)

Calderón's *El laurel de Apolo* is one of the most interesting of the many court spectacles he designed. If Lope converted Ovid's *venatio amoris* into a hunt for poetic greatness for Philip IV, Calderón turns it into a search for political grandeur for the sun king – fittingly it seems, for the laurel-tree represents attaining eternal fame in poetic and political terms.[15] *El laurel* is a clear example of José Antonio Maravall's theory of theatre, which notes the 'utilización del teatro a fin de llevar a cabo una extensa campaña a favor de los poderes establecidos y del régimen de intereses afecto a ellos' [utilization of theatre as a means to create an intensive campaign in favour of the powers-that-be and their regime] (1984, 77). Being a semi-opera – the first 'zarzuela' as Hesse has pointed out (1946, 237) – its musical component adds a sensorial element that sweetens the blatant propagandistic elements. In fact, the Austrian Habsburgs would later use such a search for universal harmony as a political tool to promote themselves.[16] Calderón's play is much more faithful to the original Ovidian text than *El Amor enamorado*. Its only departures from the sources serve to aggrandize Apollo as a symbol for royal power.

Like Lope's play, Calderón's plot starts with shepherds yelling that a beast (the snake Python) is on the loose and going after Daphne. Calderón's serpent is tinged with draconian traits, an association much exploited at the time. For early modern bibliographer Sebastián de Covarrubias, a dragon is a 'Serpiente de muchos años que con la edad ha venido a crecer desaforadamente' [an old snake that after many years has grown excessively] and which signifies 'la suma vigilancia del capitán general y el cuidado y solercia que avía de tener en todo' [the supreme vigilance of the captain general and the care and watchfulness he must have in everything] (1986, 485). Characterized as a figure taken from medieval bestiaries, the python is endowed with the power of altering the perfect order and harmony of the world (Valbuena Briones 1985, 19). Winning over the dragon is thus equivalent to restoring order

and harmony. Apollo is thus represented as the *discordia concors*, an icon
that was extensively exploited to represent kings.

At the sight of Python, two shepherds attempt to rescue Daphne, depicted as a damsel in distress. Even though Amor/Cupid tries to save her,
while accidentally dropping his weapons, it will be gallant Apollo who
will defeat the monstrous snake, thus unintentionally humiliating Cupid.
Rústico, the comic figure, organizes a dance, where all characters sing:

> Titiriti, que de Apolo es el día …
> Titiriti, que no del Amor …
> Titiriti, que el rapaz ceguezuelo …
> Titiriti, corrido ha quedado …
> Titiriti, pues de miedo ha dejado …
> Titiriti, caer el arco en el suelo …
> Titiriti, Porque el sol mató al vuelo …
> Titiriti, al monstruo traidor …

> (Titiriti, today is Apollo's day … / Titiriti, it does not belong to Love … /
> Titiriti, the blinded youth … / Titiriti, appears upset … / Titiriti, since he
> has dropped due to fear … / Titiriti, his bow on the ground … / Titiriti,
> The sun killed easily … / Titiriti, the treacherous monster …) (1969, 1.2190)

Love thus tries revenge out of spite while recognizing that his powers
are useless 'contra las fieras' [against beasts] (1969, 1.2184). Calderón
plays with the original disposition of the characters: the plumbean arrow provokes Daphne, who is not disdainful at the beginning, to turn
against her original love for Apollo; the golden arrow crazes Phoebus,
who originally has no feelings for her, into falling passionately in love
with her. But Apollo will never fulfil his eros, much to the child love-
god's rejoicing. After Amor boasts of his victory, Apollo rapidly recognizes his defeat and humiliation and accepts the laurel crown:

> para lauro de mis sienes …
> y para que más se aumente
> su honor, con él sus victorias
> han de coronar los reyes.

> [the laurel will crown me … / And to further augment / Daphne (Laurel)'s
> honour / The laurel-tree will also crown the kings.] (1969, 1.2197)

Then, Apollo crowns the young prince Charles II and hails Philip's wife Mariana of Austria as the reflection the rays of the sun (1969, 1.2195). As Brown and Elliott have asserted, the Buen Retiro Palace was intended to represent an 'ordered society [that] was supposed to move like the stars, in perfect symmetry' (1980, 141). This political cosmology had at its symbolic centre the monarch himself, who was logically identified with the sun, creating the living myth of the sun king (Mínguez 2001; Tanner 1993, 244). The whole cosmos of the Retiro Palace celebrates the sun king and the moon queen. He converts the motif of the hunt of love of Apollo for Daphne into a 'hunt of greatness' for Philip who becomes a 'Segundo césar de los orbes' (second Caesar ruler of the globe) .[17] Phoebus offers Mariana de Austria his beams of light (1969, 1.2195). Calderón presents a laudatory iconic depiction of the monarch, who, by virtue of being humble, becomes the perfect lover.[18] Through this semi-opera, Apollo/ Philip IV purges his three vices (avarice, arrogance, and lust) to become the perfect courtier through his recognition of love. As a result, we can note a social understanding of love similar to what Stephen Jaeger has termed 'ennobling love': 'a form of aristocratic self-representation. Its social function is to show forth virtue in lovers, to raise their inner worth, to increase their honor and enhance their reputation. It is, or is seen, as, a response to the virtue, charisma, saintliness of the beloved' (1999, 6). Calderón turns the Ovidian model into a mirror-of-princes for King Philip, whose greatness is reflected in the icon of Apollo.

Hapsburg imperial propaganda utilized several means to represent the vastness of the Spanish empire and the greatness of its monarchs. The metaphor of the sun was the emblematic element most commonly associated with the kings. This image intertwines a number of concepts, showing that just as the sun rules alone over the universe, the king reigns alone over his subjects. The sun provided the monarchs with the sense of eternity they wished for their reigns. The witty courtiers responsible for imperial propaganda merged the cosmological and the social, in an attempt to show the perfect symmetry of the world. The Spanish empire was intended to be a cosmos where the sun king, distant, alone, and all-powerful, illuminated his subjects with his permanent beams of light.

The organizing principle of the heliocentric metaphor finds its sequel at the Buen Retiro Palace where both Calderón's and Lope's plays were staged. Lope de Vega's El amor enamorado and Calderón's El laurel de Apolo can be better apprehended once we compare them side by side and with the original Ovidian version of the myth. Lope works through the myth to develop a poetics of patronage through a sense of derision, mockery, and parody that border on what is permissible in courtly jest. He expands an Ovidian tale of eros into a discussion of patronage and courtly politics. Calderón's version of the love affair between Daphne and Apollo shows a dialectical relation to Ovid's subtext by reelaborating the myth through medieval mythography. His version of the story, although originally more faithful to the original than Lope's, focuses on the last of the three main ideas that compose the myth: *imperium*. Calderón praises his monarchs through a clever use of myths of imperial propaganda already latent in the Ovidian version. Apollo/Philip IV's amorous defeat serves to magnify them as emperors of arms just as Lope's play intentionally converts them into the arch-patrons, the rulers of letters. Ovid's *Metamorphoses* is in itself a malleable material, capable of being transformed, 'metamorphosed' so to speak, into a disquisition on poetry and politics, *armas* and *letras*, *vates* and *imperium*.

NOTES

1 The following study stems from research projects at the Seminario de Estudios Teatrales (ref. 930128) developed with generous support of the Ramón y Cajal Program (Ministerio de Educación del Gobierno de España). I would like to express my gratitude to my colleague and friend Harley Eerdman for his corrections and suggestions.
2 In the Ptolemaic system, heavenly bodies are part of spherical shells of ether, which fit tightly around each other, without any spaces between them, in the following order: moon, Mercury, Venus, sun, Mars, Jupiter, Saturn, fixed stars. The sun lies fourth in the middle of all eight bodies.
3 All translations are mine unless otherwise noted.
4 This piece is not the first one to explore Calderón's and Lope's plays back-to-back. In her analysis of nine mythological plays by Lope de Vega, Tirso de Molina, Guillen de Castro, Calderon de la Barca, and Sor Juana Ines de la Cruz, Denise DiPuccio compares the linguistic, sociological, and psychological repercussions of the myths treated in the plays and concludes: 'Lope's play shares many similarities with Calderón's two-act zarzuela' (1998, 91). *El Amor enamorado* was staged at the Buen Retiro in 1634. *El laurel de Apolo* has two separate versions. The first one was staged 28 July 1636 with stagecraft by Cosme Loti and with an introductory *loa*. It was represented again 4 March 1658 to commemorate the birth of Prince Felipe Próspero. For an analysis of the two versions see Hesse (1946) and Valbuena-Briones (1985, 9–23).

5 'quid tibi, lascive puer, cum fortibus armis?' Unless otherwise noted, all
   translations are mine. Quotations from Ovid's *Metamorphoses* are taken
   from Anthony S. Kline online edition for the University of Virginia.
6 'tu face nescio quos esto contentus amores / inritare tua, nec laudes adsere
   nostras!'
7 'figat tus omnia, Phoebe, / te meus arcus quantoque animalia cedunt /
   cuncta deo, tanto minor est tua gloria nostra.'
8 'fugat hoc, facit illud amorem.'
9 Notice the emphasis on the sharpness and bluntness of each arrow: 'quod facit, auratum est at cuspide fulget acuta. Quod fugat, obtusum est et habet sub
   harundine plumbum' [The one that kindles is golden with a sharp glistening
   point, the one that dispels is blunt with lead beneath its shaft] (1960, 1.470–1).
10 'ut canis in vacuo leporem cum Gallicus arvo vidit.'
11 For instance, *Nueva recopilación* (New Compilation) (I. title 12, law IX). For
   a further analysis of famines in early modern Spain, see Fernández Álvarez (2004, 53–97). Also see Camporesi's *Bread of Dreams* for a dissection of
   the cultural representation of famine.
12 See Pagden (1995).
13 Many imperial propagandists such as Agustín de Mora considered the image as the most fitting for the Austrias. In his *El Sol eclipsado*, one can read:
   'no se puede negar ser el Sol la más apropiada idea, y gloriosa divisa de
   nuestros esclarecidos, y Católicos Reyes de España. Pues si aquel fue Príncipe de los Astros por ser viva imagen de Dios que retrata perfectamente
   su ser divino … quién duda, que esta es, la mayor, y más alta prenda de
   nuestros Católicos Reyes' [who can doubt that the sun is the most appropriate idea, and glorious emblem of our illustrious Catholic kings of Spain.
   The sun is prince of astral bodies, true image of God and perfect portrait
   of God's divinity … and it cannot be denied either that it is the highest gift
   of our Catholic kings] (quoted in Mínguez 1994, 210).
14 Elizabeth Wright notes 'Lope's carnival performance recreates the Renaissance ideal of a Virgilian stage – a theater full of citizens of the republic
   who listen to the public poet as he speaks to the sovereign' (2001, 62).
15 Calderón has already utilized the laurel as an imperial symbol, for instance, in *La gran Cenobia* (1969, 1.485).
16 See, for instance, *Le muse in danza d'intorno alla felicísima cuna dell'imperiale e
   regio infante* (1716) by the Academia di lettere dedicated to Leopold of Austria and staged in Trento; or Pedro Metastasio's *Il Parnaso accusato e difeso*
   (1738, 1739, 1750) series staged for Spain's Isabel Christine, Charles VI of
   Austria, and the Polish Augustus III.

17 Calderón supposedly wrote the play in honour of the late prince Felipe Próspero (1969, 1.2173).
18 José Manuel Losada Goya notes 'su lujuria tomará el cariz de un amor perfecto' [his lust has turned into perfect love] (1989, 494).

WORKS CITED

Bakhtin, Mikhail. 1984. *Rabelais and His World*. Trans. Helene Iswolsky. Bloomington: Indiana University Press.

Barnard, Mary. 1998. *The Myth of Apollo and Daphne from Ovid to Quevedo: Love, Agon, and the Grotesque*. Durham: Duke University Press.

Brown, Jonathan, and J.H. Elliott. 1980. *A Palace for a King: The* Buen Retiro *and the Court of Philip IV*. New Haven: Yale University Press.

Camporesi, Piero. 1989. *Bread of Dreams: Food and Fantasy*. Vol. 1, *Early Modern Europe*. Trans. David Gentilcore. Chicago: University of Chicago Press.

Carreño, Antonio. 1995. 'Los mitos del yo lírico: *Rimas* (1609) de Lope de Vega.' *Edad de Oro* 14:55–72.

Calderón de la Barca, Pedro. 1969. *Obras completas*. Ed. Angel Valbuena Briones. 3 vols. Madrid: Aguilar.

– 1984. *Fieras afemina Amor*. Ed. Edward Wilson. Kassel: Reichenberger.

Checa Cremades, Fernando. 1999. *Carlos V: La imagen del poder en el renacimiento*. Madrid: El Viso.

Covarrubias Orozco, Sebastián de. 1986. *Tesoro de la lengua castellana*. Ed. Martín de Riquer. Barcelona: Alta Fulla.

DiPuccio, Denise M. 1998. *Communicating Myths of the Golden Age* Comedia. Lewisburg: Bucknell University Press.

Elliott, John. H. 1989. *Spain and Its World 1500–1700: Selected Essays*. New Haven: Yale University Press.

– 1990. *El conde-duque de Olivares. El político en una época de decadencia*. Trans. Teófilo de Lozoya. Barcelona: Grijalbo.

Enríquez de Guzmán, Feliciana. 1999. 'Segunda parte de la Tragicomedia de los jardines y campos sabeos,' In *Women's Acts: Plays by Women Dramatists of Spain's Golden Age*, ed. Teresa Soufas, 229–71. Lexington: University Press of Kentucky.

Fernández Álvarez, Manuel. 2004. *Sombras y luces en la España imperial*. Madrid: Espasa-Calpe.

Hesse, Everett W. 1946. 'The Two Versions of Calderon's El laurel de Apolo.' *Hispanic Review* 14:213–34.

Huerta Calvo, Javier. 1984. 'Anatomía de una fiesta teatral burlesca del siglo XVII. (Reyes como bufones).' In *Teatro y fiesta en el Barroco*, ed. José María Díez Borque, 115–36. Madrid: Castalia.

Jaeger, Stephen J. 1999. *Ennobling Love: In Search of a Lost Sensibility*. Philadelphia: University of Pennsylvania Press.

Kenney, E.J. 1992. 'Introduction. Ovid: Sorrows of an Exile.' In *Tristia*. Trans. A.D. Melville. Oxford: Clarendon Press.

Losada Goya, José Manuel. 1989. 'Calderón de la Barca: *El laurel de Apolo*.' *Revista de Literatura* 51.102:485–94.

Maravall, José Antonio. 1984. 'Teatro, fiesta e ideología en el Barroco.' In *Teatro y fiesta en el Barroco*, ed. José María Díez Borque, 71–95. Madrid: Castalia.

Mínguez, Víctor. 1994. 'Los emblemas solares, la imagen del príncipe y los programas astrológicos en el arte efímero.' In *Actas del I Simposio Internacional de emblemática*, 209–53. Teruel: Instituto de Estudios Turolenses.

– 2001. *Los reyes solares: Iconografía astral de la monarquía hispánica*. Castelló de la Plana: Universitat Jaume I.

Morán Turina, J. Miguel, and Fernando Checa Cremades. 1986. *Las casas del Rey: Casas de Campo, Cazaderos y Jardines Siglos XVI y XVII*. Madrid: El Viso.

Ovid. 1924. *Tristia. Ex ponto*. Ed. Arthur Leslie Wheeler. London: William Heineman.

– 1960. *Metamorphoses/Metamorphoseon*. Ed. Frank Justus Miller. 2 vols. Cambridge, MA: Harvard University Press.

– 1997. *Ovid's Metamorphoses: Books 1–5*. Ed. William S. Anderson. London Oklahoma: University of Oklahoma Press.

– *Metamorphoses*. Ed. Anthony S. Kline. The Ovid Project. Online edition URL: http://etext.virginia.edu/latin/ovid/trans/Ovhome.htm

Padgen, Anthony. 1995. *Kings of All the World: Ideologies of Empire in Spain, Britain and France c. 1500–c. 1800*. New Haven: Yale University Press.

Relación de las fiestas que las imperial ciudad de Toledo hizo al nacimiento del Principe N. S. Felipe VI deste nombre. 1605. Madrid: Luis Sánchez.

Relación verdadera de las grandiosas fiestas, y regozijos, que la muy noble, y muy leal Ciudad de Valladolid hizo a nuestro Rey, y Señor Don Felipe Quarto el Grande, viniendo de Irun de entregar a la Christianissima Reyna de Francia Doña Maria tersa de Austra, su hija; donde se declaran los grandes aparatos de fuego, luminarias, toros, y cañas, y los Señores que torearon, y la mascara que hizieron. 1660. Madrid: Ioseph Fernandez de Buendia.

Segal, Charles. 1969. 'Myth and Philosophy in the *Metamorphoses*: Ovid's Augustanism and the Augustan Conclusion of Book XV.' *American Journal of Philology* 90:257–92.

Rothberg, I.E. 1983. '*El amor enamorado* de Lope de Vega y la tradición mitográfica.' In *Estudios sobre el Siglo de Oro: Homenaje a Raymond MacCurdy*, 93–101. Madrid: Cátedra.

Tanner, Marie. 1993. *The Last Descendant of Aeneas: The Hapsburg and the Mythic Image of the Emperor*. New Haven: Yale University Press.

Valbuena Briones, A. 1985. 'El tema del laurel de Apolo en Calderón.' In *Calderón and the Baroque Tradition: Proceedings of an International Symposium*, ed. Kurt L. Levy et al., 9–23. Toronto: University of Toronto Press.

Vega Carpio, Felix Lope de. 1965. *El Amor enamorado. Comedia famosa. Obras de Lope de Vega. XIV*. Ed. Marcelino Menéndez Pelayo, 239–84. Madrid: Atlas.

– 1965. *El vellocino de oro. Obras de Lope de Vega. XIV*. Ed. Marcelino Menéndez Pelayo, 99–133. Madrid: Atlas.

Vélez-Sainz, Julio. 2006. *El Parnaso español: Canon, mecenazgo y propaganda en la poesía del Siglo de Oro*. Madrid: Visor.

Wright, Elizabeth. 2001. *Pilgrimage to Patronage: Lope de Vega and the Court of Philip III: 1598–1621*. Lewisburg: Bucknell University Press.

14 Tirso's Counter-Ovidian Self-Fashioning: *Deleitar aprovechando* and the Daughters of Minyas

CHRISTOPHER B. WEIMER

In 1635, Gabriel Téllez, the Mercedarian friar better known to *corral* audiences as Tirso de Molina, published *Deleitar aprovechando* (Edifying Amusements), the second of his two miscellaneous collections of prose, poetry, and theatrical texts. Unlike its popular 1624 predecessor, *Los cigarrales de Toledo* (The Country Houses of Toledo), *Deleitar* represented a radical shift in its author's output and – still more significantly – in the fashioning of his public persona. In contrast to *Los cigarrales*'s secular novellas and *comedias*, *Deleitar* consisted instead of saints' lives and *autos sacramentales* (allegorical Eucharist plays). The volume's overt piety and explicit moral exemplarity offer a 'twist *a lo divino* of the familiar Boccaccian pattern,' according to Margaret Wilson, who considers *Deleitar* 'the prototype of the ascetic-novelistic collection, which makes its appearance in Spain as the spirit of *desengaño* begins to prevail' (1954, 20). Similarly, in his study of Tirso's prose works, André Nougué asserts: 'Ainsi, le *Deleytar aprovechando* aura un caractère résolument dévot et édifiant; vue sous cet angle, l'oeuvre de Tirso est nouvelle; les ouvrages des prédécesseurs se contentaient surtout de divertir; *Deleytar aprovechando* divertira, certes, mais en instruisant' [Thus, *Deleitar aprovechando* was to possess a resolutely devout and edifying character; seen from this angle, Tirso's work is new; his predecessors' texts were content to entertain above all else; *Deleitar aprovechando* would entertain, surely, but would do so as it taught] (1962, 210).[1] Perhaps owing to this difference, *Deleitar* – with the exception of the sometimes-excerpted novella *El bandolero* (The Bandit), a biography of San Pedro Armengol – has never won the popularity or the respect that Tirso's original audiences as well as subsequent generations have to some extent accorded the more lighthearted *Los cigarrales*. However, this often-neglected volume may well be of far greater interest in the mapping of Gabriel Téllez's public self-fashioning as an author, for it can be read as a repudiation of the Ovidian traditions which Téllez had followed and even exemplified as Tirso de Molina, especially in its frame tale's inversion of the Daughters of Minyas sequence in Ovid's *Metamorphoses*.

For any aspiring writer to realize, or even first conceive of them, literary ambitions require models of what authors are or what they do: 'no poet,' Lawrence Lipking notes, 'can become himself without inheriting an idea of what it means to be a poet' (1984, viii). From the Middle Ages onward, ideas of literary reputation and fame were often derived from the canonical writers of classical antiquity; the most compelling model of a writer's life *as a writer* was the example set by Virgil, 'who supplied the pattern of a career to so many later poets' (1984, xi). That pattern was the *rota Virgilii* (Virgilian wheel) represented by the Roman author's *Eclogues*, *Georgics*, and *Aeneid* – the movement from a pastoral apprenticeship through didactic poetry to a final empire-celebrating, *fama*-ensuring epic masterpiece, a progression which also mirrored the development of civilization from human coexistence with nature in its original state through an agrarian society to an imperial polity.[2] Aspiring dramatists, however, were bound to find Virgil's model less immediately helpful, since he did not write for the theatre. As Patrick Cheney has contended in the cases of Marlowe (1997) and Shakespeare (2004), would-be early modern playwrights might instead have turned to Virgil's younger Augustan counterpart Ovid, whose works included a lost tragedy, *Medea*, and whose *Amores* describes his poetic alter-ego's efforts to write drama (1977–89, 2:xviii, 12–18) and his personal confrontation with its muse, *Romana Tragoedia* herself (1977–89, 3.i).[3] Ovid, whose 'lifelong fascination with Virgil's poetry and his even greater fascination with Virgil's place in Roman literary history' is noted by Richard Tarrant (2002, 23), aimed at equalling or surpassing the author of the *Aeneid* with his own poetic trajectory moving from amorous elegy to tragedy to epic.[4]

Ovid's reconceptualization of the poet's career concerned subject matter as well as genre: from his earliest love poems through the *Metamorphoses*, Ovid celebrated the power of the erotic and both the glories and the pains entailed in surrender to it. He repeatedly positioned his texts in direct opposition to Virgil's glorification of the 'unflinching duty and piety' defined as imperial Rome's supreme virtues: the *Aeneid*, for example, exalted Aeneas's obedient renunciation of Dido's love in order to found Rome, but Ovid's *Heroides* (Heroines) told the same story from

Dido's point of view, giving the abandoned queen the opportunity to reproach her lover eloquently and at length for the pain his obedience caused her (*Heroides* 1977–89, 7; Braudy 1997, 135–6).[5] Moreover, if Ovid's spirited manual of seduction, his *Ars amatoria* (The Art of Love), gleefully undermined the public morality Augustus sought to buttress, the *Metamorphoses* assailed numerous Roman orthodoxies of the era:

> that poem is more political and more profoundly philosophical; more political in that it is a veiled attack on the whole basis of Augustan reform: religiosity, apotheosis, Augustus as Jupiter, Virgilian-Augustan epic, the notion that Augustan Rome is anything more than another item in the long list of metamorphoses; and more philosophical in that it is a veiled attack on some of the most basic elements of the Roman national character. (Curran 1972, 90)

Ovid thus offered a decidedly subversive, counter-Virgilian model for early modern writers who might have chosen to imitate him.

In Gabriel Téllez's Spain, writers were certainly conscious of both Virgil's and Ovid's examples, since nearly all their texts were available in Latin and in multiple translations. Among the latter, Juan del Encina had translated Virgil's *Eclogues* for publication as early as 1496, while the *Georgics* first appeared in Spanish 1586 and the *Aeneid* in 1555; Ovid's *Metamorphoses* received three complete translations during the sixteenth century, preceded by selections from the *Heroides* in 1490 and followed by a complete *Heroides* in 1608 and a *Remedia amoris* (Remedies for Love) in 1611 (Beardsley 1970). One notable example of a classically inspired literary career might well have been that of Miguel de Cervantes. Frederick de Armas has argued that Cervantes' self-conscious progress from the pastoral *Galatea* through *Don Quijote* to the decidedly epic *Persiles* can be considered an attempt to follow the Virgilian *cursus* in prose. At the same time, however, Cervantes longed for acclaim as a playwright even as many of his works return obsessively to the idea of metamorphosis and are replete with references to Ovid, including his self-inscription as 'nuestro español Ovidio' in one of *Don Quijote*'s introductory sonnets (1978, 64).[6] During the same era, just as Cervantes drew extensively upon the author of the *Metamorphoses*, his *bête noire* Lope de Vega repeatedly cited, alluded to, and imitated Ovid's works in his verse, his novels, and above all in countless examples of the *comedia nueva* (new comedy), that supremely Ovidian genre which he pioneered.[7]

Lope, of course, was the young Gabriel Téllez's own immediate literary model, and Tirso's theatrical output, especially those works written during his creative prime, abounds in Ovidian motifs and themes, from his sparkling erotic love comedies to his tales of protean cross-dressed *damas* to his most politically challenging plays.[8] Students of the *comedia* have only to recall *Don Gil de las calzas verdes* (Don Gil of the Green Stockings), in which Doña Juana's metamorphic masquerade as the fictitious Don Gil proves so contagious, or *El vergonzoso en palacio* (The Shy Man at Court), in which Serafina falls in love with a portrait of herself dressed as a man, to glimpse the inescapable Ovidian palimpsest beneath many of Tirso's plays. And it would be difficult to imagine a more Ovidian *comedia* than Tirso's *Privar contra su gusto* (The Reluctant Royal Favourite): written after Philip IV's accession to the Spanish throne at the age of sixteen, this political romantic comedy draws on the *Metamorphoses* to model its interlocking love intrigues on Ovid's accounts of Apollo and Daphne and of Diana and Actaeon while criticizing a young king's ill-considered exercises of his authority (Weimer 1998). Nor should we forget the overt Ovidianism of the 1624 *Cigarrales de Toledo*, which was the author's first published work and which contains the complete text of the above-mentioned *El vergonzoso en palacio* (1994, 105–228) along with a lengthy verse setting of the 'Fábula de Siringa y Pan' (1994, 262–70) based on Ovid's account of Syrinx and Pan in book 1 of the *Metamorphoses* (1977–89, 1:689–712).[9] When the friar Gabriel Téllez became Tirso de Molina, his art took shape as a distinctly erotic, metamorphic, and subversive one. Even his pen name evokes the thyrsus, the ivy-covered fennel staff carried by Bacchus/Dionysos and his followers during the theatre god's rites – mentioned in numerous classical texts and on more than one occasion in the *Metamorphoses*.

Tirso's literary career, however, was to follow Ovid's too closely, taking an unexpected and darkly ironic turn. Ovid's poetic ascent ended abruptly, of course, when the emperor banished him in 8 CE to a remote Roman outpost, the Black Sea port of Tomis, for reasons clouded in mystery.[10] Neither Augustus nor his successor Tiberius ever rescinded this sentence, despite Ovid's many efforts before his death in 17 CE to win a reprieve and return to Rome. Ovid writes in his post-exile *Tristia* (Sorrows) that he was punished for *carmen et error*, 'a poem and a blunder' (1977–89, 2.207; 1995, 31). The *carmen* was the *Ars amatoria*, which was removed by decree from Rome's libraries, but even today we continue to speculate as to what the *error* could have been. Ovid may have stumbled onto or even become a party to some secret with political implications, and his self-comparison to Actaeon would seem to support this interpretation:

> Ah, why did I see anything, why make my
> Eyes criminal, know guilt so imprudently?
> Actaeon all unwitting saw Diana
> Naked, yet for his hounds a prey was he. (*Tristia* 1977–89, 2.103–6; 1995, 28)

As Peter Green has argued in his case for Ovid's knowledge of a Julian conspiracy seeking to control the succession, it seems more logical to attribute Augustus's sentence to court intrigues than to his suddenly conceived disapproval of a work which had appeared a decade earlier; the *carmen* was primarily a pretext for punishing the *error*:

> Though Ovid's constant sniping at the morals and dignity of the *pax Augusta* provided an extra incentive to those selecting his place of exile, his *relegatio* had solid political motivation behind it. On the other hand, his public reputation as the arch-exponent of fashionable erotic heterodoxy provided Augustus with ideal camouflage for more crucial matters. (1998, 222)[11]

Similarly, in 1625 the Junta de la Reformación (Committee for the Reformation of Morals) recently formed by Philip IV and his influential favourite the Count-Duke of Olivares issued a decree that Tirso cease writing for the stage and that the Mercedarian Order remove him from Madrid:

> Tratóse del escándalo que causa un fraile Mercedario que se llama el maestro Téllez, por otro nombre Tirso, con comedias que hace profanas y de malos incentivos y ejemplos. Y por ser caso notorio, se acordó que se consulte a S.M. de que el confesor diga al nuncio le eche de aquí a uno de los monasterios más remotos de su Religión y le imponga excomunicación mayor, *latae sententiae*, para que no haga comedias ni otro ningún género de versos profanos. Y esto se haga luego. (cited in Kennedy 1974, 85)

> [The meeting considered the scandal caused by a Mercedarian friar named Maestro Téllez, otherwise known as Tirso, by his writing of profane plays which set a bad example. And since the affair is notorious, it was agreed to petition His Majesty that the confessor should tell the nuncio to expel him hence to one of the more remote monasteries of his order, and forbid him

on pain of excommunication to write plays or any other kind of profane verse. This to be done immediately.] (Wilson 1977, 25)

The parallels between Tirso's exile and Ovid's cannot help but fascinate. Just as Ovid was hardly the only poet to write love elegies during Augustus's reign, Tirso was one among many playwrights producing risqué romantic comedies for Madrid's public theatres in the 1620s – yet he found his case treated as unique in its alleged notoriety and in the emphatic official action it provoked. This renders suspect the Junta's moralistic verdict, especially given that Tirso's political *comedias* such as *Privar contra su gusto* could easily have antagonized powerful figures at court, including Olivares himself.[12] It is likewise worth noting that the Mercedarians chose to abide by the letter rather than the spirit of the Junta's decision, appointing the playwright *Comendador* (prior) of their monastery in Trujillo. Surely this troublesome priest's elevation to high office was not the ignominy which Olivares and the Junta de la Reformación had had in mind: 'Téllez was evidently not out of favor with his superiors, which again makes it seem likely that the real reasons for his silencing were not moral' (Wilson 1977, 27). Further evidence of the government's political animus is offered by the circumstances surrounding his second exile from Madrid in 1640. After returning to the capital as his order's chronicler, he was suddenly deprived of that office by his superiors and again banished from the city, this time never to return. On that occasion, Wilson notes, the vicar provincial 'issued an edict forbidding any of the Mercedarians of Madrid to write satires in verse or prose against the government. This edict suggests that Tirso was being censured on political grounds' (1977, 28). While Gabriel Téllez was obviously not involved with anything as explosive as whichever anti-Augustan conspiracy Ovid was unlucky enough to discover, it is quite easy to imagine Tirso de Molina's veiled criticism and mockery provoking the Count-Duke or his supporters to the point that they would twice demand this gadfly's removal from Madrid to Mercedarian monasteries far from the capital.

Gabriel Téllez was decidedly more fortunate in his misfortune than Ovid: however remote the monasteries of Trujillo and Cuenca might have seemed to him, they were still infinitely preferable to Tomis during the early first century. Nevertheless, although Téllez would continue to revise and publish his plays after 1625 with no apparent interference from his superiors and although performance of his works was not prohibited, his career as an active dramatist had effectively ended. It is extremely unlikely that we will ever know what specifically motivated the Mercedarian to publish the rigorously pious *Deleitar aprovechando* years after his involuntary return to full-time religious life, nor are the respective proportions of Téllez's sincerity or his pragmatism in writing this work ever likely to be measured. There can be no doubt, however, that this work offers an explicit repudiation of the Ovidian emulation and poetics which characterize Tirso de Molina's earlier writings.

Deleitar's first allusion to the *Metamorphoses* appears in Gabriel Téllez's fulsome dedication of the work to his patron Don Luis Fernández de Córdoba y Arce, the Spanish governor of Chile (1625–9), whose deeds the Mercedarian at one point equates to those of Jesus Christ (1994, 12). Comparing his own authorial efforts to those of his distinguished sources for the three hagiographies which will be recounted in *Deleitar*, Téllez writes of his work: 'saldrá de la competencia con la ganancia que Midas contra Apolo, que Aragnes contra Palas, y yo con el acierto, por lo menos, de habérselas dedicado a V.S., en cuya casa viven recíprocas la virtud, la afabilidad y la nobleza' [it will emerge from the competition with the reward of Midas against Apollo, of Arachne against Pallas Athena, and I (will emerge) with the wisdom, at least, of having dedicated my efforts to Your Lordship, in whose house thrive together virtue, kindness, and nobility] (1994, 9–10). Téllez here uses his protestation of his work's inferiority, a commonplace instance of the humility topos, to introduce two significant episodes involving artistic creation and performance from the *Metamorphoses*: Pan's musical contest with Apollo, which was witnessed by Midas (1977–89, bk 11.153–93), and the young Lydian weaver Arachne's challenge to Minerva (1977–89, 7.1–145). The subtlety of Téllez's syntax should be noted here: he flatters his patron by paralleling him with the immortals even as he simultaneously parallels himself to and differentiates himself from the imprudent Midas and Arachne. The reference to Midas and Apollo immediately recalls Tirso's prominent use of the 'Fábula de Siringa y Pan' in the *Cigarrales* noted above – the story of the origin of Pan's pipes, which he made from the reeds into which the determinedly chaste Syrinx was transformed in order to escape his amorous advances. It is significant that the first Ovidian allusion in *Deleitar* again evokes Pan and his pipes but in this work refers instead to the contest in which that famous instrument failed to match the sublime music of Apollo's lyre: if the eroticism of *Cigarrales* found one symbolic expression in the narration of a satyr's priapic pursuit of a reluctant nymph and the invention of new art as an unintended result, *Deleitar* distances itself from the earlier volume by dismissing Pan's rustic flutings and all that they represent – indeed, Téllez's text does not even mention Pan by name.[13] Furthermore, Pan – unlike the less fortunate Marsyas, flayed alive for his presumption (1977–89, 6.382–400) – receives no retribution in the *Metamorphoses* for daring to think himself Apollo's artistic equal; it is Midas, who witnesses the entire contest yet alone refuses to recognize the Olympian's manifest superiority, whom Apollo punishes for his 'boorish and blasphemous musical preference' by transforming his human ears into those of an ass (Barkan 1986, 260). Wise readers, Téllez implies, would do well not to emulate Midas by failing to differentiate between the earthly eroticism of *Cigarrales* and the heavenward gaze of *Deleitar*.[14]

Just as Midas's example teaches a lesson concerning discernment as well as discretion, Arachne's shows how arrogance leads both the interpretative and the creative human faculties astray. The prodigiously talented girl wilfully blinds herself to the obvious meaning of Minerva's tapestry, in which the goddess pointedly depicts not only the majesty of the Olympians but also their exemplary transformations of humans into mountains, birds, and a temple's marble steps:

> To these, Minerva added at each corner –
> so that the girl be warned of what awaits her
> audacity – a painted scene of contest.
> Each pictured warning had its own bright colors
> and figures –each distinct – in miniature.   (1977–89, 6.83–6; 1993, 180)

Worse still, Arachne refuses to submit or even defer to Minerva, either in the goddess's assumed guise of a venerable old woman or in her true divine form, and she dares to weave a tapestry accusing the gods of using metamorphosis for their most selfish, callous ends – not to maintain their majesty but to victimize mortals. Téllez here warns against such radical challenges to sovereign authority and assertions of individual autonomy, which of course won for Arachne only her own transformation into a spider. Moreover, the *Metamorphoses*' ekphrastic description of Arachne's woven portraits of the gods and their victims self-reflexively constitutes her visual 'text' as an analogue to Ovid's subversive epic itself: 'It requires no great leap of the imagination to see in Arachne's tapestry all the elements of Ovid's own poetic form in the *Metamorphoses*, which is, after all, a poem that eschews a clear narrative structure and rather creates a finely woven fabric of stories related via transformation' (Barkan 1986, 4). If Tirso de Molina's *comedias* had earned their author censure and exile by foregrounding the erotic or mocking the vices and excesses of the powerful, Gabriel Téllez – who here represents himself, by virtue of his deference to his aristocratic patron, not only as wiser than Midas but also wiser than the Lydian weaver and by extension Ovid himself – will not repeat those mistakes in *Deleitar aprovechando*. The remainder of *Deleitar's* dedication provides further evidence of this authorial self-fashioning: its lengthy, unblushing panegyric to Fernández de Córdoba y Arce's accomplishments in the New World offers the converse of Arachne's and Ovid's portraits of the immortals at their worst.

With this counter-Ovidian context in place, Téllez proceeds to construct the frame tale which will serve as a pretext for the presentation of the poems, novellas, and plays making up the bulk of *Deleitar aprovechando*. As he did in *Los cigarrales de Toledo*, Tirso followed what Wilson, cited above, labelled Boccaccio's model, placing *Deleitar aprovechando's* constituent texts within an account of noble friends narrating, reciting, and performing those works for one another over the course of three days: the mornings and afternoons of a Sunday, Monday, and Tuesday. However, these days do not fall randomly on the calendar, as the very first paragraph of the frame narrative explains. These are the pre-Lenten days of Carnival in Madrid, during which Tirso's pious young noblemen and their equally pious, equally noble wives seek refuge, not from the plague or floods, as in Boccaccio or Marguerite de Navarre, but from 'las permisiones de las Carnestolendas' [the license of Carnival] which they find so repugnant:

> – Opóngase – dijo doña Beatriz – en cuanto nos fuere posible, nuestra recreación lícita, a los reprobados festines de los profesores del siglo, y usando de lo deleitable y honesto, que en la diferencia de los tiempos, para aliviar fastidios, nos señaló la Iglesia, entretengámonos de suerte que, imitando lo regocijado de estas Carnestolendas, cercenemos los vicios que las profanan. (1994, 24)

> ['Let us oppose,' said Doña Beatriz, 'as much as possible, our moral recreation to the depraved revels of the teachers of our era, and making use of what is delightful and honest, which the church taught us in days past to relieve boredom, let us amuse ourselves in such a way that, imitating the pleasures of these days of Carnival, we may diminish the vices which profane them.']

Beatriz's companions quickly agree and adopt the proposal made by Don Luis that they should set their pastimes against 'los totalmente licenciosos del vulgo, desde el domingo hasta el martes ... término y fin de nuestra profana Pascua' [the utterly licentious (pastimes) of the common people from Sunday until Tuesday ... the end of our city's profane celebrations]:

> Si ellos se recrean con novelas ridículas, recreémonos nosotros con historias devotas; y si allá se representan comedias que proporcionan a sus comidas, representemos coloquios que solemnicen el banquete con que en los más de los templos hace el amor plato franco a sus alumnos. Adornen ellos las suyas de entremeses, músicas y bailes; vestiremos las nuestras de poemas, himnos y canciones sacras. (1994, 24)

> [If they amuse themselves with ridiculous novels, let us amuse ourselves with devout histories; and if they stage plays to go along with their feasts, let us present pious dialogues to solemnize the Holy Banquet which in most temples Love (Christ) grants freely to his disciples. Let them festoon their plays with comic interludes, music, and dances; we will garb ours with poems, hymns, and sacred songs.]

This agenda explicitly rejects the secular contents of Tirso de Molina's *Cigarrales de Toledo* a decade earlier, even as the characters likewise reject mythological tales along with more contemporary genres:

> – Poca necesidad tenemos de novelas – replicó doña Beatriz – habiendo vidas de santos, en lo prodigioso de tanta más admiración que en lo fingido, cuanto más se aventajan sus verdades a las fábulas, que, por mucho que quimericen, no las igualan. (1994, 24)

> ['Little need have we of novels,' replied Doña Beatriz, 'when we have biographies of saints, the marvels of which provoke far more admiration than mere fiction; how their truths outshine myths, which, however much they may fill people's heads with fantastic ideas, cannot equal them.']

Here the pagan magic of classical mythology – which certainly includes the transformations of mortals and immortals throughout the *Metamorphoses* – is dismissed in favour of the miracles and transfigurations which so often provide the climactic events of Christian hagiographic narratives. This religious condemnation of Ovidian storytelling, which will recur in the work's final paragraphs, further develops the opposition, initially signalled in the dedication, between *Deleitar* and those literary models offered by the Roman poet and formerly followed by the Mercedarian friar.

Most central to Gabriel Téllez's counter-Ovidian poetics, however, is the plot itself of *Deleitar*'s frame tale, which explicitly reworks and inverts the opening sequence of book 4 of the *Metamorphoses*: the account of the daughters of Minyas, or the Minyades. Book 3 of the poem concludes with Ovid's version of the events likewise depicted by Euripides in *The Bacchae*: King Pentheus's destruction and dismemberment after he refused to recognize the divinity of the newly arrived god Bacchus and outlawed his rites. Book 4 begins not only with the Theban people accepting the new god, but also with the priesthood's decree making mandatory the celebrations previously forbidden by Pentheus:

> The priest has given orders: there will be
> A Bacchic festival: all women-servants
> Must be relieved from labor on that day;
> They and their mistresses are all to wrap
> The hides of animals around their breasts,
> Loosen the bands that bind their tresses, and
> Wear garlands on their heads, and in their hands
> Hold fast the leafy thyrsus. And he adds
> That any who would slight the deity
> Will face the unrelenting Bacchus's wrath.   (1977–89, 4.4–9; 1993, 109)

All the city's families but one abide by these decrees, Ovid relates:

> And only Minyas's daughters stay at home;
> they violate the holy day; the tasks
> Minerva sets are theirs: close to the loom,
> they give their household women work to do. (1977–89, 4.32–5; 1993, 110)

The intertextuality is clear: just as Gabriel Téllez's devout aristocrats withdraw from the carnival revels enjoyed by their fellow residents of Madrid, the Minyades reject the sensual abandon of Bacchus's rites.

Revealingly, Don Luis himself foregrounds this parallel in mythological terms, lamenting of the city's excesses during these three days, '¿En qué hogar pajizo no triunfan Baco y Ceres?' [In what humble home do

Bacchus and Ceres not triumph?] (1994, 22). Moreover, the text describes the pious nobles' 'honestas conversaciones' [virtuous conversations] as 'flores del ingenio que, enemistadas con Venus, coronaban a Minerva' [flowers of ingenuity which, enemies of Venus, crowned Minerva] (1994, 19), evoking the Ovidian sisters' devotion to the weaving decreed by Minerva, cited above, and one sibling's scornful rejection of Bacchus out of devotion to that goddess:

> And one, whose thumb is agile, as she draws
> a thread, says to her sisters: 'Let us now –
> while others stop their work to join the crowd
> upon this so-called feast day – on our part
> (since we are great Minerva's votaries,
> and she is a much finer deity),
> lighten the useful labor of our hands
> with varied talk; our ears are idle; let
> each take her turn at telling tales, so that
> the hours may seem less tedious to those
> who listen.'   (1977–89, 4.36–41; 1993, 110)

Téllez thus illustrates the opposition between carnival excess and edifying godliness among an aristocratic minority in Madrid with the same opposition between the god of wine and the goddess of wisdom employed by Ovid in his account of the Minyades' defiance of Bacchus. Furthermore, as the concluding lines of the above verses from the *Metamorphoses* indicate, Téllez's nobles propose to occupy themselves during Carnival in precisely the same fashion as did the sisters during Bacchus's revels: exchanging stories. Nor do the weavers choose their tales – accounts of Pyramus and Thisbe, Mars and Venus, Leucothoe and Clytie, and Salmacis and Hermaphroditus – at random. Barkan explains: 'As holdouts against the power of Bacchus, the Minyades tell stories about the dangers of all those forces which he represents: love, sensuality, transformation' (1986, 57). The daughters of Minyas exchange cautionary tales intended to affirm their resistance to the newly recognized deity, just as *Deleitar*'s aristocrats recite saints' biographies and perform *autos sacramentales* for one another in order to edify their shared faith.

However, *Deleitar*'s perspective is diametrically opposed to the Roman poet's. Ovid's account of the daughters of Minyas does not, after all, present them in a favourable light. They defy the edicts of the priests and their refusal to acknowledge Bacchus's divinity after the god's spectacular destruction of Pentheus is both arrogant and fool-hardy. The poem itself describes their obstinacy in overtly blasphemous terms: 'The tale was done – but not the sisters' scorn / for Bacchus, and their weaving still went on, / the desecration of his holy day' (1977–89, 4.388 –9; 1993, 124–5). The sisters do not even recognize their danger as it is indicated by at least three of the stories they themselves tell. Their accounts of Pyramus and Thisbe's double suicide, of Leucothoe being buried alive by her own honour-obsessed father, and of the lovesick nymph Salmacis merging her body with her beloved's against his will all show the price to be paid when the passions are thwarted or denied – yet this is precisely the sisters' own fatal error, not only in refusing to join in the Bacchic rites themselves, but also in forbidding their maid-servants to do so. And thus Bacchus metamorphoses them into bats – blind, squeaking creatures forever consigned to the darkness: 'since they detest the day, they fly by night' (1977–89, 4.414–5; 1993, 125). In contrast, Gabriel Téllez lauds his devout young nobles for their piety and their refusal to abandon themselves to the traditional Carnival fes-tivities; their success in luring new listeners and spectators away from those revelries is as praiseworthy as the Minyades' confinement of their serving women is cruel. When the Spanish aristocrats recount pagan myths, including a 'Fábula de Píramo y Tisbe' [Myth of Pyramus and Thisbe] corresponding to the first tale told by the Minyades, their criti-cal narrative perspective affirms their moral and theological orthodoxy, while their accounts of conquered passions and the saints' transcend-ence of earthly temptations offer positive models of self-mastery rather than negative examples of the folly of denying irresistible desires.[15] In this counter-Ovidian text, Christian piety conspicuously supplants Ovid's own poetics.

In the concluding paragraphs of *Deleitar aprovechando*, Téllez offers one final, unmistakable rejection of Ovid. Summarizing the pernicious effects of profane books, he writes of how 'hazañas impropias en los de caballerías, amores vanos en los pastoriles, sucesos inútiles en las nove-las y transformaciones alegóricas en las fábulas, entorpecen costumbres y tiranizan tiempos' [improper deeds in books of chivalry, unrequited love in pastoral tales, pointless plot twists in novels, and allegorical transformations in fables dull people's customs and tyrannize the times in which they live] (1994, 949). This list of examples is significant: while the first three rank among the most persistently popular fictional genres in early modern Spain, the fourth can only refer to the far older genre of

Ovid's *Metamorphoses* and its subsequent translations, adaptations, and imitations. Téllez thus places himself as the author of *Deleitar aprovechando* in opposition not only to those writers cited disparagingly in the work's dedication to Don Luis Fernández de Córdoba y Arce – 'los autores de los Belianises, Febos, Primaleones, Dianas, Guzmanes de Alfarache, Gerardos y Persiles en nuestro castellano' [the authors of the Belianises, Febos, Primaleones, Dianas, Guzmanes de Alfarache, Gerardos and Persiles in our Castilian tongue] (1994, 9) – but he also explicitly opposes his text to the classical, Ovidian metamorphic tradition, denouncing the *Metamorphoses* and its successors in strong terms for their deleterious spiritual and moral effects.

In conclusion, *Deleitar aprovechando* can perhaps most profitably be read as an act of literary self-refashioning. In this often-neglected miscellaneous collection, Gabriel Téllez deliberately rewrote Ovid's *Metamorphoses*, appropriating and recasting the myth of the Minyades for his carefully crafted frame tale, and repeatedly condemned the Roman poet's texts and subject matter. Thus implicitly repudiating his prior emulation of Ovid's subversive example, Téllez used *Deleitar* to distance himself from the secular theatre and prose with which he had gained fame as Tirso de Molina and to construct a new, austerely devout and morally edifying public authorial persona.

NOTES

1 Unless otherwise noted, all translations are by the author.
2 See Cheney (2004, 7–9); Curtius (1953, 231–2); de Armas (2002, 269–70); and Lipking (1984, 77–8).
3 All citations from Ovid will refer to the complete Loeb edition. They refer to Ovid's book number and page number. Translations from the *Tristia* will cite Melville's *Sorrows of an Exile* by page number. Translations from the *Metamorphoses* will cite Mandelbaum by page number.
4 Consult Cheney 1997 and 2004 on the Ovidian *cursus*. Tarrant sees a conscious movement on Ovid's part as his career progressed toward a closer imitation of the Virgilian *rota* (2002, 23–7).
5 See also Tarrant (2002, 25–6).
6 Recent considerations of Cervantes' use of Ovid include McCaw (2007) and Nadeau (2002, esp. 75–105), as well as other essays in this volume. See also McFeeters's 1975 essay. Schevill's catalogue of Ovidian references in Cervantes remains useful (1913, 132–42, 174–98).

7 See Schevill (1913, 211–23) for some of Lope's most overt Ovidian allusions and borrowings.

8 Schevill considers Tirso far less given than Lope or Calderón to alluding to 'the ancients,' but he concludes this primarily on the basis of explicit textual references rather than unlabelled reworkings, thematic parallels, etc.

9 This poem may well have been written by Téllez's fellow Mercedarian Fray Plácido de Aguilar. See Cossío (1952, 460–4) for this attribution, with which Nougué (1962, 374–6) and Vázquez Fernández in his edition of *Cigarrales* (1996, 59, 261, note 543) agree, though Palomo describes the poem as 'muestra posible de un antiguo ejercicio escolar del autor' [a possible example of an old school exercise of the author's] in the introduction to her edition (1994, xxii). Whatever its paternity, Téllez's decision to include the 'Fábula' emphasizes Ovid's presence and importance in the text of *Cigarrales*.

10 Ovid's punishment was a *relegatio* (relegation) to a specified location within the empire rather than true exile, which would have stripped him of his Roman citizenship and property. *Relegatio* allowed the poet to retain both, although he could not leave Tomis as long as the relegation remained in effect. See Cohen's 2008 article on such punishments under Augustus.

11 Goold (1983) and Norwood (1963) offer similar lines of argument.

12 See Kennedy's detailed discussion of literary politics in Madrid (1974) as well as her essays on *Tanto es lo de mas como lo de menos* (1980) and *Privar contra su gusto* (1981). See also my essay on *Privar* as a work supporting one of Olivares's unsuccessful competitors for the king's favour, the Count of Villamediana (2000).

13 See Fumo's comments on the mythographic tradition foregrounding the connections between the *Metamorphoses'* two narrations involving Pan (2007, 137–9).

14 Intriguingly, Leach reads Midas as a would-be artist who flees to the pastoral world after the failure of his attempt to recuperate the Golden Age with the magical touch he received from Bacchus (1974, 131–3).

15 See Cossío (1952, 616–21) and Testa (1967) for analyses of Téllez's 'Píramo y Tisbe.' My essay 'The Poetry of Metamorphosis and the Prose of Sainthood' (2000) examines *Deleitar*'s other interpolated mythological poem, the 'Fábula de Mirra, Venus y Adonis.'

WORKS CITED

Barkan, Leonard. 1986. *The Gods Made Flesh: Metamorphosis and the Pursuit of Paganism*. New Haven: Yale University Press.

Beardsley, Theodore S., Jr. 1970. *Hispano-Classical Translations Printed between 1482 and 1699*. Pittsburgh: Duquesne University Press.

Braudy, Leo. 1997. *The Frenzy of Renown: Fame and Its History*. New York: Vintage.

Cervantes, Miguel de. 1978. *El ingenioso hidalgo don Quijote de la Mancha*. Ed. Luis Andrés Murillo. Book 1. Madrid: Castalia.

Cheney, Patrick. 1997. *Marlowe's Counterfeit Profession: Ovid, Spenser, Counter-Nationhood*. Toronto: University of Toronto Press.

– 2004. *Shakespeare, National Poet-Playwright*. Cambridge: Cambridge University Press.

Cohen, Sarah T. 2008. 'Augustus, Julia and the Development of Exile *Ad Insulam*.' *Classical Quarterly* 58.1:206–17.

Cossío, José María de. 1952. *Fábulas mitológicas en España*. Madrid: Espasa-Calpe.

Curran, Leo C. 1972. 'Transformation and Anti-Augustanism in Ovid's *Metamorphoses*.' *Arethusa* 5:71–92.

Curtius, Ernst Robert. 1953. *European Literature and the Latin Middle Ages*. Trans. Willard R. Trask. Princeton: Princeton University Press.

De Armas, Frederick A. 2002. 'Cervantes and the Virgilian Wheel: The Portrayal of a Literary Career.' In *European Literary Careers: The Author from Antiquity to the Renaissance*, ed. Patrick Cheney and Frederick A. de Armas, 268–85. Toronto: University of Toronto Press.

Fumo, Jamie C. 2007. 'Argus' Eyes, Midas' Ears, and the Wife of Bath as Storyteller.' In *Metamorphosis: The Changing Face of Ovid in Medieval and Early Modern Europe*, ed. Alison Keith and Stephen Rupp, 129–150. Toronto: Centre for Reformation and Renaissance Studies.

Goold, G.P. 1983. 'The Cause of Ovid's Exile.' *Illinois Classical Studies* 8:94–107.

Green, Peter. 1998. '*Carmen et error*: The Enigma of Ovid's Exile.' In *Classical Bearings: Interpreting Ancient History and Culture*, ed. Peter Green, 210–22. Berkeley: University of California Press.

Kennedy, Ruth Lee. 1974. *Studies in Tirso, I: The Dramatist and His Competitors, 1620–26*. Chapel Hill: University of North Carolina, Department of Romance Languages.

– 1980. 'Has Tirso Satirized the Conde-Duque de Olivares in Nineucio of *Tanto es lo de mas como lo de menos*?' In *Medieval, Renaissance and Folklore Studies in Honor of John E. Keller*, ed. Joseph R. Jones, 281–301. Newark, DE: Juan de la Cuesta.

– 1981. 'La perspectiva política de Tirso en *Privar contra su gusto*, de 1621, y la de sus comedias políticas posteriores.' In *Homenaje a Tirso*, 199–238. Madrid: Revista Estudios.

Leach, Eleanor Winsor. 1974. '*Ekphrasis* and the Theme of Artistic Failure in Ovid's *Metamorphoses*.' *Ramus* 3:102–42.

Lipking, Lawrence. 1984. *The Life of the Poet: Beginning of the Poet*. Chicago: University of Chicago Press.

McCaw, R. John. 2007. 'Transforming Phaethon: Cervantes, Ovid, and Sancho Panza's Wild Ride.' In *Metamorphosis: The Changing Face of Ovid in Medieval and Early Modern Europe*, ed. Alison Keith and Stephen Rupp, 239–250. Toronto: Centre for Reformation and Renaissance Studies.

McPheeters, Dean W. 1975. 'Ovid and the *Jealous Old Man* of Cervantes.' In *Estudios literarios de hispanistas norteamericanos dedicados a Helmut Hatzfeld con motivo de su 80 aniversario*, ed. Josep M. Sola-Sole, Alessandro Crisfulli, and Bruno Damiani, 157–65. Barcelona: Hispam.

Molina, Tirso de. 1994a. *Cigarrales de Toledo*. Ed. Pilar Palomo. Madrid: Turner.

– 1994b. *Deleitar aprovechando*. Ed. Pilar Palomo. Madrid: Turner.

– 1996. *Cigarrales de Toledo*. Ed. Luis Vázquez Fernández. Madrid: Castalia.

Nadeau, Carolyn A. 2002. *Women of the Prologue: Imitation, Myth, and Magic in Don Quixote I*. Lewisburg, PA: Bucknell University Press.

Norwood, Frances. 1963. 'The Riddle of Ovid's "Relegatio."' *Classical Philology* 58.3:150–63.

Nougué, André. 1962. *L'Oeuvre en prose de Tirso de Molina:* Los Cigarrales de Toledo *et* Deleytar aprovechando. Toulouse: Librarie des Facultes Toulouse.

Ovid. 1977–89. *Ovid*. Rev. G.P. Goold. 6 vols. 3rd ed. Loeb Classical Library. Cambridge, MA: Harvard University Press.

– 1993. *The Metamorphoses of Ovid: A New Verse Translation*. Trans. Alan Mandelbaum. San Diego: Harcourt Brace.

– 1995. *Sorrows of an Exile*. Trans. A.D. Melville. Oxford: Oxford University Press.

Schevill, Rudolph. 1913. *Ovid and the Renascence in Spain*. University of California Publications in Modern Philology 4.1. Berkeley and Los Angeles: University of California Press.

Tarrant, Richard. 2002. 'Ovid and Ancient Literary History.' In *The Cambridge Companion to Ovid*, ed. Philip Hardie, 13–33. Cambridge: Cambridge University Press.

Testa, Daniel P. 1967. 'An Analysis of Tirso de Molina's "Fábula de Pyramo y Tisbe."' *Studies in Philology* 64:132–46.

Weimer, Christopher B. 1998. 'Myth and Metamorphosis in Tirso's *Privar contra su gusto*.' In *A Star-Crossed Golden Age: Myth and the Spanish Comedia*, ed. Frederick A. de Armas, 85–107. Lewisburg PA: Bucknell University Press.

– 2000. 'The (Homo)Erotics of *Privanza*: The Count of Villamediana and Tirso's *Privar contra su gusto*.' In *Lesbianism and Homosexuality in Early Modern Spain: Literature and Theater in Context*, ed. María José Delgado and Alain Saint-Saëns, 257–79. New Orleans: University Press of the South.

– 2000. 'The Poetry of Metamorphosis and the Prose of Sainthood: Interpolated Verse Narrative in Tirso de Molina's *Deleitar aprovechando.*' *Calíope* 6.1–2:167–78.

Wilson, Margaret. 1954. 'Some Aspects of Tirso de Molina's *Cigarrales de Toledo* and *Deleytar aprovechando.*' *Hispanic Review* 22:19–31.

– 1977. *Tirso de Molina*. Boston: Twayne.

15 Noble Heirs to Apollo: Tracing African Genealogy through Ovidian Myth in Juan de Miramontes's *Armas antárticas*[1]

JASON A. MCCLOSKEY

In Juan de Miramontes Zuázola's *Armas antárticas* (Antarctic Arms) (1608–9), a former African slave named Jalonga informs the English pirate, John Oxenham, that Apollo and Andromeda are his distant ancestors. Jalonga appears to have inherited some of the talents of the classical god, as he poetically relates the tale of Apollo's pursuit of Daphne and the newly fabricated marriage of the Delphic god and Andromeda, princess of Ethiopia. These intertwined stories form an important part of Jalonga's genealogical account of his nation, and the classical mythological figures reveal a great deal about Miramontes's poem as well. Building on work by Paul Firbas (2000; 2006) and José Antonio Mazzotti (2002), this essay examines the implications of the way in which the poem casts the escaped slaves as royal descendants of Apollo and Andromeda. By focusing on the portrayal of Apollo's relation to light and on influential literary and visual representations of Andromeda, I argue that this genealogy ultimately serves to whiten the past of the former slaves. As such, the myth implicitly upholds traditional notions of nobility, an effect that Antonio Sánchez Jiménez's (2007) study of Lope de Vega's *La Dragontea* (The Dragontiad) (1598) helps to highlight. Finally, I demonstrate that the retelling of the Apollo and Daphne myth, bequeathed to Miramontes in the poems of such poets as Ovid and Garcilaso de la Vega, provides a noble literary genealogy for *Armas antárticas*.

After traversing the Isthmus of Panama with the English pirate Francis Drake in 1572, John Oxenham returned to this alluring strip of land in 1576. In fact, not only did he make it back to Panama, but Oxenham trekked across the isthmus, built a boat on the opposite coast, and proceeded to rob from isles and ships in the Pacific.[2] A poetically modified version of these exploits, and the essential assistance provided by the escaped slaves in the region, also known as maroons, form one basic plot line of the first half of *Armas antárticas*.[3] In this poem, when Oxenham first comes into contact with Jalonga, the latter introduces himself by tracing the noble genealogy of his nation to Apollo. Although he begins by launching into Ovid's well-known tale of Apollo's unsuccessful pursuit of Daphne, he continues the myth in an unexpected direction. He explains that, after Daphne had metamorphosed into a laurel tree, the god from Delphos wandered through Africa, where he encountered Andromeda, daughter of the Ethiopian king, Cepheus. Jalonga claims that he and his people are descendants of this classical royal pair: 'Nacieron de este noble ayuntamiento / los soberanos reyes de Ethiopia, / que heredan el valor, el ardimiento / de su progenitor, la ciencia propia; / tiene el reino riquísimo, opulento, / de oro y de esmeraldas grande copia, / y su sabia, ingeniosa, sutil gente / en guerra es diestra, armígera, valiente' [The sovereign kings of Ethiopia, who inherited the bravery, the ardor, and the knowledge of their progenitor, were born from this noble union. Their rich and opulent kingdom has copious stores of gold and emeralds, and its smart, clever, and deft people are skilled, battle-tested, and courageous in war] (2006, 261, stanza 345a–h).[4] Jalonga relates that his nation inherited all the virtues associated with the god Apollo, including his bravery and knowledge, not to mention all the luxuries such traits would procure, such as abundant wealth. And in keeping with their royal identity, Jalonga explains that the maroons have elected Don Luis de Mazambique their king (2006, 267, stanza 366), suggesting that they are politically well-organized.[5]

The classical genealogy plays an essential part in the noble portrayal of the maroons, and it appears to contribute to the complimentary depiction of Mazambique and his nation despite the fact that they are enemies of Spain. Their ostensibly positive portrayal has caught the attention of several critics, such as Mazzotti, who notes that 'the poem develops a sympathetic image of the maroons in order to contrast them to the British privateers. While the Englishmen are robbing and raping, the maroons are more concerned about freeing other blacks from the hands of the Spanish slave owners of Panama' (2002, 206).[6] Another way in which *Armas antárticas* creates such an image is by recounting some of the hardships that Jalonga and his fellow maroons have escaped. In his speech to Oxenham, for example, he explains: 'Aquesta servidumbre y vida amarga / sujeta a padecer tormento y pena / nos fuerza a procurar vida más larga, / como en nuestra Ethiopía, en tierra ajena, / que's dura, intolerable grave carga / collares, bragas, grillos y cadena, / palos, azotes, hierros en los gestos, / oprobios, vituperios y denuestos' [That servitude and bitter life subject to suffering, torment and pain force us to seek a longer life in a far-away land, as we had in our Ethiopia. For collars, work pants, shackles, chains, sticks, whips, iron on our faces, disgraces, offences, and insults are a tough, intolerable and heavy burden] (2006, 264, stanza 354a–h). Jalonga's description of the cruelty with which they were treated challenges certain myths associated with slavery, such as those observed by Jerome C. Branche, who writes that 'the sometimes unsubtle sophistry that produced such myths as that of happy slaves, their benign exploitation, and their equally happy integration into colonial society produced a discourse based on the silence of the subordinated' (2006, 47).[7] His report to Oxenham could thus be seen as the end of one former slave's silence, and his claim to royal ancestry through the union of Apollo and Andromeda appears to contest the common notion that slaves had no genealogical history (Branche 2006, 95).[8] *Armas antárticas* thus grants the maroon community a noble lineage, rendering them as human beings rather than items or animals for sale.[9]

However, focusing on the classical tradition from which the maroons purportedly descend reveals that the epic simultaneously deemphasizes the former slaves' African heritage.[10] Paul Firbas has observed that, in its ascription of a European mythological genealogy to the maroons, the poem follows epic conventions: 'Siguiendo la tradición del género, el poema debía inventar linajes que le confirieran al presente una relación familiar con un pasado prestigioso, como hizo Virgilio con su héroe Eneas. Así, para incorporar la novedad del cimarrón, Miramontes debia situarlo apropiadamente en alguna narración que lo legitimara y diluyera su diferencia' [Following the tradition of the genre, the poem should invent genealogies that establish a familiar relation between the present and the prestigious past, as Virgil did with his hero, Aeneas. Thus, in order to incorporate the novelty of the maroon, Miramontes must situate him appropriately in a narrative that legitimizes him and dilutes his difference] (Firbas 2006, 95). Firbas points out that genealogies constitute a fundamental aspect of epic poetry, functioning as a bridge between the past and present. Furthermore, he asserts that such a genealogy can work to mitigate what would constitute for early modern readers the strangeness of maroon protagonists by authorizing and diminishing the 'otherness' of the slaves. Accordingly, I would add that one important part of this process of making the maroons more familiar to early modern readers is the way in which the story of Apollo and Andromeda serves to whiten and brighten the past of Jalonga and his people. While this does indeed make the maroons more accessible, it also suggests that their nobility is the result of their allegedly white, European roots, and this complicates the idea of their complimentary portrayal in the epic.[11]

Mazzotti has already identified Miramontes's tendency to whiten the characters of the poem, but he does not examine the portrayal of the maroons in this context. He writes that 'the poem barely mentions the participation of Indian and black soldiers within the Spanish troops. In this way, Miramontes stresses his concept of *armas antárticas* or Antarctic arms, giving a completely white identity to the heroism of the southern hemisphere' (Mazzotti 2002, 206). From this perspective, the whitening effect noted by Mazzotti stems from neglecting to mention the contributions of the non-Spanish soldiers in defending Peru against English pirates. This appears especially revealing because, conversely, the poem does not fail to mention the historical role of the maroons when they represent enemies of the Spanish Empire. Yet this means that the epic does acknowledge their presence, so their whitening does not result from omitting them from the narrative. Instead, it arises from what the poem does say about the maroons, and what this implies about their cultural standing. Firbas remarks that 'la narración genealógica permite explicar la situación histórica del presente como una búsqueda legítima de los etíopes por recobrar su esplendor perdido' [the genealogical narration allows the historical situation to be explained as a legitimate search by the Ethiopians to recover their lost splendor] (2006, 97). Indeed, the poem suggests that, although the maroons have an illustrious history, they have lost touch with their former greatness. Moreover, Firbas's use of the word splendour ('esplendor') – in both its figurative and literal meanings – seems a quite appropriate choice to refer to the effect of making Apollo the ancestor of the maroons. On one hand, the poem depicts Jalonga and his community as endeavouring to restore the cultural sophistication (splendour) befitting a nation descended from the deity. Just as important, the genealogical link to the sun god also allows the maroons to claim inheritance to the rays of light (splendour) synonymous with Apollo.[12] Indeed, later in the epic sunlight is described as the 'luciente espl[e]ndor que Febo envía' [bright splendour that Phoebus sends] (2006, 523, stanza 1335b), and in a note to this stanza Firbas observes that splendour ('esplendor') means 'white' in the context of painting.[13] This suggests that Apollo's shine can be imagined as having a pale coloration. In addition to this connection with whiteness, moreover, the brightness of Apollo's rays naturally contrast with darkness, which was tied to explanations of African skin colour in early modern thought.[14]

This makes the light of Apollo, which Jalonga emphasizes from his first mention of his ancient forefather and throughout his ensuing narration, particularly significant. In prefacing his genealogical tale to Oxenham, the maroon underscores the resplendence of his divine ancestor, saying, 'Sabed, señor, qu'en los pasados / tiempos, por sumo dios era temido / de mi nación el *reluciente Apolo* / y aun muchos hoy por dios le tienen solo' [Know, sir, that in bygone times, *shining Apollo* was feared as the highest god, and even today many worship him alone] (2006, 257, stanza 330e–h; my emphasis). Jalonga then proceeds to tell of Apollo's unsuccessful pursuit of Daphne, who, in keeping with the Ovidian account of the story, escapes the god by transforming into a tree. From here, the familiar myth takes a surprising turn as the god, prevented from possessing Daphne, embarks on a journey that leads him to the source of the Nile River. With this introduction of sub-Saharan Africa, the narration of Apollo's wanderings plays on contrasts of light and dark, as Jalonga relates: 'Tras esto, ardiendo en cólera, impaciente, / partió, a su luz poniendo obscuro velo, / que dar señal del mal que siente, / curbrió de nubes cárdenas el cielo' [After this, impatient and burning in anger, he left, placing a dark veil over his light, and as a sign of his suffering he covered the sky with purple clouds] (2006, 260, stanza 340a–d). It is there, in this shroud of darkness, where Apollo rests, and shortly thereafter, he first sees Andromeda. His passions are rekindled by the beauty of the woman, and Apollo forgets about Daphne and tries to convince Andromeda of his virtues, introducing himself as the 'autor de la luz' [author of light] (2006, 260, stanza 342g). Once again, Jalonga's narration emphasizes the association of Apollo and light, while his description of Andromeda remains tantalizingly vague. Andromeda is said to possess 'summa beldad y hermosa cara' [utmost beauty and a lovely face] (2006, 260, stanza 342c), but Jalonga gives no indication that she excels in the typical Petrarchan standards of beauty related to whiteness, such as a bosom of alabaster attributed to Daphne before her transmutation (2006, 259, stanza 337f). It would seem that the details of Andromeda's appearance are left to the imagination of readers, but how, exactly, would they envision her?

A number of literary and artistic precedents converge in the figure of Andromeda, which contribute to her complex and contradictory image in *Armas antárticas*. In Elizabeth McGrath's article about the portrayal of Andromeda as a black woman, she surveys the representation of the mythological princess in written and visual texts of antiquity and the early modern period. McGrath concludes that, 'adherence to the "canonical" text of the *Metamorphoses* as much as to prevailing norms of beauty seems to have ensured the suppression of the black Andromeda' (1992, 16). McGrath also points out that, despite being the daughter of Cepheus and Cassiopeia (monarchs of Ethiopia), the *Metamorphoses* likened Andromeda to a marble sculpture (1992, 8–9).[15] In addition to Ovid's example in the *Metamorphoses*, Heliodorus's *Aethiopica* also exercised an enduring influence on the perception of Andromeda (McGrath 1992, 1–3). Early modern poets thought of Heliodorus's text as 'late antiquity's amorous attenuation and perfection of the epic genre' (Graf 2005, 175), and it influenceed such authors as Miguel de Cervantes, and quite possibly Miramontes's poem as well.[16] In the *Aethiopica*, the painted image of Andromeda is described as being so white that the mere sight of her induced the black Ethiopian queen, Persinna, to give birth to a white daughter named Chariclea.[17]

Of the Renaissance artists who also rendered Andromeda as a white woman, Titian is perhaps the most important in the case of sixteenth-century Spain, and his painting of her provides a visual example of how Miramontes and his readers would probably have imagined Andromeda. Titian's painting of her rescue from the sea monster by Perseus formed part of his series of mythological paintings, called the *Poesie*, which the Venetian artist had painted for the Spanish monarch, Philip II.[18] Remarking on Titian's rendering of the Ethiopian princess, Jane C. Nash writes: 'The artist builds his picture around Andromeda, who stands in the foreground and acts as the focal point from which we view the rest of the composition. The importance of Andromeda is emphasized both by her outstretched pose, which extends to the full height of the canvas, and her pale coloring, which sets her off against the dark mass of rocks' (1985, 34). Nash thus notes the whiteness of Andromeda's appearance and its importance to the composition of Titian's painting. Interestingly, McGrath also discusses the Spanish painter and poet, Francisco Pacheco, who criticized the tradition of depicting Andromeda as a fair-skinned woman, because, as he saw it, the Ethiopian princess would have been black (1992, 4–6, 8). As McGrath shows, Pacheco arrives at this conclusion with reluctance, and his 'comments make it clear that he felt that real beauty was incompatible with dark skin' (1992, 6). Apparently Pacheco felt compelled by Andromeda's identity as an Ethiopian to reason that she must have been black, but this also led him to conclude that she must have been ugly. Contrary to Pacheco's view, however, McGrath's study convincingly demonstrates that the overwhelming majority of early modern painters and poets clearly conceived of Andromeda as both white and beautiful.

Similarly, *Armas antárticas* leaves no doubt as to the attractiveness of Andromeda. When Apollo first saw the princess, as she walked across the flowers growing along the banks of the Nile, he contemplated her 'gentileza y apostura bella' [elegance and pretty looks] (Firmas 2006, 341g). In fact, Jalonga claims the god of light was so taken with Andromeda's beauty that Cupid needed to shoot no arrows to incite his amorous ardour, for he was already 'encendido' [inflamed] (2006, 260, stanza 341f), a wordplay based on Apollo's excited state and his personification of the sun's rays. Given the common association between beauty and whiteness as manifested in both Petrarchan poetry and Renaissance painting, moreover, readers of *Armas antárticas* most assuredly would assume that Andromeda, as a beautiful woman, would also necessarily be white and European in appearance. Thus, in its failure to describe Andromeda explicitly as a black African princess, *Armas antárticas* implicitly presents her as white. Considering Apollo's similarly bright image, it becomes evident that Miramontes's text evokes the way in which Africans are portrayed in early modern Spanish drama as noted by Baltasar Fra Molinero. He observes that 'el problema es que no hay nada "africano" en los negros protagonistas de comedias barrocas, por más que se insista en su origen etíope, guineano o cualquier otro lugar del África de la fantasía de cada autor. África no existe más que en el color de la piel del protagonista' [the problem is that there is nothing 'African' in the black protagonists of the baroque *comedia* regardless of the insistence on their origins from Ethiopia, Guinea, or whichever African place that exists in the imagination of each author. Africa only exists in the skin colour of the protagonist] (1995, 9). By tracing the maroons to Apollo and Andromeda, though, *Armas antárticas* appears to deny even the black skin of the escaped slaves.

And yet, this poem that, in Firbas's words, relies on a mythological genealogy 'to legitimize' the maroons and 'to dilute their difference' does not dissolve the distinction it seeks to mitigate (2006, 95).[19] Indeed, despite their supposedly white, Europeanized heritage, the poem also calls attention to the dark skin colour of the maroons by continuing the play on dark/light that begins with Apollo's arrival at the Nile.[20] For example, just before Biafara, a maroon, appeals for the aid of the Spanish in exacting revenge against an English pirate, the setting is described: 'El sol en la mitad del cielo estaba / queriendo declinarse al occeano, / cuando por el repecho de una loma / al campo enderezando un negro asoma' [The sun was in the middle of the sky, about to descend into the ocean, when a black man emerged from the slope of a hill as he made his way into the plain] (Firbas 2006, 373, stanza 762e–h). Here, the image of Biafara (referred to as simply 'un negro') emerging from behind a hill in the brightness of the day is counterposed with the sun, high in the sky, as it begins its descent toward the sea and eventual submergence into darkness. Whereas the Apollonian genealogy effectively 'brightens' the lineage of the maroons and seeks to establish a resemblance and kinship between them and the sun, this description develops a sharp contrast between Biafara and the sunlight. As a result of such portrayals in the epic, Jalonga and his people remain both African in their skin colour and yet white and Europeanized in their classical mythological ancestry – a characterization that finds an echo in the figure of Andromeda herself, although somewhat reversed.[21] Ethiopian in descent, but artistically imagined with white skin, Andromeda is both African and European during the early modern period.[22]

This ambivalent portrayal of the maroons as both dark and light parallels Miramontes's presentation of Apollo as well. For in addition to his association with resplendence, the sun god also displays occasional connections to darkness. As Jalonga describes to Oxenham, the 'apolíneo espíritu' [Apollonian spirit] (2006, 263, stanza 351d), still worshipped by some of his compatriots (2006, 257, stanza 330h), retreated to the underworld after the introduction of Christianity to the region: 'En obscuras cavernas espantosas / con voz temorizante, horrendo grito / daba falsas respuestas engañosas / el apolíneo espíritu maldito; / pero, como ilusión y vanas cosas, / en publicándose el christiano edicto / se retiró a encerrar en el infierno / ahuyentado del verbo Dios eterno' [In obscure, frightening caverns, with a terrifying voice and horrendous screams, the accursed Apollonian spirit offered false, deceitful responses, but like illusions and vanities, he withdrew to hell in flight from the word of God when the Christian edict was made known] (2006, 263, stanza 351a–h). In this context, Apollo is considered accursed, and like a demon, he resides in murky caves from which he emits frightening, deceitful screams until he is finally banished to infernal darkness. Instead of the positive, luminous characterization of the sun god, in this stanza Jalonga portrays the deity's negative influence and his relation to the absence of light.[23]

At times the *Metamorphoses* and its later Spanish interpretations evoke a similarly dark portrait of Apollo, as the light and heat attributed to the god as the sun are supposed to have resulted in physical blackness.[24] For example, in the *Metamorphoses*, Ovid relates that Phaethon's driving of Apollo's chariot too close to the earth made the blood rise to the surface of skin of the Ethiopians, giving them a dark appearance.[25] If only indirectly, this implicates Apollo in the mythical origin of the dark skin of Africans. Later in the same poem, Ovid writes that Apollo changed the originally white hue of the raven to black as punishment for the bird's inappropriate behaviour.[26] In his naturalistic interpretation of this Ovidian tale, the Spanish mythographer, Pérez de Moya, opines that this particular change of colour is said to occur as a consequence of the god's allegorical link to the heat of the sun (1995, 259). Thus, focusing on the effects of Apollo's burning attributes, as Ovid and his interpreter do in the preceding instances, tends to emphasize the god's association with darkness. However, I would argue that, contrary to this emphasis, Miramontes's genealogy presents the god in such a way as to lessen his mythical connection to obscurity.[27] Indeed, despite the mention of a satanic Apollo that lives in darkness, the god remains associated primarily with light both in Jalonga's narration and throughout the poem as a whole.

The implications of this portrayal of Jalonga and his people and their heritage emerge even more clearly when compared to Lope de Vega's *La Dragontea* (1598), an epic that depicts interactions between maroons and the English pirate, Francis Drake, on his last, fatal voyage to the Caribbean. In fact, these maroons, who reside in Santiago del Príncipe in Colonial Panama, include none other than Luis de Mazambique and a certain man named Yalonga.[28] In contrast with *Armas antárticas*, and in keeping with the historical record (Sánchez Jiménez 2007, 124–6), the maroons in *La Dragontea* fight against the English pirate and remain loyal to the Spanish king. But Sánchez Jiménez demonstrates that like the representation of Jalonga and his people in *Armas antárticas*, the maroons of *La Dragontea* also received an ambivalent treatment. He convincingly argues that Lope's description of the maroons follows the sort of contradictory portrayal of the 'other' examined by Davis and Barbara Fuchs in texts of the Spanish Empire (Sánchez Jiménez 2007, 120–3). After noting Lope's comparison of Yalonga to a 'turco azapo' [a marksman from the Ottoman Empire] (2007, 121) when he shoots Drake's nephew, Sánchez Jiménez observes that 'los cimarrones son, a un tiempo, españoles – por su lealtad – y enemigos turcos, contradicción que les describe como fieles servidores de un imperio que no acaba de aceptarles' [the maroons are simultaneously Spaniards on account of their loyalty, and enemy Turks, a contradiction that describes them as faithful servants of an empire that, in the end, does not accept them] (2007, 122–3). Similarly, in *Armas antárticas* the genealogical association of the maroons with Apollo and Andromeda casts the former slaves as having familiar, admirable, and white ancestors, but the poem also depicts them as dark-skinned enemies of the Spanish Empire.

Perhaps the most important difference between the image of the maroons in Lope's and Miramontes' epics relates to the source of nobility in the former slaves. Sánchez Jiménez contends that in *La Dragontea* 'los mulatos o negros que se distinguen por su virtud no son diferentes de los hidalgos bien nacidos, pues el color de la piel no condiciona la personalidad del individuo' [the mulato or black characters that distinguish themselves in virtue are no different than the high-born *hidalgos*, because skin colour does not condition the personality of the individual] (2007, 127).[29] However, by making Apollo, Greco-Roman god of the sun, and Andromeda, an implicitly white woman, the ancestors of the maroons, *Armas antárticas* suggests that skin colour is important and that any nobility they did have is tied to their bright, white mythological heritage. Additionally, as per epic conventions, this portrayal ultimately aggrandizes the heroism of the Spanish when they force the maroons to retreat into the mountains, for they have defeated enemies with 'illustrious,' noble ancestors rather than unknown former slaves of 'obscure' origins.[30]

Finally, I would like to note that, just as Apollo and Andromeda facilitate the construction of a particular kind of genealogical nobility, the tale of Apollo and Daphne also gives a noble literary genealogy to *Armas antárticas*. Indeed, Jalonga's versification of the Apollo and Daphne story reconstructs a myth treated by such revered poets as Ovid and, closer to his own time, Garcilaso de la Vega, and his unique rendition of the tale serves to highlight the poetic craftsmanship of Miramontes.[31] In his narration to Oxenham, Jalonga describes the beginning of Daphne's transformation thus: 'Oyola el padre y luego transformarse / en florido laurel empezó a verse: / los pies, como raíces, arraigarse / y el delicado cuerpo endurecerse, / los cabellos en hojas comutarse, / los brazos en dos ramas estenderse; / la inmaculada y virginal pureza / vestirse, poco a poco, de corteza' [Her father heard her and then she began to be seen transforming into a blooming laurel: her feet, like roots, started to anchor themselves and her delicate body began to harden; her hair, into leaves, started to change; her arms, into two branches, began to extend themselves; and the immaculate and virginal purity started to clothe itself, little by little, with bark] (2006,

259, stanza 336a–h). Jalonga's words appear to reflect the strong influence of Garcilaso de la Vega's treatment of the myth in both his 'Sonnet XIII' and in *Eclogue III*. For example, each of the first six lines of the preceding octave from *Armas antárticas* concludes with a verb, and the actions are presented with reference to the sense of sight ('empezó a verse' [began to be seen]) (2006, 259, stanza 336b). Likewise, in his sonnet, Garcilaso caps off each of the first eight lines with verbs depicting actions, which the lyric voice of the poem claims to have seen ('vi' [I saw]) (1999, 197, line 3).[32] Furthermore, in Garcilaso's eclogue, in which Apollo's chase and the nymph's transformation appear as scenes in a watery fabric, the poet also places the verbs at the ends of the first six lines of the stanza that depicts her transformation.[33] The similar construction of the lines, coupled with the emphasis on the visual element of the experience suggests that Garcilaso's descriptions provided a model for Jalonga's account of the myth.[34] Jalonga's description also presents lexical similarities with Garcilaso's portrayal of the metamorphosis in both of his poems. For example, after the nymph's transformation has finished, the Ethiopian bard says that Apollo, 'Mil veces el *bullente* tronco mudo / abraza, besa y mira enternecido' [a thousand times tenderly *hugs, kisses* and looks at the mute, *quivering* trunk] (2006, 259, stanza 338a–b; my emphasis). And in his sonnet, Garcilaso also uses the same verb of motion ('bullendo' [quivering]) (1999, 197, line 6) to describe her bark. Furthermore, the eclogue refers to the reaction of the god, '*besando* y *abrazando* aquel madero' [*kissing* and *hugging* the tree trunk] (1999, 206, line 168; my emphasis), using the identical verbs of affection that *Armas antárticas* employs.

The differences between the two versions reveal the most interesting aspects of Miramontes's creation. Of the poetic strategy used in his sonnet, Barnard writes that 'Garcilaso intensifies the illusion of dynamic unfolding by using the imperfect tense, by placing the verbs at the end of each line – creating a rhythmic, musical *ían-aban* rhyme – and by introducing enjambments' (1987, 114–15). Although the first six verbs in Jalonga's version of Daphne's transmutation appear in analogous positions, the maroon employs infinitives instead of the imperfect tense and diminishes the use of enjambments. This results in a more static account of the metamorphosis, but Jalonga's rendition displays other notable effects. The first eight lines of Garcilaso's sonnet consist of four pairs, each of which describes the transformation of one body part into a corresponding arboreal feature. The first pair describes the change of Daphne's arms into limbs, the next tells of her hair changing into leaves, the third detail the hardening of her tender skin, and the last pair gives an account of her feet becoming roots.[35] Garcilaso's eclogue follows a similar pattern, with the first six lines describing the metamorphosis of her arms, hair, and feet.[36] In Jalonga's octave cited above (2006, 259, stanza 336), however, lines c, d, e, and f showcase the changes sequentially involving the feet, body, hair, and arms – the exact opposite order presented by both of Garcilaso's texts. Furthermore, lines c, e, and f of Jalonga's account exhibit a symmetrical grammatical form unseen in Garcilaso in which the body part at the beginning of the line corresponds to the verb of metamorphosis at the end and the resultant tree characteristic in the middle. For instance, in line c, 'los pies' [her feet] and the verb 'arraigarse' [to be rooted] bracket the comparison 'como raíces' [like roots] (2006, 259, stanza 336c).

Moreover, the maroon poet literally takes Apollo in a completely new direction, as the god successfully woos Andromeda in Africa – a version of the tale recorded by neither Ovid nor Garcilaso.[37] The Ethiopian bard also leaves his mark on the myth by making the god of Parnassus undergo a unique metamorphosis of his own.[38] Jalonga depicts the reaction of Apollo to the sight of Daphne's transformation: 'Estuvo al espectáculo presente / fuera de sí, arrobado, el tierno amante; / la sangre de las venas helar siente / y enfriarse el ardor instimulante' [The tender lover, robbed of his self, was present at the spectacle, and he felt the blood in his veins freeze and his stimulating heat go cold] (2006, 259, stanza 337a–d). The experience has changed him, as the cold realization that Daphne is becoming a tree overcomes his characteristic warmth, and he notes a catalogue of traits now absent in the nymph: 'No boca que responda dulcemente, / no pecho al alabastro semejante, / no rosadas mejillas, ojo bellos, / ve, ni lazos de amor, crespos cabellos' [No mouth, which sweetly replies, no bosom similar to alabaster, no rosy cheeks, pretty eyes, nor curly locks, loops of love, does he see] (2006, 259, stanza 337e–h). Yet contrary to what happens to Daphne, the change felt by Apollo does not last, as he quickly burns again with passion – this time for Andromeda. He thus successfully defies and escapes the frozen grip of enduring metamorphosis. And it is perhaps in this spirit of defiance more than in any other respect that Jalonga and his fellow maroons resemble Apollo, as they defy the Spanish, and despite losing the military battle, manage to escape to the mountains.

The inconsistent relations of Apollo to light and dark, and of Andromeda to white and black, are passed down in *Armas antárticas* to the poetic portrayal of the maroons and their ambivalently whitened image in the epic. If the poem depicts the former slaves as admirable, it is not because of their rebellion against the Spanish and alliance with English pirates, but because of their long-lost greatness stemming, in large part, from their 'white' ancestors. This makes them more familiar to European readers, but in the process it also leaves some of the myths about slavery unaltered after all. At the beginning of the chapter, I noted that, in presenting Apollo and Andromeda as the progenitors of the maroons, the epic might be seen as challenging the idea that slaves had no lineage of their own. Yet after considering the ramifications of their alleged mythological heritage, it becomes clear that *Armas antárticas* implicitly perpetuates this stereotype. Even if it did succeed in ennobling the maroons in the eyes of early modern readers, the epic turns this royalty to the advantage of the Spanish soldiers by making them appear more heroic because they defeat enemies with an illustrious past. As for Daphne, *Armas antárticas* retells her transformation, and her new arboreal form serves as a kind of family tree. The portrayal of her metamorphosis enables Miramontes to connect a noble literary line from his poem back to Ovid through Garcilaso de la Vega. Her tree gives *Armas antárticas* poetic roots, but they may have proven just as artificial as the maroons' genealogy, because the epic never went on to bloom and flourish in popularity like its renowned literary forebears did.

NOTES

1 I would like to thank Steven Wagschal for his many helpful comments and suggestions during the development of this paper.
2 See Kenneth R. Andrews (1967, 41–2), Kris E. Lane (1998, 43–4), and Paul Firbas (2006, 246, note 283b).
3 For the origin of the term 'cimarrón' (maroon) see Firbas (2006, 92). See also Sánchez Jiménez (2007, 115, note 3).
4 All quotes of Miramontes's poem come from Firbas's edition in which he numbers the stanzas consecutively from the beginning of the epic to the end without interruption and refers to the individual lines of the stanzas by letters (a–h). Jalonga positions Apollo and Andromeda at the head of his nation's lineage, a line which he traces through such mythical kings as Senapo and Mitriandes, as well as through the historical figure of Ballano, an escaped slave. For more on Miramontes's portrayal of the maroons and their genealogy, see Firbas (2006, 91–101; 2000, 200–6). All translations are by me.

5 This is significant in the context of early modern Hispanic epic poetry, because, as Javier Cevallos points out, part of the portrayal of the Mapuche Indians as barbarians in Alonso de Ercilla's *La Araucana* (1569, 78, 89) is based
on their lack of a king (1989, 6–7). See also Elizabeth B. Davis (2000, 41).

6 See also Firbas (2006, 94–5).

7 In this way, the effect of Jalonga's description echoes what Branche says
of Gilberto Freyre, whose 'list of tools for torturing slaves in nineteenth-
century Brazil, and the frightful refinements invented by the sadistic im-
aginations of slave owners, belie, if nothing else, the facile generalizations
about the benign nature of the institution in that country, or in Latin
America as a whole' (2006, 107).

8 Branche observes: 'While the *castas* ontologically are constructed as less
than human, the subpersonhood of blacks is intrinsically associated with
their status as saleable beings, objectified by the act of commerce ... Their
condition has been described by Orlando Patterson as being literally and
metaphorically one of "social death," as he emphasized the totalitarian
premise that governed the relationship between slave and master, as well
as the slaves' alienation from ascending or descending genealogic ties and
their reduction in law to the status of a thing' (2006, 95). See also Branche
(2006, 104).

9 In their noble genealogy, the portrayal of the maroons in *Armas antárticas*
resembles that of the characters of black saints discussed by Fra Molinero
(1995, 17). As Firbas notes, their status as maroons implies their humaniza-
tion (2006, 92; 2000, 203–4).

10 Firbas also comments on the maroons' disassociation with their historical
and cultural reality (2006, 94–6).

11 Miramontes's rendering of the maroons is reminiscent of Alonso de Ercilla's
portrayal of the indigenous women in the epic, *La Araucana*. James Nicolopulos observes that 'echoing Schwartz-Lerner, Margarita Zamora remarks
that in order to make these female protagonists intelligible and palatable to
his European readers, Ercilla had to strip them of every truly indigenous
feature, except, possibly, their name. Read in this way, the amorous episodes
might well pose disturbing implications for those who would interpret Ercilla as a sympathetic defender of the rights and valor of the indigenous
peoples of the Arauco region' (1999, 228). Likewise, I would argue that the
portrayal of Apollo and Andromeda as the ancestors of the maroons produces similar interpretive complications for *Armas antárticas*. Interestingly,
Nicolopulos's discussion of Pedro de Oña's 'whitening' of Fresia (an Indian
woman) in *Arauco domado* (1596), illustrates a different effect of whitening
than that proposed here. See Nicolopulos (1999, 240).

12 Of Apollo's character, Mary E. Barnard observes: 'For the Greeks, Apollo is a brilliant figure; he is the patron god of healing, archery, music, poetry, and, as a result of the late development in Apolline cult, he is also a solar deity. The term *Phoebus*, if perhaps not originally meant to denote Apollo's solar character as was once thought, is the epithet that identifies him as a sun-god' (1987, 14). See also chapter 2 of Barnard's study in which she discusses Apollo's association with light in the moral sense of the medieval Christian tradition.

13 See Firbas (2006, 523, note 1335b). The variant spelling 'esplandor' appears in the text.

14 In her study of Alonso de Sandoval's *De instauranda Aethiopum salute* (1627), Margaret M. Olsen writes: 'classical and medieval explanations for the occurrence of black skin reflected the fear and uneasiness that such difference implied for Europeans. Thus, heat, sin, and darkness and their negative connotations for Christian society continued to play heavily in early modern theories of race' (2004, 100).

15 See *Metamorphoses* (4.672–7). McGrath argues that readers took Ovid to be referring to white marble, and not black marble (1992, 9). At the conclusion of her study, she summarizes that 'in general, in Ovidian contexts and elsewhere, the marble statue of the *Metamorphoses* effectively bleached Andromeda's colour away' (1992, 16).

16 For more on the influence of Heliodorus on Cervantes, see Eric C. Graf (2005). As for the late classical author's influence on Miramontes's text, see Firbas (2006, 69—70; 261, note 345b; 261–2, note 346a; and 470, note 1135f).

17 See McGrath (1992, 1—3).

18 The *Poesie* consisted of the paintings *Danaë*, *Venus and Adonis*, *Perseus and Andromeda*, *Diana and Acteon*, *Diana and Callisto*, and the *Rape of Europa* (Nash 1985, 13). Several scholars have written on the relation of Titian's paintings to early modern Spanish literature. For example, see Frederick A. de Armas's study on Lope de Vega and the Venetian painter (1978).

19 This is typical of epic poetry, as Davis points out: 'through the absorption and neutralization of alterity, these [early modern Hispanic] epics attempt to paint a tidy picture of the ethnic purgation of a national space that they also constitute as thoroughly gendered. When the attempt fails, disruption tears open the poetic text, exposing the seams of the epic's dominant belief systems' (2000, 17). See also Davis (2000, 12).

20 Olsen points to a similar contradiction in *De instauranda Aethiopium salute* in which Sandoval 'emphasizes blackness and diminishes it at the same time' (2004, 83). In her study, Olsen describes how Sandoval's text aims to whiten the souls of African slaves (2004, 83–91).

21 As I will discuss in greater detail below, this portrayal of the maroons as both African and European resembles Lope de Vega's depiction of the maroons in *La Dragontea* (1598), as studied by Antonio Sánchez Jiménez (2007, 120–3).

22 McGrath shows that Michel de Marolles refers explicitly to Andromeda's dual identity in his commentaries on Abraham van Diepenbeeck's illustration of a black Andromeda in *Tableau du Temple des Muses* (1655) (1992, 12–14).

23 This portrayal of Apollo recalls that of the medieval mythographer, Pierre Bersuire, as described by Barnard. She writes that 'Bersuire also declares Apollo an idol through whom the Devil gave oracles at Delphi. He signifies the evil prince or prelate exterminating the poor and innocent subjects, and he is, moreover, the image of the Devil because of his sins' (1987, 74). For more on Bersuire, see Barnard (1987, 70–5, 78).

24 Barnard notes that the moral darkness embodied by Apollo in Bersuire's readings also stemmed from the effects of the sun (1987, 74).

25 See *Metamorphoses* (2.235–6). Olsen discusses the Phaethon and Apollo myth and its connection to the skin colour of Africans (2004, 102). See also Kim F. Hall's observations on Apollo, Phaethon, and the literary portrayal of Ethiopian skin colour in English poetry of the Renaissance (1995, 96–7).

26 See *Metamorphoses* (1997, 2.626–32).

27 Hall's reading of William Basse's *Urnania* (ca. 1612) shows that the English poet also dissociated Apollo from Phaethon's burning of the earth and its mythical consequences. Hall writes: 'Lightness is associated with the order and control wrought by Apollo, whereas blackness of the Ethiopians becomes a sign of chaos and transgression. The nymph here is not only one of these pre-Phaethon, "white & faire" Ethiopians, she is in some ways a Phaethon figure herself, although in this case her transgressive nature is specifically linked to her femininity' (1995, 63).

28 Firbas notes the appearance of both Luis de Mazambique (2006, 252, note 306c) and a maroon character named Yalonga in *La Dragontea* (2006, 256, note 325f) and proposes that 'Miramontes quizá concibió el plan de imitar y superar el poema de Lope, utilizando los mismos nombres de héroes cimarrones (Jalonga y Luis de Mazambique)' [Perhaps Miramontes concebido of the plan to imitate and surpass the poem by Lope, utilizing the same names of the maroon heroes (Jalonga and Luis de Mazambique)] (2006, 29). See also Firbas (2000, 209–10, note 20; and 2006, 29). For more on the Yalonga character in *La Dragontea*, see Antonio Sánchez Jiménez (2007, 125–6).

29 Sánchez Jiménez summarizes the attitude toward nobility in *La Dragontea* writing, 'la virtud y el valor permiten obtener nobleza, al menos nobleza

de carácter, posesión que resulta más admirable que la nobleza de sangre cuando ésta no viene acompañada de hazañas gloriosas' [virtue and valour permit one to obtain nobility, at least nobility of character, a possession that results more attractive than nobility through blood when the latter is not accompanied by glorious deeds] (2007, 128).

30   Firbas correctly argues that the fate of the maroons is left open-ended in the epic (2006, 101), but this does not prevent the poem from presenting the Spanish as heroes. As Cevallos points out: 'One of the *topoi* in the epic tradition was to present the enemies as being as valiant as the heroes in order to augment the latter's greatness' (1989, 1). Cevallos argues that the ostensibly heroic depiction of the Mapuche Indians in *La Araucana* serves to enhance the image of the victorious Spaniards over formidable adversaries (1989, 17). Likewise, the noble ancestry of the maroons, whose king has no choice but to flee for his life down a river (2006, 411–12, stanza 917), ultimately glorifies the Spanish military capabilities. For more on this epic strategy, see Davis (2000, 12).

31   As Barnard has remarked, the myth has often served this purpose among Renaissance poets (1987, 4). See Barnard's study for more on the treatment of the myth in Ovid, medieval writers, Petrarch, Garcilaso de la Vega, and Francisco de Quevedo (1987).

32   Barnard discusses the significance of the voice's seeing of the metamorphosis in her study of Garcilaso (1987, 110–30). The first two quatrains of Garcilaso's sonnet read: 'A Dafne ya los brazos le crecían / y en luengos ramos vueltos se mostraban; / en verdes hojas vi que se tornaban / los cabellos qu'el oro escurecían: / de áspera corteza se cubrían / los tiernos miembros que aun bullendo 'staban; / los blancos pies en tierra se hincaban / y en torcidas raíces se volvían [Daphne's arms were growing on her and were showing themselves turned into long branches; I saw that her hair, which outshined gold, was becoming green leaves; her tender limbs were covered with a harsh bark still quivering; her white feet were fixing themselves into the ground and turning into twisted roots] (1999, 197).

33   The octave in the eclogue that deals with Daphne's transformation reads: 'Mas a la fin los brazos le crecían / y en sendos ramos vueltos se mostraban; / y los cabellos, que vencer solían / al oro fino, en hojas se tornaban; / en torcidas raíces s'estendían / los blancos pies y en tierra se hincaban; / llora el amante y busca el ser primero, / besando y abrazando aquel madero' [Yet, in the end, her arms were growing and they both showed themselves turned into branches; and her locks, which used to defeat fine gold in shine, were becoming leaves; her white feet were extending

themselves into twisted roots and fixing themselves into the ground; the lover cries and searches for her original form, kissing and hugging that tree trunk] (1999, 206, lines 161–8).

34 For more on the visual dimension of Garcilaso's description, see Barnard (1987, 117–18).

35 See Barnard on the progression and structure of Daphne's transformation (1987, 112–14).

36 As for Ovid's account, after describing a growing heaviness in Daphne's limbs, he puts her mutations in the following order: skin/bark, hair/ leaves, arms/branches, feet/roots, and finally head/treetop (*Metamorphoses* 1997, 2.549–52).

37 As Firbas observes, Miramontes's tale of Daphne and Apollo appears to imitate the general Ovidian version of the myth (2006, 258, note 332a), but the pairing of Apollo and Andromeda appears to sprout from the imagination of Miramontes (2006, 261, note 345b). Barnard discusses how Ovid's ending of the Apollo and Daphne myth was also altered by Garcilaso (1987, 116).

38 For comparison, see Barnard's discussion of the change experienced by Apollo in Francisco de Quevedo's poem 'De Dafne y Apolo, fábula' (1987, 138–9). Barnard also describes the transformation of the male lover in Petrarch's poems inspired by the Apollo and Daphne myth (1985, 94–101).

WORKS CITED

Andrews, Kenneth R. 1967. *Drake's Voyages: A Reassessment of Their Place in Elizabethan Maritime Expansion*. London: Cox & Wyman.

Barnard, Mary E. 1987. *The Myth of Apollo and Daphne from Ovid to Quevedo: Love, Agon, and the Grotesque*. Durham: Duke University Press.

Branche, Jerome C. 2006. *Colonialism and Race in Luso-Hispanic Literature*. Columbia: University of Missouri Press.

Cevallos, Francisco Javier. 1989. 'Don Alonso de Ercilla and the American Indian: History and Myth.' *Revista de estudios hispánicos* 23:1–20.

Davis, Elizabeth. 2000. *Myth and Identity in the Epic of Imperial Spain*. Columbia: University of Missouri Press.

De Armas, Frederick A. 1978. 'Lope de Vega and Titian.' *Comparative Literature* 30:338–52.

Firbas, Paul. 2000. 'Escribir en los confines: épica colonial y mundo antártico.' In *Agencias criollas: La ambigüedad 'colonial' en las letras hispanoamericanas*, ed. José Antonio Mazzotti, 191–213. Pittsburgh: Biblioteca de América.

– ed. 2006. *Armas antárticas*. Lima: Pontifica Universidad Católica del Peru.

Fra Molinero, Baltasar. 1995. *La imagen de los negros en el teatro del Siglo de Oro*. Madrid: Siglo XX de España.

Graf, Eric C. 2006. 'Heliodorus, Cervantes, La Fayette: Ekphrasis and the Feminist Origins of the Modern Novel.' In *Ekphrasis in the Age of Cervantes*, ed. Frederick A. de Armas, 175–201. Lewisburg: Bucknell University Press.

Hall, Kim F. 1995. *Things of Darkness: Economies of Race and Gender in Early Modern England*. Ithaca: Cornell University Press.

Lane, Kris E. 1998. *Pillaging the Empire: Piracy in the Americas 1500–1750*. Armonk, NY: M.E. Sharpe.

Mazzotti, José Antonio. 2002. 'The Dragon and the Seashell: British Corsairs, Epic Poetry and Creole Nation in Viceregal Peru.' In *Colonialism Past and Present: Reading and Writing about Colonial Latin America Today*, ed. Álvaro Félix Bolaños and Gustavo Verdesio, 197–214. Albany: State University of New York Press.

McGrath, Elizabeth. 1992. 'The Black Andromeda.' *Journal of the Warburg and Courtauld Institutes* 55: 1–18.

Nash, Jane C. 1985. *Veiled Images: Titian's Mythological Paintings for Philip II*. Philadelphia: Art Alliance Press.

Nicolopulos, James. 1999. 'Reading and Responding to the Amorous Episodes of the *Araucana* in Colonial Peru.' In *Ésta, de nuestra América pupila: Estudios de poesía colonial*, ed. Gerogina Sabat de Rivers, 227–47. Houston: Society for Renaissance & Baroque Hispanic Poetry.

Olsen, Margaret M. 2004. *Slavery and Salvation in Colonial Cartagena de Indias*. Tallahassee: University Press of Florida.

Ovid. *Metamorphoses*. 1997. Vol 1. Ed. William S. Anderson. Norman: University of Oklahoma Press.

Pérez de Moya, Juan. 1995. *Philosofía secreta*. Ed. Carlos Clavería. Madrid: Cátedra.

Sánchez Jiménez, Antonio. 2007. 'Raza, identidad y rebelión en los confines del imperio hispánico: Los cimarrones de Santiago del Príncipe y *La Dragontea* (1598) de Lope de Vega.' *Hispanic Review*. 75:113–33.

Vega, Garcilaso de la. 1999. *Poesía castellana completa*. Ed. Antonio Prieto. Madrid: Biblioteca Nueva.

Contributors

Timothy Ambrose is associate professor of Spanish at Indiana University Southeast. He has published articles on Rafael Alberti, Jorge Luis Borges, Pedro Calderón de la Barca, Juan Ramón Jiménez, Lope de Vega, and Cecilia Urbina. His current research project deals with the myth of Bacchus in Cervantes.

Mary E. Barnard is associate professor of Spanish and Comparative Literature at Pennsylvania State University. She is the author of *The Myth of Apollo and Daphne from Ovid to Quevedo: Love, Agon and the Grotesque*. She has published essays on early modern Spanish poetry in *PMLA, Hispanic Review, Romanic Review, Revista de Estudios Hispánicos,* and others. She is co-editing *Objects of Culture in Early Modern Spain* and is completing a book on Garcilaso de la Vega and material culture.

Marina Brownlee is Robert Schirmer Professor of Spanish and Portuguese Languages and Cultures and Comparative Literature and Chair of the Committee for Renaissance Studies at Princeton University. Her books include *The Poetics of Literary Theory: Lope and Cervantes* (1981); *The Status of the Reading Subject in the 'Libro de Buen Amor'* (1985); *The Severed Word: Ovid's 'Heroides' and the 'Novela Sentimental'* (1990); and *The Cultural Labyrinth of María de Zayas* (2000).

Keith Budner has taken graduate courses at the University of Chicago and is presently teaching English in Madrid. He expects to continue his graduate work next year. He is particularly interested in the relations between classical texts and the literature of Spain in the Age of Cervantes. His essay 'Classical Confusion: Myths, Paintings and Other Windows into Don Quixote's Erotic Life' is forthcoming.

Frederick A. de Armas is Andrew W. Mellon Professor in Humanities and professor of Spanish and Comparative Literature at the University of Chicago. His books include *The Invisible Mistress: Aspects of Feminism and Fantasy in the Golden Age* (1976); *The Return of Astraea: An Astral-Imperial Myth in Calderón* (1986); *Cervantes, Raphael and the Classics* (1998); and *Quixotic Frescoes: Cervantes and Italian Renaissance Art* (2006). He is currently President of the Cervantes Society of America.

Ryan D. Giles is assistant professor in the Department of Romance Languages and Literatures at the University of Chicago. In 2008, he received the John K. Walsh Award from the MLA Division on Medieval Spanish Language and Literature for most outstanding article published in *La corónica*. He is the author of *The Laughter of the Saints: Parodies of Holiness in Late Medieval and Renaissance Spain* (2009).

Jason A. McCloskey is assistant professor of Spanish at Bucknell University, where he studies the epic poetry of sixteenth- and seventeenth-century Spain and her exploits in the Americas. One recurring theme he finds is the use of classical myth to aggrandize Spanish endeavours.

Benjamin J. Nelson is assistant professor of Spanish at the University of South Carolina, Beaufort, where he studies the Spanish pastoral novel from the perspective of empire. He also works on the relations between the verbal and the visual and is the current president of the Early Modern Image and Text Society (Emit Society).

John C. Parrack is associate professor of Spanish at the University of Central Arkansas. He has edited *La Estrella de Sevilla* (2008) and has participated in edited volumes such as *Approaches to Teaching* Lazarillo de Tormes *and the Picaresque Tradition*. He focuses on early modern narrative discourse and is currently working on the *Guerras civiles de Granada* and Cervantes. He has published essays in journals such as *Revista Canadiense de Estudios Hispánicos, La corónica*, and *Romance Notes*.

Pablo Restrepo-Gautier is associate professor and chair of the Department of Hispanic and Italian Studies at the University of Victoria. He is the author of *La imaginación emblemática en el drama de Tirso de Molina* (2001). He has also published a number of essays on early modern and contemporary Hispanic letters in journals such as *Bulletin of the Comediantes, Revista Canadiense de Estudios Hispánicos, Anales Cervantinos Hispanic Journal*, and *Chasqui*.

Julio Vélez-Sainz has been assistant professor of Spanish at the University of Massachusetts at Amherst and now holds the post of Investigador Ramón y Cajal at the Universidad Complutense de Madrid. He is the author of *Francisco de Quevedo* (2005); *Parnaso español: canon, mecenazgo y propaganda en la poesía del Siglo de Oro* (2006); *Cervantes and/on/in the New World* (2007) (co-edited with Nieves Romero Díaz); and the critical edition of Álvaro de Luna's *Libro de las virtuosas e claras mugeres* (2009).

Steven Wagschal is associate professor of Spanish at Indiana University, Bloomington. He is the author of *The Literature of Jealousy in the Age of Cervantes* (2006) and has edited Lope de Vega's *Peribáñez y el Comendador de Ocaña* (2004). He works on various aspects of early modern Spanish literature as they intersect with other disciplines such as the history of medicine, philosophy, and art history. His articles have appeared in journals such as *Cervantes, Hispanic Review*, and *Revista Canadiense de Estudios Hispánicos*.

Chistopher Weimer is professor at Oklahoma State University, where he teaches Spanish and Humanities. With Barbara A. Simerka, he is co-founder and co-editor of *Laberinto: An Electronic Journal of Early Modern Hispanic Literatures and Cultures*. He has also co-edited with her *Echoes and Inscriptions: Comparative Approaches to Early Modern Spanish Literatures*. His essays on both early modern and contemporary Hispanic theatre have appeared in journals including *Bulletin of the Comediantes, Modern Drama, Estreno, Hispanófila*, and *Latin American Theater Review*.

Kerry Wilks is assistant professor of Spanish at Wichita State University. Her research interests focus on the theatre of the Spanish Golden Age and the myth of Circe. She has published articles in *Bulletin of the Comediantes* and *Cahiers parisiens/Parisian Notebooks*, and is now working on the little-known late seventeenth-century writer Baltasar Funes de Villalpando.

William Worden is associate professor of Spanish and director of graduate studies of the Department of Modern Languages and Classics at the University of Alabama. He has published articles on the picaresque, Cervantes, the *comedia* in the New World, and Galdós. He has just completed a book that examines Sancho Panza's role both in the narration of *Don Quixote* and in the work's reception over time.

Index